DEVELOPING YOUR

GLOBAL MINDSET

THE HANDBOOK
FOR SUCCESSFUL GLOBAL LEADERS

Mansour Javidan, Ph.D.
Jennie L. Walker, Ph.D.

ISBN 13: 978-1-59298-997-3

Library of Congress Catalog Number: 2013908850

Printed in the United States of America

First Printing: 2013

17   16   15   14   13   5   4   3   2   1

Cover and interior design by James Monroe Design, LLC.

Beaver's Pond Press, Inc.
7108 Ohms Lane
Edina, MN 55439–2129
(952) 829-8818
www.BeaversPondPress.com

To order, visit www.BeaversPondBooks.com
or call (800) 901-3480. Reseller discounts available.

Table of Contents

GLOBAL INTELLECTUAL **CAPITAL**

GLOBAL PSYCHOLOGICAL CAPITAL

GLOBAL SOCIAL CAPITAL

Introduction

Our clients and partners are deeply interested in advice on how they can better interact with people from other parts of the world to have greater personal and business success globally.

MANSOUR JAVIDAN, PH.D.
Director of Najafi Global Mindset Institute
& Garvin Distinguished Professor
Mansour.Javidan@Thunderbird.edu

This handbook was produced in response to the many requests we have received since 2007 for specific and practical development tips to develop each dimension of Global Mindset. Our clients and partners are deeply interested in advice on how they can better interact with people from other parts of the world to have greater personal and business success globally. This is probably the reason you have chosen to pick up this book as well. You're in good company.

In 2007, the Global Mindset Inventory (GMI) was first introduced to corporations and graduate business programs. The purpose of this instrument is to do a Global Mindset assessment of a manager or a group of managers. By completing this Internet-based questionnaire, managers find out which areas are their strengths and where they need to further develop. While we have always provided development suggestions during GMI coaching sessions, this handbook takes the support we offer managers to the next level.

In consultation with managers, executives, and some very senior and experienced international executive coaches, we've been able to put together a large series of advice, recommendations, and ideas on how a manager can improve on all elements of Global Mindset. You'll find that all of these ideas are very actionable and very specific, and they don't usually take much time to implement. The development tips may be used for yourself, individual direct reports or coachees, as well as for developing teams.

In addition to a rich variety of development suggestions at your fingertips, you'll find engaging narratives throughout the book illustrating the various components of Global Mindset in action. The diverse international experiences of our contributing authors bring Global Mindset to life through these narratives as well as seven intriguing case studies located at the end of the book. The case studies will transport you into complex, real-world scenarios that cross geographic and cultural borders. They will push the boundaries of your current global leadership skills to identify ways to successfully influence diverse others while working within the complex and fast-paced world of global business. The case studies may be used for individual development through self-reflection or in teams, where the discussions will no doubt be lively.

The journey to develop a Global Mindset is lifelong, and that's good news! The diversity and complexity of our twenty-first-century world is filled with unprecedented opportunities for global business interactions. At Thunderbird School of Global Management, we believe that business is much more than the exchange of goods and services. It is the mechanism that opens borders and transcends cultural differences to create sustainable prosperity worldwide.

Prosperity, for us and for our network of 40,000 alumni worldwide, includes the rich opportunity to build a deep understanding and friendships with international colleagues. A Global Mindset is the key to building these bridges across cultural, political, economic, and regulatory differences. We welcome you to our network of international bridge builders. You can join us on a variety of social media outlets at www.globalmindset.com.

Najafi Global Mindset Institute

Our team of experts performs innovative research, designs programs, and offers solutions to corporations, students, and managers on how to improve their ability to work effectively with people from other cultures and in other parts of the world.

ARVIND DESHMUKH, MBA
Manager of Operations
Najafi Global Mindset Institute
Arvind.Deshmukh@Thunderbird.edu

Najafi Global Mindset Institute, located at Thunderbird School of Global Management—ranked number one in the world for international business—is dedicated to developing managers for global roles. We help corporations succeed in pursuit of their global strategies by focusing on global leadership and global talent development. Using rigorous scientific research, including interviews with hundreds of global executives and surveys of over fifteen thousand individuals in many countries, Najafi Global Mindset Institute is able to define, measure, and develop Global Mindset using the GMI. Our team of experts performs innovative research, designs programs, and offers solutions to corporations, students, and managers on how to improve their ability to work effectively with people from other cultures and in other parts of the world.

Najafi Global Mindset Institute has developed, through rigorous scientific research, a quantitative approach to defining and assessing someone's ability to influence others. The GMI is the result of hundreds of hours of initial interviews with more than two hundred global executives and other distinguished scholars. The GMI measurement survey is comprised of less than eighty questions and takes an average of ten minutes to complete. It also is available in a 360 version. The GMI measures an individual's, a group's, or an organization's Global Mindset in terms of the three central components: Global Intellectual Capital, Global Psychological Capital, and Global Social Capital. The GMI database currently has over fifteen thousand respondents from many countries.

Najafi Global Mindset Institute is devoted to promoting and supporting research to further develop our understanding of topics such as

- leadership effectiveness in cross-cultural contexts

- theoretical and empirical linkages between Global Mindset and the effectiveness in global leadership

- practical application of Global Mindset to corporations, academic institutions, and the nonprofit and government sectors.

We invite corporate and academic organizations to partner with us on research projects.

Najafi Global Mindset Institute is dedicated to continued research and the development of new tools to develop managers and those training to become managers. The design of continued leadership development offerings is one of the main foci of the institute. We offer individual coaching sessions, half-day and full-day team development sessions, and customized development work related to Global Mindset. Our courses, workshops, and programs are focused on strengthening the global mindset in corporations, academic institutions, and nonprofit/governmental sectors.

More than 160 consultants, human resources executives, and academics worldwide have completed Global Mindset Certified Facilitator training, which provides in-depth understanding of the science behind the GMI self-assessment and 360 versions. Facilitators then learn how to provide a detailed debrief for both individuals and teams, as well as how to coach development in each dimension of Global Mindset. Certification training is two days, with an optional half-day for those who want to become certified in GMI 360 debriefs. Certified facilitators are able to administer the GMI and to facilitate both individual and team debrief and development sessions. Our website, www.globalmindset.com, offers more details on our certification programs.

Using This Handbook

We do not believe the goal of Global Mindset development is perfection in all thirty-five capabilities. We suggest you focus on developing those that are of the most immediate benefit for your role, goals, and interests.

JENNIE L. WALKER, PH.D., PHR
Director of Global Learning & Market Development
Najafi Global Mindset Institute
Jennie.Walker@Thunderbird.edu

The wealth of information in this book is ideally suited for business leaders from all nations of the world who work in global roles in various types of organizations.

In the audience description above, there are some terms we would like to further explain:

- **Business leaders** refers to those individuals who are responsible for coordinating work and influencing others in their organizations. Generally, this will include those with the titles of manager, director, or consultant, but may include many others.

- **All nations of the world** means that this book was not written for any one culture or from any one cultural point of view. Our research process included diverse international viewpoints and development suggestions. It was in that spirit that we have tried to include as many electronic resources as possible to allow the widest accessibility across the globe, at least where Internet access is possible. It is important to note that not every tip will be appropriate for all cultures, but we have included a diverse array of tips to provide you with plenty of ideas to choose from for your environment.

- **Global roles** is perhaps the most important point to define here, because *global* does not refer to simple geography. Global roles include those who are working as expatriates (i.e., outside of their home countries), and they include those who may be working in their home countries but frequently interact with colleagues, partners, suppliers, and customers from diverse cultures. Do you work with diverse people? Do your interactions include people from different parts of the world? Then chances are this book will be helpful to you.

- **Various types of organizations** refers to those who work in for-profit, nonprofit, and governmental organizations. Regardless of industry, this book will be a useful resource for you. That said, we know that we have not yet captured every industry-specific tip, so you may need to adapt some tips to fit your industry-specific resources.

The book begins with a rich overview of Global Mindset to help readers fully understand the breadth of the model and depth of the individual dimensions. We also discuss the origins and use of the GMI. The assessment is usually the beginning of our relationship with our clients, so we felt it may be an important starting point for you as well.

Following the introductory chapter, the book is divided into three sections representing the three components of Global Mindset: Global Intellectual Capital, Global Psychological Capital, and Global Social Capital. Within each section, you will find three dimensions of each respective capital broken down into the smallest capabilities. There are three to four capabilities within each dimension, and we have provided a description of each along with specific development suggestions. Each development tip includes one or more suggested resources that our expert colleagues have identified to be valuable. You'll also find rich examples of each capability in action through narrative stories and examples from real-world practitioners and experts.

Given the volume of suggestions in this handbook, you have the luxury of reflecting on a number of development activities and then choosing those that are of the most relevance and interest to you. We do not believe the goal of Global Mindset development is perfection in all thirty-five capabilities. We suggest you focus on developing those that are of the most immediate benefit for your role, goals, and interests.

We've organized the development tips into four categories:

1. **Learn:** Tips to begin developing the capability on your own. These tips involve self-directed learning, including reading, listening, watching, or observing. They are most useful for novices in the capability, but are helpful for intermediate and advanced learners to keep their knowledge current.

2. **Connect:** Tips to learn about and continue developing the capability through others. These tips involve working with another person to learn from their experiences. These tips may involve asking questions, listening to and discussing experiences, forming a new relationship, deepening an existing relationship, or receiving feedback from someone who is acting as your mentor. These tips are useful for all levels of learners.

3. **Experience:** Tips to learn about and develop skills in the capability through firsthand experience. These tips involve engaging in activities, such as exploring a new area, trying a new cultural activity, or participating in a specific business event. These tips are most useful for intermediate to advanced learners, and we suggest that novice learners prepare themselves for success by completing some of the tips in the Learn category first.

4. **Coach or Contribute:** Tips to help others learn about and develop the capability. These tips involve coaching and mentoring others. They may include creating information or experiences for individuals, teams, or your organization. These tips are designed for those who are advanced in the capability and are useful development methods to keep advanced leaders in the capability engaged in professional development at the highest level. Please note that the tips in this section may also be quite helpful for your own use if you do not have a coach or mentor.

The variety of tips in this book is intentional. Our research shows that Global Mindset is best developed through dynamic learning; that is, learning that blends cognitive, affective, and social learning. If you're new to Global Mindset, you'll probably want to start with the tips in the Learn category. Those with some familiarity and experience with Global Mindset will particularly enjoy the tips in the Connect and Explore categories. They take more effort to complete and will reward you accordingly. For our resident experts in a particular dimension of Global Mindset, you will probably be most interested in the Coach or Contribute category.

You'll see seven very diverse and engaging case studies about Global Mindset in action in the appendix. You can use these individually to reflect on how you might approach a similar situation. You can also use these as a team or class to engage in compelling dialogue and debate. We've provided discussion questions to get you started. There are also some teaching notes following each case study to provide some guidance on the responses to the discussion questions. We've highlighted how Global Mindset dimensions either were used well or needed to be better employed for a successful result.

Final Thoughts

While we have put together a variety of suggestions, we know that these are not all-encompassing. You will, no doubt, have many other useful development suggestions. We invite you to share them with us at www.globalmindset.com, so we may include them in subsequent editions of this book. We also invite your personal experiences, as you will see that those we have included throughout the book are both enlightening and entertaining.

We anticipate that this book will be a career-long, desk-side friend that you can pick up and refer to on an as-needed basis. Please feel free to join our network for up-to-date news and information from the institute. We'd love to be a partner and a resource for you in your journey to further develop your Global Mindset.

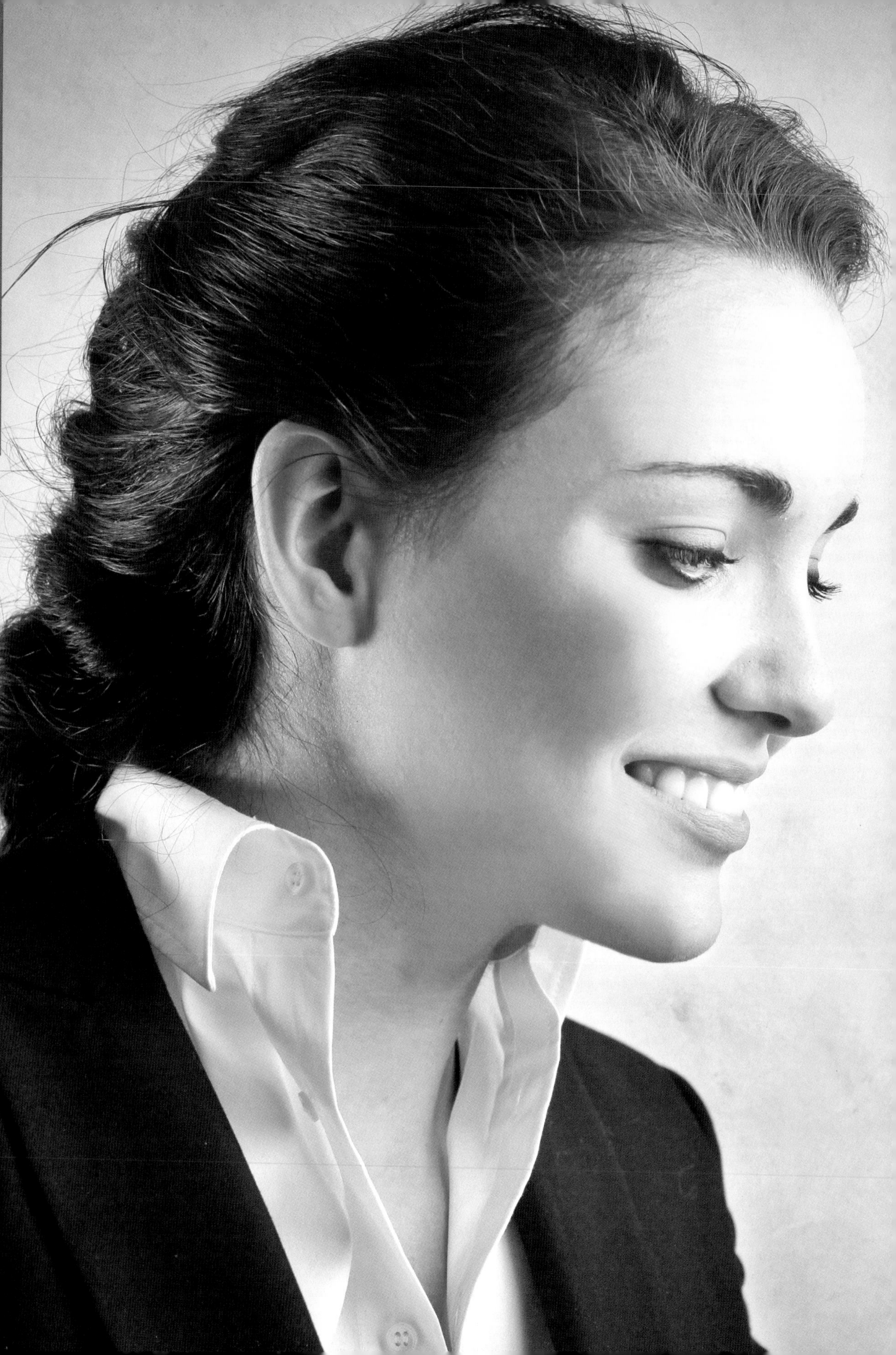

GLOBAL Mindset

Global Mindset

Global Mindset is the essence of twenty-first-century leadership, and it requires people who can think globally, who can make decisions globally, and who can understand challenges and opportunities globally and how to address them.

MANSOUR JAVIDAN, PH.D.
Director of the Najafi Global Mindset Institute
& Garvin Distinguished Professor
Mansour.Javidan@Thunderbird.edu

We've spent much time since late 2004 trying to determine precisely which knowledge, dispositions, and skills Global Mindset includes. We've interviewed hundreds of executives and global business experts in the world, and we've been able to define it in a very simple and specific way:

Global Mindset is a set of attributes and characteristics that help global leaders better influence individuals, groups, and organizations unlike themselves.

If you, as a manager, have a high level of those attributes, it makes it easier for you to work effectively with people who are different from you, regardless of where you are from. This is not strictly an American issue or a Chinese issue, for example. This is a global issue. So, those qualities and attributes that would make it easier for you to work effectively with people from other parts of the world is what we call Global Mindset.

If you look at what's going on in many companies today, the growth opportunities are beyond their borders. For companies to grow their markets and their revenue, they have to look beyond their countries. Even in cases where companies may not be looking to start up in new countries, many times their supply chains are beyond their own countries. It doesn't really matter which country, because Global Mindset applies to managers in any country who need to work with people from other cultures. Any global company and any company that's expecting to grow over the next decade is bound to look outside of its borders, because that's where the opportunities are. So, the strategic logic of the corporation is "let's go beyond our border," and it makes perfect sense.

However, the problem is that the company is now asking its managers to do something that does not come naturally to them. Implicitly, the company is saying to managers, "Now we're requiring you to work effectively with people who are from other parts of the world."

This is the essence of twenty-first-century leadership, and it requires people who can think globally, who can make decisions globally, and who can understand challenges and opportunities globally and how to address them. As companies globalize, managers are required to think beyond what they are familiar with, and that's not easy. This is what makes Global Mindset development an imperative for the success of managers and their organizations.

Global Mindset Model

In late 2004, a group of eight professors at Thunderbird asked a simple question: why is it that some executives are very effective working with people from other parts of the world? We had seen that some executives were successful in their own countries, but as soon as they were asked to work with people from other parts of the world, they either fell apart entirely or were quite ineffective. So, the question that we were trying to answer was, what distinguishes the effective ones from the ineffective ones?

We put together a very elaborate and sophisticated research project where we interviewed 217 global executives in twenty-three cities in Asia, Europe, and the United States. We also interviewed about forty of our own colleagues at Thunderbird who are experts in something global. We then worked with another group of over thirty distinguished scholars in the field of international business who helped us conceptually understand Global Mindset. This two-year process helped us identify the elements that make up Global Mindset.

Global Mindset includes three capitals (i.e., large bodies of knowledge, behaviors, and attributes): Global Intellectual Capital, Global Psychological Capital, and Global Social Capital. Within each capital, there are three dimensions (i.e., competencies). Each dimension then comprises three or four specific attributes. The structure of Global Mindset is captured in **Figure 1**.

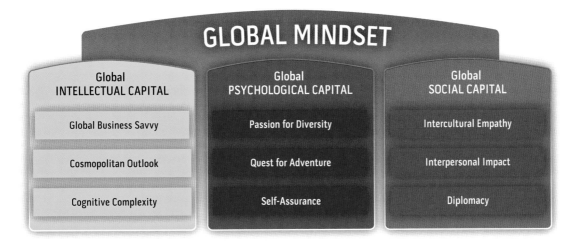

Figure 1

What Is Global Intellectual Capital?

Global Intellectual Capital is the cognitive component of Global Mindset. It is your knowledge of and ability to understand international business, business processes, and the cultural underpinnings of multiple countries around the globe. Your Global Intellectual Capital reflects your global business savvy, your cosmopolitan outlook, and your cognitive complexity. The following are the three competencies of Global Intellectual Capital.

Global Business Savvy:

- Knowledge of global industry

- Knowledge of global competitive business and marketing strategies

- Knowledge of how to transact business and assess risks of doing business internationally

- Knowledge of supplier options in other parts of the world

Cosmopolitan Outlook:

- Knowledge of cultures in different parts of the world

- Knowledge of geography, history, and important persons of several countries

- Knowledge of economic and political issues, concerns, and hot topics of major regions of the world

- Knowledge of important world events

Cognitive Complexity:

- Ability to grasp complex concepts quickly

- Ability to analyze and problem-solve

- Ability to understand abstract ideas

- Ability to take complex issues and explain the main points simply and understandably

What Is Global Psychological Capital?

Global Psychological Capital is the affective component of Global Mindset. It refers to your motives and values, and it reflects your willingness and motivation to experience and to succeed in international settings. Global Psychological Capital reflects your passion for diversity, quest for adventure, and self-assurance. The following are the three competencies of Global Psychological Capital.

Passion for Diversity:

- Enjoyment of exploring other parts of the world

- Enjoyment of getting to know people from other parts of the world

- Enjoyment of living in another country

- Enjoyment of traveling

Quest for Adventure:

- Interest in dealing with challenging situations

- Willingness to take risk

- Willingness to test one's abilities

- Enjoyment of dealing with unpredictable situations

Self-Assurance:

- Energetic

- Self-confident

- Comfortable in uncomfortable situations

- Witty in tough situations

What Is Global Social Capital?

Global Social Capital is the behavioral component of Global Mindset. It reflects your ability to interact appropriately in cultures around the world and affects your ability to build trusting relationships with individuals who are different from you. Global Social Capital reflects your intercultural empathy, interpersonal impact, and diplomacy. The following are the three competencies of Global Social Capital.

Intercultural Empathy:

- Ability to work well with people from other parts of the world

- Ability to understand nonverbal expressions of people from other cultures

- Ability to emotionally connect to people from other cultures

- Ability to engage people from other parts of the world to work together

Interpersonal Impact:

- Experience in negotiating contracts/agreements in other cultures

- Strong networks with people from other cultures and with influential people

- Reputation as a leader

Diplomacy:

- Ease of starting a conversation with a stranger

- Ability to integrate diverse perspectives

- Ability to listen to what others have to say

- Willingness to collaborate

The three capitals are highly correlated. They work together to produce the qualities, knowledge, skills, and abilities that comprise Global Mindset. They do not function in isolation. This is good news for those who are working to develop their Global Mindset. By working to develop one area, there are often improvements realized in other related areas. For example, a manager who successfully develops her passion for diversity (Global Psychological Capital) may realize gains in her intercultural empathy as well. That said, it is important to understand each part of Global Mindset to identify areas that require improvement. The detailed model of Global Mindset, including all thirty-five capabilities, is shown in **Figure 2**.

What Are the Characteristics of a Leader with a High Global Mindset?

Managers who have high Global Mindsets stand out based on their performance. These managers tend to be better able to identify market opportunities beyond their border. They tend to better identify supply chain opportunities. They identify talent across borders in other countries. They are more successful at putting together global teams who work effectively together. They also are better able to motivate people who come from different parts of the world toward the same objective. So the bottom line is that they produce better results for themselves, for their business unit, and, ultimately, for the corporation. This is because they are able to see the world from multiple perspectives.

Figure 2

Do All Levels of Managers Need a High Global Mindset?

Global Mindset is important for all levels of managers, from entry level to executive level, when they have global interactions and responsibilities. For example, the CEO or the direct reports of the CEO need Global Mindsets at the strategic level. This means CEOs must understand the global picture of their business to be able to create and drive a global competitive strategy. A mid-level manager also needs a high Global Mindset—not necessarily to think in strategic terms, but to be able to implement the global strategies. If the CEO decides that revenue needs to be increased from outside of the home country, well, guess who has to do it? The people in the middle ranks have to figure out how consumers in India, China, the United States, or Germany behave and what they want, for example. These managers then need to figure out how to build the product or deploy the service in the various ways that appeal to these clients. These managers also must figure out how to work with colleagues, supply chain partners, and joint venture partners from other countries. Their behavior has to be driven by a high Global Mindset, because if it isn't they are going to get into trouble.

Global Mindset is critical for mid-level managers all the way up to the CEO, but for different reasons. At lower levels of management, such as the supervisory level, their need for a high Global Mindset depends on the extent to which they are globally exposed. If a supervisor's team consists of people from different parts of the world, then yes, that supervisor needs a high Global Mindset. If a supervisor is working on a project basis with a group of people who are scattered in different parts of the world, he or she also needs a high Global Mindset. But if a supervisor is working with a local group of people serving a local community or a local market that is not very diverse, he or she may not need a high Global Mindset—not immediately, at least. There are more urgent problems or issues to deal with.

What Are the Characteristics of a Leader with a Low Global Mindset?

In our work with over seventeen thousand managers and in our interviews with hundreds of executives, it has become quite clear that individuals who have low Global Mindsets show very similar reactions to a global environment. To begin with, they tend to have a view that their way of doing things is the right way. If somebody else is doing it a different way, the assumption is that that person must be wrong. So these people are quite ethnocentric in their way of looking at things, and they often don't understand why things are done differently. This leads them to get frustrated, which is perhaps the most typical red flag.

Another behavior we see is that managers with low Global Mindsets tend to misunderstand the situation. They could be talking with someone from another country, for example, and they just don't understand the message. They misunderstand because they aren't able to understand the combination of words and body language coming from the other person, because it sounds and looks different than what they are used to. They simply can't step outside of their own point of view.

An example of this that we sometimes see between American and Asian managers is the difference in cultural norms around assertiveness. Many Asian managers and their employees tend to be fairly quiet in meetings. Their focus is on being respectful and deferential. This does not mean that they agree with what is being said. It is just their cultural upbringing. But if you don't know that as an American manager, and you expect everybody to raise their ideas and express opinions, you would see quiet colleagues as either being in agreement or uninterested. This common type of misunderstanding then escalates if there is low Global Mindset on the other side of the situation as well. The quiet colleagues may then interpret the more assertive colleagues as simply insensitive.

Can Global Mindset Be Developed?

Absolutely. We have a lot of scientific evidence since 2004 showing that Global Mindset can be developed. However, some dimensions are easier to develop and take less time than other dimensions. For example, the cognitive side of Global Mindset, called Global Intellectual Capital, is fairly easy to develop. It includes the manager's knowledge as well as how he or she digests and analyzes information. Development of this dimension is largely about reading, listening, and watching. It can be developed through instructor-led or self-directed training.

Global Social Capital, the behavioral side of Global Mindset, takes a bit more effort for some people to develop because it involves how a manager interacts with people from other parts of the world. Development of this area involves knowledge acquisition but largely is formed through live interactions with diverse others. So it is more challenging in that managers must have a desire to make behavioral modifications and need adequate practice with developmental coaching.

The real challenge in developing Global Mindset lies in Global Psychological Capital. It is the affective side of Global Mindset. It is about emotions and interests. Are you willing to engage? Do you like new experiences? Do you enjoy interacting with people from other parts of the world? Global Psychological Capital is the hardest dimension to develop because it is largely rooted in one's long-term life experiences and personality. Because we're working with adults, personality is less malleable than it is in children. Personality is pretty stable and doesn't change that easily. A huge improvement can be made over a short period of time on Global Intellectual Capital, but is not typical in Global Psychological Capital. Therefore, development methods become much more important in Global Psychological Capital. To improve someone's Global Psychological Capital, teaching is not going to do much good. That person needs to be immersed in experiences and coaching. Through targeted development efforts, you can create improvement through longer-term activities and personal coaching.

Global Mindset Inventory

The Global Mindset Inventory is the premier assessment tool developed by Najafi Global Mindset Institute to help determine a global leader's ability to better influence individuals, groups, and organizations unlike themselves.

ARVIND DESHMUKH, MBA
Manager of Operations
Najafi Global Mindset Institute
Arvind.Deshmukh@Thunderbird.edu

Most citizens of the world grow up as unicultural individuals who learn how to live and work with people who are like themselves. The global world of business today has brought many unicultural individuals together, expecting them to work in multicultural and cross-cultural environments. The Global Mindset Inventory (GMI) is an important tool to help determine who might be better at communicating, doing business with, and influencing other people who are unlike themselves.

The GMI is a web-based survey with fewer than eighty questions. It takes only ten to fifteen minutes to complete, but it provides a wealth of information about your Global Mindset. Your custom GMI report will show you how you currently rate in the three principle components of Global Mindset—Global Intellectual Capital, Global Psychological Capital, and Global Social Capital. You'll also see your detailed scores in the nine dimensions. The GMI is available in both a self-assessment and a 360-degree assessment in multiple languages. We offer three versions of the GMI for our clients in business firms, academic institutions, and nonprofit or government sectors. Over seventeen thousand respondents have now taken the GMI in more than seventy countries.

Is the GMI Self-Assessment Accurate?

We take our research seriously at the Najafi Global Mindset Institute! So when we decided to investigate the essential components of Global Mindset, we used a rigorous, scientific process. When it came to the creation of the GMI, we partnered with the world-renowned Dunnette Group. It comprises experts in the design and testing of psychometric instruments like the GMI. Pilot tests were done with more than one thousand global managers.

The Dunnette Group did a series of evaluations and revisions to ensure the instrument was both valid and reliable. We have a lengthy technical report available at www.globalmindset.com that describes the procedures and specific psychometric properties of the GMI.

We've also done comparative analyses of the GMI self-assessment and GMI 360 version that show that there is a strong correlation between a person's self-assessment score and the scores given by peers, managers, and clients. This means that the self-assessment does a very good job of measuring what it is supposed to measure.

What Is the Global Mindset Inventory 360?

The GMI 360 version is designed to gather the quantitative scores and qualitative feedback of a manager's peers, supervisors, and direct reports. It provides them with a wealth of information about their current knowledge, skills, and abilities. This information can be used for in-depth coaching and development. It is an ideal tool for leadership development programs, in-depth personal coaching, and a more holistic view of Global Mindset in the organization.

How Do I Register to Take the Global Mindset Inventory or Global Mindset Inventory 360?

We work closely with our clients across corporations, academia, and non-profit/government sectors to offer them the products and services that best match their needs. So we invite you to contact us to determine how we can best serve you. You'll find our most up-to-date contact information on our website: www.globalmindset.com. We look forward to partnering with you!

GLOBAL INTELLECTUAL CAPITAL

1 Global Business Savvy

2 Cosmopolitan Outlook

3 Cognitive Complexity

Global Intellectual Capital refers to how much you know about your own company's strategy globally, your competitors' strategies globally, other cultures, other governments, and other political systems, and how easy it is for your brain to handle all of that information. Think about it this way. Let's say you're a manager working for a Korean company who produces its products in Korea and sells them to its Korean market. As a manager working for this company, you need to know: What's your strategy in Korea? Who are your Korean competitors? How does your Korean consumer buy your product? What does your Korean consumer want it for, and how much is your Korean consumer willing to pay for it? You also need to be familiar with government regulations, the political environment, and the Korean culture.

Let's say your Korean company decides that there are a lot of opportunities in the United States and you, the managers and executives, need to figure out how to go after the US market. And by the way, we need you to think about how to produce the product in China and India because we can do it cheaper and more efficiently in China and India compared to Korea. As a Korean manager working for this company, now you have to learn something about the US market. Who is the US consumer? What does the US consumer want? How much is the US consumer willing to pay? Is the US consumer even interested in the same product that the Korean consumer is interested in, or does the US consumer want something totally different? Your existing product may not serve the US consumer. You'll need to know about the US political system and culture and, specifically, how people do business in the United States.

As a manager, you also need to learn about your US competitors, other competitors who do business in the United States in the market you're interested in. And on the supply chain, remember your company saying that you needed to get into China and India to produce your products? Now you have to learn about Indian culture and Indian ways of doing things. You need to learn about the Chinese way of doing things, Chinese culture, and Chinese political system.

These two decisions by the company—to go after the US market and produce supplies in India and China—have now created a huge amount of complexity for you as a Korean manager. You need to learn much more information about places and things you didn't care about before. Now the question is: Are you able to handle all of that complex information? That's what we call cognitive complexity. It's one thing to give you all of that information. It's another thing what you do with it. How do you analyze it? How do you make sense out of it, and how do you make decisions?

Global Intellectual Capital is about your knowledge of these additional markets, consumers, and suppliers and how easy it is for your brain to handle, analyze, and digest all of this information. It is really about your ability to understand and navigate the complexities of global differences and interconnectedness at the same time.

As you can see from **Figure 1**, Global Intellectual Capital consists of three main dimensions: global business savvy, cosmopolitan outlook, and cognitive complexity. In this section, we are going to explain each of the three dimensions. We'll define each dimension as well as all of its component attributes. You'll see that each dimension has three to four specific attributes that include bodies of knowledge or skills to master. You can quickly turn to a chapter on the specific attribute you'd like to develop and find a myriad of development tips and resources at your fingertips. We've also provided you with engaging examples and narratives from global leaders in the field to illustrate each attribute in action. Each of the tips and stories are intended to help you enhance your skills in the areas you most want or need to develop.

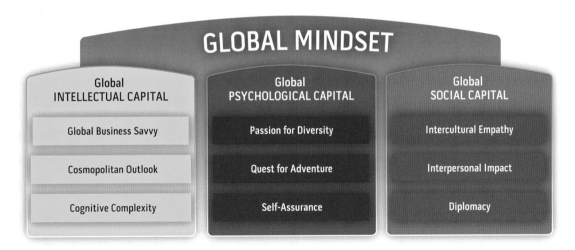

Figure 1

GLOBAL MINDSET

Global INTELLECTUAL CAPITAL

Global Business Savvy

Knowledge of global industry

Knowledge of global competitive business and marketing strategies

Knowledge of how to transact business and assess risks of doing business internationally

Knowledge of supplier options in other parts of the world

Cosmopolitan Outlook

Knowledge of cultures in different parts of the world

Knowledge of geography, history, and important persons of several countries

Knowledge of economic & political issues, concerns, & hot topics of major regions of the world

Up-to-date knowledge of important world events

Cognitive Complexity

Ability to grasp complex topics quickly

Strong analytical and problem solving skills

Ability to understand abstract ideas

Ability to take complex issues and explain the main points simply and understandably

Global PSYCHOLOGICAL CAPITAL

Passion for Diversity

Enjoy exploring other parts of the world

Enjoy getting to know people from other parts of the world

Enjoy living in another country

Enjoy traveling

Quest for Adventure

Interest in dealing with challenging situations

Willingness to take risk

Willingness to test one's abilities

Enjoy dealing with unpredictable situations

Self-Assurance

Energetic

Self-confident

Comfortable in uncomfortable situations

Witty in tough situations

Global SOCIAL CAPITAL

Intercultural Empathy

Ability to work well with people from other parts of the world

Ability to understand nonverbal expressions of people from other cultures

Ability to emotionally connect to people from other cultures

Ability to engage people from other parts of the world to work together

Interpersonal Impact

Experience in negotiating contracts/agreements in other cultures

Strong networks with people from other cultures and with influential people

Reputation as a leader

Diplomacy

Ease of starting a conversation with a stranger

Ability to integrate diverse perspectives

Ability to listen to what others have to say

Willingness to collaborate

Figure 1-1

1

Global Business Savvy

As seen in **Figure 1-1** on page 32, this chapter examines Global Business Savvy, which is a key dimension of Global Intellectual Capital. Global business savvy refers to your understanding of the consumers, markets, and competitors in your industry in different parts of the world. It requires that you are knowledgeable about what's going on in the parts of the world that are currently of interest to your organization as well as emerging markets in your industry. Most importantly, it requires you to have 360 eyes: the ability to look at the same business issue from multiple perspectives.

Business executives who are very good at Global Business Savvy don't think, for example, "I'm a British executive in a British company." They approach business issues and decisions by looking from the perspective of the particular culture and environment in question. For example, a senior executive of a huge retail operation was in a meeting to discuss global sourcing strategy. The rest of the leaders were discussing the typical sourcing countries for their industry, namely China and India. But this executive began asking questions about countries they had not yet explored, such as Bangladesh. Even though they had not yet done business in Bangladesh, he wanted to explore the possibility. He wanted to figure out how

INTERNATIONAL CARGO SHIPMENT

they might adapt their operations for this new market, from the perspective of the people of Bangladesh.

This comes more naturally to those managers who have high global business savvy. They develop this savvy through a combination of practical experience, curiosity, and continuous learning. Those with high global business savvy are able to look beyond the markets they are currently in to explore new frontiers with confidence and grace.

In this chapter, we provide development suggestions for each of the following capabilities within global business savvy:

- Knowledge of global industry

- Knowledge of global competitive business and marketing strategies

- Knowledge of how to transact business and assess risks of doing business internationally

- Knowledge of supplier options in other parts of the world

CHEESE PROCESSING PLANT, SWITZERLAND

Tan Wei Ming / Shutterstock.com

Knowledge of Global Industry

Knowledge of global industry refers to the depth and breadth of your knowledge about your industry on a global scale. Global industry is dynamic and rapidly changing. So while the tips here are a good starting point for those new to global business, they are also a point of continuous education for all levels. To stay sharp, you must keep your finger on the pulse of what is happening globally.

Consider the case of the manufacturing sector. A 2009 Global Intelligence Analyst survey of forty-six senior executives at some of the world's largest manufacturing companies revealed that market opportunities are changing quickly due to population changes, such as a fast-growing middle class in China and aging populations in parts of Western Europe. Competitors are quickly cropping up in these markets to meet consumer needs, largely through international expansion of existing companies. More competitors in the market have led to pricing pressures and to long-established companies being challenged to respond more quickly to the changing market needs. The market leaders in the manufacturing sector today may not stay competitive for long if they do not keep up with the pace of changing consumer needs and keep informed about their competitors.

The tips in this section will help you get up to speed with current knowledge about global industry. Because of the fast pace of change in the global marketplace, these tips will help you stay informed. Hold on tight; you're in for a wild ride.

Knowledge of Global Industry in Action

In 2007, our association had members in sixty-seven countries and three international offices in the Netherlands, India, and the United States. At the time, one of our main strategic goals was to expand our international presence, particularly in China.

ŞIRIN Z. KÖPRÜCÜ, MBA
International Business Consultant
StrategicStraits Inc.

In 2007, our association had members in sixty-seven countries and three international offices in the Netherlands, India, and the United States. At the time, one of our main strategic goals was to expand our international presence, particularly in China. Our association formed a relationship with a marketing company in China to advance our brand in the Chinese market. We were referred to the company by our staff in our European office.

Our objectives in China were to

- serve as the official regional representative of the association

- build alliances with partners and affiliate associations in China

- aggressively focus on building membership in China

- assist with the implementation of international projects conducted in the China region

- participate in international project business development exercises by working with potential donors (USDA, USAID, foreign governments, etc.)

- achieve a financial breakeven point in 2007 with surplus goals in future years.

After a year of operating in China, we noticed some strategic flaws with our presence in China. While we were successfully hosting well-attended events, membership development was slow and we were having trouble making the strategic connections with national associations and large corporations necessary to succeed in China. We decided to conduct a comprehensive assessment of our China office and strategy.

We interviewed several actors involved in our activities in China, including headquarters staff, our China representative, our leadership, and leaders of national associations in China. We realized through these interviews that we may have erred in developing our approach in China. We realized that we had a serious diplomacy gap in our China strategy. Our representative was exactly who we would want to help us develop membership in North America or Europe, but in China, where relationships are highly valued, our representative and our association were seen as an upstart.

These interviews highlighted the cultural differences between doing business in China and doing business in the United States. We learned that the directness we so value in the United States does not typically transfer to communications in China. Our constructive criticism could easily be deemed an insult. We also realized that communicating solely via email or phone was not enough. Operating in China meant visiting China a lot. We needed to have face-to-face conversations with partners to foster relationships.

After the interviews, we came to the conclusion, like many international companies realize when operating in China, that we needed an established partner in China. We needed a representative with both the drive and the personal finesse to navigate the sometimes tricky turf of the Chinese industry and build a strong network. Ideally, our representative would be someone with preexisting industry contacts and expertise.

We also needed to learn more about our industry in China and a representative who could collect and disseminate market intelligence. Finally, we needed

ROTTERDAM, NETHERLANDS

an in-country representative who would focus on serving members in China and international members interested in developing business in China.

We revised our strategy to put greater emphasis on relationship building and collecting market intelligence. We established the following as the objectives for our new representative:

- Serve as the official regional association in China.

- Build alliances with partners and affiliate associations in China.

- Serve existing members.

- Collect market intelligence on the industry, and initiate development of Chinese resources.

We felt that this less aggressive approach in China would help build our brand and guanxi, as they name personalized networks of relationships or influence in China. Now, almost three years later, we have established some very powerful relationships in China. Our brand is more recognizable, and we are about to once again revise our strategy in China to actively build membership. The willingness to be flexible and rapidly adapt to changes is perhaps the most valuable lesson we took away from our experiences in China. International growth is a fluid process. You have to be willing to adapt to changing markets and the needs of your constituents in order to succeed.

DEVELOPMENT SUGGESTIONS
for Knowledge of Global Industry

LEARN

Tips to learn about and begin developing the capability on your own. These tips involve self-directed learning, including reading, listening, watching, or observing, that you can do on your own at your own pace. They are most useful for novices in the capability, but are helpful for intermediate and advanced learners to keep knowledge current.

Development Activity	Suggested Resource(s) and Tips
Read books about company history (e.g., Walmart, Nike) to get a sense of what/how they learned as they globalized.	Corporations Who Changed the World series: • *Apple Inc.* (O'Grady, 2008) • *Google* (Scott, 2008) • *Harley-Davidson* (Scott, 2008) • *Starbucks* (Bussing-Burks, 2009) • *Nike* (Carbasho, 2010)
Learn about global role models.	• The annual *Time* 100 Most Influential People in the World (www.time.com) • The annual *Forbes* Most Powerful People List (www.forbes.com)
Read about fast-growing *Fortune* 500 companies and the Global *Fortune* 500.	• The *Fortune* 500 annual listing of "Top Companies: Fastest Growing" (money.cnn.com/magazines/fortune/fortune500/2012/performers/companies/fastgrowprofits) • The Global *Fortune* 500 annual listing (http://money.cnn.com/magazines/fortune/global500/2011)
Listen to analyst calls, and use/purchase analyst reports on industries and specific countries of interest.	• Economist Intelligence Unit (www.eiu.com) • World Bank (www.worldbank.org)
Watch Hans Rosling's graphic illustrations of global statistics to understand trends in developing countries.	Hans Rosling's work can be found at www.gapminder.org and www.ted.com/talks/hans_rosling_at_state.html.
Read industry journals.	Find trade publications by industry at www.webwire.com/industrylist.asp.

DEVELOPMENT SUGGESTIONS
for Knowledge of Global Industry

LEARN

Tips to learn about and begin developing the capability on your own. These tips involve self-directed learning, including reading, listening, watching, or observing, that you can do on your own at your own pace. They are most useful for novices in the capability, but are helpful for intermediate and advanced learners to keep knowledge current.

Development Activity	Suggested Resource(s) and Tips
Read world business news websites to understand what is going on in the world of business—trends, issues, economic development.	• *The Wall Street Journal* (available in editions for the United States, Asia, Europe, and the Americas) (http://online.wsj.com) • *The Economist* (www.economist.com) • *Financial Times* (www.ft.com) • CNN Money (money.cnn.com/news/world) • Reuters (www.reuters.com) • *Forbes* (www.forbes.com) • BBC (www.bbc.com) • *Foreign Affairs* (www.foreignaffairs.com) • *BusinessWeek Asia* (www.businessweek.com/asia) • *China Business Review* (www.chinabusinessreview.com) • *BusinessWeek Europe* (www.businessweek.com/europe) • Latin Finance (www.latinfinance.com) • Latin Focus (www.latin-focus.com) • *Latin Trade* (http://latintrade.com) • America Economia (www.americaeconomica.com)

DEVELOPMENT SUGGESTIONS
for Knowledge of Global Industry

CONNECT

Tips to learn about and continue developing the capability through others. These tips involve working with another person to learn from their experiences. These tips may involve asking questions, listening to and discussing experiences, forming a new relationship, deepening an existing relationship, or receiving feedback from someone who is acting as your mentor. These tips are useful for all levels of learners.

Development Activity	Suggested Resource(s) and Tips
Identify successful global executives in your organization and within your industry. Look at what they do and how they do it. Ask to meet with them to ask questions about what they do.	• Ask your manager. • Ask your human resources department. • Ask colleagues. • Follow your organization's public relations and communications. • Read your organization's newsletters, blogs, intranet, and external web page. • Follow trade publications in your industry. • Follow trade and industry conferences in your field.

DEVELOPMENT SUGGESTIONS
for Knowledge of Global Industry

EXPERIENCE

Tips to learn about and develop skills in the capability through firsthand experience. These tips involve engaging in activities, such as exploring a new area, trying a new cultural activity, or participating in a specific business event. These tips are most useful for intermediate to advanced learners, and we suggest that novice learners prepare themselves for success by completing some of the tips in the Learn category first.

Development Activity	Suggested Resource(s) and Tips
Attend global conferences and trade shows, and listen for differences in cultural approaches in different parts of the world.	<ul><li>Ask your manager.</li><li>Ask colleagues.</li><li>Follow your organization's public relations and communications.</li><li>Read your organization's newsletters, blogs, intranet, and external web page.</li><li>Follow trade publications in your industry.</li></ul>
Create a list of questions related to global business savvy that you need answered in your current job.	Self-assess what you already know well and where your knowledge gaps are. Consider the following global bodies of knowledge:<ul><li>supply chain</li><li>marketing</li><li>commercial sales</li><li>finance</li><li>tax</li><li>social responsibility</li><li>ethics</li><li>regulatory environments/law</li><li>industry-specific knowledge.</li></ul>
Seek out global positions to gain knowledge of global industry and business.	<ul><li>Join global teams inside and outside of your organization.</li><li>Ask your manager if you can be assigned to work on global projects.</li></ul>

DEVELOPMENT SUGGESTIONS
for Knowledge of Global Industry

COACH OR CONTRIBUTE

Tips to help others learn about and develop this capability. These tips involve coaching and mentoring others. They may include creating information or experiences for individuals, teams, or your organization. These tips are designed for those who are advanced in the capability and are useful development methods to keep advanced leaders in the capability engaged in professional development at the highest level. Please note that the tips in this section may also be quite helpful for individual use if you do not have a coach or mentor.

Development Activity	Suggested Resource(s) and Tips
Share your expertise to develop others.	Create teaching moments for your direct reports in your interactions and in staff functions through: • storytelling • dialogue • presentations • guest speakers.
Hire people with diverse experiences and backgrounds.	Post jobs and solicit applicants from: • diverse locations • diverse interest groups • diverse network/affinity groups in your organization • your global network inside and outside of your organization.
Have an ethics policy or credo.	• Know how ethics is defined and implemented by the company and from a manager's point of view. • Implement ethics training. • Use ethics consultants such as Oxford Analytica (www.oxan.com). • Look to global role models in ethics policies like J&J (www.jnj.com).

Additional Reading

The readings listed here provide you with additional study of the Global Mindset capability in this section. You will find that many of these resources provide you with a specific and detailed look at using this capability in a particular context or location.

··

Title: "The Transfer of Knowledge and the Retention of Expertise: The Continuing Need for Global Assignments"

Publication: *Journal of Knowledge Management*

Date: 2000

Authors: Silke Bender and Alan Fish

Executive Summary: A general overview of knowledge management and a discussion of the transfer of knowledge and expertise throughout organizations operating on a global scale are given. A particular emphasis is placed on the importance of global assignments in transferring knowledge and, furthermore, on the implications of human resources management practices to ensure the successful and effective retention of expertise.

··

Title: "Top Executives' International Expertise Commitment: Exploring Potential Antecedents"

Publication: *Leadership & Organization Development Journal*

Date: 2010

Authors: Tejinder K. Billing, Debmalya Mukherjee, Ben L. Kedia, and Somnath Lahiri

Executive Summary: The purpose of this paper is to explore the immediate antecedents of top executives' international expertise commitment. More specifically, the study focuses on the effect of top management characteristics and the international business performance of firms on top management's commitment to developing international expertise in their workforce.

Title: "Managing Executive Attention in the Global Company"

Publication: *MIT Sloan Management Review*

Date: 2007

Authors: Julian Birkinshaw, Cyril Bouquet, and Tina C. Ambos

Executive Summary: For executives running global companies, the challenge of keeping abreast of events in markets around the world is mind-boggling. The problem is not a lack of information; it is having the time and energy to process the information. How should executives prioritize their time to ensure that it is focused on the countries and subsidiaries that need the attention? Which markets should they emphasize, and which ones can they allow to fall off their radar? The authors researched executive attention at global companies for five years, interviewing fifty executives at thirty corporations including ABB, Dun & Bradstreet, Nestlé, and Sara Lee. They found that executives end up prioritizing a handful of markets at the expense of the others, but they don't always select the most promising ones.

Title: "Effect of Global Business Curriculum on Student Attitudes"

Publication: *Business Education Innovation Journal*

Date: 2011

Authors: David W. Brasfield, James P. McCoy, and Mary Tripp Reed

Executive Summary: Business schools have internationalized their curriculum to prepare students for work in the global economy. This internationalization rests on the assumption that exposure to international business content will lead students to be more open to doing international business. Traditionally, schools infused core courses with international business content. However, while we find that international knowledge is gained, there is little effect on student attitudes. Rather, we find evidence that more experiential approaches such as exchange and study abroad programs may enhance a global curriculum through encouraging desired attitudinal changes regarding doing business with other cultures and nations. While additional research is needed to make firm conclusions, international content with experiential, international learning activities may increase the global knowledge base and skills of students as well as increase the likelihood that they actually make use of these skills.

Title: "Born-Globals and Culturally Proximate Markets"

Publication: *Management International Review*

Date: 2012

Authors: Susan Freeman, Kate Hutchings, and Sylvie Chetty

Executive Summary: The article presents the business styles of born-globals and older firms in terms of expansion and revenues. It discusses born-globals as more of small and medium enterprises, compared to multinational structure of older firms, but the born-globals have more aggressive and proactive approaches. It describes technological knowledge used by born-globals as leverage to pursue international markets and establish foreign partnerships with the pressure of limited cash flow and lack of stable resources as drawbacks.

Title: "The Role of Managerial Curiosity in Organizational Learning: A Theoretical Inquiry"

Publication: *International Journal of Management*

Date: 2012

Authors: Nancy H. McIntyre, Michael Harvey, and Miriam Moeller

Executive Summary: Organizational learning is a means to improve the chances of the organization surviving in today's highly competitive global marketplace. Organizational knowledge creation and knowledge transfer represent imperative for attaining and sustaining a competitive advantage in a global business environment. Yet organizations are unable to learn unless the individuals in the organizations are committed to the learning process. Curiosity provides the platform for global managers to inquire into why things happen and what can be done to effectively meet the goals of the organization. Learning managers with curiosity need to heed the importance of their level of mindfulness (i.e., focusing curiosity to meet goals) so that curiosity is an effective tool to learn and solve problems. This paper explores the concept of curiosity by linking individual curiosity and learning style to organizational learning. The traits/characteristics of knowledge activists are discussed as a means to cultivate organizational learning.

Title: "Analytical Perspectives on the Integration and Diffusion of Knowledge in Multicultural Business Schools to Build Global Image"

Publication: *ICFAI Journal of Knowledge Management*

Date: 2009

Authors: William Henry Steinwascher and Rajagopal

Executive Summary: Multicultural phenomenon in organizations has been studied in this paper from educational and business perspectives. It discusses the pattern of organizational behavior of business schools seeking a global image in a multicultural environment. The study focuses on the process of knowledge diffusion and its effect on the variability of corporate and organizational image, reviews literature from both perspectives, and tries to integrate the contributions in the multicultural education model to gain a global image. To get a better understanding of the literature about multicultural education and organizational goals, a matrix was developed to explain both criteria. Two kinds of educational orientation and organizational goals were identified. The local and multicultural organizational platforms that demonstrate tenure goals—short and long term—were analyzed to assess the variability factors in building the global image. The analysis of both criteria revealed four orientations in the previous contributions made on the topic: traditional, integrative, expansive, and global. Different prepositions were developed on the basis of critical review of literature by identifying gaps in the conceptual dimensions and a model that explains the variability factors in building a global image under multicultural environment was suggested. The model explains how business schools can reach global orientation through their organizational goals and educational perspectives.

SHOPPING MALL ▪ CHENGDU, CHINA

Knowledge of Global Competitive Business and Marketing Strategies

Developing your knowledge of global competitive business and marketing strategies lands in two categories: what you should know about global business and marketing strategies to stay ahead of the curve and what you need to know to be competitive in your industry. You need both to succeed in today's volatile market. The use of social media for marketing is an example of how worldwide trends must be customized for your particular industry and consumers.

Social media is increasingly en vogue for marketing efforts across the globe and has been shown to be effective when used well. However, social media marketers are quickly learning a lesson that manufacturing and consumer services companies learned in the late twentieth century: communication, products, and services must all be customized to meet consumer needs in different cultures. Attempts to use the same social media marketing strategies across countries have not worked well. The content of marketing communications, not just the language, must be relevant to a local market to engage them (Global Business Hub, 2012).

Being knowledgeable about globalization and global business trends across industries will help you fine-tune your strategic understanding of the broader forces at play in the markets. Expertise in your own industry helps you with the strategy in that specific context, and it also helps you figure out how to tactfully implement and manage business on your own playing field. It's a bit like the Olympics. We may be most invested in our own sport, but it is always interesting to see how the ripple effects of individual wins and losses affect the overall morale, motivation, and eventual success of countries across all of the sports. Let the games begin.

Knowledge of Global Competitive Business and Marketing Strategies in Action

I was leading an American business delegation of senior executives, all from different companies, to various cities throughout China, to assist them in learning how to do business there.

CARI E. GUITTARD, MPA
Principal
Global Engagement Partners

The formality and pace of doing business in China is very different from the typical American style. Seniority and protocol are extremely important when conducting business in China, as is gifting and the cultural experience. For every business meeting, we would have two cultural events complete with lavish, over-the-top gifts.

Most of the executives were tuned out or annoyed during the opening cultural events, perhaps in part due to jetlag, but also because many seemed anxious to get down to business. They were trying to approach competitive business in China as they do in the United States. Irritated with the cultural differences in business dealings, they began plotting their disappearance during the cultural events in the coming days. I knew that evening we'd have to pull the group together and give them a crash course in business in China before their attitudes deteriorated any further.

During our discussion, I stressed that competitive business relationships in China go beyond traditional networking to involve in-depth social time and cultural events. This involves dinners that typically include up to ten courses over a period of several hours, many formal toasts, and traditional foods that they may not be prepared for. We discussed in-depth the business rituals and protocol, so they could reset their expectations. Once they had a clear sense of how important the protocol and cultural events were to doing competitive business in China, many seemed to relax and enjoy the experience.

DEVELOPMENT SUGGESTIONS
for Knowledge of Global Competitive Business and Marketing Strategies

LEARN

Tips to learn about and begin developing the capability on your own. These tips involve self-directed learning, including reading, listening, watching, or observing, that you can do on your own at your own pace. They are most useful for novices in the capability, but are helpful for intermediate and advanced learners to keep knowledge current.

Development Activity	Suggested Resource(s) and Tips
Learn relevant demographic data in countries of interest.	• United Nations Statistics Division (http://unstats.un.org) • The World Factbook (www.cia.gov/library/publications/the-world-factbook/rankorder/2119rank.html)
Find articles, books, and videos on how companies are globalizing.	• *World 3.0* (Ghemawat, 2011) • *The Quest for Global Dominance* (Gupta, Govindarajan, & Wang, 2008) • *Redefining Global Strategy* (Ghemawat, 2007) • Dr. Justin Paul's public-facing Facebook page, which links to many videos on global competitive business and marketing topics around the world (www.facebook.com/drjustinpaul)
Learn about role models by watching biographies and documentaries and through reading.	• CNBC Managing Asia (www.cnbc.com/id/15838822) • Bloomberg TV Game Changers (www.bloomberg.com/tv/shows/game-changers)
Read specific global industry/trade reports.	• Oxford Analytica (www.oxam.com) • Euromonitor International (www.euromonitor.com) • Business Without Borders (www.businesswithoutborders.com)
Learn about your own company's global initiatives and product launches, and learn from its successes and failures.	• Regularly read internal communications on your organization's intranet, newsletter, and blog. • Follow your organization's external news including press releases, news stories, magazine articles, and books. • Talk to colleagues who have been at the organization longer than you to learn about the history from those in the trenches.
Read about how to anticipate trends.	• Develop an understanding of the history of trends in your industry and responses to those trends by people inside and outside your organization. • Stay tuned into trends across your industry, not just within your organization or among main competitors. • Read news and forecasts about your industry in trade journals (www.webwire.com/industrylist.asp).

DEVELOPMENT SUGGESTIONS
for Knowledge of Global Competitive Business and Marketing Strategies

CONNECT

Tips to learn about and continue developing the capability through others. These tips involve working with another person to learn from their experiences. They may involve asking questions, listening to and discussing experiences, forming a new relationship, deepening an existing relationship, or receiving feedback from someone who is acting as your mentor. These tips are useful for all levels of learners.

Development Activity	Suggested Resource(s) and Tips
Take part in global project teams to gain exposure to different environments and worldviews.	• Join global teams inside and outside of your organization. • Ask your manager to work on global projects. • Participate in international corporate volunteering (www.worldactionteams.com).

DEVELOPMENT SUGGESTIONS
for Knowledge of Global Competitive Business and Marketing Strategies

EXPERIENCE

Tips to learn about and develop skills in the capability through firsthand experience. These tips involve engaging in activities, such as exploring a new area, trying a new cultural activity, or participating in a specific business event. These tips are most useful for intermediate to advanced learners, and we suggest that novice learners prepare themselves for success by completing some of the tips in the Learn category first.

Development Activity	Suggested Resource(s) and Tips
Interact with the local culture of business.	Visit local hot spots for business such as: • local markets • malls and other commercial centers • street markets and bazaars • local pubs, tea houses, and coffee shops.
Benchmark business and marketing practices within your industry in different countries.	Visit competitor stores and/or business sites specific to your industry and trade.

DEVELOPMENT SUGGESTIONS
for Knowledge of Global Competitive Business and Marketing Strategies

COACH OR CONTRIBUTE

Tips to help others learn about and develop this capability. These tips involve coaching and mentoring others. They may include creating information or experiences for individuals, teams, or your organization. These tips are designed for those who are advanced in the capability and are useful development methods to keep advanced leaders in the capability engaged in professional development at the highest level. Please note that the tips in this section may also be quite helpful for individual use if you do not have a coach or mentor.

Development Activity	Suggested Resource(s) and Tips
Identify ways to train and develop employees, direct reports, and customers in emerging markets.	• Emerging Markets News, Analysis, and Opinion (www.emergingmarkets.com) • Bloomberg Emerging Markets News (www.bloomberg.com/news/emerging-markets) • ISI Emerging Markets (www.securities.com) • Economist Education: Emerging Markets Essentials Program (www.economisteducation.com/courses/emerging-markets-essentials-programme)
Learn how to manage geographically diverse and virtual teams.	• "Managing a Virtual Team" (Mortenson and O'Leary, 2012) (http://blogs.hbr.org/cs/2012/04/how_to_manage_a_virtual_team.html) • "How to Manage Virtual Teams" (Siebdrat, Hoegl, and Ernst, 2009) (http://sloanreview.mit.edu/the-magazine/2009-summer/50412/how-to-manage-virtual-teams)

Additional Reading

The readings listed here provide you with additional study of the Global Mindset capability in this section. You will find that many of these resources provide you with a specific and detailed look at using this capability in a particular context or location.

···

Title: "Global Marketing: Overcoming a Little Local Difficulty"

Publication: *Marketing Week*

Date: October 2008

Authors: Not listed

Executive Summary: New global brand leaders are typically quite comfortable developing the what of global marketing—insights, innovation, and communication. However, what keeps many global brand leaders awake at night is the challenge of global leverage or the how of global marketing—working with local marketers on executing a single global brand strategy, enabling global marketing team alignment, improving speed to market, and sharing brand expertise across geographies. The critical underlying challenge to address is often a lack of real trust and interdependence between the local and global marketing teams. Defining the operating model and roles on key decisions is important, but enforcing the model and required behaviors is even more important. Many global brands' operating models have taken innovation and communication development responsibilities away from the countries and into global brand teams, allowing an increase in the focus on local market activation.

···

Title: "Global Branding, Country of Origin and Expertise"

Publication: *International Marketing Review*

Date: 2007

Authors: Anthony Pecotich and Steven Ward

Executive Summary: The globalization of markets combined with the paradoxical rise of nationalism has created an increased concern about the importance of the interaction of global brands with other cues such as the country of origin (COO) of products and services. The purpose of this paper is to evaluate the decision-making processes of experts and novices with respect to international brand names, COO, and intrinsic quality differences.

Knowledge of How to Transact Business and Assess Risks of Doing Business Internationally

As the old adage goes, almost anything worth doing involves risk. This is certainly the case when we're doing business in different countries. It doesn't just look and feel different than doing business at home, it is different. The spectrum of differences can range from minor to major; so can the risk.

The first step then is to determine how business is transacted in the location of interest. This includes consideration of the local customs, politics, economics, regulations, technologies, infrastructure, etc. (Be thorough in your investigation!) Your due diligence should include the perspectives of both natives to the local culture and foreigners working there. Foreigners will probably have a keener sense of where the differences lie, but natives will have a better sense of what actually works.

After doing your homework, you'll be better prepared to identify potential risks and then quantify them. But we invite you to examine your findings not through the lens of skepticism, rather through one of possibility. In the global market, where there is great risk there is also great opportunity for those who have business savvy and are able to assess and manage risks appropriately. It takes a mix of curiosity, courage, and vision to be successful. It may also take a little help from your risk management partners.

 INTERNATIONAL CURRENCY

Pedro Salaverría / Shutterstock.com

Knowledge of How to Transact Business and Assess Risks of Doing Business Internationally in Action

I was asked to facilitate a team-building session for a management team of twelve individuals representing seven nationalities. I was introduced to the president, Herr Doktor (Mr. Dr.) Schmidt who was Swiss German...

KATHERINE JOHNSTON, MBA
Speaker, Author, and Consultant

I was asked to facilitate a team-building session for a management team of twelve individuals representing seven nationalities. I was introduced to the president, Herr Doktor (Mr. Dr.) Schmidt who was Swiss-German, as was the human resources director. When I asked about the team's main challenge, the human resources director responded "communication" but struggled to explain why.

The solution, or at least the first step, was surprisingly simple. In the process of establishing team ground rules, one member suggested they use first names when addressing each other.

The subsequent discussion was revealing. For the Swiss-Germans, the use of formal titles was a sign of respect. For other team members, particularly those from Scandinavia, formal titles created distance and implied a lack of trust.

Herr Dr. Schmidt's intent was not to alienate his team members but rather to engage them. He understood that working well with people from other parts of the world was critical to his success. The challenge was that many members of his global management team were from countries with more egalitarian cultural expectations of leaders.

ZURICH, SWITZERLAND

So Herr Dr. Schmidt decided that first names would be used. From then on, he was Martin when the management team conducted their meetings in English. Language also seemed to provide psychological flexibility for the president and human resources director to address each other by first names when speaking English in team meetings. Interestingly enough, they reverted to the more formal Herr Dr. when speaking Swiss-German together.

DEVELOPMENT SUGGESTIONS
for Knowledge of How to Transact Business and Assess Risks of Doing Business Internationally

LEARN

Tips to learn about and begin developing the capability on your own. These tips involve self-directed learning, including reading, listening, watching, or observing, that you can do on your own at your own pace. They are most useful for novices in the capability, but are helpful for intermediate and advanced learners to keep knowledge current.

Development Activity	Suggested Resource(s) and Tips
Take risk management training.	• The Risk Management Society (www.rims.org) • The Institute of Risk Management (www.theirm.org) • CREATE Homeland Security Center at the University of Southern California (http://create.usc.edu)
Read the global section from *Successful Manager's Handbook*.	*Successful Manager's Handbook* (Gebelein, Nelson-Neuhaus, Skube, and Lee, 2010)
Review business/strategy books from other cultures.	• *The India Way* (Cappelli, Singh, Singh, and Useem, 2010) • *Chinese Leadership* (Wang and Chee, 2011)
Read about globalization around the world.	• Globalization 101 (www.globalization101.org) • *Globality* (Sirkin, Hemerling, and Bhattacharya, 2008) • *Globalization: A Very Short Introduction* (Steger, 2009) • *Fifty Key Thinkers on Globalization* (Coleman and Sajed, 2012)
Read how business is done in different cultures.	• Do an Internet search for how to transact business in your country of interest, including personnel practices, marketing, and distribution. • Subscribe to GlobeSmart (www.globesmart.com). • Visit Kwintessential country profiles (www.kwintessential.co.uk/resources/country-profiles.html). • Read *Kiss, Bow, or Shake Hands: The Bestselling Guide to Doing Business in More Than 60 Countries* (Morrison and Conaway, 2006). • Use the app "Business Practices" by the Brannen Group, which tells you how to conduct business in different countries. • Use the app "Business Traveler's Passport Series," which provides guides on international business and travel. • Use the app "International Business Etiquette" to learn about business dos and don'ts in 150 countries.
Find out the cost of moving into a particular market from various angles including global mobility of employees, social responsibility, ethical considerations, labor regulations, and overall risk management.	• "Global Mobility Risk Advisory: Taking Hold of Global Mobility Cost (Ernst & Young, 2010) (www.ey.com/Publication/vwLUAssets/2011_HC_Global_Mobility_Risk_Advisory/$FILE/EY_HC_GM_Risk_Advisory_engl.pdf) • Global Mobility Solutions (www.gmsmobility.com) • Worldwide ERC: The Association for Workforce Mobility (www.worldwideerc.org) • The Forum for Expatriate Management (www.totallyexpat.com)

DEVELOPMENT SUGGESTIONS
for Knowledge of How to Transact Business and Assess Risks of Doing Business Internationally

LEARN

Tips to learn about and begin developing the capability on your own. These tips involve self-directed learning, including reading, listening, watching, or observing, that you can do on your own at your own pace. They are most useful for novices in the capability, but are helpful for intermediate and advanced learners to keep knowledge current.

Development Activity	Suggested Resource(s) and Tips
Look for speakers, courses, and workshops through your local business school to learn about different marketing approaches.	• Global Marketing Essentials (http://online.thunderbird.edu/global-marketing-essentials) • International Marketing Program (http://executive.education.insead.edu/international_marketing)
Keep current on trends/issues in the world.	• *The Wall Street Journal* (available in editions for the United States, Asia, Europe, and the Americas) (http://online.wsj.com) • *The Economist* (www.economist.com) • *Financial Times* (www.ft.com) • CNN Money (http://money.cnn.com/news/world) • Reuters (www.reuters.com) • *Forbes* (www.forbes.com) • BBC (www.bbc.com) • *Foreign Affairs* (www.foreignaffairs.com) • *BusinessWeek Asia* (www.businessweek.com/asia) • *China Business Review* (www.chinabusinessreview.com) • *BusinessWeek Europe* (www.businessweek.com/europe) • Latin Finance (www.latinfinance.com) • Latin Focus (www.latin-focus.com) • *Latin Trade* (http://latintrade.com) • America Economia (www.americaeconomica.com) • Local news sites in the region(s) of interest for a deeper dive into the local news
Read about focusing on three horizons for sustainable economic growth: core business, new business, and future business.	*The Alchemy of Growth* (Baghai, Coley, White, and Coley, 2000)

DEVELOPMENT SUGGESTIONS
for Knowledge of How to Transact Business and Assess Risks of Doing Business Internationally

CONNECT

Tips to learn about and continue developing the capability through others. These tips involve working with another person to learn from their experiences. They may involve asking questions, listening to and discussing experiences, forming a new relationship, deepening an existing relationship, or receiving feedback from someone who is acting as your mentor. These tips are useful for all levels of learners.

Development Activity	Suggested Resource(s) and Tips
Use risk management services.	• The Risk Management Society (www.rims.org) • The Institute of Risk Management (www.theirm.org) • CREATE Homeland Security Center at the University of Southern California (http://create.usc.edu) • Oxford Analytica (www.oxam.com)
Talk to someone in your own company or industry who is knowledgeable about marketing approaches.	• Ask your manager. • Ask your marketing department. • Ask human resources.

DEVELOPMENT SUGGESTIONS
for Knowledge of How to Transact Business and Assess Risks of Doing Business Internationally

EXPERIENCE

Tips to learn about and develop skills in the capability through firsthand experience. These tips involve engaging in activities, such as exploring a new area, trying a new cultural activity, or participating in a specific business event. These tips are most useful for intermediate to advanced learners, and we suggest that novice learners prepare themselves for success by completing some of the tips in the Learn category first.

Development Activity	Suggested Resource(s) and Tips
Attend industry risk management conferences and trade workshops on risk.	The Institute of Risk Management lists conferences and workshops in the industry (www.theirm.org).
Get an expatriate assignment—short or long term.	• Express interest to your manager. • Talk to your international human resources managers about how to be considered for an assignment and how you would need to prepare.
Participate in a global bidding project to see global business savvy in action.	• Express interest to your manager. • Find out from your human resources department who would have responsibility for global bids, and contact them to see how you may be able to participate or observe.

DEVELOPMENT SUGGESTIONS

for Knowledge of How to Transact Business and Assess Risks of Doing Business Internationally

COACH OR CONTRIBUTE

Tips to help others learn about and develop this capability. These tips involve coaching and mentoring others. They may include creating information or experiences for individuals, teams, or your organization. These tips are designed for those who are advanced in the capability and are useful development methods to keep advanced leaders in the capability engaged in professional development at the highest level. Please note that the tips in this section may also be quite helpful for individual use if you do not have a coach or mentor.

Development Activity	Suggested Resource(s) and Tips
Put together a risk management plan that includes specific scenario plans and crisis management protocols for your industry.	• Use expert consultants to form your plan, such as Crisis Management International (www.cmiatl.com). • Take a course in crisis management, such as Crisis Management: Introduction to the Response Plan and Advanced Topics through ASIS International (www.asisonline.org/store/program_detail.xml?id=42944694). • Look at companies who have well-developed risk management plans, such as Shell (www.shell.com/home/content/environment_society).
In discussions, prompt for risks including downsides and upsides.	Figure out how to minimize the downside and maximize the upside.

Additional Reading

The readings listed here provide you with additional study of the Global Mindset capability in this section. You will find that many of these resources provide you with a specific and detailed look at using this capability in a particular context or location.

....

Title: "Building a Global Leadership Pipeline"

Publication: *Chief Learning Officer*

Date: 2012

Author: John Gillis Jr.

Executive Summary: The article reports on the importance of global leadership. It explores how globalization drove major changes in the business environment and the benefits of having the right leaders in international and multinational companies. It details the shortage in global leaders and developing global leaders. It also discusses several strategies to make a global leadership framework work.

....

Title: "How to Conquer New Markets with Old Skills"

Publication: *Harvard Business Review*

Date: 2010

Authors: Mauro F. Guillén and Esteban García-Canal

Executive Summary: In examining the international expansion of Spanish firms over the past twenty-five years, we found that the leaders used acquisitions to extend their reach but focused them on just a few industries and geographic areas. They then strengthened their positions by drawing on their homegrown political and networking skills, project execution knowledge, and vertical integration expertise—capabilities that many companies in emerging markets also possess.

Title:　　　　　"Future Leadership Competencies: From Foresight to Current Practice"

Publication:　*Journal of European Industrial Training*

Date:　　　　　2009

Authors:　　　　Emma O'Brien and Phillipa Robertson

Executive Summary: With tectonic plates shifting change and continuous uncertainty, a reliance on leadership competencies rooted in the past will no longer be successful. Instead, it is argued that the emerging business environment now demands a new set of leadership skills that are aligned to the requirements of the future.

MICROCHIP PRODUCTION, CHINA

Knowledge of Supplier Options in Other Parts of the World

As the world of commerce has flattened, we are now able to connect across greater distances and cultural divides. This is because access to many foreign markets is easier through diplomacy and deregulation efforts. For example, the seemingly simple process of transporting goods across Europe was a bureaucratic nightmare for a trucker in the 1990s. Prior to the formation of the European Union and the subsequent deregulation within it, a trucker had to have individual permits for every country on his route to deliver goods. This slowed down delivery and limited the distance a trucker was willing to travel. It also meant that truckers might only carry their loads one way to avoid more delays and paperwork on the way home. Post–European Union, truckers can now travel with one permit across multiple countries. Delivery is faster. Partnerships are also more fluid in that truckers can take on multiple loads without more red tape. Technology also makes these partnerships possible and more fluid through more sophisticated supply chain management.

You see in this example that supply chain requires knowledge of not only who can supply the products we need and want at a good price, but also political and regulatory environments, cultural differences in production and delivery of goods, and familiarity with the technologies that enable us to partner with suppliers who may be geographically distant and culturally distinct. There's a lot to know, but the road of discovery is paved with new possibilities, new friendships, and innovative products that make the journey worthwhile.

Knowledge of Supplier Options in Other Parts of the World in Action

We do three things to ensure that we have backup options for suppliers in other parts of the world. First, we recognize that volatility and shelf life of suppliers may be short and is at least somewhat unpredictable.

SUSAN GEBELEIN
CEO
Business and Leadership Consulting

We do three things to ensure that we have backup options for suppliers in other parts of the world. First, we recognize that volatility and shelf life of suppliers may be short and is at least somewhat unpredictable. This requires constant scanning of the environment to identify signals indicating a change is needed and to identify new possible vendors in the same or different parts of the world. Second, we identify possible new vendors by using our competitive intelligence group to look at who our competitors are using. This involves understanding where new capabilities are being developed by similar or related industries that can be used in our own industry. We do this by building relationships with executives in similar or related industries, asking consultants or education institutions we work with, and reading trade publications. Third, we use teams of high potentials from a particular region to investigate possible sourcing options. This provides them with a great development experience while providing our leadership team with knowledge of regions or country resources that may be unfamiliar to us.

Building and maintaining trusting relationships is especially important, because trust is a critical issue in supply chain partnerships. Take China as an example. Between 2007 and 2012, we've seen recalls on children's toys containing lead, pet food laced with melamine, and a series of suicides in a well-known high-tech factory with accusations of working employees to death. These are all supply chain problems involving trust. The parent companies trusted the suppliers to produce safe products and treat employees fairly. Customers trusted they were getting safe products that were produced humanely. It is important to keep in mind that a supply chain rarely involves one or two companies. In the first two examples, there were dozens of supply partners contributing various parts of the products. That's why it took time to track down the sources of the problems. Chinese suppliers in these supply chains were equally disturbed along with the rest of the world with these terrible incidents. This is why trust is particularly low among supply chain partners in China. They do not want to be a part of bad business practices. This means that companies rely very heavily on known partners and deep relationships. These issues are not just isolated to China, however. To build a supply chain in most cultures will require skill in forming and maintaining trusting relationships. So before jumping on a new supply prospect in another culture, we do a little homework about how relationships and trust are formed there because it could affect the health and well-being of employees, partners, and clients.

DEVELOPMENT SUGGESTIONS
for Knowledge of Supplier Options in Other Parts of the World

LEARN

Tips to learn about and begin developing the capability on your own. These tips involve self-directed learning, including reading, listening, watching, or observing, that you can do on your own at your own pace. They are most useful for novices in the capability, but are helpful for intermediate and advanced learners to keep knowledge current.

Development Activity	Suggested Resource(s) and Tips
Take a course in supply chain.	Courses and certification in supply chain management can be found at: • The Institute for Supply Management (www.ism.ws) • Supply Chain Online (www.supplychainonline.com) • The Association for Operations Management (www.apics.com) • The International Supply Chain Education Alliance (www.iscea.org) • Your local business school
Familiarize yourself with the global supply chain trends, as well as specific issues in your industry.	• Deloitte's 2010 Global Benchmark Study "The Challenge of Complexity in Manufacturing: Trends in Supply Chain Management" (www.deloitte.com/view/en_GX/global/insights/deloitte-research/2d61c5275d0fb110VgnVCM100000ba42f00aRCRD.htm) • The annual Supply Chain Foresight report published by Barlowworld Logistics (www.barloworld-logistics.com/industry-insight) • Bob Ferrari's blog on industry-specific supply chain issues (www.theferrarigroup/supply-chain-matters) • The industry-focused resource guide for supply chain (http://logistics.about.com/od/industryfocus/Industry_Focus.htm) • Internal supply chain experts
Learn about the political and regulatory environments in the countries and regions of interest to you.	• The CIA World Factbook (www.cia.gov/library/publications/the-world-factbook) • The US State Department country guide (www.state.gov/countries) • Custom country reports produced by Country Reports (www.countryreports.org) • Country guides, information, and media through Aperian Global's Globe Smart tool (www.aperianglobal.com)

DEVELOPMENT SUGGESTIONS
for Knowledge of Supplier Options in Other Parts of the World

LEARN

Tips to learn about and begin developing the capability on your own. These tips involve self-directed learning, including reading, listening, watching, or observing, that you can do on your own at your own pace. They are most useful for novices in the capability, but are helpful for intermediate and advanced learners to keep knowledge current.

Development Activity	Suggested Resource(s) and Tips
Learn about supply chain technologies.	• Supply Chain Digest offers current articles and videocasts on supply chain issues and technologies (www.scdigest.com). • The Supply Chain Council publishes supply chain standards and benchmarks (http://supply-chain.org). • The Supply Chain Management Review publishes articles, white papers, blogs, webcasts, and message boards on supply chain topics, including technology (www.scmr.com). • The Supply Chain Management Research Association publishes links to resources and sponsors an annual conference on supply chain issues, including technology (http://scmr.uark.edu).
Learn about how trust is developed in the country or region of interest to you.	• You may want to begin by reading a country guide describing how relationships are built and maintained in other cultures. See the country guide suggestions above. • After a general understanding of relationships in the culture of interest, ask a colleague who has worked successfully in that culture how to build and maintain trust there.

DEVELOPMENT SUGGESTIONS
for Knowledge of Supplier Options in Other Parts of the World

CONNECT

Tips to learn about and continue developing the capability through others. These tips involve working with another person to learn from their experiences. They may involve asking questions, listening to and discussing experiences, forming a new relationship, deepening an existing relationship, or receiving feedback from someone who is acting as your mentor. These tips are useful for all levels of learners.

Development Activity	Suggested Resource(s) and Tips
Meet with supply chain experts in your organization to learn about the past, present, and future of supply chain.	• Identify the supply chain experts in your organization through your supply chain department. The department may be called procurement or may be classified under operations. • Ask what has been done in terms of supply chain, what is currently done, and what the future looks like for supply chain in your organization.
Meet with local suppliers in other countries to see how they operate and partner with your organization.	• Identify who your organization's local suppliers are by working with your in-country counterparts. • Arrange to meet with each of the suppliers to walk through their operations.
Participate in professional organizations and conferences dedicated to supply chain management.	• Investigate where there are local chambers of commerce organizations for your home country in the country of interest, for example AmChams is the name of US Chamber of Commerce organizations located in 102 countries across the world (www.uschamber.com/international/directory). • Join the Institute for Supply Management (www.ism.ws). • Join the Association for Operations Management (www.apics.com). • Attend the annual conference sponsored by the Supply Chain Management Research Association (http://scmr.uark.edu).
Ask local nationals who are inside your organization or inside your industry how trust is developed in their culture, especially in terms of supply chain.	• Identify your local national counterparts in the country of interest through your organization's directory or through colleague recommendations. • Ask to spend time with specific people to learn more about supply chain relationships in their country. • Ask how trusting business relationships are both formed and maintained over time.

DEVELOPMENT SUGGESTIONS
for Knowledge of Supplier Options in Other Parts of the World

EXPERIENCE

Tips to learn about and develop skills in the capability through firsthand experience. These tips involve engaging in activities, such as exploring a new area, trying a new cultural activity, or participating in a specific business event. These tips are most useful for intermediate to advanced learners, and we suggest that novice learners prepare themselves for success by completing some of the tips in the Learn category first.

Development Activity	Suggested Resource(s) and Tips
Visit supplier production facilities, warehouses, and distribution centers to see supply chain in action firsthand.	<ul><li>Identify who your organization's local suppliers are by working with your in-country counterparts.</li><li>Arrange to meet with each of the suppliers to walk through their operations.</li></ul>
Participate in supply chain meetings in your organization to see how decisions are made and how plans are operationalized.	<ul><li>Identify the supply chain experts in your organization through your supply chain department. The department may be called procurement or may be classified under operations.</li><li>Arrange to participate in a few meetings to see how decisions are made and how operational plans unfold.</li></ul>
Shadow a supply chain manager for a day to see what that person does.	<ul><li>Identify the supply chain managers in your organization through your supply chain department. The department may be called procurement or may be classified under operations.</li><li>Arrange to spend a few hours or a day with the supply chain managers to see what the job entails firsthand.</li></ul>

DEVELOPMENT SUGGESTIONS
for Knowledge of Supplier Options in Other Parts of the World

COACH OR CONTRIBUTE

Tips to help others learn about and develop this capability. These tips involve coaching and mentoring others. They may include creating information or experiences for individuals, teams, or your organization. These tips are designed for those who are advanced in the capability and are useful development methods to keep advanced leaders in the capability engaged in professional development at the highest level. Please note that the tips in this section may also be quite helpful for individual use if you do not have a coach or mentor.

Development Activity	Suggested Resource(s) and Tips
Ensure suppliers have an ethics policy/credo that aligns with your organization.	The best way to see what a supplier ethics policy looks like is to read examples from major global businesses: • Cisco (technology industry) (www.cisco.com/web/about/ac50/ac142/docs/ethics_policy.pdf) • HSBC (financial industry) (www.hsbc.com/1/2/purchasing/ethical-code-of-conduct) • BBC (media industry) (http://bbcworldwide.com/media/34660/bbcw%20ethical%20code%20of%20conduct.pdf) • Coca-Cola (consumer products industry) (www.thecoca-colacompany.com/ourcompany/pdf/COBC_English.pdf)
Invite a supply chain manager to your department meeting to share how the products and services your department helps to produce reach clients.	• Identify the supply chain managers in your organization through your supply chain department. The department may be called procurement or may be classified under operations. • Invite the supply chain managers to speak to your department about how supply chain works in your organization.
Invite your team to investigate potential suppliers in a new market and report back. The idea is to learn about a new market, identify innovative new products and suppliers, and discover how operational decisions are made in terms of supply chain.	Use resources from supply chain organizations like the following: • Supply Chain Digest offers current articles and videocasts on supply chain issues and technologies (www.scdigest.com). • Supply Chain Council publishes supply chain standards and benchmarks (http://supply-chain.org). • Supply Chain Management Review publishes articles, white papers, blogs, webcasts, and message boards on supply chain topics (www.scmr.com). • Supply Chain Management Research Association publishes links to resources and sponsors an annual conference on supply chain issues (http://scmr.uark.edu).

Additional Reading

The readings listed here provide you with additional study of the Global Mindset capability in this section. You will find that many of these resources provide you with a specific and detailed look at using this capability in a particular context or location.

....

Title: "Knowledge Acquisition and Sharing: A Sustainable Source of Competitive Advantage in Supply Chains"

Publication: *Proceedings of the International Conference on Global Intellectual Capital, Knowledge Management & Organizational Learning*

Date: 2011

Author: Ikechukwu Diugwu

Executive Summary: The level of success enjoyed by an organization is dependent upon the level of competitive advantage it enjoys over its competitors. Competitive advantage is known to be a function of the extent to which an organization adapts and applies its resources in the exploitation of prevailing market conditions, and this is in turn dependent on the level of knowledge about existing market conditions, modern production techniques, and processes. Although it was previously believed that tangible or physical economic assets of an organization were the major sources of sustainability and profitability, there has been a gradual but steady change in perception of a firm's real source of competitive advantage, sustainability, and profitability. The contemporary view is that sustainability, profitability, and competitive advantage no longer come from tangible economic assets but rather from sources that ensure adequate use of the knowledge or Global Intellectual Capital inherent in an organization. While it is possible that several organizations may have access to the same or similar knowledge at the same time, the level of use of this knowledge varies from organization to organization. It is this variation that holds the key to sustainable competitive advantage. Although more of a theoretical and qualitative work, this paper shall, through a literature review of competitive advantage, knowledge acquisition and sharing, learning, partnerships and networking, supply chain management, as well as citing results from earlier research surveys, as well as Ph.D. research conducted by the author, highlight how organizations in supply chains can improve their competitiveness by leveraging on the intellectual capabilities and resources of their partners. Sustained competitive advantage through improved customer relationship/loyalty, greater awareness of business processes and performance, faster and better management decision making, as well as effective product/service development is the motivation for engagement in knowledge acquisition and sharing activities by organizations.

. . . .

Title: "Selection of Planned Supply Initiatives: The Role of Senior Management Expertise"

Publication: *International Journal of Operations & Production Management*

Date: 2007

Authors: P. Fraser Johnson, Robert D. Klassen, Michiel R. Leenders, and Amrou Awaysheh

Executive Summary: The purpose of this paper is to assess the selection of planned supply initiatives and the role of senior management expertise. The drivers that influence the selection of particular supply initiatives by firms are of major interest to both practitioners and academics, because choices indicate priorities for resources, potential performance gaps, and needs for future research. Moreover, theory indicates that senior management expertise and firm-level resources might influence the likelihood of selecting particular initiatives. Senior management expertise has received relatively little attention in prior research, yet was found to be a significant factor influencing strategic-, process-, and network-related supply initiatives. Moreover, the framework of supply initiatives provides a basis for assessing and benchmarking firm-level supply chain strategy and investment patterns. Finally, empirical evidence emerged that both firm- and individual-level factors influenced the probability of selecting particular initiatives.

. . . .

Title: "The Hollow Corporation Revisited: Can Governance Mechanisms Substitute for Technical Expertise in Managing Buyer–Supplier Relationships?"

Publication: *European Management Review*

Date: 2010

Authors: Anne Parmigiani and Will Mitchell

Executive Summary: This article considers how a firm's system of exchange skills including internal technical expertise and supplier governance mechanisms influence supplier performance, both independently and jointly. The core question is whether interfirm governance mechanisms, including both relational and contractual mechanisms, can substitute for a firm's internal technical skills in maintaining supplier performance or, alternatively, whether a firm risks hollowing itself out by de-emphasizing internal expertise when it outsources. The arguments build on the capabilities, interorganizational governance, and supply management literatures. We find that internal technical expertise influences multiple dimensions of supplier performance, including cooperation, price, quality, delivery, and communication, while relational governance also affects supplier performance though in a more focused way. In turn, combinations of technical expertise, relational governance, and contractual agreements jointly affect supplier performance. Thus, firms generate superior supplier performance if they retain internal technical skills as well as increase their use of external governance mechanisms to manage buyer–supplier relationships.

FESTIVAL • CUZCO, PERU

John Kershner / Shutterstock.com

2

Cosmopolitan Outlook

As seen in **Figure 2-1** on page 82, this chapter examines Cosmopolitan Outlook, which is a key dimension of Global Intellectual Capital. Cosmopolitan outlook refers to understanding that the world is full of diversity. There are many ways in which things can be done in different parts of the world. It doesn't mean that one way is better or worse. It just means that they're different. For example, someone who has a high cosmopolitan outlook understands different political systems. So a Chilean executive, for example, would understand that the Chinese system is very different than the Chilean system. It doesn't mean it's better or worse. It just means for the executive to do business with a Chinese corporation, or in China, the executive needs to deal with a different political environment. It also means that the executive has to have an understanding of how other societies function in different parts of the world. How do people interact with each other? How do they make decisions? How do they get things done? The approaches may be very different across regions and countries.

When a person with high cosmopolitan outlook is working with someone from another culture who is thinking very differently about things, her reaction is not, "He doesn't get it. He's not competent." Her first reaction is, "Hmm, this is very interesting. He has a very different way of understanding and interpreting the

GLOBAL MINDSET

Global INTELLECTUAL CAPITAL

Global Business Savvy

Knowledge of global industry

Knowledge of global competitive business and marketing strategies

Knowledge of how to transact business and assess risks of doing business internationally

Knowledge of supplier options in other parts of the world

Cosmopolitan Outlook

Knowledge of cultures in different parts of the world

Knowledge of geography, history, and important persons of several countries

Knowledge of economic & political issues, concerns, & hot topics of major regions of the world

Up-to-date knowledge of important world events

Cognitive Complexity

Ability to grasp complex topics quickly

Strong analytical and problem solving skills

Ability to understand abstract ideas

Ability to take complex issues and explain the main points simply and understandably

Global PSYCHOLOGICAL CAPITAL

Passion for Diversity

Enjoy exploring other parts of the world

Enjoy getting to know people from other parts of the world

Enjoy living in another country

Enjoy traveling

Quest for Adventure

Interest in dealing with challenging situations

Willingness to take risk

Willingness to test one's abilities

Enjoy dealing with unpredictable situations

Self-Assurance

Energetic

Self-confident

Comfortable in uncomfortable situations

Witty in tough situations

Global SOCIAL CAPITAL

Intercultural Empathy

Ability to work well with people from other parts of the world

Ability to understand nonverbal expressions of people from other cultures

Ability to emotionally connect to people from other cultures

Ability to engage people from other parts of the world to work together

Interpersonal Impact

Experience in negotiating contracts/agreements in other cultures

Strong networks with people from other cultures and with influential people

Reputation as a leader

Diplomacy

Ease of starting a conversation with a stranger

Ability to integrate diverse perspectives

Ability to listen to what others have to say

Willingness to collaborate

Figure 2-1

same situation. So let's have a conversation about that. Let's see how we can come to an agreement." This is in contrast to someone with low cosmopolitan outlook who would get frustrated that her approach was not shared by the other person. Cosmopolitan outlook requires openness to learning about diversity of thoughts and actions and, ultimately, a deep understanding and appreciation for global diversity.

In this chapter, we will cover the following areas:

- Knowledge of cultures in different parts of the world

- Knowledge of geography, history, and important persons of several countries

- Knowledge of economic and political issues, concerns, and hot topics of major regions of the world

- Knowledge of important world events

MADAGASCAR MUSICIAN

Pierre-Yves Babelon / Shutterstock.com

Knowledge of Cultures in Different Parts of the World

Obviously, cultures across the world vary politically, socially, economically, and individually. They're just different, and the first thing is to know that. It's important to understand not just how the cultures differ but also why. For example, research on some eastern European countries shows a tendency for people in these cultures to be guarded toward new or unknown situations and people. The GLOBE (Global Leadership and Organizational Behavior Effectiveness) study *Culture, Leadership, and Organizations: The GLOBE Study of 62 Societies* (House, et al., 2004) has produced an exceptional body of research that supports this, showing how national cultures vary in terms of their values and practices. GLOBE revealed that eastern European cultures, such as Germany, show a strong cultural value for uncertainty avoidance, compared to some western European cultures, like that of the United Kingdom. Why? There are certainly many variables that contribute to this. However, knowledge of the history of the region points to many invasions in eastern Europe over the past two thousand years. They are located in a very important, strategic area for resources. They are in the passage from the east to the west and vice versa. This long history of invasions has, no doubt, contributed to a psyche in the culture that uncertain situations and unknown people are things to be avoided. In contrast, the United Kingdom, while it has had numerous conflicts within the region, has quite a different tradition of having been the dominant power in both its own region and much of the rest of the world. Therefore uncertainty and the unknown are not as strongly valued as things to be avoided. In fact, they may be viewed as exciting new frontiers instead of things to be feared.

These differences in cultural psyche affect the way people tend to think, and that affects business. For example, people may view foreign companies that want to invest in their country quite differently. Someone who has a high cosmopolitan outlook will have done a proper investigation about the culture where she is working and will understand both how the culture differs and why. She will have an appreciation for the differences and will then figure out a way to bridge differences for a successful outcome.

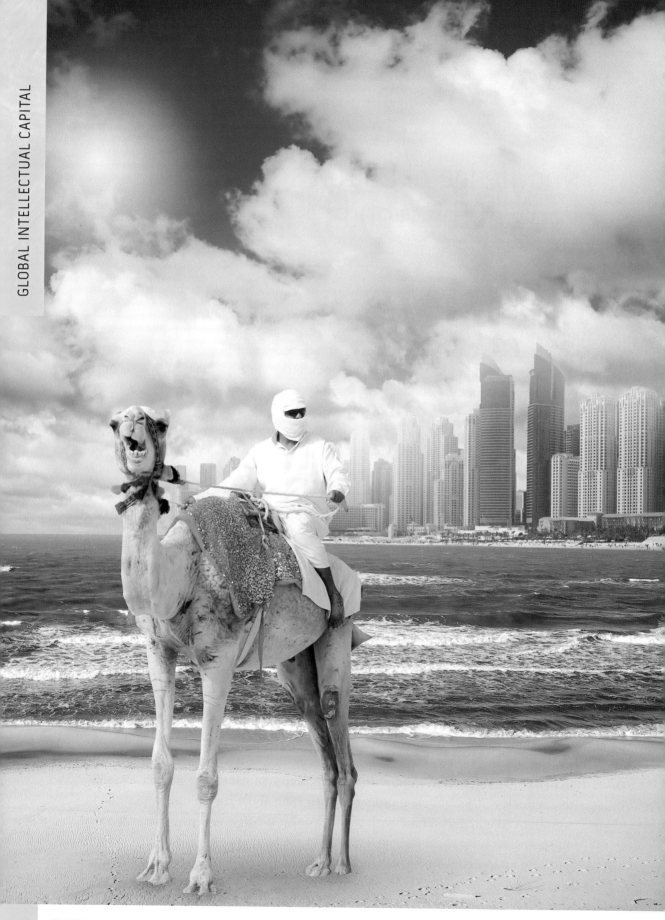

DUBAI, UNITED ARAB EMIRATES

Knowledge of Cultures in Different Parts of the World in Action

While leading an American business delegation of middle managers to various cities throughout the Middle East, I noticed that many were having difficulty easing into their normal networking modes.

CARI E. GUITTARD, MPA
Principal
Global Engagement Partners

While leading an American business delegation of middle managers to various cities throughout the Middle East, I noticed that many were having difficulty easing into their normal networking modes. Many became quiet and withdrawn during meetings and social activities. Appreciating this was their first trip to the region, I began each morning with a short briefing on the country we were visiting to include the geopolitical landscape, cultural and business customs, and stories from my past experiences there. I then asked them to practice within our group how to greet a peer in a business setting. This included everything from saying hello in the local language to proper handshakes and noting appropriate eye contact, posture, and so on. We also discussed Insha'Allah, which in the local business culture is a more relaxed environment where time is a fluid rather than a fixed notion. This helped ease their trepidation and manage their expectations. However, I still felt they were holding back during our meetings and, as such, were not benefiting as much as they could from the experience.

So one evening, after an exhausting day of back-to-back meetings, I directly asked them about their concerns and reasons for being withdrawn. I did this with the understanding that Americans tend to respond well to directness in business settings. Unanimously, the group responded, albeit somewhat sheepishly, that they were both exhausted and impatient. In an attempt to pack everything in, as they had originally requested, we hadn't allowed enough time for them to just enjoy and absorb the local culture on their own. Once they were able to share their concerns and shift their focus from being output driven to one of learning and building relationships, it was as if a weight was lifted. They began to open up more and just enjoy the experience.

DEVELOPMENT SUGGESTIONS

for Knowledge of Cultures in Different Parts of the World

LEARN

Tips to learn about and begin developing the capability on your own. These tips involve self-directed learning, including reading, listening, watching, or observing, that you can do on your own at your own pace. They are most useful for novices in the capability, but are helpful for intermediate and advanced learners to keep knowledge current.

Development Activity	Suggested Resource(s) and Tips
Read, watch, or listen to world news from a variety of sources to have a current and broad understanding of cultures around the world.	• World News Network (http://wn.com) • BBC World News (www.bbc.co.uk/news/world) • GlobalPost (www.globalpost.com) • CNN International (http://edition.cnn.com) • NPR World News (www.npr.org/sections/world) • Aljazeera (www.aljazeera.com) • *The Wall Street Journal* (available in editions for the United States, Asia, Europe, and the Americas) (http://online.wsj.com) • *The Economist* (www.economist.com) • *Financial Times* (www.ft.com) • CNN Money (money.cnn.com/news/world) • *Reuters* (www.reuters.com) • *Forbes* (www.forbes.com) • BBC (www.bbc.com) • *Foreign Affairs* (www.foreignaffairs.com) • *BusinessWeek Asia* (www.businessweek.com/asia) • *China Business Review* (www.chinabusinessreview.com) • *BusinessWeek Europe* (www.businessweek.com/europe) • Latin Finance (www.latinfinance.com) • Latin Focus (www.latin-focus.com) • *Latin Trade* (http://latintrade.com) • America Economia (www.americaeconomica.com)

DEVELOPMENT SUGGESTIONS
for Knowledge of Cultures in Different Parts of the World

LEARN

Tips to learn about and begin developing the capability on your own. These tips involve self-directed learning, including reading, listening, watching, or observing, that you can do on your own at your own pace. They are most useful for novices in the capability, but are helpful for intermediate and advanced learners to keep knowledge current.

Development Activity	Suggested Resource(s) and Tips
Learn about the dynamics between countries in the same region.	• Read the GLOBE studies: "Culture, Leadership, and Organizations: The GLOBE Studies of 62 Societies" (House, et al., 2004) and "Culture and Leadership across the World: The GLOBE Book of In-Depth Studies of 25 Societies" (Chhokar, et al., 2007). • Look at side-by-side comparisons of cultures using Dr. Geert Hofstedes' dimensions (http://geert-hofstede.com). • Compare cultures by subscribing to the GlobeSmart tool through Aperian Global (www.aperianglobal.com). • Take a course through your local business school on doing business in a particular region of the world, such as "Regional Business Environment" courses at Thunderbird School of Global Business (www.thunderbird.edu). • Read world region reports through the World Bank to get a sense of issues and trends in these areas (www.worldbank.org). Click on the "countries" tab, and then "browse by region." • Compare economic trends among countries in a region by using the International Monetary Fund's Country Information Page (www.imf.org/external/country/index.htm). • Connect with a local World Trade Center Association for information and events on regional trade issues (www.wtcaonline.com).

DEVELOPMENT SUGGESTIONS
for Knowledge of Cultures in Different Parts of the World

LEARN

Tips to learn about and begin developing the capability on your own. These tips involve self-directed learning, including reading, listening, watching, or observing, that you can do on your own at your own pace. They are most useful for novices in the capability, but are helpful for intermediate and advanced learners to keep knowledge current.

Development Activity	Suggested Resource(s) and Tips
Develop specific cultural knowledge in regions of interest through self-guided study, especially as it relates to doing business in that culture.	• Read about and watch travel documentaries through *National Geographic* (http://travel.nationalgeographic.com/travel). • Watch Michael Palin's popular travel documentaries (www.palinstravels.co.uk). • Learn about demographic information for an area or region through the United Nations' Statistics Division (http://unstats.un.org/unsd/demographic) or the World Factbook produced by the CIA (www.cia.gov/library/publications/the-world-factbook). • Attend public lectures about other cultures by universities, libraries, museums, etc. • Read your local newspaper's events section, or contact these locations personally. • Take open enrollment (i.e., free and easily accessible), online university courses and lectures on cultural topics like history and political science. You can find a robust list of these online courses through various universities (www.openculture.com). • Watch online courses through iTunesU either on your computer or on a mobile device (www.apple.com/education/itunes-u). • Learn about the relationship between culture and how business is done in a specific society through websites like GlobeSmart (www.aperianglobal.com). • Know the relative importance of hierarchy in a culture by learning about research on cultural frameworks like the GLOBE Study (House, et al., 2004; and Chhokar, et al., 2007), and Dr. Geert Hofstede's work (http://geert-hofstede.com). • Learn about the firsthand experience of foreigners in that culture by surfing expatriate websites and websites designed to serve expatriates like InterNations (www.internations.org), Transitions Abroad (www.transitionsabroad.com), Escape Artist (www.escapeartist.com), and Expat Exchange (www.expatexchange.com). • Use the app "Questiorama" by Mind of Two to test your knowledge of international sports, entertainment, and general cultural knowledge.

DEVELOPMENT SUGGESTIONS
for Knowledge of Cultures in Different Parts of the World

LEARN

Tips to learn about and begin developing the capability on your own. These tips involve self-directed learning, including reading, listening, watching, or observing, that you can do on your own at your own pace. They are most useful for novices in the capability, but are helpful for intermediate and advanced learners to keep knowledge current.

Development Activity	Suggested Resource(s) and Tips
Develop specific cultural knowledge in regions of interest through self-guided study, especially as it relates to doing business in that culture.	• Test your international cultural knowledge using the app "Cultural Connections" by Mobile Learning Design. • Use the app "Cultural GPS" to learn about cultural differences in many countries of the world. • Use the app "World Customs and Cultures" for at-a-glance information on 165 countries. • Use the app "World Customs" by Hooked in Motion, which includes a comprehensive guide of greetings, communication styles, and other topics in more than 150 countries.
Watch or read popular media in other cultures to see how people think and interact with one another.	• Watch local television or listen to local radio broadcasts. If you are outside the country of interest, you can find local channels on satellite television (www.directv.com and www.dishnetwork.com). You can also subscribe to foreign news radio broadcasts through SiriusXM Satellite Radio (www.siriusxm.com/worldradionetwork). • Watch reality shows like *Pop Idol* in forty-two countries around the world or Got Talent (http://en.wikipedia.org/wiki/Got_Talent#Got_Talent_around_the_world) in more than fifty countries. A complete listing of countries and networks for *Pop Idol* is on Wikipedia (http://en.wikipedia.org/wiki/Idol_(TV_series)#Idol_around_the_world). • Watch global documentaries from local perspectives through PBS Global Voices (www.pbs.org/itvs/globalvoices). • Watch popular local sporting events. If you are outside of the country of interest, you can subscribe to international sporting channels on satellite television (e.g., www.directv.com or www.dishnetwork.com) or watch highlights on ESPN (https://espn.go.com) or FoxSports (https://msn.foxsports.com). • Read or watch a biography or historical account of a local hero. Very popular heroes may be covered on History Channel International (www.history.com/schedule/h2), while others may only be covered in locally produced publications. • Follow fan pages of influential people in that culture (e.g., www.facebook.com and www.twitter.com).

DEVELOPMENT SUGGESTIONS
for Knowledge of Cultures in Different Parts of the World

LEARN

Tips to learn about and begin developing the capability on your own. These tips involve self-directed learning, including reading, listening, watching, or observing, that you can do on your own at your own pace. They are most useful for novices in the capability, but are helpful for intermediate and advanced learners to keep knowledge current.

Development Activity	Suggested Resource(s) and Tips
Learn the language in a region of interest. Words, phrases, and popular sayings capture the history and sentiments of a people.	• Take a language course locally in the culture of interest through language institutes geared toward foreigners. • Take a language course at your local community college or university. • Learn a language online through Rosetta Stone (www.rosettastone.com). • Decide how you want to learn the language of interest through Berlitz (www.berlitz.com). Courses are offered in a variety of formats, including travel courses. • Use the app "Tests de Langues" by Learnorama SA to test your knowledge in five languages.

DEVELOPMENT SUGGESTIONS
for Knowledge of Cultures in Different Parts of the World

CONNECT

Tips to learn about and continue developing the capability through others. These tips involve working with another person to learn from their experiences. They may involve asking questions, listening to and discussing experiences, forming a new relationship, deepening an existing relationship, or receiving feedback from someone who is acting as your mentor. These tips are useful for all levels of learners.

Development Activity	Suggested Resource(s) and Tips
Talk with others who have traveled to a culture of interest.	• Ask your manager and/or your human resources department for referrals to colleagues who have been to that culture for business. • Contact expatriate coworkers who are currently living in the location of interest or who have lived there in the past. Your international human resources representatives may be able to help you with this request. • Contact international organizations for information on local cultures, such as World Economic Forum (www.weforum.org), the World Bank (www.worldbank .org), InterNations (www.internations.org), and the United Nations (www.un.org).
Find a guide to introduce you to local culture.	• Hire a guide through local guide services. Your company may have a trusted list of guides used previously in that area. Your travel agency or hotel concierge may be good resources for referrals to guides as well. • When possible and appropriate, try to arrange for guided tours with local employees to build relationships and learn more deeply about local culture.

DEVELOPMENT SUGGESTIONS
for Knowledge of Cultures in Different Parts of the World

CONNECT

Tips to learn about and continue developing the capability through others. These tips involve working with another person to learn from their experiences. They may involve asking questions, listening to and discussing experiences, forming a new relationship, deepening an existing relationship, or receiving feedback from someone who is acting as your mentor. These tips are useful for all levels of learners.

Development Activity	Suggested Resource(s) and Tips
Show interest in another person's culture by asking questions.	• Use icebreakers to start conversations with local people. We recommend that you select icebreakers based on what is appropriate for the local customs. Here are some conversation topics that will work well across most cultures: • local sporting events • local dining and entertainment • local cultural attractions. Here are some conversations topics that you will generally want to avoid discussing until a trusting relationship is established (ask trusted local experts for a list of conversation topics that are too sensitive to discuss): • religion • politics • history • money/economics. • For ideas on conversation starters, read Over 600 Icebreakers and Games (Carter, 2011), or 300+ Sizzling Icebreakers (Puffett, 2010).
Get to know a local person by finding local friends.	• When you are in the location of interest, be sure to make conversation with local people, such as merchants, taxi drivers, hotel staff, and restaurant staff. • If your company has local employees who work in the location you are in, contact them in advance of your travel to arrange to meet socially to learn about the local culture.

DEVELOPMENT SUGGESTIONS

for Knowledge of Cultures in Different Parts of the World

CONNECT

Tips to learn about and continue developing the capability through others. These tips involve working with another person to learn from their experiences. They may involve asking questions, listening to and discussing experiences, forming a new relationship, deepening an existing relationship, or receiving feedback from someone who is acting as your mentor. These tips are useful for all levels of learners.

Development Activity	Suggested Resource(s) and Tips
Join groups that explore other cultures.	• InterNations (www.internations.org) is an invitation-only website for expatriates worldwide to provide them with information, guides, and a forum to connect with one another. Find clubs focused on international/global issues through MeetUp (www.meetup.com). • Join local language and culture groups through community group listings in your local online newspaper or language and culture professors at local community colleges and universities.
Invite an exchange student or international colleague to dinner to discuss their culture.	Ask them: • What does it take to trust someone in your culture? • What does it mean to be a good colleague in your culture? • What does good leadership look like in your culture? • What are some communication taboos in your culture?

DEVELOPMENT SUGGESTIONS
for Knowledge of Cultures in Different Parts of the World

EXPERIENCE

Tips to learn about and develop skills in the capability through firsthand experience. These tips involve engaging in activities, such as exploring a new area, trying a new cultural activity, or participating in a specific business event. These tips are most useful for intermediate to advanced learners, and we suggest that novice learners prepare themselves for success by completing some of the tips in the Learn category first.

Development Activity	Suggested Resource(s) and Tips
Host an exchange student. The organizations listed all work to place international high school students with families. Their focus is on placing students in the United States, so if you are located in another country you may want to contact them for referrals to local placement agencies.	• The Council on International Education Exchange (www.ciee.org/highschool/host-families/benefits.html) • AFS (www.afsusa.org/host-family) • International Student Exchange (www.iseusa.com/meet-our-students.cfm) • The Center for Cultural Exchange (www.cci-exchange.com/about.aspx) • The EF Foundation for Foreign Study (www.effoundation.org)
Make plans to travel outside of your borders.	The idea of a border (i.e., a geographical, political, or cultural boundary) will vary depending upon your experience. Crossing borders for you may mean: • visiting other countries • visiting different regions within countries • spending time with different cultural groups within countries or regions • exploring new cultural activities • trying new foods • learning a new language or dialect.
On vacation, create a plan before you depart to learn about local culture in meaningful ways.	• Read guidebooks before traveling, such as Lonely Planet (www.lonelyplanet.com), Fodor's (www.fodors.com), Frommer's (www.frommers.com), and Rough (www.roughguides.com) guides, and create a checklist of places you want to explore in-depth and experiences you want to have on your trip. • Think of local exploration less in terms of sightseeing and more in terms of experience-gathering. That is, plan to participate in local customs and events that are off the beaten tourist path. • Plan to use tour guides to learn more about local culture than you would on your own. Find trusted guides through your company, travel agency, or hotel concierges.

DEVELOPMENT SUGGESTIONS
for Knowledge of Cultures in Different Parts of the World

EXPERIENCE

Tips to learn about and develop skills in the capability through firsthand experience. These tips involve engaging in activities, such as exploring a new area, trying a new cultural activity, or participating in a specific business event. These tips are most useful for intermediate to advanced learners, and we suggest that novice learners prepare themselves for success by completing some of the tips in the Learn category first.

Development Activity	Suggested Resource(s) and Tips
While you are in another country, immerse yourself as much as possible and as is safe in the local culture.	• Spend time at local gathering places (e.g., city centers, pubs, clubs) rather than tourist spots. • Stay at bed and breakfasts instead of large chain hotels to experience local hospitality and living customs. • Seek out differences in the local culture (as compared to your own culture or other cultures with which you are familiar), and plan to experience these differences firsthand. • Explore new cultural activities that are popular or commonplace in the area. • Try new foods. • Learn a new language or dialect.

DEVELOPMENT SUGGESTIONS
for Knowledge of Cultures in Different Parts of the World

COACH OR CONTRIBUTE

Tips to help others learn about and develop this capability. These tips involve coaching and mentoring others. They may include creating information or experiences for individuals, teams, or your organization. These tips are designed for those who are advanced in the capability and are useful development methods to keep advanced leaders in the capability engaged in professional development at the highest level. Please note that the tips in this section may also be quite helpful for individual use if you do not have a coach or mentor.

Development Activity	Suggested Resource(s) and Tips
Share your travel experiences in regions of interest to your organization with your colleagues and direct reports.	When you return from business travel, share highlights and learnings with your staff during staff meetings or through a communication.
Adequately prepare your direct reports or coachees for work in another culture, and actively support them while they are away.	• Meet with your direct reports or coachees well in advance of international travel to review their preparation and suggest resources. • In advance of travel, introduce your direct reports or coachees to colleagues or partners based in the region they will be visiting. • While they are traveling, provide them with information on how to contact you or appropriate parties for questions or support.

Additional Reading

The readings listed here provide you with additional study of the Global Mindset capability in this section. You will find that many of these resources provide you with a specific and detailed look at using this capability in either a particular context or location.

Title: "Cross-Cultural Knowledge Management"

Publication: *Informatica Economica*

Date: 2009

Authors: Felicia Albescu, Irina Pugna, and Dorel Paraschiv

Executive Summary: The success of international companies in providing high-quality products and outstanding services is subject, on the one hand, to the increasing dynamic of the economic environment and, on the other hand, to the adoption of worldwide quality standards and procedures. As the marketplace is becoming more and more global, products and services offered worldwide by international companies must face the multicultural environment challenges. These challenges manifest themselves not only at the customer relationship level, but also at the employee level. Important support in facing all of these challenges has been provided at the cognitive level by management system models and at the technological level by information cutting-edge technologies. Business Intelligence & Knowledge Management Business Intelligence is already delivering its promised outcomes at internal business environment and, with the explosive deployment of public databases, expanding its analytical power at the national, regional, and international levels. Quantitative measures of economic environment, wherever available, may be captured and integrated in companies' routine analyses. As for qualitative data, some effort is still to be done in order to integrate measures of social, political, legal, natural, and technological environment in companies' strategic analyses. An increased difficulty is found in treating cultural differences, common knowledge making the most hidden part of any foreign environment. Managing cultural knowledge is crucial to success in cultivating and maintaining long-term business relationships in multicultural environments. Knowledge management provides the long-needed technological support for cross-cultural management in the tedious task of improving knowledge sharing in multinational companies and using knowledge effectively in international joint ventures. The paper is approaching the conceptual frameworks of knowledge management and

proposes a unified model of knowledge-oriented enterprise and a structural model of a global knowledge management system.

....

Title: "Cultural Intelligence"

Publication: *Harvard Business Review*

Date: 2004

Authors: P. Christopher Earley and Elaine Mosakowski

Executive Summary: Cultural intelligence, or CQ, is the ability to make sense of unfamiliar contexts and then blend in. It has three components—the cognitive, the physical, and the emotional/motivational. While it shares many of the properties of emotional intelligence, CQ goes one step further by equipping a person to distinguish behaviors produced by the culture in question from behaviors that are peculiar to particular individuals and those found in all human beings. In their surveys of 2,000 managers in 60 countries, the authors found that most managers are not equally strong in all 3 of these areas of cultural intelligence.

....

Title: "The Cosmopolitan Corporation"

Publication: *Harvard Business Review*

Date: 2011

Author: Pankaj Ghemawat

Executive Summary: Today's global landscape is marked by unbalanced growth, protectionism, and ethnic, religious, and linguistic divides. Differences still do matter. This article discusses the importance of a cognitive framework encompassing political, geographical, and economic knowledge.

....

Title: "Remapping Your Strategic Mind-Set"

Publication: *McKinsey Quarterly*

Date: 2011

Author: Pankaj Ghemawat

Executive Summary: The article discusses the need for executives to have at their disposal better tools to visualize the state of globalization. Despite the view of some that globalization has presented equal opportunities across all countries, the reality of the matter is different. Differences among nations in culture and policy cannot be ignored, and neither can the geographic distance between nations. The author observes that he has sought to make these distinctions clearer through the use of a perceptual tool called a rooted map.

....

Title: "The Broad Dimensions of Doing Business Abroad"

Publication: *The Business Review*

Date: 2007

Author: Coen Heijes

Executive Summary: Management literature on cross-cultural cooperation generally adopts a standardized approach that is based on the classic dimensions of researchers such as Hofstede (1980, 1991) and Trompenaars (1993). In this exploratory study, we show the importance of a broader perspective and discuss the ambivalences and ambiguities inherent in cultural identity.

....

Title: "Developing a Global Mindset: The Relationship between an International Assignment and Cultural Intelligence"

Publication: *International Journal of Business & Social Science*

Date: 2011

Authors: Al S. Lovvorn and Chen Jiun-Shiu

Executive Summary: Global mindsets are argued to be critical for managers to develop their firm's current and future international success. An international assignment is considered one of the most powerful means of developing a global mindset. The skill sets, cognitive complexity, and expanded networks resulting from an international assignment provide expatriates with unique and often tacit knowledge. Yet, every overseas assignment is not successful, and not every foreign assignment results in the expatriate gaining a broadened perspective and enhanced skill sets. We develop a model that explicates how an individual's cultural intelligence will affect the relationship between an international assignment experience and the development of a global mindset, and we suggest that a moderator—cultural intelligence—must play a role in the transformation of the international experience into a global mindset.

Title: "3 Skills Every 21st-Century Manager Needs"

Publication: *Harvard Business Review*

Date: 2012

Authors: Andrew L. Molinsky, Thomas H. Davenport, Bala Iyer, and Cathy Davidson

Executive Summary: Over the past decade, companies have become more global and employee groups more diverse than ever before. Organizations are less hierarchical and more collaborative. And today's offices are full of once unimaginable technological distractions. We asked experts in cross-cultural communication, information networks, and the science of attention what skills executives should cultivate to tackle these new challenges. Molinsky thinks that managers must overcome psychological barriers in order to act in ways that other cultures find appropriate.

Title: "The Role of Cultural Intelligence in Achievement of Iran's Small and Medium Enterprise Managers"

Publication: *Interdisciplinary Journal of Contemporary Research in Business*

Date: 2011

Authors: Gholamreza Rahimi, Alireza Razmi, and Qader Vazifeh Damirch

Executive Summary: A study of SMEs in Iran showing a strong correlation between cultural intelligence and achievement.

Title: "The Effects of Cultural Intelligence on Cross-Cultural Adjustment and Job Performance amongst Expatriates in Malaysia"

Publication: *International Journal of Business & Social Science*

Date: 2011

Authors: Subramaniam A/L Sri Ramalu, Wei Chuah Chin, and Raduan Che Rose

Executive Summary: This study investigates the effects of cultural intelligence (CQ) and its dimensions on cross-cultural adjustment (CCA) and job performance in a sample of 332 expatriates working in Malaysia. The findings of this study reveal that CQ is a vital cross-cultural competency that facilitates expatriate CCA and job performance in international assignments. Specifically, the results of this study reveal that expatriates in Malaysia with greater meta-cognitive and motivational CQ fared better in their general adjustment. Greater interaction adjustment was related to greater meta-cognitive, greater cognitive, and greater motivational CQ. Greater work adjustment was related to greater motivational CQ. Secondly, it was found that greater contextual performance in expatriates was related to greater meta-cognitive and behavioral CQ, while greater assignment-specific performance was related to greater behavioral CQ. However, there was no support for the relationship between CQ and task performance. The findings of this study contribute to the body of knowledge in the cross-cultural management field as well as practical implication to expatriating firms especially in the area of selection and hiring of international candidates.

Title: "Expatriate Performance in International Assignments: The Role of Cultural Intelligence as Dynamic Intercultural Competency"

Publication: *International Journal of Business & Management*

Date: 2010

Authors: Raduan Che Rose, Subramaniam Sri Ramalu, Jegak Uli, and Naresh Kumar Samy

Executive Summary: This paper investigates the effects of dynamic intercultural competency of cultural intelligence and its dimensions on expatriate job performance. Based on a sample of 332 expatriates working in Malaysia, cultural intelligence found to be a vital intercultural competency that facilitates expatriate job performance in international assignments. Specifically, the results of this study reveal that expatriates in Malaysia with greater meta-cognitive and behavioral cultural intelligence fared better in their contextual performance. Greater assignment-specific performance related to greater behavioral cultural intelligence. The findings of this study contribute to the body of knowledge in the cross-cultural management field as well as practical implication to expatriating firms especially in the area of selection and hiring of international candidates.

Title: "Cultural Intelligence in Organizations"

Publication: *Group & Organization Management*

Date: 2006

Author: Harry C. Triandis

Executive Summary: Successful interaction across cultures requires cultural intelligence. Several aspects of cultural intelligence in organizations are described: suspending judgment until enough information about the other person becomes available; paying attention to the situation; training cross-cultural mindsets to increase isomorphic attributions, appropriate affect, and appropriate behaviors; matching personal and organizationally attributes; and increasing the probability of appropriate organizational practices.

VINTAGE MAP

Knowledge of Geography, History, and Important Persons of Several Countries

One of our authors found herself in a predicament over historical knowledge on her first trip to Argentina. During her first week of a three-month trip to Argentina in 1996, a peer asked her pointedly about her point of view on the Malvinas Islands. She wasn't sure what to say. She had no idea where these islands were or why he was asking about them. She had simply never heard of them. She admitted her ignorance, and he graciously explained the conflict between Britain and Argentina over the islands. She learned that there was a long history of contention over the control of these islands off the coast of Argentina by the British. That contention came to a head in the 1980s. While there was no active conflict in motion in 1996, the historical disagreement was alive and well in the very name of the islands. Argentines called them the Malvinas; British called them the Falklands. Now, she had just met this peer that very day and he eagerly wanted to know which side she stood on. This is one example of the importance of knowing the geography, history, and important persons of the countries where you are doing business. The fabric of a culture is woven by these very elements and is alive and well in its people. So the point is not to produce a book report in your head. The idea is to understand the psyche of the people who live and work in that region. Chances are that their customs, values, and motivations are tied to the geography, history, and heroes in their country. Therefore, you should know at least some basic information on these topics before going. It might even help you to avoid putting your foot in your mouth or looking uninformed.

WARSAW, POLAND

Knowledge of Geography, History, and Important Persons of Several Countries in Action

Recently I coached the country manager for Poland for a global conglomerate. Mark was a US national and a well-regarded executive who was on his first expatriate assignment.

JOY MCGOVERN, PH.D.
Principal
The McGovern Group

Recently I coached the country manager for Poland for a global conglomerate. Mark was a US national and a well-regarded executive who was on his first expatriate assignment. He had been in Poland for three months, realized he was floundering, and reached out for coaching support.

In preparation for his expatriate assignment, Mark had been to cross-cultural training, which compared the culture of the United States to that of Poland. He had also learned some rudimentary Polish, although everyone who reported to him was able to speak basic English. English was a requirement for employment at his organization.

He approached the assignment with great energy and enthusiasm at first, but became discouraged when he realized that he was very uncomfortable in almost every interaction with his employees. Because he normally had a high degree of self-confidence, these feelings of discomfort perplexed him. I suggested to him that it might be helpful if he analyzed this discomfort to identify exactly what about the interactions bothered him most. After some thought, he noted that he felt lost in conversations with his employees. Half the time he could not figure out what they were talking about. It wasn't a language issue, because they were all speaking English. And he tried to ask questions during conversations to understand the subject of conversation, but after two or three questions he felt awkward asking more. So he withdrew from conversations.

After some more reflection and discussion, he noted that his employees were always alluding to people, places, and events unknown to him. It turned out that in his preparation for the assignment, he had not learned anything about Poland's geography, history, or the key people in Polish politics and society. This was quickly remedied with a crash course and readings on these topics.

I recently checked in with Mark who is now one year into his assignment. He told me that this simple fix, to learn more about the country, politics, and society, had helped him regain his self-confidence. He was now thriving in his country manager role.

DEVELOPMENT SUGGESTIONS
for Knowledge of Geography, History, and Important Persons of Several Countries

LEARN

Tips to learn about and begin developing the capability on your own. These tips involve self-directed learning, including reading, listening, watching, or observing, that you can do on your own at your own pace. They are most useful for novices in the capability, but are helpful for intermediate and advanced learners to keep knowledge current.

Development Activity	Suggested Resource(s) and Tips
Read country facts and figures from a variety of resources to get a broad overview.	• Browse the World Fact Book produced by the CIA (www.cia.gov/library/publications/the-world-factbook). • Explore country information on Wikipedia (www.wikipedia.com). It will give you ideas to explore further. • Browse WorldAtlas (www.worldatlas.com). • Read resources at Oxford Analytica (www.oxan.com). • Read country guides for purchase produced by CultureGrams (www.culturegrams.com). • Use the GlobeSmart subscription tool to explore countries in depth (www.aperianglobal.com). • Search *The Economist* Intelligence Unit website for economic information on your country of interest (www.eiu.com). • Use the app "The Big Chinese Quiz" by Onteca to test your knowledge about China's history and geography.
When traveling, look at different types of guidebooks because they will give you different perspectives and different types of information. Rick Steve's, a popular European travel guide on television, provides detailed reviews of guidebooks on his website (www.ricksteves.com/plan/tips/guidetip.htm).	• Lonely Planet (www.lonelyplanet.com) guides are comprehensive and provide country facts and on-the-ground travel tips. • Fodor's (www.fodors.com) publishes a wide range of country, regional, and specialty travel books. They also have apps for major cities. • Frommer's (www.frommers.com) guides are written for less experienced travelers and are particularly focused on large cities. • Rough (www.roughguides.com) guides are a British series that offers in-depth historical insight as well as a solid understanding of contemporary social scenes. • Joe Sent Me is an online resource guide for business travelers (www.joesentme.com). • Use the app "Beautiful Cities of the World" by NEC BIGLOBE Ltd., which provides images and tips for exploring cities around the world. • Use the app "Metropolis" by Halcyon Creations LC, which provides a gallery of images of cities around the world.
Read the local and regional newspapers.	You can browse a list of local newspapers around the world online (www.onlinenewspapers.com and www.newslink.org).

DEVELOPMENT SUGGESTIONS
for Knowledge of Geography, History, and Important Persons of Several Countries

LEARN

Tips to learn about and begin developing the capability on your own. These tips involve self-directed learning, including reading, listening, watching, or observing, that you can do on your own at your own pace. They are most useful for novices in the capability, but are helpful for intermediate and advanced learners to keep knowledge current.

Development Activity	Suggested Resource(s) and Tips
Read, listen to, or watch a variety of news sources including alternative news publications and broadcasts.	• Because freedom of speech and censorship will vary across countries, these sources may not be publicized widely and you may want to inquire locally about them from trusted advisors. • Read and watch world news in fifty languages at World News Network (http://wn.com). • Read and watch BBC World News (www.bbc.co.uk/news/world). • Read and watch global news through GlobalPost (www.globalpost.com). • Read and watch CNN International (http://edition.cnn.com). • Read and listen to news NPR World News (www.npr.org/sections/world). • Read and watch region-specific news on Aljazeera (www.aljazeera.com). • Watch Fareed Zakaria's GPS show on CNN and browse his website for blogs, podcasts, and breaking news (http://globalpublicsquare.blogs.cnn.com). • Read the Wall Street Journal (available in editions for the United States, Asia, Europe, and the Americas) (http://online.wsj.com). • Review *The Economist* (www.economist.com). • Scan the *Financial Times* (www.ft.com). • Read CNN Money (money.cnn.com/news/world). • Scan Reuters (www.reuters.com). • Read *Forbes* (www.forbes.com). • Review BBC (www.bbc.com). • Peruse *Foreign Affairs* (www.foreignaffairs.com). • Read *BusinessWeek Asia* (www.businessweek.com/asia). • Scan *China Business Review* (www.chinabusinessreview.com). • Review *BusinessWeek Europe* (www.businessweek.com/europe). • Peruse Latin Finance (www.latinfinance.com). • Review Latin Focus (www.latin-focus.com). • Scan *Latin Trade* (http://latintrade.com). • Read America Economia (www.americaeconomica.com).
Read publications and watch programs that illustrate the geography of the location of interest.	• Read and watch *National Geographic* (www.nationalgeographic.com). • Read *National Geographic* Traveler (http://travel.nationalgeographic.com/travel/traveler-magazine), and browse the website for information and tips. • Watch *Amazing Race*, an international travel competition (www.cbs.com/shows/amazing_race).

DEVELOPMENT SUGGESTIONS
for Knowledge of Geography, History, and Important Persons of Several Countries

LEARN

Tips to learn about and begin developing the capability on your own. These tips involve self-directed learning, including reading, listening, watching, or observing, that you can do on your own at your own pace. They are most useful for novices in the capability, but are helpful for intermediate and advanced learners to keep knowledge current.

Development Activity	Suggested Resource(s) and Tips
Use online map tools to understand the geography of an area. These tools allow you to look at topographical and satellite views of countries around the world.	• National Geographic's Map Machine (http://maps.nationalgeographic.com/map-machine) • Google Maps (https://maps.google.com) • The US Geological Survey scientific map tool with exact coordinates (http://earthexplorer.usgs.gov) • Google Earth's virtual adventures in 3D around the world (www.google.com/earth/index.html) • App "iGeo World" by Vendep, which includes world geography of about 500 destinations
Learn about major historical events and people in the country of interest.	• Watch the History Channel (www.history.com). • Read historical novels written from the perspective of local national authors. • Use the app "Current World Leaders" by Fuzzy Peach, which includes comprehensive lists of heads of state and cabinet members of governments around the world.
Read about the reputation of your home country and countries of interest around the world.	The Reputation Institute produces country reputation reports based on global surveys for purchase (www.reputationinstitute.com).

DEVELOPMENT SUGGESTIONS
for Knowledge of Geography, History, and Important Persons of Several Countries

CONNECT

Tips to learn about and continue developing the capability through others. These tips involve working with another person to learn from their experiences. They may involve asking questions, listening to and discussing experiences, forming a new relationship, deepening an existing relationship, or receiving feedback from someone who is acting as your mentor. These tips are useful for all levels of learners.

Development Activity	Suggested Resource(s) and Tips
Get the insider's perspective.	• Ask a local national about his or her perspective on history, politics, and important persons for their culture. • Spend as much time as possible interacting with local people; this kind of information will naturally surface in conversations over time.
Talk to people who travel internationally on business.	Ask your colleagues and friends who have traveled to the country of interest to you about geography, history, and important persons in that culture.

DEVELOPMENT SUGGESTIONS
for Knowledge of Geography, History, and Important Persons of Several Countries

EXPERIENCE

Tips to learn about and develop skills in the capability through firsthand experience. These tips involve engaging in activities, such as exploring a new area, trying a new cultural activity, or participating in a specific business event. These tips are most useful for intermediate to advanced learners, and we suggest that novice learners prepare themselves for success by completing some of the tips in the Learn category first.

Development Activity	Suggested Resource(s) and Tips
Take a sightseeing flight over a region of interest.	Arrange sightseeing flights through your company, travel agent, or hotel concierge.
Bike, hike, and explore by foot when possible and safe.	Arrange for guided bike, hiking, or walking tours through your company, travel agent, or hotel concierge.
Visit local museums and historical sites/monuments.	Museums and historical sites/monuments should be readily identifiable in travel guides, such as Lonely Planet (www.lonelyplanet.com), Fodor's (www.fodors.com), Frommer's (www.frommers.com), and Rough (www.roughguides.com).
Attend public lectures and events featuring important people.	Read and watch the local news to identify opportunities to hear local people of importance speak.

DEVELOPMENT SUGGESTIONS
for Knowledge of Geography, History, and Important Persons of Several Countries

COACH OR CONTRIBUTE

Tips to help others learn about and develop this capability. These tips involve coaching and mentoring others. They may include creating information or experiences for individuals, teams, or your organization. These tips are designed for those who are advanced in the capability and are useful development methods to keep advanced leaders in the capability engaged in professional development at the highest level. Please note that the tips in this section may also be quite helpful for individual use if you do not have a coach or mentor.

Development Activity	Suggested Resource(s) and Tips
Share your knowledge and insights about regions of interest to your organization with your colleagues and direct reports.	When you return from business travel, share highlights and learnings with your staff during staff meetings or through a communication.
Adequately prepare your direct reports or coachees for work in another culture by making sure they have sufficient background information and understanding.	• Meet with your direct reports or coachees well in advance of international travel to review their preparation and suggest resources. • In advance of travel, introduce your direct reports or coachees to colleagues or partners based in the region they will be visiting to make local connections that can provide them with detailed insights.

Additional Reading

The readings listed here provide you with additional study of the Global Mindset capability in this section. You will find that many of these resources provide you with a specific and detailed look at using this capability in a particular context or location.

....

Title: "Cross-Cultural Knowledge Management"

Publication: *Informatica Economica*

Date: 2009

Authors: Felicia Albescu, Irina Pugna, and Dorel Paraschiv

Executive Summary: The success of international companies in providing high-quality products and outstanding services is subject, on the one hand, to the increasing dynamic of the economic environment and, on the other hand, to the adoption of worldwide quality standards and procedures. As the marketplace is becoming more and more global, products and services offered worldwide by international companies must face the multicultural environment challenges. These challenges manifest themselves not only at the customer relationship level, but also at the employee level. Important support in facing all of these challenges has been provided at the cognitive level by management system models and at the technological level by information cutting-edge technologies. Business Intelligence & Knowledge Management Business Intelligence is already delivering its promised outcomes at internal business environment and, with the explosive deployment of public databases, expanding its analytical power at the national, regional, and international levels. Quantitative measures of economic environment, wherever available, may be captured and integrated in companies' routine analyses. As for qualitative data, some effort is still to be done in order to integrate measures of social, political, legal, natural, and technological environment in companies' strategic analyses. An increased difficulty is found in treating cultural differences, common knowledge making the most hidden part of any foreign environment. Managing cultural knowledge is crucial to success in cultivating and maintaining long-term business relationships in multicultural environments. Knowledge management provides the long-needed technological support for cross-cultural management in the tedious task of improving knowledge sharing in multinational companies and using knowledge effectively in international joint ventures. The paper is approaching the conceptual frameworks of knowledge management and proposes a unified model of knowledge-oriented enterprise and a structural model of a global knowledge management system.

Title: "Cultural Intelligence"

Publication: *Harvard Business Review*

Date: 2004

Authors: P. Christopher Earley and Elaine Mosakowski

Executive Summary: Cultural intelligence, or CQ, is the ability to make sense of unfamiliar contexts and then blend in. It has three components—the cognitive, the physical, and the emotional/motivational. While it shares many of the properties of emotional intelligence, CQ goes one step further by equipping a person to distinguish behaviors produced by the culture in question from behaviors that are peculiar to particular individuals and those found in all human beings. In their surveys of 2,000 managers in 60 countries, the authors found that most managers are not equally strong in all 3 of these areas of cultural intelligence.

Title: "The Cosmopolitan Corporation"

Publication: *Harvard Business Review*

Date: 2011

Author: Pankaj Ghemawat

Executive Summary: Today's global landscape is marked by unbalanced growth, protectionism, and ethnic, religious, and linguistic divides. Differences still do matter. This article discusses the importance of a cognitive framework encompassing political, geographical, and economic knowledge.

Title: "Remapping Your Strategic Mind-set"

Publication: *McKinsey Quarterly*

Date: 2011

Author: Pankaj Ghemawat

Executive Summary: The article discusses the need for executives to have at their disposal better tools to visualize the state of globalization. Despite the view of some that globalization has presented equal opportunities across all countries, the reality of the matter is different. Differences among nations in culture and policy cannot be ignored, and neither can the geographic distance between nations. The author observes that he has sought to make these distinctions clearer through the use of a perceptual tool called a rooted map.

Title: "The Broad Dimensions of Doing Business Abroad"

Publication: *The Business Review*

Date: 2007

Author: Coen Heijes

Executive Summary: Management literature on cross-cultural cooperation generally adopts a standardized approach that is based on the classic dimensions of researchers such as Hofstede (1980, 1991) and Trompenaars (1993). In this exploratory study, we show the importance of a broader perspective and discuss the ambivalences and ambiguities inherent in cultural identity.

Title: "Developing a Global Mindset: The Relationship between an International Assignment and Cultural Intelligence"

Publication: *International Journal of Business & Social Science*

Date: 2011

Authors: Al S. Lovvorn and Chen Jiun-Shiu

Executive Summary: Global mindsets are argued to be critical for managers to develop their firms' current and future international success. An international assignment is considered one of the most powerful means of developing a global mindset. The skill sets, cognitive complexity, and expanded networks resulting from an international assignment provide expatriates with unique and often tacit knowledge. Yet, every overseas assignment is not successful and not every foreign assignment results in the expatriate gaining a broadened perspective and enhanced skill sets. We develop a model that explicates how an individual's cultural intelligence will affect the relationship between an international assignment experience and the development of a global mindset, and we suggest that a moderator—cultural intelligence—must play a role in the transformation of the international experience into a global mindset.

···

Title:	"3 Skills Every 21st-Century Manager Needs"
Publication:	*Harvard Business Review*
Date:	2012
Authors:	Andrew L. Molinsky, Thomas H. Davenport, Bala Iyer, and Cathy Davidson

Executive Summary: Over the past decade, companies have become more global and employee groups more diverse than ever before. Organizations are less hierarchical and more collaborative. And today's offices are full of once unimaginable technological distractions. We asked experts in cross-cultural communication, information networks, and the science of attention what skills executives should cultivate to tackle these new challenges. Molinsky thinks that managers must overcome psychological barriers in order to act in ways that other cultures find appropriate.

···

Title:	"The Role of Cultural Intelligence in Achievement of Iran's Small and Medium Enterprise Managers"
Publication:	*Interdisciplinary Journal of Contemporary Research in Business*
Date:	2011
Authors:	Gholamreza Rahimi, Alireza Razmi, and Qader Vazifeh Damirch

Executive Summary: A study of SMEs in Iran showing a strong correlation between cultural intelligence and achievement.

···

Title:	"The Effects of Cultural Intelligence on Cross-Cultural Adjustment and Job Performance amongst Expatriates in Malaysia"
Publication:	*International Journal of Business & Social Science*
Date:	2011
Authors:	Subramaniam A/L Sri Ramalu, Wei Chuah Chin, and Raduan Che Rose

Executive Summary: This study investigates the effects of cultural intelligence (CQ) and its dimensions on cross-cultural adjustment (CCA) and job performance in a sample of 332 expatriates working in Malaysia. The findings of this study reveal that CQ is a vital cross-cultural competency that facilitates expatriate CCA and job performance in international assignments. Specifically, the results of this study reveal that expatriates in Malaysia with greater meta-cognitive and motivational

CQ fared better in their general adjustment. Greater interaction adjustment was related to greater meta-cognitive, greater cognitive, and greater motivational CQ. Greater work adjustment was related to greater motivational CQ. Secondly, it was found that greater contextual performance in expatriates was related to greater meta-cognitive and behavioral CQ, while greater assignment-specific performance was related to greater behavioral CQ. However, there was no support for the relationship between CQ and task performance. The findings of this study contribute to the body of knowledge in the cross-cultural management field as well as practical implication to expatriating firms especially in the area of selection and hiring of international candidates.

Title: "Expatriate Performance in International Assignments: The Role of Cultural Intelligence as Dynamic Intercultural Competency"

Publication: *International Journal of Business & Management*

Date: 2010

Authors: Raduan Che Rose, Subramaniam Sri Ramalu, Jegak Uli, and Naresh Kumar

Executive Summary: This paper investigates the effects of dynamic intercultural competency of cultural intelligence and its dimensions on expatriate job performance. Based on a sample of 332 expatriates working in Malaysia, cultural intelligence found to be a vital intercultural competency that facilitates expatriate job performance in international assignments. Specifically, the results of this study reveal that expatriates in Malaysia with greater meta-cognitive and behavioral cultural intelligence fared better in their contextual performance. Greater assignment-specific performance related to greater behavioral cultural intelligence. The findings of this study contribute to the body of knowledge in the cross-cultural management field as well as practical implication to expatriating firms especially in the area of selection and hiring of international candidates.

Title: "Cultural Intelligence in Organizations"

Publication: *Group & Organization Management*

Date: 2006

Author: Harry C. Triandis

Executive Summary: Successful interaction across cultures requires cultural intelligence. Several aspects of cultural intelligence in organizations are described: suspending judgment until enough information about the other person becomes available; paying attention to the situation; training cross-cultural mindsets to increase isomorphic attributions, appropriate affect, and appropriate behaviors; matching personal and organizationally attributes; and increasing the probability of appropriate organizational practices.

Knowledge of Economic and Political Issues, Concerns, and Hot Topics of Major Regions of the World

Regional issues are important to be aware of not only for operational reasons, like supply chain partnerships and expansion into neighboring countries, but also for security and political reasons. The Middle East is perhaps the most vivid current example of regional tensions escalating into security concerns and political unrest. But even wine distributors in South America, for example, must walk the proverbial line with regional tensions. Both Chile and Argentina are wine-producing countries. Some of the region's most bountiful for wine production in each country neighbor one another (i.e., the Central Valley in Chile and the Mendoza Province in Argentina). However, Chile and Argentina have a long-standing history of disagreements over a variety of political and social topics. Wine distributors in either of these countries would need to be aware that comparisons between Chilean and Argentine wines, for example, would be particularly unwelcome. As is the case with many regional neighbors throughout the world, relationships are characterized by a long history of issues, concerns, and hot topics. As you prepare to do business in another country, expand your aperture beyond the country of interest to learn about regional dynamics between neighboring countries. This will add a layer of sophistication to your cultural knowledge and will help you avoid missteps in your communications and business dealings.

Portokalis / Shutterstock.com

Knowledge of Economic and Political Issues, Concerns, and Hot Topics of Major Regions of the World in Action

For several decades, I have consulted and facilitated negotiation training in the global real estate market. Since the 2008 worldwide collapse of lending, bank bail outs, foreclosures, and unemployment, I have witnessed a crisis of trust and uncertainty among real estate buyers and sellers.

KAREN S. WALCH, PH.D.
Associate Professor
Thunderbird School of Global Management

For several decades, I have consulted and facilitated negotiation training in the global real estate market. Since the 2008 worldwide collapse of lending, bank bail outs, foreclosures, and unemployment, I have witnessed a crisis of trust and uncertainty among real estate buyers and sellers. In most recent negotiation seminars, I have observed that the agents and brokers who continue to excel financially and maintain a strong client base have particular attributes that set them apart from those who have been crushed by this volatile market.

Jenna, a real estate agent from Northern California who works in a very diverse cultural and global market, developed a practice after a recent negotiation workshop, which she states has increased her ability to succeed despite the bleak realities. For example, she now spends additional preparation time before any negotiation to understand her own fears, uncertainties, and needs and how she can prepare to explore with more curiosity and patience the needs and concerns of her clients and mortgage brokers, even her competitor agents.

Not only is her business savvy about the global and local real estate market trends a focus of preparation, but she now also is more mindful of how her self-understanding, self-assurance, and empathy have increased her interpersonal effect and trust she is building, one client at a time in a very hostile environment. Jenna provides a great example of the vision, clarity, and agility that has become a fundamental negotiation leadership capability as a means to create new solutions, effective problem solving, and sharing of finite resources that have been diminished at a global scale.

SAN FRANCISCO, CALIFORNIA · UNITED STATES OF AMERICA

DEVELOPMENT SUGGESTIONS

for Knowledge of Economic and Political Issues, Concerns, and Hot Topics of Major Regions of the World

LEARN

Tips to learn about and begin developing the capability on your own. These tips involve self-directed learning, including reading, listening, watching, or observing, that you can do on your own at your own pace. They are most useful for novices in the capability, but are helpful for intermediate and advanced learners to keep knowledge current.

Development Activity	Suggested Resource(s) and Tips
Read about regional conflicts and dynamics between countries of the same region.	Here are some news sources that tend to have regional news coverage internationally: <ul><li>*The Wall Street Journal* (available in editions for the United States, Asia, Europe, and the Americas) (http://online.wsj.com)</li><li>*The Economist* (www.economist.com)</li><li>*The Financial Times* (www.ft.com)</li><li>*Foreign Affairs* (www.foreignaffairs.com)</li><li>*LeMonde Diplomatique* (English Edition of LeMonde) (http://mondediplo.com)</li><li>Welt Online (English edition of Die Welt) (www.welt.de/international)</li><li>China Daily (English Edition) (www.chinadaily.com.cn/english/cndy/cdtop.html)</li><li>Aljazeera News (www.aljazeera.com)</li><li>The Times of India (http://timesofindia.indiatimes.com)</li><li>*BusinessWeek Asia* (www.businessweek.com/asia)</li><li>*China Business Review* (www.chinabusinessreview.com)</li><li>*BusinessWeek Europe* (www.businessweek.com/europe)</li><li>Latin Finance (www.latinfinance.com)</li><li>Latin Focus (www.latin-focus.com)</li><li>*Latin Trade* (http://latintrade.com)</li><li>America Economia (www.americaeconomica.com)</li></ul>

DEVELOPMENT SUGGESTIONS

for Knowledge of Economic and Political Issues, Concerns, and Hot Topics of Major Regions of the World

LEARN

Tips to learn about and begin developing the capability on your own. These tips involve self-directed learning, including reading, listening, watching, or observing, that you can do on your own at your own pace. They are most useful for novices in the capability, but are helpful for intermediate and advanced learners to keep knowledge current.

Development Activity	Suggested Resource(s) and Tips
Follow news on topics of importance in a particular country through international media, as well as through local media.	• Read and watch world news in fifty languages at World News Network (http://wn.com). • Read and watch BBC World News (www.bbc.co.uk/news/world). • Read and watch global news through GlobalPost (www.globalpost.com). • Read and watch CNN International (http://edition.cnn.com). • Read and listen to news NPR World News (www.npr.org/sections/world). • Read and watch region-specific news on Aljazeera (www.aljazeera.com). • Read the *The Wall Street Journal* (available in editions for the United States, Asia, Europe, and the Americas) (http://online.wsj.com). • Browse a list of local newspapers around the world (www.onlinenewspapers.com and www.newslink.org).

DEVELOPMENT SUGGESTIONS

for Knowledge of Economic and Political Issues, Concerns, and Hot Topics of Major Regions of the World

LEARN

Tips to learn about and begin developing the capability on your own. These tips involve self-directed learning, including reading, listening, watching, or observing, that you can do on your own at your own pace. They are most useful for novices in the capability, but are helpful for intermediate and advanced learners to keep knowledge current.

Development Activity	Suggested Resource(s) and Tips
Learn about the business implications of differences between regions and between countries in a region by following regional trade agreements. These agreements are not simply about trade. Their primary function is to facilitate economic, social, political, and cultural harmony in a region (Barbarinde, 2012).	<ul><li>Follow the European Union's twenty-seven member countries (http://europa.eu).</li><li>Follow NAFTA (Canada, United States, and Mexico) (www.ustr.gov/trade-agreements/free-trade-agreements/north-american-free-trade-agreement-nafta).</li><li>Follow MercoSur (Argentina, Brazil, Paraguay, Uruguay) (www.mercosur.int/msweb/portal%20intermediario).</li><li>Follow the Andean Community (Bolivia, Columbia, Ecuador, Peru) (www.comunidadandina.org/endex.htm).</li><li>Follow CARICOM (Caribbean Community including fifteen member states) (www.caricom.org).</li><li>Follow CAFTA (Dominican Republic, five nations in Central America, United States) (www.ustr.gov/trade-agreements/free-trade-agreements/cafta-dr-dominican-republic-central-america-fta).</li><li>Follow SAARC (eight South Asian countries) (www.saarc-sec.org).</li><li>Follow CCASG (six Arab countries bordering the Persian Gulf) (www.gcc-sg.org/eng).</li><li>Follow the African Union (fifty-four African countries) (www.au.int).</li><li>Follow ECOWAS (fifteen West African countries) (www.ecowas.int).</li><li>Follow ECCAS (six Central African countries) (www.ceeac-eccas.org).</li><li>Follow EAC (five East African countries) (www.eac.int).</li><li>Follow SACU—the oldest free trade association in the world (five Southern African countries) (www.sacu.int).</li></ul>

DEVELOPMENT SUGGESTIONS
for Knowledge of Economic and Political Issues, Concerns, and Hot Topics of Major Regions of the World

LEARN

Tips to learn about and begin developing the capability on your own. These tips involve self-directed learning, including reading, listening, watching, or observing, that you can do on your own at your own pace. They are most useful for novices in the capability, but are helpful for intermediate and advanced learners to keep knowledge current.

Development Activity	Suggested Resource(s) and Tips
Learn about the current economy of the country or region of interest and the effect on the world.	• Read *The Economist* (www.economist.com). • Read the *Financial Times* (www.ft.com). • Purchase reports from *The Economist* Intelligence Unit (www.eiu.com). • Browse information through the World Bank website (www.worldbank.org). • Read information at the International Monetary Fund website (www.imf.org).
Follow travel warnings and advisories through your local and national government.	For US travel warnings and advisories, visit the US Department of State (www.state.gov).
Learn about holidays, both historical and religious.	• You can find worldwide public holidays at Q++ Studio (www.qppstudio.net/publicholidays.htm). • You can search worldwide public holidays in several languages through Bank Holidays (www.bank-holidays.com).
Follow nongovernmental organizations (NGOs) to understand the issues they are facing in specific countries. There are thousands of NGOs throughout the world, so you will want to research those most active in your area of interest. Types of NGOs you may want to research include: • international NGOs • national NGOs • community-based NGOs • charitable organizations • service organizations • professional associations • participatory organizations.	• Global Journal's Top 100 Best NGO list (http://theglobaljournal.net/article/view/585). • The Development Studies program at University of Wisconsin-Madison lists major NGOs (http://devstudies.wisc.edu/resources_ngo.html).

DEVELOPMENT SUGGESTIONS
for Knowledge of Economic and Political Issues, Concerns, and Hot Topics of Major Regions of the World

CONNECT

Tips to learn about and continue developing the capability through others. These tips involve working with another person to learn from their experiences. They may involve asking questions, listening to and discussing experiences, forming a new relationship, deepening an existing relationship, or receiving feedback from someone who is acting as your mentor. These tips are useful for all levels of learners.

Development Activity	Suggested Resource(s) and Tips
Reach out to colleagues and business partners in the region of the world in which you are interested to get the most current news.	Ask colleagues and business partners in countries of interest to discuss economic, political, and social topics that are of most current importance there.
Join international business organizations in the region you are in or are going to.	<ul><li>Join a local Rotary International club (www.rotaryinternational.org).</li><li>Join chamber of commerce organizations in countries of interest, for example AmChams is the name of US Chamber of Commerce organizations located in 102 countries across the world (www.uschamber.com/international/directory).</li></ul>
Join expatriate organizations to connect with people who are currently living in or who have lived in the region of interest to you.	Join an expatriate forum:<ul><li>InterNations (www.internations.org)</li><li>Transitions Abroad (www.transitionsabroad.com)</li><li>Escape Artist (www.escapeartist.com)</li><li>Expat Exchange (www.expatexchange.com).</li></ul>

DEVELOPMENT SUGGESTIONS

for Knowledge of Economic and Political Issues, Concerns, and Hot Topics of Major Regions of the World

EXPERIENCE

Tips to learn about and develop skills in the capability through firsthand experience. These tips involve engaging in activities, such as exploring a new area, trying a new cultural activity, or participating in a specific business event. These tips are most useful for intermediate to advanced learners, and we suggest that novice learners prepare themselves for success by completing some of the tips in the Learn category first.

Development Activity	Suggested Resource(s) and Tips
Participate in a nongovernmental organization (NGO) service project to learn about regional issues firsthand.	• Global Journal's Top 100 Best NGO list (http://theglobaljournal.net/article/view/585) • The Development Studies program at University of Wisconsin-Madison lists major NGOs (http://devstudies.wisc.edu/resources_ngo.html)
Participate in an international corporate volunteering project.	These short-term projects led by organizations such as World Action Teams (www.worldactionteams.com) allow you to work in corporate teams to understand regional and local issues firsthand on a team-based project.

DEVELOPMENT SUGGESTIONS

for Knowledge of Economic and Political Issues, Concerns, and Hot Topics of Major Regions of the World

COACH OR CONTRIBUTE

Tips to help others learn about and develop this capability. These tips involve coaching and mentoring others. They may include creating information or experiences for individuals, teams, or your organization. These tips are designed for those who are advanced in the capability and are useful development methods to keep advanced leaders in the capability engaged in professional development at the highest level. Please note that the tips in this section may also be quite helpful for individual use if you do not have a coach or mentor.

Development Activity	Suggested Resource(s) and Tips
When coaching a direct report or mentee on doing business in another country, be sure to include regional perspectives.	• Provide your direct report or mentee with the resources listed in this chapter for further exploration. • Share your experience and insights of having worked in a particular region.
When presenting project updates and plans to your team, include regional concerns and effects.	• Highlight pertinent regional issues, concerns, and hot topics for your stakeholders and team. • Be sure to address these issues in your contingency plans.

Additional Reading

The readings listed here provide you with additional study of the Global Mindset capability in this section. You will find that many of these resources provide you with a specific and detailed look at using this capability in either a particular context or location.

....

Title: "Cross-Cultural Knowledge Management"

Publication: *Informatica Economica*

Date: 2009

Authors: Felicia Albescu, Irina Pugna, and Dorel Paraschiv

Executive Summary: The success of international companies in providing high-quality products and outstanding services is subject, on the one hand, to the increasing dynamic of the economic environment and, on the other hand, to the adoption of worldwide quality standards and procedures. As the marketplace is becoming more and more global, products and services offered worldwide by international companies must face the multicultural environment challenges. These challenges manifest themselves not only at the customer relationship level, but also at the employee level. Important support in facing all of these challenges has been provided at the cognitive level by management system models and at the technological level by information cutting-edge technologies. Business Intelligence & Knowledge Management Business Intelligence is already delivering its promised outcomes at internal business environment and, with the explosive deployment of public databases, expanding its analytical power at the national, regional, and international levels. Quantitative measures of economic environment, wherever available, may be captured and integrated in companies' routine analyses. As for qualitative data, some effort is still to be done in order to integrate measures of social, political, legal, natural, and technological environment in companies' strategic analyses. An increased difficulty is found in treating cultural differences, common knowledge making the most hidden part of any foreign environment. Managing cultural knowledge is crucial to success in cultivating and maintaining long-term business relationships in multicultural environments. Knowledge management provides the long-needed technological support for cross-cultural management in the tedious task of improving knowledge sharing in multinational companies and using knowledge effectively in international joint ventures. The paper is approaching the conceptual frameworks of knowledge management and

proposes a unified model of knowledge-oriented enterprise and a structural model of a global knowledge management system.

....

Title:	"Cultural Intelligence"
Publication:	*Harvard Business Review*
Date:	2004
Authors:	P. Christopher Earley and Elaine Mosakowski

Executive Summary: Cultural intelligence, or CQ, is the ability to make sense of unfamiliar contexts and then blend in. It has three components—the cognitive, the physical, and the emotional/motivational. While it shares many of the properties of emotional intelligence, CQ goes one step further by equipping a person to distinguish behaviors produced by the culture in question from behaviors that are peculiar to particular individuals and those found in all human beings. In their surveys of 2,000 managers in 60 countries, the authors found that most managers are not equally strong in all 3 of these areas of cultural intelligence.

....

Title:	"The Cosmopolitan Corporation"
Publication:	*Harvard Business Review*
Date:	2011
Author:	Pankaj Ghemawat

Executive Summary: Today's global landscape is marked by unbalanced growth, protectionism, and ethnic, religious, and linguistic divides. Differences still do matter. This article discusses the importance of a cognitive framework encompassing political, geographical, and economic knowledge.

....

Title:	"Remapping Your Strategic Mind-Set"
Publication:	*McKinsey Quarterly*
Date:	2011
Author:	Pankaj Ghemawat

Executive Summary: The article discusses the need for executives to have at their disposal better tools to visualize the state of globalization. Despite the view of some that globalization has presented equal opportunities across all countries, the reality of the matter is different. Differences among nations in culture and policy cannot be ignored, and neither can the geographic distance between nations. The author observes that he has sought to make these distinctions clearer through the use of a perceptual tool called a rooted map.

....

Title: "The Broad Dimensions of Doing Business Abroad"

Publication: *The Business Review*

Date: 2007

Author: Coen Heijes

Executive Summary: Management literature on cross-cultural cooperation generally adopts a standardized approach that is based on the classic dimensions of researchers such as Hofstede (1980, 1991) and Trompenaars (1993). In this exploratory study, we show the importance of a broader perspective and discuss the ambivalences and ambiguities inherent in cultural identity.

....

Title: "Developing a Global Mindset: The Relationship between an International Assignment and Cultural Intelligence"

Publication: *International Journal of Business & Social Science*

Date: 2011

Authors: Al S. Lovvorn and Chen Jiun-Shiu

Executive Summary: Global mindsets are argued to be critical for managers to develop their firms' current and future international success. An international assignment is considered one of the most powerful means of developing a global mindset. The skill sets, cognitive complexity, and expanded networks resulting from an international assignment provide expatriates with unique and often tacit knowledge. Yet, every overseas assignment is not successful and not every foreign assignment results in the expatriate gaining a broadened perspective and enhanced skill sets. We develop a model that explicates how an individual's cultural intelligence will affect the relationship between an international assignment experience and the development of a global mindset, and we suggest that a moderator—cultural intelligence—must play a role in the transformation of the international experience into a global mindset.

Title: "3 Skills Every 21st-Century Manager Needs"

Publication: *Harvard Business Review*

Date: 2012

Authors: Andrew L. Molinsky, Thomas H. Davenport, Bala Iyer, and Cathy Davidson

Executive Summary: Over the past decade, companies have become more global and employee groups more diverse than ever before. Organizations are less hierarchical and more collaborative. And today's offices are full of once unimaginable technological distractions. We asked experts in cross-cultural communication, information networks, and the science of attention what skills executives should cultivate to tackle these new challenges. Molinsky thinks that managers must overcome psychological barriers in order to act in ways that other cultures find appropriate.

Title: "The Role of Cultural Intelligence in Achievement of Iran's Small and Medium Enterprise Managers"

Publication: *Interdisciplinary Journal of Contemporary Research in Business*

Date: 2011

Authors: Gholamreza Rahimi, Alireza Razmi, and Qader Vazifeh Damirch

Executive Summary: A study of SMEs in Iran showing a strong correlation between cultural intelligence and achievement.

Title: "The Effects of Cultural Intelligence on Cross-Cultural Adjustment and Job Performance amongst Expatriates in Malaysia"

Publication: *International Journal of Business & Social Science*

Date: 2011

Authors: Subramaniam A/L Sri Ramalu, Wei Chuah Chin, and Raduan Che Rose

Executive Summary: This study investigates the effects of cultural intelligence (CQ) and its dimensions on cross-cultural adjustment (CCA) and job performance in a sample of 332 expatriates working in Malaysia. The findings of this study reveal that CQ is a vital cross-cultural competency that facilitates expatriate CCA and job performance in international assignments. Specifically, the results of this study reveal that expatriates in Malaysia with greater meta-cognitive and motivational

CQ fared better in their general adjustment. Greater interaction adjustment was related to greater meta-cognitive, greater cognitive, and greater motivational CQ. Greater work adjustment was related to greater motivational CQ. Secondly, it was found that greater contextual performance in expatriates was related to greater meta-cognitive and behavioral CQ, while greater assignment-specific performance was related to greater behavioral CQ. However, there was no support for the relationship between CQ and task performance. The findings of this study contribute to the body of knowledge in the cross-cultural management field as well as practical implication to expatriating firms especially in the area of selection and hiring of international candidates.

....

Title: "Expatriate Performance in International Assignments: The Role of Cultural Intelligence as Dynamic Intercultural Competency"

Publication: *International Journal of Business & Management*

Date: 2010

Authors: Raduan Che Rose, Subramaniam Sri Ramalu, Jegak Uli, and Naresh Kumar

Executive Summary: This paper investigates the effects of dynamic intercultural competency of cultural intelligence and its dimensions on expatriate job performance. Based on a sample of 332 expatriates working in Malaysia, cultural intelligence found to be a vital intercultural competency that facilitates expatriate job performance in international assignments. Specifically, the results of this study reveal that expatriates in Malaysia with greater meta-cognitive and behavioral cultural intelligence fared better in their contextual performance. Greater assignment-specific performance related to greater behavioral cultural intelligence. The findings of this study contribute to the body of knowledge in the cross-cultural management field as well as practical implication to expatriating firms especially in the area of selection and hiring of international candidates.

....

Title: "Cultural Intelligence in Organizations"

Publication: *Group & Organization Management*

Date: 2006

Author: Harry C. Triandis

Executive Summary: Successful interaction across cultures requires cultural intelligence. Several aspects of cultural intelligence in organizations are described: suspending judgment until enough information about the other person becomes available; paying attention to the situation; training cross-cultural mindsets to increase isomorphic attributions, appropriate affect, and appropriate behaviors; matching personal and organizationally attributes; and increasing the probability of appropriate organizational practices.

Knowledge of Important World Events

It's an Olympic year as we're writing this book, which is always a visual reminder of how the world is constantly changing. They'll be some new flags at the opening ceremonies. For example, South Sudan is a recognized country as of 2011. But there will also be some missing flags. The Netherlands Antilles is no longer one nation, having been dissolved in 2010 by the Kingdom of the Netherlands. We also see sociopolitical changes in the Olympics. Saudi Arabia, Qatar, and Brunei sent the first women athletes to represent their nations, further closing gender gaps in sport. The announcers for the Olympic games (and their staff writers!) are role models for having up-to-date knowledge of important world events. They may be experts in track and field, but they also enlighten us on the political and human front of what is going on in and between the countries at play. We gather around our televisions this year to watch swimming and gymnastics, but by the closing ceremonies we will have learned a little more about the world we share with so many talented athletes from hundreds of nations. And we see that they all produce excellence in a myriad of ways.

FOR A
WORKING
IRELAND

VOTE YES
www.voteyes2012.ie   FINE GAEL

It's about
STABILITY
Vote YES
labour.ie   Labour

YES for
STABILITY
Labour

AUSTERITY
ISN'T
WORKING

VOTE
NO

STAND UP FOR IRELAND
Sinn Féin

Knowledge of Important World Events in Action

Fareed Zakaria's Global Public Square blog (http://globalpublicsquare.blogs.cnn.com) and television show are great examples of up-to-date knowledge of world events in action.

JENNIE L. WALKER, PH.D., PHR
Director of Global Learning and Market Development
Najafi Global Mindset Institute

Fareed Zakaria's Global Public Square blog (http://globalpublicsquare.blogs.cnn.com) and television show are great examples of up-to-date knowledge of world events in action. The Global Public Square is described as a website where "you can make sense of the world every day with insights and explanations from leading journalists and other international thinkers." While there are a number of international news websites that provide information, Global Public Square really demonstrates the true meaning of up-to-date knowledge of important world events. It is not just about knowing information by watching a thirty-second news story or reading a headline. It is about understanding what is behind the headline. Global Public Square does this by explaining what the backstory is for major news events as well as the implications for the future. They share the perspectives and stories of the people within the cultures where the events are unfolding and make sense of them in the context of the region.

There is a lot going on in the world, and even the most avid news follower cannot be expected to understand every news event in-depth. But when you are working with and in different countries around the world, it is important to investigate more fully the headlines coming out of those particular regions. Global Public Square is one good source of information to do that.

DEVELOPMENT SUGGESTIONS
for Knowledge of Important World Events

LEARN

Tips to learn about and begin developing the capability on your own. These tips involve self-directed learning, including reading, listening, watching, or observing, that you can do on your own at your own pace. They are most useful for novices in the capability, but are helpful for intermediate and advanced learners to keep knowledge current.

Development Activity	Suggested Resource(s) and Tips
Keep current on issues in the world through a variety of sources.	• *The International Herald Tribune* (the global version of the *New York Times* produced by forty-five bureaus across the world) (www.ihtinfo.com) • News360 app (www.news360app.com) • SiloBreaker (www.silobreaker.com) • WorldPulse (global women's voices) (www.worldpulse.com) • *The Wall Street Journal* (available in editions for the United States, Asia, Europe, and the Americas) (http://online.wsj.com) • *The Economist* (www.economist.com) • *Financial Times* (www.ft.com) • CNN Money (money.cnn.com/news/world) • *Reuters* (www.reuters.com) • *Forbes* (www.forbes.com) • BBC (www.bbc.com) • *Foreign Affairs* (www.foreignaffairs.com) • *BusinessWeek Asia* (www.businessweek.com/asia) • *China Business Review* (www.chinabusinessreview.com) • *BusinessWeek Europe* (www.businessweek.com/europe) • Latin Finance (www.latinfinance.com) • Latin Focus (www.latin-focus.com) • *Latin Trade* (http://latintrade.com) • America Economia (www.americaeconomica.com)
Follow major international organizations, which will provide you with insight on important world political, social, and economic events.	• The United Nations is committed to maintaining international peace and security, developing friendly relations among nations, and promoting social progress, better living standards, and human rights (www.un.org). • UNESCO encourages international peace and universal respect by promoting collaboration among nations (www.unesco.org). • For a comprehensive list of major international organizations with headquarters across the world, visit the US Department of State (www.state.gov/p/io/empl/125507.htm).
Learn about and watch international sporting events, especially those that are popular in your country or region of interest.	• Browse a list of "The 25 Coolest International Sporting Events" at the Bleacher Report by Yahoo! Sports (http://bleacherreport.com/articles/669379-the-25-coolest-international-sporting-events). • Scan WikiTravel, which hosts a list of international sporting events by region (http://wikitravel.org/en/International_sporting_events). • You can subscribe to international channels, including several specialty sport channels through satellite television services, such as DirectTV (www.directv.com) and DISH Network (www.dishnetwork.com).

DEVELOPMENT SUGGESTIONS
for Knowledge of Important World Events

LEARN

Tips to learn about and begin developing the capability on your own. These tips involve self-directed learning, including reading, listening, watching, or observing, that you can do on your own at your own pace. They are most useful for novices in the capability, but are helpful for intermediate and advanced learners to keep knowledge current.

Development Activity	Suggested Resource(s) and Tips
Follow trade organizations in your industry to understand important world events as they affect your specific industry.	• Find trade publications by industry (www.webwire.com/industrylist.asp). • Ask your manager for recommendations on trade organizations to follow.
Learn about world religious holidays and how they are celebrated.	• Find worldwide public holidays at Q++ Studio (www.qppstudio.net/publicholidays.htm). • Search worldwide public holidays in several languages through Bank Holidays (www.bank-holidays.com).
Learn about global interconnectedness and sustainable business practices from social, economic, political, and environmental perspectives.	• Take a course at your local business school or community college on world political economy. • Take World Trade Center Association courses in your city or region (www.worldtradecenterassociation.com). • Take a course at your local community college or university in development practices. These are usually through departments of international studies. • Follow major nongovernmental organizations (NGOs) (http://devstudies.wisc.edu/resources_ngo.html) in your field of interest (e.g., social, economic, political, or environmental development). • Watch TED videos on global issues (www.ted.com).

DEVELOPMENT SUGGESTIONS
for Knowledge of Important World Events

CONNECT

Tips to learn about and continue developing the capability through others. These tips involve working with another person to learn from their experiences. They may involve asking questions, listening to and discussing experiences, forming a new relationship, deepening an existing relationship, or receiving feedback from someone who is acting as your mentor. These tips are useful for all levels of learners.

Development Activity	Suggested Resource(s) and Tips
Call or meet with local national colleagues in countries of interest to learn more about world events affecting the people in those regions as they unfold.	Ask for your colleague's understanding of the issues as well as for his or her experience of them.
Join international business organizations in the region you are in or are going to learn about world events affecting business in the region.	• Join a local Rotary International club (www.rotaryinternational.org). • Join chamber of commerce organizations in countries of interest, for example AmChams is the name of US Chamber of Commerce organizations located in 102 countries across the world (www.uschamber.com/international/directory).

DEVELOPMENT SUGGESTIONS
for Knowledge of Important World Events

CONNECT

Tips to learn about and continue developing the capability through others. These tips involve working with another person to learn from their experiences. They may involve asking questions, listening to and discussing experiences, forming a new relationship, deepening an existing relationship, or receiving feedback from someone who is acting as your mentor. These tips are useful for all levels of learners.

Development Activity	Suggested Resource(s) and Tips
Join expatriate organizations to connect with people who are currently living in or who have lived in the region of interest to you to learn about world events affecting the region from an insider's perspective.	Join an expatriate forum: • InterNations (www.internations.org) • Transitions Abroad (www.transitionsabroad.com) • Escape Artist (www.escapeartist.com) • Expat Exchange (www.expatexchange.com).

DEVELOPMENT SUGGESTIONS
for Knowledge of Important World Events

EXPERIENCE

Tips to learn about and develop skills in the capability through firsthand experience. These tips involve engaging in activities, such as exploring a new area, trying a new cultural activity, or participating in a specific business event. These tips are most useful for intermediate to advanced learners, and we suggest that novice learners prepare themselves for success by completing some of the tips in the Learn category first.

Development Activity	Suggested Resource(s) and Tips
Participate in global business simulations to analyze political, social, economic, and environmental effects and interconnectedness.	• OS Earth's Global Simulation Workshop is an interactive experience for academic, community, and professional organizations to work in teams to solve world problems from the perspective of corporations, governments, and NGOs (www.osearth.com). • Glo-Bus is an entirely online simulation for business schools and corporations to work in teams to run a global company while making decisions related to global competitive business decisions, corporate citizenship, and social responsibility (www.glo-bus.com). • You can have a custom simulation designed for your organization and even compete in a global tournament with colleagues across the world in an online simulation through BTS (www.bts.com).
To the extent possible, participate in global nongovernmental organization (NGO) projects in a field of interest to you to have a hands-on effect on an important world event or issue.	• Review Global Journal's Top 100 Best NGO list (http://theglobaljournal.net/article/view/585). • The Development Studies program at University of Wisconsin-Madison lists major NGOs (http://devstudies.wisc.edu/resources_ngo.html).

DEVELOPMENT SUGGESTIONS
for Knowledge of Important World Events

EXPERIENCE

Tips to learn about and develop skills in the capability through firsthand experience. These tips involve engaging in activities, such as exploring a new area, trying a new cultural activity, or participating in a specific business event. These tips are most useful for intermediate to advanced learners, and we suggest that novice learners prepare themselves for success by completing some of the tips in the Learn category first.

Development Activity	Suggested Resource(s) and Tips
Attend international conferences in your industry to learn more about world events affecting your industry.	• Ask your manager for recommendations. • Ask colleagues for recommendations. • Follow your organization's public relations and communications. • Read your organization's newsletters, blogs, intranet, and external website. • Follow trade publications in your industry.

DEVELOPMENT SUGGESTIONS
for Knowledge of Important World Events

COACH OR CONTRIBUTE

Tips to help others learn about and develop this capability. These tips involve coaching and mentoring others. They may include creating information or experiences for individuals, teams, or your organization. These tips are designed for those who are advanced in the capability and are useful development methods to keep advanced leaders in the capability engaged in professional development at the highest level. Please note that the tips in this section may also be quite helpful for individual use if you do not have a coach or mentor.

Development Activity	Suggested Resource(s) and Tips
Encourage your direct reports and coachees to keep current on important world events.	• Discuss important world events affecting your business, industry, and/or countries where you do business at staff meetings and in communications. • Ask team members to further investigate and report back on critical issues. • Create an intranet that links to important global news sources, industry associations, industry conferences, and partner nongovernmental organizations (NGOs).
Encourage your direct reports and mentees to be active in NGOs sponsored by your organization or industry.	• Provide them with information and updates about these partnerships and how they can get involved if they choose. • Consider organizing team-building events that involve your NGO partner organizations.

Additional Reading

The readings listed here provide you with additional study of the Global Mindset capability in this section. You will find that many of these resources provide you with a specific and detailed look at using this capability in either a particular context or location.

··

Title: "Cross-Cultural Knowledge Management"

Publication: *Informatica Economica*

Date: 2009

Authors: Felicia Albescu, Irina Pugna, and Dorel Paraschiv

Executive Summary: The success of international companies in providing high-quality products and outstanding services is subject, on the one hand, to the increasing dynamic of the economic environment and, on the other hand, to the adoption of worldwide quality standards and procedures. As the marketplace is becoming more and more global, products and services offered worldwide by international companies must face the multicultural environment challenges. These challenges manifest themselves not only at the customer relationship level, but also at the employee level. Important support in facing all of these challenges has been provided at the cognitive level by management system models and at the technological level by information cutting-edge technologies. Business Intelligence & Knowledge Management Business Intelligence is already delivering its promised outcomes at internal business environment and, with the explosive deployment of public databases, expanding its analytical power at the national, regional, and international levels. Quantitative measures of economic environment, wherever available, may be captured and integrated in companies' routine analyses. As for qualitative data, some effort is still to be done in order to integrate measures of social, political, legal, natural, and technological environment in companies' strategic analyses. An increased difficulty is found in treating cultural differences, common knowledge making the most hidden part of any foreign environment. Managing cultural knowledge is crucial to success in cultivating and maintaining long-term business relationships in multicultural environments. Knowledge management provides the long-needed technological support for cross-cultural management in the tedious task of improving knowledge sharing in multinational companies and using knowledge effectively in international joint ventures. The paper is approaching the conceptual frameworks of knowledge management and

proposes a unified model of knowledge-oriented enterprise and a structural model of a global knowledge management system.

....

Title: "Cultural Intelligence"

Publication: *Harvard Business Review*

Date: 2004

Authors: P. Christopher Earley and Elaine Mosakowski

Executive Summary: Cultural intelligence, or CQ, is the ability to make sense of unfamiliar contexts and then blend in. It has three components—the cognitive, the physical, and the emotional/motivational. While it shares many of the properties of emotional intelligence, CQ goes one step further by equipping a person to distinguish behaviors produced by the culture in question from behaviors that are peculiar to particular individuals and those found in all human beings. In their surveys of 2,000 managers in 60 countries, the authors found that most managers are not equally strong in all 3 of these areas of cultural intelligence.

....

Title: "The Cosmopolitan Corporation"

Publication: *Harvard Business Review*

Date: 2011

Author: Pankaj Ghemawat

Executive Summary: Today's global landscape is marked by unbalanced growth, protectionism, and ethnic, religious, and linguistic divides. Differences still do matter. This article discusses the importance of a cognitive framework encompassing political, geographical, and economic knowledge.

....

Title: "Remapping Your Strategic Mind-Set"

Publication: *McKinsey Quarterly*

Date: 2011

Author: Pankaj Ghemawat

Executive Summary: The article discusses the need for executives to have at their disposal better tools to visualize the state of globalization. Despite the view of some that globalization has presented equal opportunities across all countries, the reality of the matter is different. Differences among nations in culture and policy cannot be ignored, and neither can the geographic distance between nations. The author observes that he has sought to make these distinctions clearer through the use of a perceptual tool called a rooted map.

....

Title: "The Broad Dimensions of Doing Business Abroad"

Publication: *The Business Review*

Date: 2007

Author: Coen Heijes

Executive Summary: Management literature on cross-cultural cooperation generally adopts a standardized approach that is based on the classic dimensions of researchers such as Hofstede (1980, 1991) and Trompenaars (1993). In this exploratory study, we show the importance of a broader perspective and discuss the ambivalences and ambiguities inherent in cultural identity.

....

Title: "Developing a Global Mindset: The Relationship between an International Assignment and Cultural Intelligence"

Publication: *International Journal of Business & Social Science*

Date: 2011

Authors: Al S. Lovvorn and Chen Jiun-Shiu

Executive Summary: Global mindsets are argued to be critical for managers to develop their firms' current and future international success. An international assignment is considered one of the most powerful means of developing a global mindset. The skill sets, cognitive complexity, and expanded networks resulting from an international assignment provide expatriates with unique and often tacit knowledge. Yet, every overseas assignment is not successful and not every foreign assignment results in the expatriate gaining a broadened perspective and enhanced skill sets. We develop a model that explicates how an individual's cultural intelligence will affect the relationship between an international assignment experience and the development of a global mindset, and we suggest that a moderator—cultural intelligence—must play a role in the transformation of the international experience into a global mindset.

Title: "3 Skills Every 21st-Century Manager Needs"

Publication: *Harvard Business Review*

Date: 2012

Authors: Andrew L. Molinsky, Thomas H. Davenport, Bala Iyer, and Cathy Davidson

Executive Summary: Over the past decade, companies have become more global and employee groups more diverse than ever before. Organizations are less hierarchical and more collaborative. And today's offices are full of once unimaginable technological distractions. We asked experts in cross-cultural communication, information networks, and the science of attention what skills executives should cultivate to tackle these new challenges. Molinsky thinks that managers must overcome psychological barriers in order to act in ways that other cultures find appropriate.

Title: "The Role of Cultural Intelligence in Achievement of Iran's Small and Medium Enterprise Managers"

Publication: *Interdisciplinary Journal of Contemporary Research in Business*

Date: 2011

Authors: Gholamreza Rahimi, Alireza Razmi, and Qader Vazifeh Damirch

Executive Summary: A study of SMEs in Iran showing a strong correlation between cultural intelligence and achievement.

Title: "The Effects of Cultural Intelligence on Cross-Cultural Adjustment and Job Performance amongst Expatriates in Malaysia"

Publication: *International Journal of Business & Social Science*

Date: 2011

Authors: Subramaniam A/L Sri Ramalu, Wei Chuah Chin, and Raduan Che Rose

Executive Summary: This study investigates the effects of cultural intelligence (CQ) and its dimensions on cross-cultural adjustment (CCA) and job performance in a sample of 332 expatriates working in Malaysia. The findings of this study reveal that CQ is a vital cross-cultural competency that facilitates expatriate CCA and job performance in international assignments. Specifically, the results of this study reveal that expatriates in Malaysia with greater meta-cognitive and motivational CQ fared better in their general adjustment. Greater interaction adjustment was related to greater meta-cognitive, greater cognitive, and greater motivational CQ. Greater work adjustment was related to greater motivational CQ. Secondly, it was found that greater contextual performance in expatriates was related to greater meta-cognitive and behavioral CQ, while greater assignment-specific performance was related to greater behavioral CQ. However, there was no support for the relationship between CQ and task performance. The findings of this study contribute to the body of knowledge in the cross-cultural management field as well as practical implication to expatriating firms especially in the area of selection and hiring of international candidates.

....

Title: "Expatriate Performance in International Assignments: The Role of Cultural Intelligence as Dynamic Intercultural Competency"

Publication: *International Journal of Business & Management*

Date: 2010

Authors: Raduan Che Rose, Subramaniam Sri Ramalu, Jegak Uli, and Naresh Kumar

Executive Summary: This paper investigates the effects of dynamic intercultural competency of cultural intelligence and its dimensions on expatriate job performance. Based on a sample of 332 expatriates working in Malaysia, cultural intelligence found to be a vital intercultural competency that facilitates expatriate job performance in international assignments. Specifically, the results of this study reveal that expatriates in Malaysia with greater meta-cognitive and behavioral cultural intelligence fared better in their contextual performance. Greater assignment-specific performance related to greater behavioral cultural intelligence. The findings of this study contribute to the body of knowledge in the cross-cultural management field as well as practical implication to expatriating firms especially in the area of selection and hiring of international candidates.

Title: "Cultural Intelligence in Organizations."

Publication: *Group & Organization Management*

Date: 2006

Author: Harry C. Triandis

Executive Summary: Successful interaction across cultures requires cultural intelligence. Several aspects of cultural intelligence in organizations are described: suspending judgment until enough information about the other person becomes available; paying attention to the situation; training cross-cultural mindsets to increase isomorphic attributions, appropriate affect, and appropriate behaviors; matching personal and organizationally attributes; and increasing the probability of appropriate organizational practices.

ALBERT EINSTEIN MEMORIAL ▪ WASHINGTON, D.C.   Cristina CIOCHINA / Shutterstock.com

3

Cognitive Complexity

As shown in **Figure 3-1** on page 150, this chapter examines Cognitive Complexity, which is a key dimension of Global Intellectual Capital. Cognitive complexity really boils down to the way our brains process information and how much information they can handle at any given time. What does cognitive complexity mean in the context of Global Mindset? It means that there are many more variables to consider in decision making when working across cultures and global markets. We see examples of low-cognitive complexity in action particularly when we examine the numerous examples throughout the twentieth century when products and services that had done well in one market were launched internationally without modifications for the local cultures, needs, and preferences.

The simplest way of describing a person with high cognitive complexity is someone who is not looking for easy, quick solutions to a problem. He or she understands that the world is a little complicated. Things may be done in my country in a particular way, but there may be fifty other ways that same thing is done in other countries. So someone who has high cognitive complexity is thoughtful, is curious, and asks a lot of questions before coming up with a solution. In contrast, people with low cognitive complexity have a pocketful of solutions looking for problems. They're so quick. "Oh, you have a problem? Here's a solution." They may not even

GLOBAL MINDSET

Global INTELLECTUAL CAPITAL

Global Business Savvy

Knowledge of global industry

Knowledge of global competitive business and marketing strategies

Knowledge of how to transact business and assess risks of doing business internationally

Knowledge of supplier options in other parts of the world

Cosmopolitan Outlook

Knowledge of cultures in different parts of the world

Knowledge of geography, history, and important persons of several countries

Knowledge of economic & political issues, concerns, & hot topics of major regions of the world

Up-to-date knowledge of important world events

Cognitive Complexity

Ability to grasp complex topics quickly

Strong analytical and problem solving skills

Ability to understand abstract ideas

Ability to take complex issues and explain the main points simply and understandably

Global PSYCHOLOGICAL CAPITAL

Passion for Diversity

Enjoy exploring other parts of the world

Enjoy getting to know people from other parts of the world

Enjoy living in another country

Enjoy traveling

Quest for Adventure

Interest in dealing with challenging situations

Willingness to take risk

Willingness to test one's abilities

Enjoy dealing with unpredictable situations

Self-Assurance

Energetic

Self-confident

Comfortable in uncomfortable situations

Witty in tough situations

Global SOCIAL CAPITAL

Intercultural Empathy

Ability to work well with people from other parts of the world

Ability to understand nonverbal expressions of people from other cultures

Ability to emotionally connect to people from other cultures

Ability to engage people from other parts of the world to work together

Interpersonal Impact

Experience in negotiating contracts/agreements in other cultures

Strong networks with people from other cultures and with influential people

Reputation as a leader

Diplomacy

Ease of starting a conversation with a stranger

Ability to integrate diverse perspectives

Ability to listen to what others have to say

Willingness to collaborate

Figure 3-1

understand what the problem is, but in their mind everything is simple because they don't have the capacity, the training, or the experience of understanding the complexity of the issue. So cognitive complexity begins with an openness to learn about these many variables. It then takes a particular level of savvy and sophistication to be able to respond well.

In this chapter, we will cover the following areas:

- Ability to grasp complex concepts quickly

- Ability to analyze and problem-solve

- Ability to understand abstract ideas

- Ability to take complex issues and explain the main points simply and understandably

360-DEGREE VIEW OF TOWN SQUARE ▪ ULAN UDE, RUSSIA   Mikhail Markovskiy / Shutterstock.com

Ability to Grasp Complex Concepts Quickly

Grasping complex concepts quickly is a science. It's a process of critical thinking, analysis, and synthesis. Critical thinking is the ability to mentally dissect the many pieces of information into their individual parts, so you can see their full spectrum. Analysis involves seeing how those individual pieces interact with one another. Once we've done those two important steps, we can then synthesize the complex concept into a more simplified understanding. Let's consider our previous example in supply chain management. In its simplest conceptualization, it consists of where products are sourced and how they are distributed. But to create and manage a supply chain, you have to break down that process into its component parts: suppliers, products, technology, governments, employees, and clients, among others. You then need to understand the interactions between each of these individual parts: trust among companies, suppliers, employees, and clients; government regulations with respect to products and technologies; etc. So to say a supply chain consists of only sourcing and distribution assumes all of these factors among savvy supply chain managers.

It's important to note that *quickly* is relative to the issue. We're not talking about snap judgments here. It means that you are able to efficiently move through the process of critical and analytical thinking to reach synthesis. This may take a few minutes with a small issue or a few hours, days, or weeks with a more complex issue. Of course, there also are some incredibly complex issues like world hunger, poverty, peace, and globalization that we may generally grasp over time but are not on a timetable for understanding or solving quickly. So while developing this skill set, it is more important to focus on how to grasp complex concepts rather than on the speed with which you do it. As you become more experienced and savvy with a particular issue, speed will increase.

GOLD COAST, AUSTRALIA

Ability to Grasp Complex Concepts Quickly in Action

I have found my biggest barrier to grasping complex issues quickly is that I do not realize something is more complex than what I see.

SUSAN GEBELEIN
CEO
Business and Leadership Consulting

I have found my biggest barrier to grasping complex issues quickly is that I do not realize something is more complex than what I see. Because I see myself as an efficient problem solver and leader, when I see something needs to be done, I do it. When I see an answer to a problem and an explanation of a situation, I go with it. Over time, though, I have trained myself in what I call my 360-degree scan. I identify a situation and then figure out who or what else is involved from the point of view of all of the people, teams, companies, and institutions that may be involved in the situation or affected by it. This process allows me to see how the situation is more complex than I originally assessed. It may take slightly more time up front to do this, but, ultimately, it allows me to really grasp a complex situation more quickly than having to circle back and address issues later that I didn't catch right away.

DEVELOPMENT SUGGESTIONS
for Ability to Grasp Complex Concepts Quickly

LEARN

Tips to learn about and begin developing the capability on your own. These tips involve self-directed learning, including reading, listening, watching, or observing, that you can do on your own at your own pace. They are most useful for novices in the capability, but are helpful for intermediate and advanced learners to keep knowledge current.

Development Activity	Suggested Resource(s) and Tips
Learn about paradoxes in global environments. Note: a paradox is a statement that is seemingly contradictory or opposed to common sense and yet is perhaps true (www.merriam-webster.com).	• Read about the paradoxes inherent in globalization in books like The Globalization Paradox (Rodrik, 2011) and *Paradoxes of Culture and Globalization* (Gannon, 2007). • Watch the Commanding Heights PBS series on the paradoxes in globalization (www.pbs.org/wgbh/commandingheights).
As you read, analyze and synthesize information for comprehension and application.	• As you read one of the recommended texts, stop at the end of each chapter to note the main points as well as the central message of the chapter. • Create a thirty-second summary you could use to quickly explain the main points and their significance to a colleague.
Read blogs from experts and people from other countries with different points of view.	• Global Voices (http://globalvoicesonline.org) is an international community of bloggers who report on blogs and citizen media from around the world. • Oxfam International is a global confederation comprised of seventeen aid organizations in ninety-two countries, and its website (www.blogs.oxfam.org) consists of blogs written from Oxfam aides across the globe.
Learn about the complexity of music, especially in studio-quality recordings.	• This video by C2C (produced by 20syl and Francis Cutter, 2011) duplicates and layers clips of the band playing for a perfectly timed, choreographed video that parallels the complexity of an electronic music recording (www.theatlantic.com/video/archive/2011/12/f-u-y-a-c2c/250549). • Watch the complexity of live music performed during the opening ceremony of the Beijing 2008 Summer Olympic Games (www.youtube.com/watch?v=JsDY1Ha83M8&feature=related).

DEVELOPMENT SUGGESTIONS
for Ability to Grasp Complex Concepts Quickly

CONNECT

Tips to learn about and continue developing the capability through others. These tips involve working with another person to learn from their experiences. They may involve asking questions, listening to and discussing experiences, forming a new relationship, deepening an existing relationship, or receiving feedback from someone who is acting as your mentor. These tips are useful for all levels of learners.

Development Activity	Suggested Resource(s) and Tips
Bring in other perspectives and other people.	• Invite colleagues from other teams related to the complex topic to provide their perspectives on a given issue, including what questions they have about that same issue. This will help you identify all of the variables. • Bring in outside consultants to provide a different perspective. • Host a blog or chat topic on a related professional organization's site to invite other perspectives, opinions, and commentary.
Take complex issues and have others define what they mean to them.	• When you are faced with understanding a complex issue, ask colleagues and mentors both inside and outside of your organization how they view the issue. • Browse your professional organizations' websites for explanations and commentary on the complex issue by colleagues in your profession.
Find people who have had success with a similar assignment or project.	• Ask for advice from colleagues and managers who have worked on similar assignments or projects in your organization in the past. • Once you've identified someone to talk to, ask him or her to describe his or her experience including success strategies and resources.
Use ask-the-expert tools on the Internet.	• Ask Jeeves (www.ask.com) allows you to ask a question on any topic and receive both the results of an Internet search as well as access to subject matter experts in the ask.com community who can answer your question. • For specific questions pertaining to your industry or field, look on your professional organizations' websites for ask-the-expert tools. If they don't have any online, call them to see who they recommend you speak with to find answers.

DEVELOPMENT SUGGESTIONS
for Ability to Grasp Complex Concepts Quickly

EXPERIENCE

Tips to learn about and develop skills in the capability through firsthand experience. These tips involve engaging in activities, such as exploring a new area, trying a new cultural activity, or participating in a specific business event. These tips are most useful for intermediate to advanced learners, and we suggest that novice learners prepare themselves for success by completing some of the tips in the Learn category first.

Development Activity	Suggested Resource(s) and Tips
Ask different types and depths of questions when you are faced with a complex issue.	• Visit Mind Tools (www.mindtools.com/pages/article/newTMC_88 .htm) for tips on types of questions to ask. • You can also purchase a Mind Tools app (www.mindtools.com/ Apps) for iPhone. • Changing Minds (http://changingminds.org/techniques/ questioning/questioning.htm) has a useful list of question types with definitions and examples.
Take courses and workshops to develop your critical thinking skills.	• Look into courses in critical thinking in your local community college or other higher education institution. • Visit the Critical Thinking Community (www.criticalthinking.org) for articles, workshops, conferences, and other resources on the topic.
Participate in an international corporate immersion experience to gain firsthand experience with complex projects in a cross-cultural setting.	• International corporate immersion experiences are generally short-term international projects to work in a community of interest on a complex issue. • You can learn more about these kinds of programs offered through World Action Teams (www.worldactionteams.com).
Practice using these abilities in a safe environment (e.g., with trusted friends and family) first.	• Explain complex business issues succinctly to people in your life who have little to no knowledge of the issues (e.g., friends, family), and see if they understand the issue after you've explained it. • Rehearse presentations on complex issues with colleagues and/ or your manager prior to the final presentation.
Once you've developed a foundation in critical thinking, pick a specific project with identified stakeholders and then rehearse your explanations to those stakeholders.	• Identify a particularly complex project within your current responsibilities, and break it down into the various components on paper. • Note how the various components are affected by other components (i.e., the relationships among the variables). • Create a quick summary of the main theme and key points. • Identify the various stakeholders on this project and how your communication with each may vary. • Practice explaining the complex issue to various stakeholders in a succinct and clear way.

DEVELOPMENT SUGGESTIONS
for Ability to Grasp Complex Concepts Quickly

COACH OR CONTRIBUTE

Tips to help others learn about and develop this capability. These tips involve coaching and mentoring others. They may include creating information or experiences for individuals, teams, or your organization. These tips are designed for those who are advanced in the capability and are useful development methods to keep advanced leaders in the capability engaged in professional development at the highest level. Please note that the tips in this section may also be quite helpful for individual use if you do not have a coach or mentor.

Development Activity	Suggested Resource(s) and Tips
To help coachees begin to understand a complex topic, you'll want to help them break the issue down and identify what must be understood, solved, and/or produced.	• Identify the various parts of the issue and general themes. • Apply existing models and tools used in your organization to understand the issue and organize information. • Generate problem statements about what specifically needs to be understood or solved. • Identify expected output or results.
To help your coachee understand the complex themes underlying specific events and the various points of view of a particular issue, introduce him or her to different models of thinking, such as systems thinking (Senge, 2006) and six thinking hats (de Bono, 1999).	Systems Thinking: • Dr. Peter Senge popularized the concept of systems thinking, where we systematically analyze underlying themes in an issue, in his book *The Fifth Discipline* (Senge, 2006). • The concept of the systems thinking iceberg is explained in a video by Chancellor University (2012) (www.youtube.com/watch?v=K8xNCySfwC0). • PDI Ninth House offers an online course in systems thinking called Forging Breakthroughs (www.pdinh.com). Six Thinking Hats: • Dr. Edward de Bono (1999) created the six thinking hats model in his book by the same title, discussing the various types of thinking that should be used to produce a clear understanding of a complex issue and produce creative and sensible solutions. • The concept is explained by Dr. de Bono (www.youtube.com/watch?v=o3ew6h5nHcc). • Workshops for six thinking hats can be found at Indigo Business (www.indigobusiness.co.uk).
Help your coachees put ideas and problems into cultural contexts.	• Connect your coachee with a manager from the culture of interest to explain how he or she understands and approaches the same challenge. • Put your coachee on a project team in the cultural environment to learn about the cultural approaches firsthand. • Remind your coachee to consider all of the cultural perspectives on the issue. • Remind your coachee to remain nonjudgmental and not to make final decisions until the issues are truly understood and analyzed.

DEVELOPMENT SUGGESTIONS
for Ability to Grasp Complex Concepts Quickly

COACH OR CONTRIBUTE

Tips to help others learn about and develop this capability. These tips involve coaching and mentoring others. They may include creating information or experiences for individuals, teams, or your organization. These tips are designed for those who are advanced in the capability and are useful development methods to keep advanced leaders in the capability engaged in professional development at the highest level. Please note that the tips in this section may also be quite helpful for individual use if you do not have a coach or mentor.

Development Activity	Suggested Resource(s) and Tips
Encourage your coachee to organize his or her thoughts visually to manage the quantity and complexity of information and to help him or her see the issues. This process is sometimes called visual thinking or mind mapping.	• Ask your coachee to use paper, a white board, a flow chart, or mind-mapping software to show each of the parts of the complex issue and how they interact with one another. • Find tutorials on how to mind map and how to use mind-mapping software and iPhone apps through Tony Buzan and NovaMind (www.thinkbuzan.com/us and www.novamind.com).
Provide your coachee with regular opportunities to practice using critical thinking skills to reduce anxiety and fine-tune his or her skills.	• Use case study activities during either individual or team development time, such as the case studies in the appendix of this book. • Do scenario-planning, where your coachee or team takes an anticipated or potential problem for your organization and goes through a similar process to solve it. • Have the individual or team read the case study and come up with both an analysis and a solution. • Provide plenty of time for analysis and discussion, especially if this is done in a group. More experienced people will generally converge on a solution more quickly, but novices need time to break apart the issues. • Ask them to present their understanding of the case and how they would solve the issue(s). • Discuss alternative understandings and solutions within the group to illustrate diverse viewpoints and approaches. • Share what was ultimately done in the case, and discuss how similar situations may be approached in the future in the organization.

Additional Reading

The readings listed here provide you with additional study of the Global Mindset capability in this section. You will find that many of these resources provide you with a specific and detailed look at using this capability in either a particular context or location.

....

Title: "Cognitive Style and Entrepreneurial Drive of New and Mature Business Owner-Managers"

Publication: *Journal of Business and Psychology*

Date: 2009

Authors: Steven J. Armstrong and Andrew Hird

Executive Summary: The purpose of this study was to investigate whether cognitive style and entrepreneurial drive are important for identifying individuals who have the potential to become successful entrepreneurs and for discriminating between owner-managers operating in mature and early stages of venture creation and growth.

....

Title: "Cognitive Complexity Implications for Research on Sustainable Competitive Advantage"

Publication: *Journal of Business Research*

Date: 2010

Authors: Shu-Ling Cheng and Hae-Ching Chang

Executive Summary: Cognitive complexity of top managers gains increasing attention in the management field. Performance implication of cognitive complexity is an important one. This article clarifies several of the original points to reply to Huang's commentary. In particular, we comment on some issues of testability and measurement of cognitive complexity and internal/external related dimensions.

Title: "Assessment Issues in Estimating Managerial Potential in a Global Context"

Publication: *International Management Review*

Date: 2011

Author: Thomas A. Clerkin

Executive Summary: Business leaders are predicting a talent shortage of high-quality senior managers and executives. Companies are establishing programs to identify managerial potential early in a career. The early identification of management potential (EIMP) process depends on selection tools (e.g., ability tests, personality tests, assessment-center exercises, weighted biographical data, and past performance reviews) that were typically developed in Western Europe or the United States and validated using Western research samples, but they are now being used in other parts of the world to evaluate non-Western managers and professionals. In this paper, the author hypothesizes, reviews, and analyzes potential problems using these tools across cultures.

Title: "Decision-Making Competence, Executive Functioning, and General Cognitive Abilities"

Publication: *Journal of Behavioral Decision Making*

Date: 2012

Authors: Fabio Del Missier, Timo Mäntylä, and Wändi Bruine Bruin

Executive Summary: Although previous studies investigated the relationship between general cognitive abilities and decision making, few have characterized specific cognitive abilities underlying decision-making competence. In this paper, we focus on executive functions-control processes involved in the regulation of cognition. Specifically, we report on an individual-differences study that investigated the relationship of executive functioning (EF) and general cognitive abilities (fluid intelligence and numeracy) with different aspects of decision-making competence. Individual differences in EF components explained aspects of decision-making competence even after controlling for fluid intelligence and numeracy. However, different aspects of decision-making competence varied in the extent to which they relied on different executive functions. In particular, resistance to framing effects, the ability to apply decision rules, and successful engagement in cognitive reflection partially depend on individual differences on the monitoring/inhibition dimension of EF. The ability to provide consistent judgments in risk perception is related to the shifting aspect of EF. The ability to recognize social norms and resistance to sunk costs were not significantly related to EF, thus supporting the idea that executive control is not a major determinant of these aspects of decision-making competence. Finally, substantial variance in some of the decision-making tasks remained unexplained, suggesting that other cognitive or noncognitive abilities need to be considered in future studies.

....

Title: "Developing Executive Leaders: The Relative Contribution of Cognitive Ability, Personality, and the Accumulation of Work Experience in Predicting Strategic Thinking Competency"

Publication: *Personnel Psychology*

Date: 2011

Authors: Lisa Dragoni, In-Sue Oh, Paul Vankatwyk, and Paul E. Tesluk

Executive Summary: We conceptually define and empirically investigate the accumulation of work experience—a concept that refers to the extent to which executives have amassed varied levels of roles and responsibilities (e.g., contributor, manager, lead strategist) in each of the key work activities that they have encountered over the course of their careers. In studying executives' work experience accumulation, we consider key antecedents such as executives' cognitive ability and personality traits, namely Extraversion and Openness to Experience, and examine the value of work experience accumulation on executives' strategic thinking competency. Analyses of multisource data from 703 executives revealed three key findings: (1) accumulated work experience positively relates to executives' strategic thinking competency after controlling for individual characteristics and other measures of work experience, (2) executives' cognitive ability demonstrates the strongest and most positive relationship to executives' strategic thinking competency, and (3) extraverted executives tend to achieve higher levels of work experience accumulation. Relative weight analyses also indicated that cognitive ability and accumulated work experience are the two most important predictors for executives' strategic thinking competency among the other predictors. These findings are discussed in light of their practical implications.

Title:	"Cognitive Fitness"
Publication:	*Harvard Business Review*
Date:	2007
Authors:	Roderick Gilkey and Clint Kilts

Executive Summary: Recent neuroscientific research shows that the health of your brain isn't, as experts once thought, just the product of childhood experiences and genetics; it reflects your adult choices and experiences as well. Professors Gilkey and Kilts of Emory University's medical and business schools explain how you can strengthen your brain's anatomy, neural networks, and cognitive abilities and prevent functions such as memory from deteriorating as you age. The brain's alertness is the result of what the authors call cognitive fitness—a state of optimized ability to reason, remember, learn, plan, and adapt. Certain attitudes, lifestyle choices, and exercises enhance cognitive fitness. Mental workouts are the key. Brain-imaging studies indicate that acquiring expertise in areas as diverse as playing a cello, juggling, speaking a foreign language, and driving a taxicab expands your neural systems and makes them more communicative. In other words, you can alter the physical makeup of your brain by learning new skills. The more cognitively fit you are, the better equipped you are to make decisions, solve problems, and deal with stress and change. Cognitive fitness will help you be more open to new ideas and alternative perspectives. It will give you the capacity to change your behavior and realize your goals. You can delay senescence for years and even enjoy a second career. Drawing from the rapidly expanding body of neuroscience research as well as from well-established research in psychology and other mental health fields, the authors have identified four steps you can take to become cognitively fit: understand how experience makes the brain grow, work hard at play, search for patterns, and seek novelty and innovation. Together, these steps capture some of the key opportunities for maintaining an engaged, creative brain.

Title:	"Critical Thinking: A Critical Strategy for Financial Executives"
Publication:	*Financial Executive*
Date:	2009
Author:	Susan Schott Karr

Executive Summary: Analytical thinking, skepticism, and good judgment are increasingly the key ingredients financial executives must add to their intellectual/educational mix to remain competitive in a world economy that now places

more emphasis on critical thinking than ever before. Those skills will be even more essential with the potential transition to International Financial Reporting Standards and a greater reliance on subjectivity in applying fair value measurements and other standards. The principles-based system demands an ability to make inferences and use sound judgment. To enhance critical-thinking skill development, some universities and organizations are undertaking various initiatives. Leadership-development programs have begun to offer current and potential leaders ways to improve their skills. For companies, there's a need to create processes that are smarter, take into account the value of critical thinking, and address low-probability high-impact risk. Today's financial executive will face a different combination of challenges, a different package in terms of issues and risks.

....

Title: "Managing Complexity: How to Capture Latent Value from Products, Customers, and Operations"

Publication: *Business Performance Management Magazine*

Date: 2007

Author: Sonny Saksena

Executive Summary: Achieving the optimal level of complexity in products, services, and operations is one of the best ways that companies can attract customers, maximize revenues, and grow market capitalization. Complexity eats away at corporate profits by diverting scarce resources from where they are most valuable, diluting the management team's focus, raising operating costs, masking the true drivers of profitability, and exhausting the organization. All of which result not in competitive advantage and a company's focused differentiation from its peers, but in the exact opposite: competitive disadvantage and diffusion. A recent study by PricewaterhouseCoopers found that only 5 percent of CEOs believe they have the capabilities to manage complexity effectively. They understand the importance of managing complexity, but many do not know its true causes, let alone its true costs. Measuring complexity and establishing appropriate metrics and baselines are often difficult and require specialized skills and dedicated resources. Companies must develop their complexity measures based on their areas of concern and desired results.

....

Title:	"Why Some Leaders Succeed and Others Fail"
Publication:	*Leader to Leader*
Date:	2011
Author:	Paul B. Thornton

Executive Summary: The article offers the author's insights regarding how to become an effective leader. The author discusses the attributes of a great leader, claiming that leaders should know how to identify opportunities, elaborate ideas, and implement change. According to author Jim Collins, great leaders should have the discipline to confront facts in different situations in which they should ask questions; assess the situations; and organize, interpret, and analyze the gathered hard and soft data. The author also relates on why other leaders fail when implementing change and explores the common problems associated with the implementation including lack of clarity, inadequate training, and selection of an ineffective manager.

....

Title:	"Measuring Complexity: Things that Go Wrong and How to Get It Right"
Publication:	*Emergence: Complexity and Organization*
Date:	2008
Author:	Vincent Vesterby

Executive Summary: Seven problems that occur in attempts to measure complexity are pointed out as they occur in four proposed measurement techniques. Each example method is an improvement over the previous examples. It turns out, however, that none are up to the challenge of complexity. Apparently, there is no currently available method that truly gets the measure of complexity. There are two reasons. First, the most natural approach, quantitative analysis, is rendered inadequate by the very nature of complexity. Second, the intrinsic magnitude of complexity is still holding at bay attempts to use both quantitative and qualitative methods combined. Further progress in complexity science and in systems science is required. Any method that simplifies will fail because it ignores what complexity is. Techniques of understanding that do not simplify, but rather provide ways for the mind to grasp and work with complexity, are more effective in getting its measure.

Ability to Analyze and Problem-Solve

Problem solving. It's a term we throw around a lot in organizations. Most job descriptions require it, and we are rated on it in our performance reviews. There is much less attention, in our experience, on how to actually develop it, though. Problem solving effectively requires an understanding of what it means to problem-solve and what it takes to do it well. Many managers have developed this skill through years of hands-on experience. They may not be able to tell you how they did it. They just became pretty good at solving problems. And when we are talking about global work, past success in problem solving in local environments will not guarantee success globally. Many a successful local manager has packed a suitcase early on a global assignment and headed home. Check out the humbling statistics on expatriate managers for proof of this.

If we want to develop ourselves and our employees in problem solving, we need to start with defining it. Problem solving is really a process that involves multiple steps:

- breaking an issue down into its smaller parts

- identifying how the parts work together

- figuring out where a problem truly lies

- brainstorming all feasible solutions

- weighing solutions to determine the best fit considering time, resources, and goals

- implementing the solution

- anticipating potential problems

- circling back periodically to see how the solution is working and course correcting where necessary.

The resources in this section will help you develop each of these skills more fully.

TEAM PROBLEM SOLVING

Ability to Analyze and Problem-Solve in Action

I knew an Asian executive who was working as the new country manager in Cuba for an Asian consumer electronics company. His company had decided that Cuba was a growing market. So he needed to hire five salespeople there.

MANSOUR JAVIDAN, PH.D.
Director of Najafi Global Mindset Institute
& Garvin Distinguished Professor

I knew an Asian executive who was working as the new country manager in Cuba for an Asian consumer electronics company. His company had decided that Cuba was a growing market. So he needed to hire five salespeople there.

In most countries, the way you do that is to advertise or ask your contacts for references. Not in Cuba; it's illegal there. You cannot advertise a position. There's only one thing you can do. You write a request to an office in the Cuban government, and that agency, over some time, will ship you five people. They may or may not have any experience in sales. Whatever labor is available is sent to you. So for this Asian executive, the first learning was to work with the Cuban government to figure out how to build a workforce given these constraints. Knowledge of the regulatory system, the government, and the political system were critically important.

Six months later, I checked back with him to find that he was very successful. Their product was selling in Cuba, and the sales office was doing well. Given their success, naturally the manager wanted to reward his effective salespeople. There was just one problem: that too is illegal in Cuba. You can't do it. You cannot distinguish one person from another. He really wanted to motivate them to continue achieving, though.

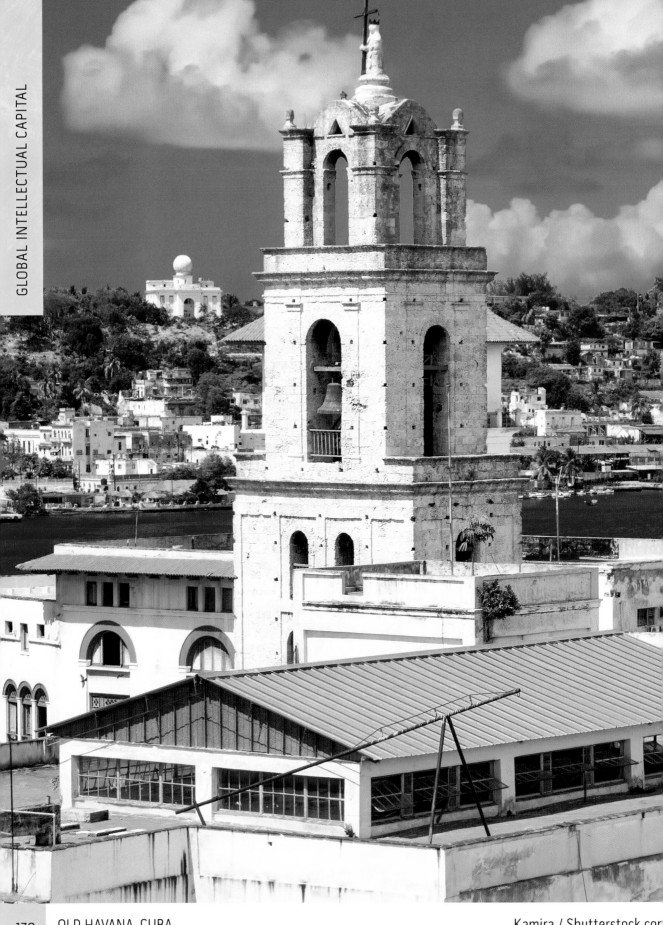

OLD HAVANA, CUBA

So what did he do? There is a supermarket in Havana that only caters to foreigners. Cuban citizens are not allowed into that store, unless they're accompanied by a foreigner. The currency of transaction is the US dollar. So he identified his top seller for the past six months, put him in his car, and drove to the supermarket. They walked into the supermarket. He then gave a cart to the Cuban fellow and said, "You have fifteen minutes. Whatever you put in the cart, I'll pay for it." He used this clever solution to reward his employee in a way that was possible in the local environment.

To me, that was a perfect example of cognitive complexity in action. This Asian executive did his homework. He understood what the realities were. But instead of sitting in his office and complaining about it, he came up with solutions that were perfectly acceptable in this constrained political environment and achieved his objectives.

DEVELOPMENT SUGGESTIONS
for Ability to Analyze and Problem-Solve

LEARN

Tips to learn about and begin developing the capability on your own. These tips involve self-directed learning, including reading, listening, watching, or observing, that you can do on your own at your own pace. They are most useful for novices in the capability, but are helpful for intermediate and advanced learners to keep knowledge current.

Development Activity	Suggested Resource(s) and Tips
To fully understand the complex themes underlying specific events and the various points of view of a particular issue, learn to use different models of thinking, such as systems thinking (Senge, 2006) and six thinking hats (de Bono, 1999).	Systems Thinking: • Dr. Peter Senge popularized the concept of systems thinking, where we systematically analyze underlying themes in an issue, in his book *The Fifth Discipline* (Senge, 2006). • The concept of the systems thinking iceberg is explained in a video by Chancellor University (2012) (www.youtube.com/watch?v=K8xNCySfwC0). • PDI Ninth House offers an online course in systems thinking called Forging Breakthroughs (www.pdinh.com). Six Thinking Hats: • Dr. Edward de Bono (1999) created the six thinking hats model in his book by the same title, discussing the various types of thinking that should be used to produce a clear understanding of a complex issue and produce creative and sensible solutions. • The concept is explained by Dr. de Bono (www.youtube.com/watch?v=o3ew6h5nHcc). • Workshops for six thinking hats can be found at Indigo Business (www.indigobusiness.co.uk).
Learn about data-driven problem-solving techniques, like Six Sigma and TRIZ (Theory of Inventive Problem Solving), through books, online resources, and courses.	Six Sigma: • Six Sigma is a patented process for quality improvement that you can learn about through courses, workshops, and certifications (www.isixsigma.com). • Lean Six Sigma is a course that is particularly relevant for managers who are interested in building problem-solving skills to address process-improvement issues. • Lean Six Sigma Academy offers resources, training, and a community for Six Sigma users (http://Lssaacademy.com). • You can find a free Lean Six Sigma tutorial as well as subscriber resources (www.leandeployment.com). TRIZ (Theory of Inventive Problem Solving): • TRIZ is a problem-solving method based on logic and data. It is most relevant for those in technical industries and engineering environments. • Learn about the TRIZ process and access an online journal and other resources (www.triz-journal.com). • Read about using the TRIZ process to solve very difficult technical problems in "Trizics" (Cameron, 2010).

DEVELOPMENT SUGGESTIONS
for Ability to Analyze and Problem-Solve

LEARN

Tips to learn about and begin developing the capability on your own. These tips involve self-directed learning, including reading, listening, watching, or observing, that you can do on your own at your own pace. They are most useful for novices in the capability, but are helpful for intermediate and advanced learners to keep knowledge current.

Development Activity	Suggested Resource(s) and Tips
Learn about the methods used to approach analysis and problem solving in different cultures through organizations with cultural expertise, like Aperian Global and CultureGrams.	• Subscribe to Aperian Global's Globesmart tool to learn about different methods in the culture of interest (www.aperianglobal.com). • Buy CultureGrams reports on cultures of interest (www.culturegrams.com).

DEVELOPMENT SUGGESTIONS
for Ability to Analyze and Problem-Solve

CONNECT

Tips to learn about and continue developing the capability through others. These tips involve working with another person to learn from their experiences. They may involve asking questions, listening to and discussing experiences, forming a new relationship, deepening an existing relationship, or receiving feedback from someone who is acting as your mentor. These tips are useful for all levels of learners.

Development Activity	Suggested Resource(s) and Tips
Ask to meet with local national consultants, employees, managers, and business partners to understand analysis and decision making in that culture.	• Use cultural consultants based in the culture of interest to you to provide you with insight relevant to your specific industry. • Consult with local national employees, managers, and business partners to learn more about cultural preferences and norms for analysis and decision making.
Invite others, especially those from the cultures you are working in, to join with you in solving a problem.	• Form problem-solving teams that include members with both technical and cultural expertise. • Create a diverse team to provide you with many perspectives and ideas.
When you think you have fully analyzed a problem, test your assumptions objectively by running them by another person.	• Invite a colleague with basic knowledge of the technical and cultural issues you are exploring to discuss your analysis and provide his or her perspective. • Share your analysis and potential solution with friends or family who may not know much about the issues; sometimes novices identify very important issues we have taken for granted.

DEVELOPMENT SUGGESTIONS
for Ability to Analyze and Problem-Solve

CONNECT

Tips to learn about and continue developing the capability through others. These tips involve working with another person to learn from their experiences. They may involve asking questions, listening to and discussing experiences, forming a new relationship, deepening an existing relationship, or receiving feedback from someone who is acting as your mentor. These tips are useful for all levels of learners.

Development Activity	Suggested Resource(s) and Tips
Contact IDEO group and ask them to help you solve your problem.	IDEO (www.ideo.com/about) is a global design consultancy that specializes in innovation and growth.

DEVELOPMENT SUGGESTIONS
for Ability to Analyze and Problem-Solve

EXPERIENCE

Tips to learn about and develop skills in the capability through firsthand experience. These tips involve engaging in activities, such as exploring a new area, trying a new cultural activity, or participating in a specific business event. These tips are most useful for intermediate to advanced learners, and we suggest that novice learners prepare themselves for success by completing some of the tips in the Learn category first.

Development Activity	Suggested Resource(s) and Tips
To begin to analyze and problem-solve a complex topic, break the issue down and identify what must be understood, solved, and/or produced.	• Identify the various parts of the issue and general themes. • Challenge yourself to identify as many angles of the problem as possible. • Apply existing models and tools used in your organization to understand the issue and organize information. • Generate problem statements about what specifically needs to be understood or solved. • Identify expected output or results.

DEVELOPMENT SUGGESTIONS
for Ability to Analyze and Problem-Solve

EXPERIENCE

Tips to learn about and develop skills in the capability through firsthand experience. These tips involve engaging in activities, such as exploring a new area, trying a new cultural activity, or participating in a specific business event. These tips are most useful for intermediate to advanced learners, and we suggest that novice learners prepare themselves for success by completing some of the tips in the Learn category first.

Development Activity	Suggested Resource(s) and Tips
Put ideas and problems into cultural contexts.	• Speak with a manager from the culture of interest about how he or she understands and approaches the same challenge. • Join a project team in the cultural environment to learn about the cultural approaches firsthand. • Organize premeetings (i.e., meetings before official meetings) when you are in other cultures to provide colleagues with focused, individual time to explain their points of view. This is particularly important in some Asian cultures. • Remember to consider all of the cultural perspectives on the issue. • Remember to remain nonjudgmental and not to make final decisions until the issues are truly understood and analyzed. You can do this by practicing both-and thinking, rather than either-or thinking. Both-and thinking means that you do not rule out any ideas or opinions; you consider them all equally and explore them fully. It allows multiple points of view to exist at the same time. To read more about this from a cultural standpoint, look at *The Geography of Thought* (Nisbett, 2004).
Organize your thoughts visually to manage the quantity and complexity of information and to be able to see the issues. This process is sometimes called visual thinking or mind mapping.	• Use paper, a white board, a flow chart, or mind-mapping software to show each of the parts of the complex issue and how they interact with one another. • Find tutorials on how to mind map and how to use mind-mapping software and iPhone apps through Tony Buzan and NovaMind (www.thinkbuzan.com/us and www.novamind.com).

DEVELOPMENT SUGGESTIONS
for Ability to Analyze and Problem-Solve

EXPERIENCE

Tips to learn about and develop skills in the capability through firsthand experience. These tips involve engaging in activities, such as exploring a new area, trying a new cultural activity, or participating in a specific business event. These tips are most useful for intermediate to advanced learners, and we suggest that novice learners prepare themselves for success by completing some of the tips in the Learn category first.

Development Activity	Suggested Resource(s) and Tips
Practice using critical-thinking skills regularly to reduce anxiety and fine-tune your skills.	• Use case study activities, such as the case studies in the appendix of this book. • Do scenario-planning, where you take an anticipated or potential problem for your organization and work through a similar process to solve it. • Find a colleague to work with you on the case study or scenario. • Read the case study and come up with an analysis and a solution. • Discuss your understanding of the case and how you would solve the issue(s) with your colleague. • Discuss alternative understandings and solutions with your colleague. • Read about what was ultimately done in the case, and discuss how similar situations may be approached in the organization.

DEVELOPMENT SUGGESTIONS
for Ability to Analyze and Problem-Solve

COACH OR CONTRIBUTE

Tips to help others learn about and develop this capability. These tips involve coaching and mentoring others. They may include creating information or experiences for individuals, teams, or your organization. These tips are designed for those who are advanced in the capability and are useful development methods to keep advanced leaders in the capability engaged in professional development at the highest level. Please note that the tips in this section may also be quite helpful for individual use if you do not have a coach or mentor.

Development Activity	Suggested Resource(s) and Tips
Help your coachee work through the analysis of an issue by listening to him or her process out loud and by asking questions.	• Ask probing questions to challenge your coachee to explain his or her logic. • Help him or her identify issues or points of view that may have been overlooked, especially cultural perspectives. • Challenge him or her to explain why the solution chosen is the best one for the situation. • Ask him or her to identify alternative and equally feasible solutions to expand his or her thinking.

DEVELOPMENT SUGGESTIONS
for Ability to Analyze and Problem-Solve

COGNITIVE COMPLEXITY

COACH OR CONTRIBUTE

Tips to help others learn about and develop this capability. These tips involve coaching and mentoring others. They may include creating information or experiences for individuals, teams, or your organization. These tips are designed for those who are advanced in the capability and are useful development methods to keep advanced leaders in the capability engaged in professional development at the highest level. Please note that the tips in this section may also be quite helpful for individual use if you do not have a coach or mentor.

Development Activity	Suggested Resource(s) and Tips
Provide your coachee with regular opportunities to practice using critical-thinking skills to reduce anxiety and fine-tune his or her skills.	• Use case study activities during either individual or team development time, such as the case studies in the appendix of this book. • Do scenario-planning, where your coachee or team takes an anticipated or potential problem for your organization and goes through a similar process to solve it. • Have the individual or team read the case study and come up with an analysis and a solution. • Provide plenty of time for analysis and discussion, especially if this is done in a group. More experienced people will generally converge on a solution more quickly, but novices need time to break apart the issues. • Ask them to present their understanding of the case and how they would solve the issue(s). • Discuss alternative understandings and solutions within the group to illustrate diverse viewpoints and approaches. • Share what was ultimately done in the case, and discuss how similar situations may be approached in the organization.
Once the issue has been understood and analyzed, help your coachee move to action.	• Help your coachee define the specific deliverables the issue requires. • Help your coachee identify the actions needed to produce those deliverables. • Ask your coachee to practice explaining how the issue was defined, analyzed, and solved with you as if you were a stakeholder. Help your coachee fine-tune his or her communication for different audiences.

Additional Reading

The readings listed here provide you with additional study of the Global Mindset capability in this section. You will find that many of these resources provide you with a specific and detailed look at using this capability in either a particular context or location.

....

Title: "Leading with Competence: Problem-Solving by Leaders and Followers"

Publication: *Leader to Leader*

Date: 2010

Author: Thomas S. Bateman

Executive Summary: Charisma without substance and competence is meaningless, even dangerous, according to Thomas S. Bateman. The leadership field focuses so heavily on personality and interpersonal skills that the need for genuine competence is easily overlooked, he argues. Bateman explains three critical imperatives for leaders that some would say are obvious but that leaders and followers ignore all of the time. "If leaders are willing to take the challenge," he says, "this process offers a clear, actionable, competence-based path to higher performance."

....

Title: "Problem Solving in Small Firms: An Interpretive Study"

Publication: *Journal of Small Business and Enterprise Development*

Date: 2009

Author: Isabelle Giroux

Executive Summary: The purpose of this research is to present the results of a recent interpretive study of eleven small Central Vancouver Island firms in British Columbia, Canada, which yield new interpretations of the nature of problem-solving processes within the wider context of managerial capability as a critical contributor to small-business survival.

Title: "Solving Problems"

Publication: *Leadership Excellence*

Date: 2012

Author: Chris Griffiths

Executive Summary: It's now common knowledge that leaders can achieve phenomenal results when they apply more of the brain's skills to what they're doing. They've all heard the theory about the brain being split into two parts—the left side, which exhibits rational and logical skills, and the right side, which is emotional, holistic, and intuitive. Left-brain skills include things like words, numbers, language, and lists, while the skills of the right brain deal with images, color, shape, and imagination. In the author's business, he likes to use an approach he devised called the 3S Analysis System (Sort, Screen, Select) to evaluate ideas and come to a decision. During the screening phase, he uses a mind map to assess the more promising ideas based on head vs. reds and greens vs. reds.

Title: "Cultivating Problem-Solving Skills through Problems-Based Approaches to Professional Development"

Publication: *Human Resources Development Quarterly*

Date: 2002

Author: Margaret C. Lohman

Executive Summary: An extensive literature review was conducted of four problem-based approaches to professional development: case study, goal-based scenario, problem-based learning, and action learning. The review comparatively analyzed the training designs of these four approaches and found key differences in the nature of their case problems and training strategies. Specifically, the analysis found that case problems are ill structured in action learning and problem-based learning, are moderately structured in a goal-based scenario, and are fairly well structured in the case study approach. In addition, it was found that prototypical problems are used to a much greater extent in the problem-based learning and goal-based scenario approaches than they are in the other two approaches.

....

Title: "Smart Rules: Six Ways to Get People to Solve Problems Without You"

Publication: *Harvard Business Review*

Date: 2011

Author: Yves Morieux

Executive Summary: The article discusses six rules managers can implement to help those under them make smart decisions and solve problems. A first step is to gain a better understanding of the goals and challenges of subordinates by interacting with them and observing how they do their jobs. Individuals who interface with multiple stakeholders should be empowered to mediate conflicts between different parts of the organization. Accountability among employees can be enhanced by taking steps to ensure they are affected by the consequences of their actions.

....

Title: "Toward Group Problem Solving Guidelines for 21st-Century Teams"

Publication: *Performance Improvement Quarterly*

Date: 2004

Author: Kathryn L. Ranieri

Executive Summary: Effective problem-solving skills are critical in dealing with ambiguous and often complex issues in the present-day leaner and globally diverse organizations. Yet respected, well-established problem-solving models may be misaligned within the current work environment, particularly within a team context. Models learned from a more bureaucratic, homogeneously functional organizational structure were not designed specifically to acknowledge and capitalize on the intellectual and functional diversity of teams, to appropriate a range of technologies in the process, and to work within a more holistic, contextualized view of the problem. Using a case study of a software integration project within a global training company, this article describes possible guidelines for problem solving for twenty-first-century teams.

Ability to Understand Abstract Ideas

If you love art, you are probably already good at understanding abstract ideas. *Abstract*, according to Merriam-Webster dictionary, means "expressing a quality apart from an object." So it means that an object or idea can be interpreted in a variety of ways. Salvador Dali's "The Persistence of Memory" (1931) is one of our favorite examples of abstract thinking in art. In the Western world, we generally consider time and space to be fixed concepts. Time is broken down into its smallest parts—minutes, seconds, milliseconds. We organize our working lives around time—calendar appointments, project deadlines, working hours. But Dali saw it differently. In his famous painting, he shows clocks bending, contorting, melting. The image on page 182 shows an example of Dali's contorted clocks. You may have different and equally compelling interpretations of Dali's message, but the idea here is that he presents an abstract idea that challenges the fixed notion of time. For him, time and space were relative concepts. Dali, like many artists, liked to view what many of us consider reality in a myriad of alternative ways. You can see Dali's painting at the Museum of Modern Art in New York (www.moma .org/collection/object.php?object_id=79018).

Understanding abstract ideas in global business increasingly involves grasping different cultural views. It also requires the ability to envision a new product, service, or partnership that has never been forged before. Who would have envisioned, for example, that cellular telephones would thrive in rural markets like those in China, India, and Africa? The visionaries who put those cell phone towers in the ground certainly did. Their vision has connected populations who had very little access outside of their locale to a worldwide network.

Sybase Inc. estimates that 70 percent of the world now has a mobile phone and presents an intriguing video on the history of mobile phone growth since its introduction in 1956 (http://www.youtube.com/watch?v=0aUQLIPdtg8). So we see that the concept of abstract itself involves an understanding of diversity, innovation, and creativity.

Understanding the abstract is first about being able to move outside of our own views of the world to recognize alternative views and realities. Once we are able to see them, it becomes apparent that multiple and contradictory realities may exist at the same time. When we've reached the point of both recognizing alternative realities and the fact that they may exist in parallel with other realities is when the really hard work begins. It is then that we must contemplate how we can work and live in these different realities in a way that respects the local culture but also aligns with our personal and cultural values.

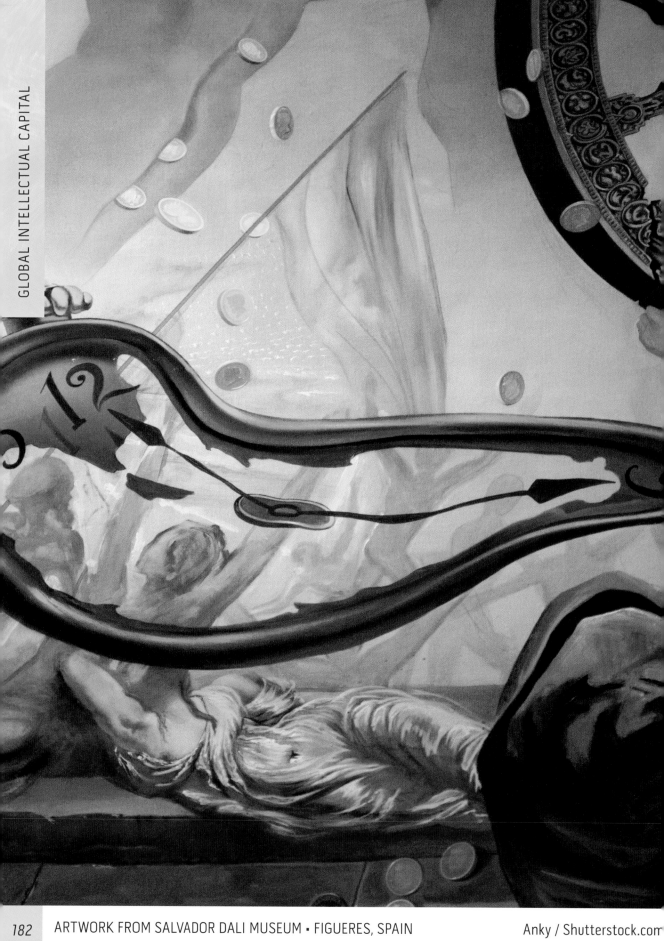

ARTWORK FROM SALVADOR DALI MUSEUM · FIGUERES, SPAIN

Ability to Understand Abstract Ideas in Action

Understanding the abstract is first about being able to move outside of our own views of the world to recognize alternative views and realities.

JENNIE L. WALKER, PH.D., PHR
Director of Global Learning and Market Development
Najafi Global Mindset Institute

Understanding the abstract is first about being able to move outside of our own views of the world to recognize alternative views and realities. Once we are able to see them, it becomes apparent that multiple and contradictory realities may exist at the same time. For example, I once heard an argument from a business student that discrimination against women in the workplace was a thing of the past. She stated this quite confidently. When she was asked to explain her statement, she cited US employment laws.

This sparked a lively debate among the class wherein US students discussed the fact that the presence of the laws did not mean that women were not discriminated against. In fact, there are many reported cases annually of various forms of discrimination in the workplace. Many international students in the room shared this experience as well. However, it was the international students who also added their real-life experiences of discrimination against women that was neither illegal nor discouraged in some cultures. The student quietly listened to her peers, and it became evident that her eyes were opened to the many different and sometimes contradictory realities of women in the workplace around the world. The very concept of discrimination was opened up in all of its abstractions.

INDIAN FASHION FUSION · CHENNAI, INDIA

When we've reached the point of both recognizing alternative realities and the fact that they may exist in parallel with other realities is when the really hard work begins. It is then that we must contemplate how we can work and live in these different realities in a way that respects the local culture but also aligns with our personal and cultural values.

At a recent conference for human resources professionals, for example, I was in a session where a vice president for diversity and inclusion for a large multinational firm said that she simply would not condone separate work environments for men and women in her company's Saudi Arabian office, as was the local custom. She and a very experienced cross-cultural consultant had a lively dialogue about what a decision like that would mean for the company and for the employees in those offices. Both were concerned about the women, but from very different points of view. The cross-cultural consultant believed the women would be uncomfortable breaking with local traditions and may be exposed to heightened discrimination as a result. The vice president wanted to make a clear statement with her policy that women were equal in that organization and should not be segregated. There were many diverse opinions on this issue, and it showed just how layered an abstract concept like equality in the workplace really is.

Because we're looking at abstract ideas in this section, we have included a real-world dialogue between a senior human resources executive in India, Satish Pradhan, and an esteemed professor of global business in Australia, Dr. Steven Segal. Their dialogue captures the essence of an abstract idea: the fundamental differences between Eastern and Western worldviews. It was part of a larger conversation we host monthly with our Global Mindset partners about the realities of doing business globally.

"Our major challenge seems to be [that] the Western thinking on [global leadership] seems inadequate. This may sound provocative, and it is. It is provocative to us, as we are all saddled with the paradigms of very good research, theory, and assumptions of thought emerging from great work done in the west. Yet this work seems to require some challenge and rethinking."

SATISH PRADHAN
Chief, Group HR, Tata Sons Limited

"I think it is crucial to make our own preconceptions about Global Mindset explicit. There is a methodology in thought practices called hermeneutic phenomenology that makes explicit our assumptions and examines our preconceptions when doing research on any topic, such as Global Mindset. The idea is that when we are in our own mindset we do not see the mindset that we are in. We need to cross boundaries and borders not only to see how others do things but to see the preconceptions that inform our own way of doing things."

"When we can begin to observe our preconceptions, we can begin to go beyond them, not in the sense of denying them but in the sense of opening a greater range of perspectives through which to see things. Thus it allows us to see how being Western influences our way of perceiving Global Mindset. It allows us to create a dialogue or conversation across different ways of seeing things such that through the encounter with another, I am not only learning about the other but I am also learning about that which informs my taken for granted assumptions in terms of which I experience another."

STEVEN SEGAL, PH.D.
Senior Lecturer, Macquarie Graduate School of Management

"Steven, you have hit the sweet spot of our thinking here! The good news is that we share strengths in the methodological rigor in both the East and the West—we are required to state our priors up front and hence are subject to our own scrutiny and that of others for our assumption set. But let me give an example of how deep our struggle is. The basic building blocks of thinking and logic, that which is a is not b, leads us to an either-or approach. This is useful in an analytical teardown of the components of reality to understand the elements and their interrelationships better. The challenge is that, viscerally, my Asian self lives the reality of simultaneous presence of opposites in the real world and the

multiplicity of reality. For example, that which is red may not appear to be green, but the reality is it is both red and green at that same time. There are many other realities and perceptions involved as well. Reality is messy. It doesn't lend itself to my analytical categorization. So what does this mean for human sciences theory and how we classify and explain experiences?"

SATISH PRADHAN
Chief, Group HR, Tata Sons Limited

"Yes, I do agree with you, Satish. What I will call my logical self always works in terms of the law of noncontradiction (black cannot be white at the same time), but my existential self experiences opposites as being part of the same whole. For example, I can simultaneously feel excited and frightened by something—say, going on a date or beginning a new job. I feel both fear and desire. To me these different ways of being attuned are different dimensions of our being. When I am a subject viewing an object from a discrete distance, I am in a logical attunement to being. But when I am committing myself to something, I am in an engaged relationship to being. It is in the latter context that both fear and excitement can coexist in one whole. These different ways of being attuned are different dimensions of being in the world. The limitation of the West is that it has reduced being in the world to one mode, that is the logical mode, rather than seeing that not only are there multiple ways of being but also that being in the world is always more than what we can say of it! And this paradoxically is what keeps the curiosity, humility, and mystery open. These are the key elements of Global Mindset."

STEVEN SEGAL, PH.D.
Senior Lecturer, Macquarie Graduate School of Management

DEVELOPMENT SUGGESTIONS
for Ability to Understand Abstract Ideas

LEARN

Tips to learn about and begin developing the capability on your own. These tips involve self-directed learning, including reading, listening, watching, or observing, that you can do on your own at your own pace. They are most useful for novices in the capability, but are helpful for intermediate and advanced learners to keep knowledge current.

Development Activity	Suggested Resource(s) and Tips
Learn about how abstract thinking is learned from a human development perspective and from a philosophical perspective.	Human Development Perspective: • Dr. Jean Piaget's work on cognitive development showed that abstract thinking is the highest order of thinking and the last to be developed by adolescents. A brief explanation of his findings are explained at Simply Psychology (www.simplypsychology.org/formal-operational.html). Philosophical Perspective: • Stanford's Encyclopedia of Philosophy describes several viewpoints on abstract ideas (http://plato.stanford.edu/entries/abstract-objects).
Learn about the distinction between abstract and concrete concepts.	Watch medical doctor Charles Limb's fascinating video illustrating the difference between concrete sounds like language and abstract sounds like music as they are perceived by hearing restoration patients (www.ted.com/talks/charles_limb_building_the_musical_muscle.html).
Learn about abstract ideas in business.	Read John Sviokla's *Harvard Business Review* article "Getting Buy-In for Abstract Ideas" (http://blogs.hbr.org/sviokla/2009/11/getting_buyin_for_abstract_ide.html).
Learn about how to reframe ideas to expand thinking beyond static beliefs and values.	• Changing Minds offers a detailed explanation of reframing (http://changingminds.org/techniques/general/reframing.htm). • Mind Tools provides an explanation and a tool called the Reframing Matrix (www.mindtools.com/pages/article/newCT_05.htm).
Learn about paradoxes as both a form of abstract thinking and a representation of multiple realities.	• Read Human Capital Institute's blog on "Opening Our Mind to Paradoxical Thinking" (www.hci.org/lib/opening-our-mind-paradoxical-thinking). • Read Francis Cholle's (2011) book *The Intuitive Compass*, which uses paradoxes in successful businesses to illustrate new ways of thinking and working.

DEVELOPMENT SUGGESTIONS
for Ability to Understand Abstract Ideas

LEARN

Tips to learn about and begin developing the capability on your own. These tips involve self-directed learning, including reading, listening, watching, or observing, that you can do on your own at your own pace. They are most useful for novices in the capability, but are helpful for intermediate and advanced learners to keep knowledge current.

Development Activity	Suggested Resource(s) and Tips
Learn about the difference between divergent thinking, which is a thought process used to generate multiple creative ideas, and convergent thinking, which is a thought process used to come to one conclusion.	Problem Solving Techniques has a brief explanation of the difference between these two thinking processes (www.problem-solving-techniques.com/Convergent-Thinking.html).

DEVELOPMENT SUGGESTIONS
for Ability to Understand Abstract Ideas

CONNECT

Tips to learn about and continue developing the capability through others. These tips involve working with another person to learn from their experiences. They may involve asking questions, listening to and discussing experiences, forming a new relationship, deepening an existing relationship, or receiving feedback from someone who is acting as your mentor. These tips are useful for all levels of learners.

Development Activity	Suggested Resource(s) and Tips
Identify a leader in your organization who is particularly good at understanding abstract ideas, and ask to meet with him or her to understand how he or she has developed this skill.	• Ask what experiences he or she has had to develop this skill. • If he or she does not readily know, inquire about his or her education, experiences, and professional experience prior to his or her current position to identify what may have led to this ability. • Identify a recent example where you have seen him or her work to understand an abstract idea, and ask him or her to explain what information he or she gathered to aid in that understanding.
When faced with understanding an abstract idea, ask to meet with people who are involved with the same issue who have diverse perspectives and experiences.	• Ask them to explain their understanding of the idea and how they came to that understanding. • Seek multiple perspectives to understand the many views on the issue.

DEVELOPMENT SUGGESTIONS
for Ability to Understand Abstract Ideas

EXPERIENCE

Tips to learn about and develop skills in the capability through firsthand experience. These tips involve engaging in activities, such as exploring a new area, trying a new cultural activity, or participating in a specific business event. These tips are most useful for intermediate to advanced learners, and we suggest that novice learners prepare themselves for success by completing some of the tips in the Learn category first.

Development Activity	Suggested Resource(s) and Tips
Practice abstract thinking skills with tests that measure this ability.	• *How to Pass Diagramatic Reasoning Tests* (Bryon, 2008) includes tests for abstract reasoning among others. • *The Complete Book of Intelligence Tests* (Carter, 2005) includes 500 exercises to enhance mind strength. • Mensa, the high IQ society, offers free quizzes that include problems designed for abstract thinking (www.mensa.org).
Work to keep yourself physically alert and mentally ready to use advanced thinking skills.	• Do regular physical exercise. • Eat balanced meals throughout the day. • Get plenty of rest. • Recharge your mental batteries by taking regular short breaks at work.

DEVELOPMENT SUGGESTIONS
for Ability to Understand Abstract Ideas

COACH OR CONTRIBUTE

Tips to help others learn about and develop this capability. These tips involve coaching and mentoring others. They may include creating information or experiences for individuals, teams, or your organization. These tips are designed for those who are advanced in the capability and are useful development methods to keep advanced leaders in the capability engaged in professional development at the highest level. Please note that the tips in this section may also be quite helpful for individual use if you do not have a coach or mentor.

Development Activity	Suggested Resource(s) and Tips
Create environments that stimulate abstract thinking.	• Encourage diverse viewpoints and ideas by actively inviting them during meetings, projects, and events. • Stimulate creativity and innovation in your department/environment by fostering diverse team formation for projects as well as a culture of divergent thinking and brainstorming, and by allowing people to have control over their working styles and environment. • Encourage your coachees to explore how top-rated innovative workplaces differentiate themselves. Some of these companies include MindLab (Denmark), Red Bull (UK), VW (Germany), and Google (United States) (http://positivesharing.com/2006/10/10-seeeeeriously-cool-workplaces).

Additional Reading

The readings listed here provide you with additional study of the Global Mindset capability in this section. You will find that many of these resources provide you with a specific and detailed look at using this capability in either a particular context or location.

....

Title: "Cognitive Style and Entrepreneurial Drive of New and Mature Business Owner-Managers"

Publication: *Journal of Business and Psychology*

Date: 2009

Authors: Steven J. Armstrong and Andrew Hird

Executive Summary: The purpose of this study was to investigate whether cognitive style and entrepreneurial drive are important for identifying individuals who have the potential to become successful entrepreneurs, and for discriminating between owner-managers operating in mature and early stages of venture creation and growth.

....

Title: "Cognitive Complexity Implications for Research on Sustainable Competitive Advantage"

Publication: *Journal of Business Research*

Date: 2010

Authors: Shu-Ling Cheng and Hae-Ching Chang

Executive Summary: Cognitive complexity of top managers gains increasing attention in the management field. Performance implication of cognitive complexity is an important one. This article clarifies several of the original points to reply to Huang's commentary. In particular, we comment on some issues of testability and measurement of cognitive complexity and internal/external related dimensions.

Title: "Assessment Issues in Estimating Managerial Potential in a Global Context"

Publication: *International Management Review*

Date: 2011

Author: Thomas A. Clerkin

Executive Summary: Business leaders are predicting a talent shortage of high-quality senior managers and executives. Companies are establishing programs to identify managerial potential early in a career. The early identification of management potential (EIMP) process depends on selection tools (e.g., ability tests, personality tests, assessment-center exercises, weighted biographical data, and past performance reviews) that were typically developed in Western Europe or the United States and validated using Western research samples, but they are now being used in other parts of the world to evaluate non-Western managers and professionals. In this paper, the author hypothesizes, reviews, and analyzes potential problems using these tools across cultures.

Title: "Decision-Making Competence, Executive Functioning, and General Cognitive Abilities"

Publication: *Journal of Behavioral Decision Making*

Date: 2012

Authors: Fabio Del Missier, Timo Mäntylä, and Wändi Bruine Bruin

Executive Summary: Although previous studies investigated the relationship between general cognitive abilities and decision making, few have characterized specific cognitive abilities underlying decision-making competence. In this paper, we focus on executive functions-control processes involved in the regulation of cognition. Specifically, we report on an individual-differences study that investigated the relationship of executive functioning (EF) and general cognitive abilities (fluid intelligence and numeracy) with different aspects of decision-making competence. Individual differences in EF components explained aspects of decision-making competence even after controlling for fluid intelligence and numeracy. However, different aspects of decision-making competence varied in the extent to which they relied on different executive functions. In particular, resistance to framing effects, the ability to apply decision rules, and successful engagement in cognitive reflection partially depend on individual differences on the monitoring/inhibition dimension of EF. The ability to provide consistent judgments in risk perception is related to the shifting aspect of EF. The ability to recognize social norms and resistance to sunk costs were not significantly related to EF, thus supporting the idea that executive control is not a major determinant of these aspects of decision-making competence. Finally, substantial variance in some of the decision-making tasks remained unexplained, suggesting that other cognitive or noncognitive abilities need to be considered in future studies.

. . . .

Title: "Developing Executive Leaders: The Relative Contribution of Cognitive Ability, Personality, and the Accumulation of Work Experience in Predicting Strategic Thinking Competency"

Publication: *Personnel Psychology*

Date: 2011

Authors: Lisa Dragoni, In-Sue Oh, Paul Vankatwyk, and Paul E. Tesluk

Executive Summary: We conceptually define and empirically investigate the accumulation of work experience—a concept that refers to the extent to which executives have amassed varied levels of roles and responsibilities (e.g., contributor, manager, lead strategist) in each of the key work activities that they have encountered over the course of their careers. In studying executives' work experience accumulation, we consider key antecedents such as executives' cognitive ability and personality traits, namely Extraversion and Openness to Experience, and examine the value of work experience accumulation on executives' strategic thinking competency. Analyses of multisource data from 703 executives revealed three key findings: (1) accumulated work experience positively relates to executives' strategic thinking competency after controlling for individual characteristics and other measures of work experience, (2) executives' cognitive ability demonstrates the strongest and most positive relationship to executives' strategic thinking competency, and (3) extraverted executives tend to achieve higher levels of work experience accumulation. Relative weight analyses also indicated that cognitive ability and accumulated work experience are the two most important predictors for executives' strategic thinking competency among the other predictors. These findings are discussed in light of their practical implications.

••

Title: "Cognitive Fitness"

Publication: *Harvard Business Review*

Date: 2007

Authors: Roderick Gilkey and Clint Kilts

Executive Summary: Recent neuroscientific research shows that the health of your brain isn't, as experts once thought, just the product of childhood experiences and genetics; it reflects your adult choices and experiences as well. Professors Gilkey and Kilts of Emory University's medical and business schools explain how you can strengthen your brain's anatomy, neural networks, and cognitive abilities and prevent functions such as memory from deteriorating as you age. The brain's alertness is the result of what the authors call cognitive fitness—a state of optimized ability to reason, remember, learn, plan, and adapt. Certain attitudes, lifestyle choices, and exercises enhance cognitive fitness. Mental workouts are the key. Brain-imaging studies indicate that acquiring expertise in areas as diverse as playing a cello, juggling, speaking a foreign language, and driving a taxicab expands your neural systems and makes them more communicative. In other words, you can alter the physical makeup of your brain by learning new skills. The more cognitively fit you are, the better equipped you are to make decisions, solve problems, and deal with stress and change. Cognitive fitness will help you be more open to new ideas and alternative perspectives. It will give you the capacity to change your behavior and realize your goals. You can delay senescence for years and even enjoy a second career. Drawing from the rapidly expanding body of neuroscience research as well as from well-established research in psychology and other mental health fields, the authors have identified four steps you can take to become cognitively fit: understand how experience makes the brain grow, work hard at play, search for patterns, and seek novelty and innovation. Together, these steps capture some of the key opportunities for maintaining an engaged, creative brain.

••

Title: "Critical Thinking: A Critical Strategy for Financial Executives"

Publication: *Financial Executive*

Date: 2009

Author: Susan Schott Karr

Executive Summary: Analytical thinking, skepticism, and good judgment are increasingly the key ingredients financial executives must add to their intellectual/educational mix to remain competitive in a world economy that now places

more emphasis on critical thinking than ever before. Those skills will be even more essential with the potential transition to International Financial Reporting Standards and a greater reliance on subjectivity in applying fair value measurements and other standards. The principles-based system demands an ability to make inferences and use sound judgment. To enhance critical-thinking skill development, some universities and organizations are undertaking various initiatives. Leadership-development programs have begun to offer current and potential leaders ways to improve their skills. For companies, there's a need to create processes that are smarter, take into account the value of critical thinking, and address low-probability high-impact risk. Today's financial executive will face a different combination of challenges, a different package in terms of issues and risks.

....

Title: "Managing Complexity: How to Capture Latent Value from Products, Customers, and Operations"

Publication: *Business Performance Management Magazine*

Date: 2007

Author: Sonny Saksena

Executive Summary: Achieving the optimal level of complexity in products, services, and operations is one of the best ways that companies can attract customers, maximize revenues, and grow market capitalization. Complexity eats away at corporate profits by diverting scarce resources from where they are most valuable, diluting the management team's focus, raising operating costs, masking the true drivers of profitability, and exhausting the organization. All of which result not in competitive advantage and a company's focused differentiation from its peers, but in the exact opposite: competitive disadvantage and diffusion. A recent study by PricewaterhouseCoopers found that only 5 percent of CEOs believe they have the capabilities to manage complexity effectively. They understand the importance of managing complexity, but many do not know its true causes, let alone its true costs. Measuring complexity and establishing appropriate metrics and baselines are often difficult and require specialized skills and dedicated resources. Companies must develop their complexity measures based on their areas of concern and desired results.

••

Title: "Why Some Leaders Succeed and Others Fail"

Publication: *Leader to Leader*

Date: 2011

Author: Paul B. Thornton

Executive Summary: The article offers the author's insights regarding how to become an effective leader. The author discusses the attributes of a great leader, claiming that leaders should know how to identify opportunities, elaborate ideas, and implement change. According to author Jim Collins, great leaders should have the discipline to confront facts in different situations in which they should ask questions; assess the situations; and organize, interpret, and analyze the gathered hard and soft data. The author also relates on why other leaders fail when implementing change and explores the common problems associated with the implementation including lack of clarity, inadequate training, and selection of an ineffective manager.

••

Title: "Measuring Complexity: Things that Go Wrong and How to Get It Right"

Publication: *Emergence: Complexity and Organization*

Date: 2008

Author: Vincent Vesterby

Executive Summary: Seven problems that occur in attempts to measure complexity are pointed out as they occur in four proposed measurement techniques. Each example method is an improvement over the previous examples. It turns out, however, that none are up to the challenge of complexity. Apparently, there is no currently available method that truly gets the measure of complexity. There are two reasons. First, the most natural approach, quantitative analysis, is rendered inadequate by the very nature of complexity. Second, the intrinsic magnitude of complexity is still holding at bay attempts to use both quantitative and qualitative methods combined. Further progress in complexity science and in systems science is required. Any method that simplifies will fail because it ignores what complexity is. Techniques of understanding that do not simplify, but rather provide ways for the mind to grasp and work with complexity, are more effective in getting its measure.

Ability to Take Complex Issues and Explain the Main Points Simply and Understandably

There is no shortage of complexity in global business, and surely the senior leaders and managers in your organization do not have time to learn about every complex business issue in detail. Leaders and managers might be interested and eager to know more about a topic, such as how the organization's Indonesian truck drivers will be able to observe daily prayers on an operations timeline, but they may not have the luxury of time to learn about every detail. So you need to communicate an overview of the operations plan quickly. Or your manager may have very little interest in the details of a topic, like how precisely your information technology group is going to install network connections in the Columbia operations. He or she may just want to know the high-level plan. If you are the point-person for these operational issues, you need to understand the full complexity of the issues to determine the appropriate operational approach. In contrast, the communication of that needs to be simple and understandable for others in the organization who are not subject matter experts.

This is a challenging skill to master for many subject matter experts, because you may be very excited about the details and history of an issue. Your enthusiasm and engagement have probably made you very knowledgeable. So you are going to have to reign in some of that enthusiasm to master this skill.

The first step is to do a stakeholder analysis:

- Who do you need to communicate with?

- What do they already know?

- What do they need to know?

- How much time do you have to communicate your message?

- How will you be communicating your message?

You need to define the issue, briefly explain the problem or opportunity, briefly explain the solution, and highlight implementation steps. The level of detail you provide will depend on your audience.

MAPPING COMPLEX ISSUES

Ability to Take Complex Issues and Explain the Main Points Simply and Understandably in Action

As I am a person skilled in taking any situation and making it more complex, talking with people for whom my language is not their native language can be a challenge.

Susan Gebelein
CEO
Business and Leadership Consulting

As I am a person skilled in taking any situation and making it more complex, talking with people for whom my language is not their native language can be a challenge. To speak in a way that can be understood, I have developed some useful strategies for simplifying my language. There are a number of things I do. First, I consider what my main point is, and I make sure I say that clearly. I then provide a very brief explanation about my main point. I do not say more than four or five sentences at a time. I typically will make one or two points at a time, rather than my usual many. I also have used video coaching to help me speak more concisely. I review video of my speaking to others, and I identify language that I use that needs to be simplified. This has helped me become more succinct and clear. This is a high priority for me when talking with people whose first language is different from mine.

ARABIC-ENABLED KEYBOARD

DEVELOPMENT SUGGESTIONS
for Ability to Take Complex Issues and Explain the Main Points Simply and Understandably

LEARN

Tips to learn about and begin developing the capability on your own. These tips involve self-directed learning, including reading, listening, watching, or observing, that you can do on your own at your own pace. They are most useful for novices in the capability, but are helpful for intermediate and advanced learners to keep knowledge current.

Development Activity	Suggested Resource(s) and Tips
Learn how to summarize complex issues.	• Read eHow's Guide to Writing Issue Briefing Papers to see how to isolate key information for concise communication (www.ehow.com/how_8551495_write-issue-briefing-papers.html). • Read *Technically Speaking* (D'Arcy, 1998) about how to communicate complex information. • Learn how to speak clearly and concisely in the book *Make Your Point* (Elliott and Carroll, 2005).

DEVELOPMENT SUGGESTIONS
for Ability to Take Complex Issues and Explain the Main Points Simply and Understandably

CONNECT

Tips to learn about and continue developing the capability through others. These tips involve working with another person to learn from their experiences. They may involve asking questions, listening to and discussing experiences, forming a new relationship, deepening an existing relationship, or receiving feedback from someone who is acting as your mentor. These tips are useful for all levels of learners.

Development Activity	Suggested Resource(s) and Tips
Meet with your stakeholders on this topic to understand their expectations prior to formal meetings or presentations.	• Ask to meet with each stakeholder briefly. • Ask him or her to describe how he or she best receives information and what types of information are most useful to him or her. • Find out what are the top two or three most important concerns or areas of interest to him or her on the topic.
Ask diverse colleagues to partner with you in creating communications about complex issues.	• Ask your colleague to explain his or her understanding of the issues to see if and how it converges with yours. • Ask your colleague which points he or she identifies as the most relevant to share.

DEVELOPMENT SUGGESTIONS
for Ability to Take Complex Issues and Explain the Main Points Simply and Understandably

CONNECT

Tips to learn about and continue developing the capability through others. These tips involve working with another person to learn from their experiences. They may involve asking questions, listening to and discussing experiences, forming a new relationship, deepening an existing relationship, or receiving feedback from someone who is acting as your mentor. These tips are useful for all levels of learners.

Development Activity	Suggested Resource(s) and Tips
Once your message is prepared, have a colleague listen to or read it for improvement.	• Ask your colleague what he or she understood from the message. • Ask him or her to point out information that needs to be added, edited, or cut altogether. • Invite feedback on how you can improve your communication skills. • Time yourself during practice sessions to get a good understanding of how long your message really is. Identify places to make it even more concise.

DEVELOPMENT SUGGESTIONS
for Ability to Take Complex Issues and Explain the Main Points Simply and Understandably

EXPERIENCE

Tips to learn about and develop skills in the capability through firsthand experience. These tips involve engaging in activities, such as exploring a new area, trying a new cultural activity, or participating in a specific business event. These tips are most useful for intermediate to advanced learners, and we suggest that novice learners prepare themselves for success by completing some of the tips in the Learn category first.

Development Activity	Suggested Resource(s) and Tips
Use a mind-mapping process to visually identify the main points and key issues in the topic of interest.	• Use paper, a white board, a flow chart, or mind-mapping software to show each of the parts of the complex issue and how they interact with one another. • Find tutorials on how to mind map and how to use mind-mapping software and iPhone apps through Tony Buzan and NovaMind (www.thinkbuzan.com/us/ and www.novamind.com).

DEVELOPMENT SUGGESTIONS
for Ability to Take Complex Issues and Explain the Main Points Simply and Understandably

EXPERIENCE

Tips to learn about and develop skills in the capability through firsthand experience. These tips involve engaging in activities, such as exploring a new area, trying a new cultural activity, or participating in a specific business event. These tips are most useful for intermediate to advanced learners, and we suggest that novice learners prepare themselves for success by completing some of the tips in the Learn category first.

Development Activity	Suggested Resource(s) and Tips
Practice synthesizing and explaining complex issues.	• Listen to or read a complex news story. • Identify the main points and key issues. • Practice explaining it to a friend, family member, or colleague. • If your language is not simple enough, imagine you are explaining it to a child. • Ask your friend, family member, or colleague to give you feedback on how to make the message even more understandable and concise. • If there is a disconnect between your view of how clear the message was and that of your friends, you may want to videotape yourself so you can analyze your presentation along with a coach or mentor. • Participate in Toastmaster's International meetings where you have regular opportunities to practice short speeches on complex topics (www.toastmasters.org).
Adjust your language and style for the particular audience and topic.	After you have had a chance to discuss your stakeholders' needs and preferences, adapt your message to meet their needs and expectations.

DEVELOPMENT SUGGESTIONS
for Ability to Take Complex Issues and Explain the Main Points Simply and Understandably

COACH OR CONTRIBUTE

Tips to help others learn about and develop this capability. These tips involve coaching and mentoring others. They may include creating information or experiences for individuals, teams, or your organization. These tips are designed for those who are advanced in the capability and are useful development methods to keep advanced leaders in the capability engaged in professional development at the highest level. Please note that the tips in this section may also be quite helpful for individual use if you do not have a coach or mentor.

Development Activity	Suggested Resource(s) and Tips
Provide your coachee with examples of how to explain complex issues simply and understandably in your organization.	Show examples of communications you have written or videos of you explaining a particular issue.
Host a Toastmaster's International club at your workplace.	Contact Toastmaster's International for information on how to establish and run a successful club through your organization. (www.toastmasters.org)

Additional Reading

The readings listed here provide you with additional study of the Global Mindset capability in this section. You will find that many of these resources provide you with a specific and detailed look at using this capability in either a particular context or location.

....

Title:	"Cognitive Style and Entrepreneurial Drive of New and Mature Business Owner-Managers"
Publication:	*Journal of Business and Psychology*
Date:	2009
Authors:	Steven J. Armstrong and Andrew Hird

Executive Summary: The purpose of this study was to investigate whether cognitive style and entrepreneurial drive are important for identifying individuals who have the potential to become successful entrepreneurs and for discriminating between owner-managers operating in mature and early stages of venture creation and growth.

....

Title:	"Cognitive Complexity Implications for Research on Sustainable Competitive Advantage"
Publication:	*Journal of Business Research*
Date:	2010
Authors:	Shu-Ling Cheng and Hae-Ching Chang

Executive Summary: Cognitive complexity of top managers gains increasing attention in the management field. Performance implication of cognitive complexity is an important one. This article clarifies several of the original points to reply to Huang's commentary. In particular, we comment on some issues of testability and measurement of cognitive complexity and internal/external related dimensions.

Title: "Assessment Issues in Estimating Managerial Potential in a Global Context"

Publication: *International Management Review*

Date: 2011

Author: Thomas A. Clerkin

Executive Summary: Business leaders are predicting a talent shortage of high-quality senior managers and executives. Companies are establishing programs to identify managerial potential early in a career. The early identification of management potential (EIMP) process depends on selection tools (e.g., ability tests, personality tests, assessment-center exercises, weighted biographical data, and past performance reviews) that were typically developed in Western Europe or the United States and validated using Western research samples, but they are now being used in other parts of the world to evaluate non-Western managers and professionals. In this paper, the author hypothesizes, reviews, and analyzes potential problems using these tools across cultures.

Title: "Decision-Making Competence, Executive Functioning, and General Cognitive Abilities"

Publication: *Journal of Behavioral Decision Making*

Date: 2012

Authors: Fabio Del Missier, Timo Mäntylä, and Wändi Bruine Bruin

Executive Summary: Although previous studies investigated the relationship between general cognitive abilities and decision making, few have characterized specific cognitive abilities underlying decision-making competence. In this paper, we focus on executive functions-control processes involved in the regulation of cognition. Specifically, we report on an individual-differences study that investigated the relationship of executive functioning (EF) and general cognitive abilities (fluid intelligence and numeracy) with different aspects of decision-making competence. Individual differences in EF components explained aspects of decision-making competence even after controlling for fluid intelligence and numeracy. However, different aspects of decision-making competence varied in the extent to which they relied on different executive functions. In particular, resistance to framing effects, the ability to apply decision rules, and successful engagement in cognitive reflection partially depend on individual differences on the monitoring/inhibition dimension of EF. The ability to provide consistent judgments in risk perception is related to the shifting aspect of EF. The ability to recognize social norms and resistance to sunk costs were not significantly related to EF, thus supporting the idea that executive control is not a major determinant of these aspects of decision-making competence. Finally, substantial variance in some of the decision-making tasks remained unexplained, suggesting that other cognitive or noncognitive abilities need to be considered in future studies.

....

Title: "Developing Executive Leaders: The Relative Contribution of Cognitive Ability, Personality, and the Accumulation of Work Experience in Predicting Strategic Thinking Competency"

Publication: *Personnel Psychology*

Date: 2011

Authors: Lisa Dragoni, In-Sue Oh, Paul Vankatwyk, and Paul E. Tesluk

Executive Summary: We conceptually define and empirically investigate the accumulation of work experience—a concept that refers to the extent to which executives have amassed varied levels of roles and responsibilities (e.g., contributor, manager, lead strategist) in each of the key work activities that they have encountered over the course of their careers. In studying executives' work experience accumulation, we consider key antecedents such as executives' cognitive ability and personality traits, namely Extraversion and Openness to Experience, and examine the value of work experience accumulation on executives' strategic thinking competency. Analyses of multisource data from 703 executives revealed three key findings: (1) accumulated work experience positively relates to executives' strategic thinking competency after controlling for individual characteristics and other measures of work experience, (2) executives' cognitive ability demonstrates the strongest and most positive relationship to executives' strategic thinking competency, and (3) extraverted executives tend to achieve higher levels of work experience accumulation. Relative weight analyses also indicated that cognitive ability and accumulated work experience are the two most important predictors for executives' strategic thinking competency among the other predictors. These findings are discussed in light of their practical implications.

Title: "Cognitive Fitness"

Publication: *Harvard Business Review*

Date: 2007

Authors: Roderick Gilkey and Clint Kilts

Executive Summary: Recent neuroscientific research shows that the health of your brain isn't, as experts once thought, just the product of childhood experiences and genetics; it reflects your adult choices and experiences as well. Professors Gilkey and Kilts of Emory University's medical and business schools explain how you can strengthen your brain's anatomy, neural networks, and cognitive abilities, and prevent functions such as memory from deteriorating as you age. The brain's alertness is the result of what the authors call cognitive fitness—a state of optimized ability to reason, remember, learn, plan, and adapt. Certain attitudes, lifestyle choices, and exercises enhance cognitive fitness. Mental workouts are the key. Brain-imaging studies indicate that acquiring expertise in areas as diverse as playing a cello, juggling, speaking a foreign language, and driving a taxicab expands your neural systems and makes them more communicative. In other words, you can alter the physical makeup of your brain by learning new skills. The more cognitively fit you are, the better equipped you are to make decisions, solve problems, and deal with stress and change. Cognitive fitness will help you be more open to new ideas and alternative perspectives. It will give you the capacity to change your behavior and realize your goals. You can delay senescence for years and even enjoy a second career. Drawing from the rapidly expanding body of neuroscience research as well as from well-established research in psychology and other mental health fields, the authors have identified four steps you can take to become cognitively fit: understand how experience makes the brain grow, work hard at play, search for patterns, and seek novelty and innovation. Together, these steps capture some of the key opportunities for maintaining an engaged, creative brain.

Title: "Critical Thinking: A Critical Strategy for Financial Executives"

Publication: *Financial Executive*

Date: 2009

Author: Susan Schott Karr

Executive Summary: Analytical thinking, skepticism, and good judgment are increasingly the key ingredients financial executives must add to their intellectual/educational mix to remain competitive in a world economy that now places

more emphasis on critical thinking than ever before. Those skills will be even more essential with the potential transition to International Financial Reporting Standards and a greater reliance on subjectivity in applying fair value measurements and other standards. The principles-based system demands an ability to make inferences and use sound judgment. To enhance critical-thinking skill development, some universities and organizations are undertaking various initiatives. Leadership-development programs have begun to offer current and potential leaders ways to improve their skills. For companies, there's a need to create processes that are smarter, take into account the value of critical thinking, and address low-probability high-impact risk. Today's financial executive will face a different combination of challenges, a different package in terms of issues and risks.

....

Title: "Managing Complexity: How to Capture Latent Value from Products, Customers, and Operations"

Publication: *Business Performance Management Magazine*

Date: 2007

Author: Sonny Saksena

Executive Summary: Achieving the optimal level of complexity in products, services, and operations is one of the best ways that companies can attract customers, maximize revenues, and grow market capitalization. Complexity eats away at corporate profits by diverting scarce resources from where they are most valuable, diluting the management team's focus, raising operating costs, masking the true drivers of profitability, and exhausting the organization. All of which result not in competitive advantage and a company's focused differentiation from its peers, but in the exact opposite: competitive disadvantage and diffusion. A recent study by PricewaterhouseCoopers found that only 5 percent of CEOs believe they have the capabilities to manage complexity effectively. They understand the importance of managing complexity, but many do not know its true causes, let alone its true costs. Measuring complexity and establishing appropriate metrics and baselines are often difficult and require specialized skills and dedicated resources. Companies must develop their complexity measures based on their areas of concern and desired results.

Title: "Why Some Leaders Succeed and Others Fail"

Publication: *Leader to Leader*

Date: 2011

Author: Paul B. Thornton

Executive Summary: The article offers the author's insights regarding how to become an effective leader. The author discusses the attributes of a great leader, claiming that leaders should know how to identify opportunities, elaborate ideas, and implement change. According to author Jim Collins, great leaders should have the discipline to confront facts in different situations in which they should ask questions; assess the situations; and organize, interpret, and analyze the gathered hard and soft data. The author also relates on why other leaders fail when implementing change and explores the common problems associated with the implementation including lack of clarity, inadequate training, and selection of an ineffective manager.

Title: "Measuring Complexity: Things that Go Wrong and How to Get It Right"

Publication: *Emergence: Complexity and Organization*

Date: 2008

Author: Vincent Vesterby

Executive Summary: Seven problems that occur in attempts to measure complexity are pointed out as they occur in four proposed measurement techniques. Each example method is an improvement over the previous examples. It turns out, however, that none are up to the challenge of complexity. Apparently, there is no currently available method that truly gets the measure of complexity. There are two reasons. First, the most natural approach, quantitative analysis, is rendered inadequate by the very nature of complexity. Second, the intrinsic magnitude of complexity is still holding at bay attempts to use both quantitative and qualitative methods combined. Further progress in complexity science and in systems science is required. Any method that simplifies will fail because it ignores what complexity is. Techniques of understanding that do not simplify, but rather provide ways for the mind to grasp and work with complexity, are more effective in getting its measure.

TOURISTS ON A CAMEL CARAVAN TOUR, EGYPT

GLOBAL PSYCHOLOGICAL CAPITAL

4 Passion for Diversity

5 Quest for Adventure

6 Self-Assurance

Global Psychological Capital is really about an individual's interests. Is he willing to engage in global situations? Does he have a willingness to spend the extra energy needed to navigate business cross-culturally? Think about a top world soccer player. He has to be willing to not only get off the bench and onto the field, but also give his full attention to where the ball is at, how to pass it to the right team members, and how to score goals all while navigating a field full of people with both shared and competing objectives. Each team he plays will be from a different culture and will require different approaches. This takes a lot of energy and commitment. Global roles are similar in that they tend to be fast-paced, complex, and full of diverse peoples. The willingness to engage, which is represented by a high level of Global Psychological Capital, is a critical starting point.

In our experience, we have seen quite a few managers with a long history of success in their home market fail in global roles. It can be quite devastating for them, because they've done a great job previously. Then they're told, for a variety of reasons, "If you want to go to the next level in the company, you need to complete an international assignment or take on global responsibilities." Some multinational companies require this check on the résumé before moving managers into more senior roles. For the unprepared or disinterested manager, this can be painful. For example, one of our authors was working for a Middle Eastern executive who was in charge of his company's operations in an African country. When the author asked him about his experience and how things were going, he said, "To be honest with you, I dislike every minute of my experience in this country." When the author asked him why he felt so strongly, he said, "Because they're so different. Everything is so different. I don't like it. I don't like the way these people do things." When the author asked him why he continued to stay in the role given his disdain for it, he simply pulled out the drawer in front of him, took out his last paycheck stub, and pointed to all the zeros. He was making a lot of money and hating every minute of it.

Assigning someone to a global role who is unprepared or disinterested in it can have long-term effects on both the individual and the company. Clearly, the employee and his family, in the previous example, were living unhappy lives. Also, the local employees and business partners picked up on his displeasure. People who have no passion for diversity communicate that very quickly through their words, body language, and expressions. This leads to an erosion of trust. Local employees and business partners may continue to do their jobs, but will interact minimally with the manager. Worst-case scenario, they decide that they will not cooperate at all. Over time, the relationships dissolve and trust becomes difficult to recover, even when that manager is replaced.

The good news is that Global Psychological Capital can be both measured (through the Global Mindset Inventory) and developed. Our research at the Najafi Global Mindset Institute since 2007 has consistently shown that managers can improve their Global Psychological Capital over time through carefully designed development experiences. It's important to gradually introduce managers to diversity experiences, so they experience success that, in turn, builds their confidence and interest. It takes time, because motivations and attitudes are deeply imbedded in a person's life experiences, upbringing, and personality.

When working to develop people's Global Psychological Capital, it's important to have open conversations with them about why their scores are low. What about their backgrounds, personalities, and life experiences resulted in low scores? Once you identify that, then you can create development experiences for them that include supportive coaching. Coaching is key to developing Global Psychological Capital so people can make sense of the experiences they are having and course correct along the way. It is important that managers are set up for success and supported along the way. Building someone's Global Psychological Capital has positive ripple effects that touch each person the coachee interacts with across cultures. It's hard work, but it's worth it.

As you can see in **Figure 1**, Global Psychological Capital consists of three main dimensions: passion for diversity, quest for adventure, and self-assurance.

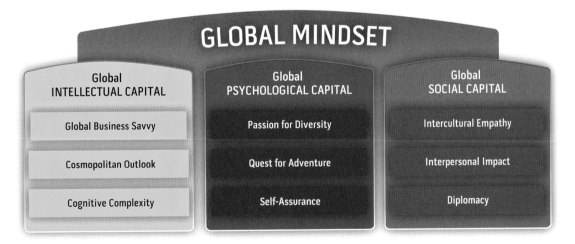

Figure 1

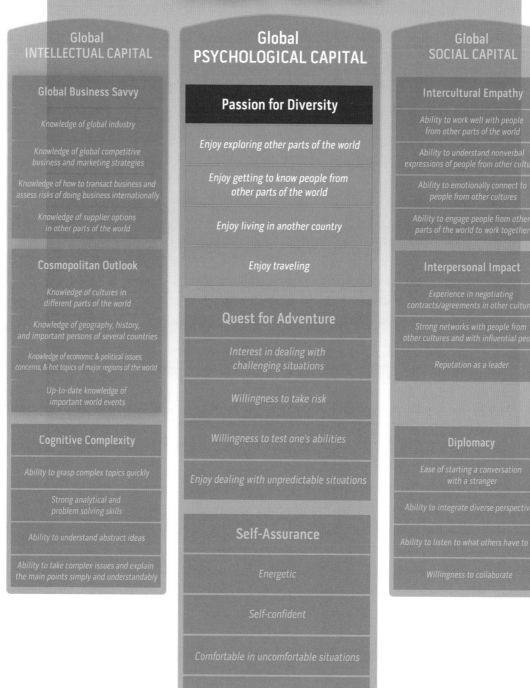

GLOBAL MINDSET

Global INTELLECTUAL CAPITAL

Global Business Savvy

Knowledge of global industry

Knowledge of global competitive business and marketing strategies

Knowledge of how to transact business and assess risks of doing business internationally

Knowledge of supplier options in other parts of the world

Cosmopolitan Outlook

Knowledge of cultures in different parts of the world

Knowledge of geography, history, and important persons of several countries

Knowledge of economic & political issues, concerns, & hot topics of major regions of the world

Up-to-date knowledge of important world events

Cognitive Complexity

Ability to grasp complex topics quickly

Strong analytical and problem solving skills

Ability to understand abstract ideas

Ability to take complex issues and explain the main points simply and understandably

Global PSYCHOLOGICAL CAPITAL

Passion for Diversity

Enjoy exploring other parts of the world

Enjoy getting to know people from other parts of the world

Enjoy living in another country

Enjoy traveling

Quest for Adventure

Interest in dealing with challenging situations

Willingness to take risk

Willingness to test one's abilities

Enjoy dealing with unpredictable situations

Self-Assurance

Energetic

Self-confident

Comfortable in uncomfortable situations

Witty in tough situations

Global SOCIAL CAPITAL

Intercultural Empathy

Ability to work well with people from other parts of the world

Ability to understand nonverbal expressions of people from other cultures

Ability to emotionally connect to people from other cultures

Ability to engage people from other parts of the world to work together

Interpersonal Impact

Experience in negotiating contracts/agreements in other cultures

Strong networks with people from other cultures and with influential people

Reputation as a leader

Diplomacy

Ease of starting a conversation with a stranger

Ability to integrate diverse perspectives

Ability to listen to what others have to say

Willingness to collaborate

Figure 4-1

GLOBAL PSYCHOLOGICAL CAPITAL

Passion for Diversity

As seen in **Figure 4-1** on page 214, this chapter examines Passion for Diversity, which is a key dimension of Global Intellectual Capital. Passion for diversity includes the level of interest a person has in traveling, trying new foods and experiences, and, most importantly, getting to know diverse peoples. Is he willing to spend time with people from other parts of the world? Is he willing to learn about them and from them? For example, one of our authors was working with an upper-middle level executive who had just received notice that he was being posted outside the country for the first time. He was so excited that he couldn't stop talking about it. He said, "This is wonderful! We [my family] are going to do all kinds of interesting things." The author asked him if he knew anything about the country. He didn't, but his passion for diversity was contagious. "That's what makes it more exciting," he said. "I am so excited to learn about these people and explore this new place." That tremendous energy and excitement about a new experience, place, and people is what passion for diversity is all about.

In this chapter, we will focus on passion for diversity, which consists of:

- Enjoyment of exploring other parts of the world

- Enjoyment of getting to know people from other parts of the world

- Enjoyment of living in another country

- Enjoyment of traveling

EXCHANGE OF BUSINESS CARDS · JAPAN

Enjoyment of Exploring Other Parts of the World

Exploring other parts of the world has become easier through technology. While you may have a tremendous desire to visit a culture of interest, such as Japan, perhaps your schedule or resources do not currently allow it. The good news is that travel is just one way of exploring the world. You could read fiction or nonfiction books set in Japan written by Japanese writers to get a sense of the place and the people. You could watch documentaries online or on television about Japanese culture, events, and geography. Or you could have a conversation with a colleague who has been to Japan to discuss his experiences of doing business there. For people who are nervous about exploring new places, the nontravel options are an excellent starting point to prepare for new experiences. Even for those people who are anxious to hit the road, the nontravel tips are helpful to develop a more sophisticated understanding of the location to be explored. There are many ways to explore the world. The tips here will give you some ideas on how to do that.

PASSION FOR DIVERSITY

Enjoyment of Exploring Other Parts of the World in Action

SID NACHMAN, PH.D.
Principal, Sound Insight
Consulting

**MARGARET BUTTERISS,
M.SC.** Principal, M A
Butteriss & Associates

PAUL MAYER,
Head of HR, Americas
ALTANA AG

*We were working with a privately held German company
with several US-based, wholly owned subsidiaries. For
years, it had run a business education program for its high-
potential employees in Germany. In 2005, the decision was
made to start a similar program for American employees.*

We were working with a privately held German company with several US-based, wholly owned subsidiaries. For years, it had run a business education program for its high-potential employees in Germany. In 2005, the decision was made to start a similar program for American employees.

Even though the company was a global player in its industry and it employed very educated and skilled professionals, there was an opportunity to sharpen their sensitivities to working across cultures. During the second iteration of this program, it became apparent that there was a cultural disconnect. The North American employees did not have a full appreciation of their German counterparts. It was important to build an understanding of German culture and the culture of

HEIDELBERG, GERMANY

GLOBAL PSYCHOLOGICAL CAPITAL

the parent company. By learning more about Germany and German culture and language, we hoped to increase their sensitivity and effectiveness in working with their colleagues abroad.

Because the program was hosted in North America, they did not have the opportunity to explore Germany and German culture firsthand. We had to be creative. So we invited a representative from the German Chamber of Commerce in New York to join us. In the session, the participants learned many things about Germany and German culture. For example, they learned that in Germany people do not jay-walk (i.e., cross a street without a proper signal or crosswalk). They actually do not walk in the street at all; they stay on the sidewalk. And if someone were to see you from his window doing the wrong thing, he would shout out to you. They learned the importance of rules in Germany and how they translate in real-life situations. This gave the North American employees deeper insight as to why there was such a great adherence to protocols, rules, and regulations by their German colleagues.

This type of session was as lively as it was enlightening. It was an important addition to the program to build cross-cultural understanding. This nontravel option allowed us to explore Germany and German culture while maintaining our budget and the objectives of the program.

DEVELOPMENT SUGGESTIONS
for Enjoyment of Exploring Other Parts of the World

LEARN

Tips to learn about and begin developing the capability on your own. These tips involve self-directed learning, including reading, listening, watching, or observing, that you can do on your own at your own pace. They are most useful for novices in the capability, but are helpful for intermediate and advanced learners to keep knowledge current.

Development Activity	Suggested Resource(s) and Tips
Watch videos about another country to see what intrigues you. You can search by region, country, or particular local issues of interest to you.	• YouTube (www.YouTube.com) has a variety of professionally produced and user-produced videos. • BBC World Service has a variety of documentary videos and podcasts on regions and countries (www.bbc.co.uk/worldservice/programmes). • PBS Global Voices offers documentaries featuring local perspectives (www.pbs.org/itvs/globalvoices). • *National Geographic Traveler* hosts photos, blogs, and videos (http://travel.nationalgeographic.com/travel/?source=NavTravHome).
Read novels set in foreign locations. These can be fiction or nonfiction to give you a sense of the place and people.	• You can browse or search travel writers' books and blogs through the Society of American Travel Writers (www.satw.org). • You can browse travel fiction by region (http://librarybooklists.org/fiction/adult/travel.htm). • On Amazon.com, you can search "travel writing" and add the country name to find a list of books on your country of interest.
Take World Trade Center Association courses and attend their conferences to learn more about doing business in and with other countries.	Find your closest World Trade Center Association (www.wtcaonline.com/cms_wtca).

DEVELOPMENT SUGGESTIONS
for Enjoyment of Exploring Other Parts of the World

CONNECT

Tips to learn about and continue developing the capability through others. These tips involve working with another person to learn from their experiences. They may involve asking questions, listening to and discussing experiences, forming a new relationship, deepening an existing relationship, or receiving feedback from someone who is acting as your mentor. These tips are useful for all levels of learners.

Development Activity	Suggested Resource(s) and Tips
Spend time with locals when you are traveling.	• While planning your trip, contact local national colleagues to spend time with during your travels. • Work with your travel agent or hotel concierge to find local tour groups and guides. • Spend time in local gathering places (e.g., pubs, clubs, markets, town squares) when possible.
Find friends who like to explore other parts of the world, and go on trips with them.	• If you want support and company while traveling to a certain location, ask your well-traveled friends to accompany you. • Join tour groups to have the built-in support and company of others. • Join local travel clubs and cultural interest groups (www.meetup.com).
Use LinkedIn and Facebook to connect to people in other parts of the world.	• Network through your friends to build your cross-cultural network. • Ask your friends from other cultures what social networking sites are popular in their cultures.

PASSION FOR DIVERSITY

DEVELOPMENT SUGGESTIONS
for Enjoyment of Exploring Other Parts of the World

EXPERIENCE

Tips to learn about and develop skills in the capability through firsthand experience. These tips involve engaging in activities, such as exploring a new area, trying a new cultural activity, or participating in a specific business event. These tips are most useful for intermediate to advanced learners, and we suggest that novice learners prepare themselves for success by completing some of the tips in the Learn category first.

Development Activity	Suggested Resource(s) and Tips
Start exploring other parts of the world through interests you are already passionate about and expand out to interests you have not already explored.	• If you enjoy dining out, dine in local ethnic restaurants. • If you like sports, try a new sport that is popular in your culture of interest. • If you like dancing, take a dance class featuring a dance from a culture of interest.
Explore different parts of your own city or country.	• Become a AAA member (www.aaa.com) for access to travel planning, maps, guidebooks, and other resources around the world. • Talk with your local travel agent about new places to experience. • Read the culture or society section in your local newspaper or magazine to find new places and events to explore.
While you are in another country, plan to experience activities just like the locals do to get a sense of their culture and daily lives.	• Visit a local market. • Go to a local movie. • Go to a local concert or other kind of cultural entertainment event. • Attend a local sporting event. • Visit a local museum.
Get a passport, if you do not already have one, or make a plan to use it more often.	Plan an international trip to a country of interest within the next twelve months.
Volunteer to work on a project in a country of interest.	• Global Volunteer Network can connect you with projects around the world (www.globalvolunteernetwork.org). • Go Volunteer lists volunteer programs around the world and shows reviews of the programs by active volunteers (www.go-volunteerabroad.com). • Inquire within organizations and activities you already participate in for global volunteer opportunities.

DEVELOPMENT SUGGESTIONS
for Enjoyment of Exploring Other Parts of the World

COACH OR CONTRIBUTE

Tips to help others learn about and develop this capability. These tips involve coaching and mentoring others. They may include creating information or experiences for individuals, teams, or your organization. These tips are designed for those who are advanced in the capability and are useful development methods to continue to keep advanced leaders in the capability engaged in professional development at the highest level. Please note that the tips in this section may also be quite helpful for individual use if you do not have a coach or mentor.

Development Activity	Suggested Resource(s) and Tips
When coaching your direct reports or mentees, ask open-ended questions to help them understand their current motivations and barriers to exploring other parts of the world.	Ask questions such as the following: • Think about your past experience learning about or experiencing new parts of the world. What are three things that you enjoyed about these experiences? Why? • What are three things you did not enjoy about past experiences learning about or exploring new parts of the world? Why? • What are the top two or three reasons you have to explore another part of the world? • What are the consequences to you of not exploring the other part of the world you have identified? • What would make your exploration of other parts of the world more comfortable and enjoyable? • What are two or three things you are genuinely interested in learning more about in this other part of the world? Why? How can you learn more about these? • Who can you call on to support you in preparing to explore other parts of the world and during those explorations?

Additional Reading

The readings listed here provide you with additional study of the Global Mindset capability in this section. You will find that many of these resources provide you with a specific and detailed look at using this capability in either a particular context or location.

....

Title: "Three Keys to Getting an Overseas Assignment Right"

Publication: *Harvard Business Review*

Date: 2009

Authors: Mark Alan Clouse and Michael D. Watkins

Executive Summary: An international assignment can be among the most exciting and challenging transitions that an aspiring leader can undertake. With the right planning and attitudes, taking on that kind of leadership role can stretch capabilities, challenge assumptions, and steer both people and profits in a positive direction. But an expat assignment can also be a harrowing journey. Indeed, if they've never made an international move before, emerging leaders can fall into common traps that can severely stress their family bonds, negatively affect their performance at work, damage their businesses, and even lead to outright career derailment.

....

Title: "Exploring the Motives of Company-Backed and Self-Initiated Expatriates"

Publication: *Human Resource Management*

Date: 2011

Authors: Noeleen Doherty, Michael Dickmann, and Timothy Mills

Executive Summary: Few studies have investigated the range of issues considered important to the decision to move abroad for expatriates, particularly comparing the company-backed and self-initiated expatriate experiences. This study contributes to an important gap in current research about the drivers of company-backed and self-initiated expatriation. It reveals details about the diverse motivations to undertake an expatriation and the similarities and differences between these two groups. Through a web-based study, the structure of the motivational components considered influential to the decision to move abroad was explored and quantitatively assessed. Principal component analysis (PCA) suggested an eight-factor model. Scales developed from the model highlighted significant differences between the motivations of the self-initiated and company-backed across three key areas. Location and host reputation motives were significantly more important to the self-initiated suggesting that the desire to move to a particular country and characteristics of that country were primary drivers. Company-backed individuals placed significantly more emphasis on specific career motives including job, skills, and career impact.

....

Title: "Compelled to Go Abroad? Motives and Outcomes of International Assignments"

Publication: *The International Journal of Human Resource Management*

Date: 2012

Authors: Luísa H. Pinto, Carlos Cabral-Cardoso, and William B. Werther, Jr.

Executive Summary: This article examines the motives of expatriates and repatriates to accept international assignments and how these motives relate to individuals' perceptions of expatriation outcomes. Issues of adjustment, satisfaction, withdrawal intentions, willingness to relocate again, and recommendation of an assignment to others were considered as outcomes. The data were collected through semistructured interviews of thirty Portuguese expatriates and repatriates. The results indicate that a considerable number of participants relocated because they felt compelled to do so by their employing companies. Moreover, the extent to which organizations persuade these originally unwilling expatriates seems to have negative implications in terms of their perceptions of the adjustment process, general satisfaction with the assignment, and withdrawal intentions. Compelling behavior also has career implications and affects individual receptiveness to relocate in the future.

PASSION FOR DIVERSITY

BUSINESS NETWORKING EVENT

Enjoyment of Getting to Know People from Other Parts of the World

At a recent globally focused conference at Thunderbird, Dr. Mansour Javidan asked the crowd of about one thousand people how many of them had grown up in environments that taught them to interact with people from other cultures. About fifteen people raised their hands. The audience was full of diverse people from around the world, and most of them, regardless of home country, had the shared experience of growing up without much diversity interaction.

It is human nature to gravitate toward people who are like us, who have similar interests and shared life experiences. We see this in young children as they sit with similar peers in the school cafeteria at lunch or select teams for sports on the playground. And we know, from business diversity literature, that these tendencies persist into the workplace for adults. Now, in the previous example, fifteen people did indeed raise their hands to say, "Yes, I grew up interacting with diverse others." So this may be your reality as well. But it is important to understand that some people, maybe it's your direct reports or your colleagues, did not have the good fortune to have these experiences. This is why getting to know people from other parts of the world can sometimes be intimidating or even scary for those new to the experience.

The twenty-first century has ushered in a strong focus on building diversity and inclusion in both schools and the workplace for many organizations. We are hopeful that these efforts will foster a greater appreciation for the diversity of peoples in our world and encourage more and more people to strike up conversations and friendships with diverse others. The experiences to be had are rich and paved with new friendships.

GLOBAL PSYCHOLOGICAL CAPITAL

Enjoyment of Getting to Know People from Other Parts of the World in Action

I have found people from other cultures to be so helpful to understanding the culture in their part of the world.

SUSAN GEBELEIN
CEO
Business and Leadership Consulting

I have found people from other cultures to be so helpful to understanding the culture in their part of the world. When I ask people from cultures other than my own what I should understand about their culture, I get two great benefits. I learn about the culture, but I also get what is important to that person about their culture. It is a great way to get to know that person more deeply.

Many times I have found the information helpful as I work to establish a relationship with the person and work with them. For example, I learned from a Japanese colleague how difficult it is for many Japanese people to apologize or say, "I'm sorry." That is a fairly common thing to do in my culture, and I did not realize this was not shared. It also helped me to understand later why my Japanese team wanted much more training and education on a new service; they did not want to make a mistake. Whereas, in my culture, one can simply say, "I made a mistake with the new process; I am sorry. Can we set it up again?" This is not something easy to do in Japan. Thanks to my Japanese colleague, I now know that.

DEVELOPMENT SUGGESTIONS
for Enjoyment of Getting to Know People from Other Parts of the World

LEARN

Tips to learn about and begin developing the capability on your own. These tips involve self-directed learning, including reading, listening, watching, or observing, that you can do on your own at your own pace. They are most useful for novices in the capability, but are helpful for intermediate and advanced learners to keep knowledge current.

Development Activity	Suggested Resource(s) and Tips
Read the business case for diversity.	• Start by reading your organization's diversity and inclusion statements and policies. • Diversity Inc. posts articles, videos, and a list of the top Diversity employers (http://diversityinc.com). • Diversity Executive hosts news, video, and a magazine (http://diversity-executive.com). • The Multicultural Advantage posts current articles from a variety of news sources on diversity in the workplace topics and metrics (www.multiculturaladvantage.com/business-case-for-diversity-recruiting.asp).
Learn about Emergenetics (an alternate thinking styles assessment) to understand the various ways people think and behave around the world.	Emergenetics International provides a framework, assessment tools, and training on the various ways people think and behave (www.emergenetics.com).
Do cross-cultural comparisons of cuisine, fine arts, crafts, music, and any other activity of interest to you.	• Dine in ethnic restaurants. • Visit ethnic art galleries or exhibits. • Visit ethnic artesian markets. • Listen to ethnic music. • Try a new sport that is popular in your culture of interest. • Take a dance class featuring a dance from a culture of interest.

DEVELOPMENT SUGGESTIONS
for Enjoyment of Getting to Know People from Other Parts of the World

CONNECT

Tips to learn about and continue developing the capability through others. These tips involve working with another person to learn from their experiences. They may involve asking questions, listening to and discussing experiences, forming a new relationship, deepening an existing relationship, or receiving feedback from someone who is acting as your mentor. These tips are useful for all levels of learners.

Development Activity	Suggested Resource(s) and Tips
Diversify your circle of contacts and friends by networking and forming friendships with people who are from other cultures.	• Identify people in your existing network who are from other cultures and make plans to spend time with them. • Ask people in your network to introduce you to new colleagues from other cultures. • Use Poken, an electronic device to exchange contact information (www.poken.com). • Reach out to foreign national colleagues to spend time with them, especially in local gathering spots. • Join local cultural interest groups to meet like-minded friends and friends from other cultures (www.meetup.com). • Learn some of the local language to be able to interact with local people in markets and other local gathering spots.

DEVELOPMENT SUGGESTIONS
for Enjoyment of Getting to Know People from Other Parts of the World

EXPERIENCE

Tips to learn about and develop skills in the capability through firsthand experience. These tips involve engaging in activities, such as exploring a new area, trying a new cultural activity, or participating in a specific business event. These tips are most useful for intermediate to advanced learners, and we suggest that novice learners prepare themselves for success by completing some of the tips in the Learn category first.

Development Activity	Suggested Resource(s) and Tips
Participate in experiential learning activities to explore the concept and emotions around diversity issues.	• Find courses and workshops through your local community colleges and universities. • Attend Thunderbird School of Global Management's course "Communicating and Negotiating with a Global Mindset" (www.thunderbird.edu/executive_education/classroom_programs/communicating_negotiating.htm). • Attend programs through the Intercultural Communications Institute (www.intercultural.org).
Take advantage of international and cross-cultural orientation programs offered by your company.	• Ask your manager or human resources representative for information on classes and workshops. • Ask your colleagues through LinkedIn or other social networking sites for recommendations on cultural orientation programs they have completed.
Create or attend diversity forums within your organization to debrief your experiences.	• Ask your manager or human resources representative for information on diversity forums in your organization. • Attend meetings of the local chapters of the professional organizations you belong to, and inquire about diversity resources and groups.
Pursue your passions across cultures.	• Dine in ethnic restaurants. • Visit ethnic art galleries or exhibits. • Visit ethnic artesian markets. • Listen to ethnic music. • Try a new sport that is popular in your culture of interest. • Take a dance class featuring a dance from a culture of interest.

DEVELOPMENT SUGGESTIONS
for Enjoyment of Getting to Know People from Other Parts of the World

EXPERIENCE

Tips to learn about and develop skills in the capability through firsthand experience. These tips involve engaging in activities, such as exploring a new area, trying a new cultural activity, or participating in a specific business event. These tips are most useful for intermediate to advanced learners, and we suggest that novice learners prepare themselves for success by completing some of the tips in the Learn category first.

Development Activity	Suggested Resource(s) and Tips
Join international business organizations in the region you are in to connect with local business people.	• Join a local Rotary International club (www.rotaryinternational.org). • Join Chamber of Commerce organizations in countries of interest (www.uschamber.com/international/directory).
Join expatriate organizations to connect with people who are currently living in or who have lived in the region of interest to you.	Join an expatriate forum online: • InterNations (www.internations.org) • Transitions Abroad (www.transitionsabroad.com) • Escape Artist (www.escapeartist.com) • Expat Exchange (www.expatexchange.com)
Host an exchange student. The organizations listed all work to place international high school students with families. Their focus is on placing students in the United States, so if you are located in another country you may want to contact them for referrals to local placement agencies.	• The Council on International Education Exchange (CIEE) (www.ciee.org/highschool/host-families/benefits.html) • AFS (www.afsusa.org/host-family) • International Student Exchange (www.iseusa.com/meet-our-students.cfm) • The Center for Cultural Exchange (www.cci-exchange.com/about.aspx) • The EF Foundation for Foreign Study (www.effoundation.org)
Participate in philanthropic activities that have an international scope.	• Global Volunteer Network can connect you with projects around the world (www.globalvolunteernetwork.org). • Go Volunteer lists volunteer programs around the world and shows reviews of the programs by active volunteers (www.go-volunteerabroad.com). • Inquire within organizations and activities you already participate in for global volunteer opportunities.

DEVELOPMENT SUGGESTIONS
for Enjoyment of Getting to Know People from Other Parts of the World

COACH OR CONTRIBUTE

Tips to help others learn about and develop this capability. These tips involve coaching and mentoring others. They may include creating information or experiences for individuals, teams, or your organization. These tips are designed for those who are advanced in the capability and are useful development methods to keep advanced leaders in the capability engaged in professional development at the highest level. Please note that the tips in this section may also be quite helpful for individual use if you do not have a coach or mentor.

Development Activity	Suggested Resource(s) and Tips
Be a connector of others in your organization (i.e., create ways to help others meet and get to know one another).	• Invest sufficient time for members of the team to get to know one another as a part of the group process in global teams. • Host meetings and other gatherings with mentors who are well connected. • Start a conversation blog with diverse people in the company.
When you are coaching your direct reports or others who are new to the idea of getting to know people from other parts of the world, use open-ended coaching questions to engage them in dialogue.	Here is a list of potential coaching questions to ask: • How do you feel about people who are strangers to you? Why? • What is the value in spending time with these people? What is the cost of not interacting with them? • Identify visible and invisible differences between your own and another culture. What about each difference is particularly appealing/interesting? • Think about past cross-cultural experiences you have had. What did you enjoy? What did you not enjoy?
When working with direct reports or others who are uncomfortable with getting to know people who are from other parts of the world, you may want to start by discussing less sensitive diversity topics like differences between thinking styles before diving into deeper topics like diversity of values and belief systems.	The following psychometric assessments can be used with those you are coaching to assess their personality/behavioral profiles: • Meyers-Briggs Type Indicator (www.myersbriggs.org) • DiSC (www.thediscpersonalitytest.com) • Insights (www.insights.com)
When you are preparing for an expatriate assignment, act as a mentor to your children and significant other to help expand their passion for diversity.	• Involve your family in your predeparture training to prepare them as well. • Share the resources and support you are receiving from your company with your family during your assignment. • Have open conversations frequently with your family to see how they are feeling.

DEVELOPMENT SUGGESTIONS

for Enjoyment of Getting to Know People from Other Parts of the World

COACH OR CONTRIBUTE

Tips to help others learn about and develop this capability. These tips involve coaching and mentoring others. They may include creating information or experiences for individuals, teams, or your organization. These tips are designed for those who are advanced in the capability and are useful development methods to keep advanced leaders in the capability engaged in professional development at the highest level. Please note that the tips in this section may also be quite helpful for individual use if you do not have a coach or mentor.

Development Activity	Suggested Resource(s) and Tips
When coaching your direct reports or mentees, ask open-ended questions to help them understand their current motivations and barriers to getting to know people from other parts of the world.	Ask questions such as: • Think about your past experience getting to know people from other parts of the world. What are three things that you enjoyed about these experiences? Why? • What are three things you did not enjoy about past experiences getting to know people from other parts of the world? Why? • What are the top two or three reasons you have to get to know people from other parts of the world? • What are the consequences to you of not getting to know people from other parts of the world? • What would make getting to know people from other parts of the world more comfortable and enjoyable? • What are two or three things you are genuinely interested in learning about from people in the other part of the world you have identified? Why? • Who can you call on to support you in getting to know people from other parts of the world?

Additional Reading

The readings listed here provide you with additional study of the Global Mindset capability in this section. You will find that many of these resources provide you with a specific and detailed look at using this capability in either a particular context or location.

....

Title: "Expatriate Performance in Overseas Assignments: The Role of Big Five Personality"

Publication: *Asian Social Science*

Date: 2010

Authors: Raduchan Che Rose, Subramaniam Sri Ramalu, Jegak Uli, and Naresh Kumar Samy

Executive Summary: This paper investigates the effects of Big Five personality and its dimensions on expatriate job performance. Based on a sample of 332 expatriates working in Malaysia, personality factor was found to be a significant determinant of expatriate job performance in international assignments. Specifically, the results of this study reveal that expatriates in Malaysia with greater conscientiousness personality fared better in their task and contextual performance. Those with greater openness to experience were found to perform better in their task, contextual and assignment-specific performance.

....

Title: "Expatriates Social Networks: The Role of Company Size"

Publication: *The International Journal of Human Resource Management*

Date: 2010

Authors: Christina Stroppa and Erika Spiess

Executive Summary: This study is an extension as well as a test of Caligiuri and Lazarova's model (2002) for the influence of support provided by network partners (supervisors, coworkers, friends, spouses) on received socioemotional and instrumental support. We extended this model by examining this relationship in connection with company size. Ninety expatriates were questioned during their foreign assignment: forty-five from small- and medium-sized enterprises and forty-five from large companies. Consistent with our hypothesis, expatriates who received support from their coworkers during their foreign sojourn also received more instrumental support. In addition, the type of company moderated the relationship between the network partner friends and socioemotional and instrumental support. Implications for expatriate adjustment research and practice are discussed.

....

Title: "Effects of Cross-Cultural and Language Training on Expatriates' Adjustment and Job Performance in Vietnam"

Publication: *Asia Pacific Journal of Human Resources*

Date: 2012

Authors: Yu-Lin Wang and Emma Tran

Executive Summary: The purpose of this study is to explore the relationships among predeparture cross-cultural training, postarrival cross-cultural training, language training, expatriates' adjustment (general, interaction, work), and job performance. Questionnaire data were collected from 114 expatriates and their supervisors, who evaluated the expatriates' job performance in Vietnam. The results indicate that predeparture cross-cultural training, postarrival cross-cultural training, and language training all are positively associated with general, interaction, and work adjustment ability.

PASSION FOR DIVERSITY

RIYADH, SAUDI ARABIA

Enjoyment of Living in Another Country

Living in another country is an excellent way to strengthen a person's Global Mindset. Our research at Najafi Global Mindset Institute has shown that managers who have lived in one or more countries over the span of six months to two years have much higher overall scores on the Global Mindset Inventory than their peers. But even for the most well-traveled among us, adapting to life in a new country is a process. Companies who regularly send employees abroad to work (i.e., expatriates) understand this and usually provide training and coaching before, during, and after life abroad. Pretrip preparation is not just about learning the new culture and customs. A very good program will also discuss the range of emotions a person will typically experience during the first several months in a new country.

For example, someone may feel quite excited predeparture but will likely encounter some uncomfortable or unexpected situations early on that discourage her. It is also likely that she will miss some of the comforting customs and amenities of her home country. For the well-prepared employee, she will recognize and manage her emotions while adapting to life in the new country. She'll also draw on the support of her company and her colleagues. However, without the understanding that the adaptation process takes time and personal reflection, she may want to pack up her bags and leave early on. This is a common and unfortunate reality for too many expatriate employees and their families. With the right preparation before, during, and after the immersion, the experience can be fulfilling, rewarding, and enjoyable.

Enjoyment of Living in Another Country in Action

When I was offered the position of plant manager in the Shanghai facility, my wife immediately agreed that I should take the role and move to China.

VALERIE WHITE, PH.D.
Principal
Change Perspectives

"When I was offered the position of plant manager in the Shanghai facility, my wife immediately agreed that I should take the role and move to China. This would be our third relocation in the course of seven years, and we were thrilled. We had embraced our previous opportunities to live and work in Eastern Europe (my wife is Polish and I am American) and in South Africa. This would be yet another opportunity to experience life different from what we have known.

"We hoped that my tenure in the role would be long enough for us to be truly inculcated to life in China, to the extent that educated, city-dwelling Chinese people would experience. Although we travel at every opportunity, we have come to realize that getting to truly know another culture means becoming a part of it. This requires participating in the local community for a significant period of time. When possible, we have always extended our time as ex-pats until we feel that we have learned a way of life that is unique to the country we are residing in."

*This example was shared with Dr. White by a coaching client.

DEVELOPMENT SUGGESTIONS
for Enjoyment of Living in Another Country

LEARN

Tips to learn about and begin developing the capability on your own. These tips involve self-directed learning, including reading, listening, watching, or observing, that you can do on your own at your own pace. They are most useful for novices in the capability, but are helpful for intermediate and advanced learners to keep knowledge current.

Development Activity	Suggested Resource(s) and Tips
Before moving to another country, prepare yourself for the experience with both cultural knowledge and analysis of what you may need during your acclimation.	• Anticipate predictable surprises and possible surprises when living in another country, and have solutions in mind. You can identify these during your study of the country, customs, and culture. • Read travel writers' books and blogs about the location you'll be living in to get a firsthand account. You can browse or search travel writers' books and blogs through the Society of American Travel Writers (www.satw.org). • On Amazon.com, you can search "travel writing" and add the country name to find a list of books on your country of interest. • Watch the movie *Lost in Translation* (2003) to reflect on culture shock.
Plan ahead for ways to quickly start connecting with social life in the new country.	• Use guidebooks and local media sources to identify social activities and events you would like to participate in. • Once you are in-country, use technology, like an iPad, to link you to local entertainment.
Keep a log or journal of your experiences while living in another country.	• Create an online blog using WordPress (www.wordpress.com). • Join an expatriate forum online such as InterNations (www.internations.org), Transitions Abroad (www.transitionsabroad.com), Escape Artist (www.escapeartist.com), and Expat Exchange (www.expatexchange.com).

GLOBAL PSYCHOLOGICAL CAPITAL

DEVELOPMENT SUGGESTIONS
for Enjoyment of Living in Another Country

CONNECT

Tips to learn about and continue developing the capability through others. These tips involve working with another person to learn from their experiences. They may involve asking questions, listening to and discussing experiences, forming a new relationship, deepening an existing relationship, or receiving feedback from someone who is acting as your mentor. These tips are useful for all levels of learners.

Development Activity	Suggested Resource(s) and Tips
Join communities of foreigners/expats in the country where you are living to learn about their experience living in that country.	• Join a local Rotary International club to participate in service activities there (www.rotaryinternational.org). • Join an expatriate forum online such as InterNations (www.internations.org), Transitions Abroad (www.transitionsabroad.com), Escape Artist (www.escapeartist.com), and Expat Exchange (www.expatexchange.com).
When living in another country, use local professional or social networks to build your own community on several levels.	• Ask new friends and community members in your new country about popular professional or social networks to join. • Continue with social activities that fulfilled you in your home country, such as sports, entertainment, spiritual, and educational pursuits.
Seek out a senior executive mentor with experience in the country you'll be living in to discuss his or her experiences and insights, especially as they relate to how to grow your career while abroad.	• Ask your manager or human resources representative for referrals to senior executives with experience in the country you'll be living in. • Ask the executive what she or he enjoyed most about living in the country and why.
Maintain your network of personal and professional contacts in your home country while living in another country.	• Use international calling cards or Skype (www.skype.com) to talk to your friends, family, and colleagues often. • Use social media sites regularly like LinkedIn and Facebook to stay connected. • Invite your friends and colleagues to come visit you and experience the culture with you.
When living in another country, create a network of native informants (i.e., locals who can give you firsthand insight on life in that location).	• Talk to local people you interact with on a daily basis about their lives (e.g., taxi drivers, store clerks, waiters). • Find a local member of the community who can act as your guide and mentor.

PASSION FOR DIVERSITY

DEVELOPMENT SUGGESTIONS
for Enjoyment of Living in Another Country

EXPERIENCE

Tips to learn about and develop skills in the capability through firsthand experience. These tips involve engaging in activities, such as exploring a new area, trying a new cultural activity, or participating in a specific business event. These tips are most useful for intermediate to advanced learners, and we suggest that novice learners prepare themselves for success by completing some of the tips in the Learn category first.

Development Activity	Suggested Resource(s) and Tips
When living in another country, participate in local holidays, try local foods, and try using the local dress.	• Identify major events and customs through guide books, such as Lonely Planet (www.lonelyplanet.com), Fodor's (www.fodors.com), Frommer's (www.frommers.com), and Rough Guides (www.roughguides.com). • Frequently ask locals about upcoming events and inquire about traditions to learn more.
Identify something you are passionate about, and replicate that in the new country where you are living.	Continue with social activities that fulfilled you in your home country, such as sports, entertainment, spiritual, and educational pursuits.

DEVELOPMENT SUGGESTIONS
for Enjoyment of Living in Another Country

COACH OR CONTRIBUTE

Tips to help others learn about and develop this capability. These tips involve coaching and mentoring others. They may include creating information or experiences for individuals, teams, or your organization. These tips are designed for those who are advanced in the capability and are useful development methods to keep advanced leaders in the capability engaged in professional development at the highest level. Please note that the tips in this section may also be quite helpful for individual use if you do not have a coach or mentor.

Development Activity	Suggested Resource(s) and Tips
Volunteer while you are living in the new country to contribute to your new community, or encourage someone you are mentoring to live in another country to do so.	• Global Volunteer Network can connect you with projects around the world (www.globalvolunteernetwork.org). • Go Volunteer lists volunteer programs around the world and shows reviews of the programs by active volunteers (www.go-volunteerabroad.com). • Inquire within organizations and activities you already participate in for global volunteer opportunities. • Locally inquire about volunteer opportunities.

DEVELOPMENT SUGGESTIONS
for Enjoyment of Living in Another Country

COACH OR CONTRIBUTE

Tips to help others learn about and develop this capability. These tips involve coaching and mentoring others. They may include creating information or experiences for individuals, teams, or your organization. These tips are designed for those who are advanced in the capability and are useful development methods to keep advanced leaders in the capability engaged in professional development at the highest level. Please note that the tips in this section may also be quite helpful for individual use if you do not have a coach or mentor.

Development Activity	Suggested Resource(s) and Tips
Ensure that your family has an enjoyable experience living in the new country.	• Involve your family in your predeparture training to prepare them as well. • Share the resources and support you are receiving from your company with your family during your assignment. • Have open conversations frequently with your family to see how they are feeling.
Develop a manual that provides insights into the basics of living in that country.	• While many of the expatriate forums provide or sell guidebooks for a number of locations in the world, consider creating your own personal guide with your insights and preferred social activities specific to your location and to your organization. Some expatriate communities include: • InterNations (www.internations.org) • Transitions Abroad (www.transitionsabroad.com) • Escape Artist (www.escapeartist.com) • Expat Exchange (www.expatexchange.com)
When coaching a direct report or mentee to live in another country, ask open-ended questions to get them mentally ready.	• What are you excited about when you think about living in this other country? • What would make this experience extremely enjoyable for you? • What makes you nervous about living in this other country? What can you do to mitigate or eliminate these fears? • Think about your previous experiences with new environments. What were your positive and negative experiences, and how did you respond to them? • What lessons can you take from past experiences to make your current experience very enjoyable? • Who can support you in preparing to live in the new country? • Who can support you while you are living in the new country? • When you think ahead to the day that you leave the new country for home or for another location, what are some things that you would like to be able to say about your experience there? How can you make sure that this vision becomes a reality?

PASSION FOR DIVERSITY

Additional Reading

The readings listed here provide you with additional study of the Global Mindset capability in this section. You will find that many of these resources provide you with a specific and detailed look at using this capability in either a particular context or location.

Title: "Three Keys to Getting an Overseas Assignment Right"

Publication: *Harvard Business Review*

Date: 2009

Authors: Mark Alan Clouse and Michael D. Watkins

Executive Summary: An international assignment can be among the most exciting and challenging transitions that an aspiring leader can undertake. With the right planning and attitudes, taking on that kind of leadership role can stretch capabilities, challenge assumptions, and steer both people and profits in a positive direction. But an expat assignment can also be a harrowing journey. Indeed, if they've never made an international move before, emerging leaders can fall into common traps that can severely stress their family bonds, negatively affect their performance at work, damage their businesses, and even lead to outright career derailment.

Title: "Exploring the Motives of Company-Backed and Self-Initiated Expatriates"

Publication: *Human Resource Management*

Date: 2011

Authors: Noeleen Doherty, Michael Dickmann, and Timothy Mills

Executive Summary: Few studies have investigated the range of issues considered important to the decision to move abroad for expatriates, particularly comparing the company-backed and self-initiated expatriate experiences. This study contributes to an important gap in current research about the drivers of both company-backed and self-initiated expatriation. It reveals details about the diverse motivations to undertake an expatriation and the similarities and differences between these two groups. Through a web-based study, the structure of the motivational components considered influential to the decision to move abroad was explored and quantitatively assessed. Principal component analysis (PCA) suggested an eight-factor model. Scales developed from the model highlighted significant differences between the motivations of the self-initiated and company-backed across three key areas. Location and host reputation motives were significantly more important to the self-initiated suggesting that the desire to move to a particular country and characteristics of that country were primary drivers. Company-backed individuals placed significantly more emphasis on specific career motives including job, skills, and career impact.

....

Title: "Compelled to Go Abroad? Motives and Outcomes of
                 International Assignments"

Publication: *The International Journal of Human Resource Management*

Date: 2012

Authors: Luísa H. Pinto, Carlos Cabral-Cardoso, and William B. Werther, Jr.

Executive Summary: This article examines the motives of expatriates and repatriates to accept international assignments and how these motives relate to individuals' perceptions of expatriation outcomes. Issues of adjustment, satisfaction, withdrawal intentions, willingness to relocate again, and recommendation of an assignment to others were considered as outcomes. The data were collected through semistructured interviews of thirty Portuguese expatriates and repatriates. The results indicate that a considerable number of participants relocated because they felt compelled to do so by their employing companies. Moreover, the extent to which organizations persuade these originally unwilling expatriates seems to have negative implications in terms of their perceptions of the adjustment process, general satisfaction with the assignment, and withdrawal intentions. Compelling behavior also has career implications and affects individual receptiveness to relocate in the future.

Enjoyment of Traveling

Travel is a word that conjures many images. What's the first image that comes to your mind? For one of our colleagues, she thinks of long airplane rides to exciting foreign places to sightsee in major metropolitan areas. For another colleague, his vision is quite different. It still involves airplanes and foreign places, but travel for him is connected with backpacks, hiking through tucked-away historical spots, and discovering local adventures. The beauty of travel is that you can do it in a myriad of ways to suit your desires, comfort level, and budget.

We typically find that the people we work with who already have a high degree of enjoyment for travel, especially the global kind, don't need much help in this area. So while our tips do range from novice to expert, they are most helpful for those looking to build an appreciation for travel and for those who want to deepen their cross-cultural experiences.

PASSION FOR DIVERSITY

MALAGA, SPAIN

Enjoyment of Traveling in Action

Every year, I try to select an international conference to share my research ideas with international colleagues and explore a foreign culture. This year, I was excited to present my research at a large academic conference in Malaga, Spain.

YULIA TOLSTIKOV-MAST, PH.D.
Assistant Professor Global Leadership
IndianaTech

Every year, I try to select an international conference to share my research ideas with international colleagues and explore a foreign culture. This year, I was excited to present my research at a large academic conference in Malaga, Spain. Because some European countries have been going through economic or political turmoil, I kept up with world news and felt I had realistic expectations about my trip. I did not speak Spanish, but I had purchased a small dictionary with handy Spanish words and phrases (and had even tried to learn some of them). Equipped with some knowledge of Spain and a printed itinerary for my four-day conference, I was ready.

Even though I had traveled to Europe before, it was my first trip to Spain. I was excited not only to reconnect with international researchers that I had met at previous conferences but also to get to know Spaniards. One of the parts of the trip I was most excited about was an excursion to Malaga and the neighboring towns. Malaga is a part of the Andalusia region in the south, which is the birthplace of the famous Spanish flamenco. This passionate dance always fascinated me. An opportunity to see real flamenco at a local flamenco bar was one of the wishes in my bucket list.

The first part of the trip was uneventful: a routine check-in at the airport, an on-time flight, and pleasant passengers sitting next to me. The only thing that concerned me at that time was that my connecting flight in Madrid had been scheduled very close to my arrival time. But I tried not to worry too far in advance. When we landed, I realized that we were at least half an hour behind schedule. I looked around the plane and noticed concerned faces. It seemed that I was not the only one with the possibility of a missed connection. I became anxious. By missing my connecting flight, I would probably miss a keynote presenter, a leading content expert in my field. As my anxiety was building, I told myself to relax and follow the course of the event.

When passengers were allowed to leave the plane, most of them were rushing to get to customs. Although I did speed up as I was walking down a long and dark hall that connected the international terminal to customs, I felt comfortable and relaxed. I noticed I was not the only calm person in the crowd. A slim, tanned lady in a colorful top, tall leather boots, and oversized stylish bag was the picture of confidence herself. She was smiling and walked with a steady pace. The moment I saw her, I immediately decided to strike up a conversation. I learned that Sharon was an American who moved to Malaga several years ago and was in love with everything Spanish. She was my kind of person!

We got separated when we were going through customs, so I came out of customs by myself in a sea of panicked people. Airport officials were not able to provide accurate instructions regarding connecting flights, and people had become angry. At first, influenced by the panicked crowd, I raised my voice and demanded assistance in English from the polite but unhelpful officials who spoke broken English. I could not find information on where and when the next flight to Malaga was.

Thankfully, I spotted Sharon again. She was acting like a local. She was relaxed and smiling while speaking perfect Spanish, not to airline representatives, but to local clerks. She knew from experience who the right people were to talk to in a situation like this. She said we could get new tickets for connecting flights in the baggage claim area. And so we did. When we returned to the main terminal, the masses were still angry. I tried to help a few people by sharing what I had learned.

As I was boarding my plane to Malaga, I thanked Sharon for being my guide to Spanish culture. She smiled confidently and replied, "Welcome to Spain! Don't you love this country?"

DEVELOPMENT SUGGESTIONS
for Enjoyment of Traveling

LEARN

Tips to learn about and begin developing the capability on your own. These tips involve self-directed learning, including reading, listening, watching, or observing, that you can do on your own at your own pace. They are most useful for novices in the capability, but are helpful for intermediate and advanced learners to keep knowledge current.

Development Activity	Suggested Resource(s) and Tips
Prepare yourself to enjoy the new location by learning in advance about the country, people, and culture.	• YouTube (www.YouTube.com) has a variety of professionally produced and user-produced videos on international travel. • BBC World Service has a variety of documentary videos and podcasts on regions and countries (www.bbc.co.uk/worldservice/programmes). • PBS Global Voices offers documentaries featuring local perspectives (www.pbs.org/itvs/globalvoices). • *National Geographic Traveler* hosts photos, blogs, and videos (http://travel.nationalgeographic.com/travel/?source=NavTravHome. Read travel books). • Read travel writers' books and blogs about the location you'll be living in to get a firsthand account. You can browse or search travel writers' books and blogs through the Society of American Travel Writers (www.satw.org). • On Amazon.com, you can search "travel writing" and add the country name to find a list of books on your country of interest.
Create a travel budget to keep any concerns about finances at bay.	• Read *101 Money-Saving Travel Tips* (Davidson, 2012). • Read *Travel Happy, Budget Low* (Zaraysky, 2009). • Read *Budget Travel Magazine* (www.budgettravel.com).

DEVELOPMENT SUGGESTIONS
for Enjoyment of Traveling

CONNECT

Tips to learn about and continue developing the capability through others. These tips involve working with another person to learn from their experiences. They may involve asking questions, listening to and discussing experiences, forming a new relationship, deepening an existing relationship, or receiving feedback from someone who is acting as your mentor. These tips are useful for all levels of learners.

Development Activity	Suggested Resource(s) and Tips
Travel with either new or established friends.	• If you want support and company while traveling to a certain location, ask your well-traveled friends to accompany you. • Join tour groups to have the built-in support and company of others. You can identify these through your travel agent. • Join local travel clubs and cultural interest groups (www.meetup.com).
Learn more about what makes travel enjoyable for other people. You may discover some new ideas to fuel your own enjoyment.	Talk to your friends and colleagues who enjoy travel. Ask them what they specifically enjoy about it.

DEVELOPMENT SUGGESTIONS
for Enjoyment of Traveling

EXPERIENCE

Tips to learn about and develop skills in the capability through firsthand experience. These tips involve engaging in activities, such as exploring a new area, trying a new cultural activity, or participating in a specific business event. These tips are most useful for intermediate to advanced learners, and we suggest that novice learners prepare themselves for success by completing some of the tips in the Learn category first.

Development Activity	Suggested Resource(s) and Tips
If you are nervous about travel, mentally prepare yourself by creating success strategies to overcome your fears.	• List your top three concerns about travel. For each, identify at least one possible solution. • List the top three exciting things about travel. Keep these in a visible place as you plan your travel. • Pick your top two or three personal interests to try in the country you are traveling to. • Make a plan to travel within the next six months.

DEVELOPMENT SUGGESTIONS
for Enjoyment of Traveling

EXPERIENCE

Tips to learn about and develop skills in the capability through firsthand experience. These tips involve engaging in activities, such as exploring a new area, trying a new cultural activity, or participating in a specific business event. These tips are most useful for intermediate to advanced learners, and we suggest that novice learners prepare themselves for success by completing some of the tips in the Learn category first.

Development Activity	Suggested Resource(s) and Tips
Start by exploring places that are similar to where you are comfortable first.	• Dine in ethnic restaurants. • Visit ethnic art galleries or exhibits. • Visit ethnic artesian markets.
Explore the local area while you are on business trips.	Add in an extra day or two of exploration as a rule on a business trip.
Reflect on what you enjoy about your travel experiences as you have them, including new insights.	• Keep a journal. • Create a travel blog on WordPress (www.wordpress.com).
Connect your travel interests with your philanthropic interests through volunteer work.	• Global Volunteer Network can connect you with projects around the world (www.globalvolunteernetwork.org). • Go Volunteer lists volunteer programs around the world and shows reviews of the programs by active volunteers (www.go-volunteerabroad.com). • Inquire within organizations and activities you already participate in for global volunteer opportunities. • As a manager, arrange to do international corporate volunteer work with your team through an organization like World Action Teams (www.worldactionteams.org).

DEVELOPMENT SUGGESTIONS
for *Enjoyment of Traveling*

COACH OR CONTRIBUTE

Tips to help others learn about and develop this capability. These tips involve coaching and mentoring others. They may include creating information or experiences for individuals, teams, or your organization. These tips are designed for those who are advanced in the capability and are useful development methods to keep advanced leaders in the capability engaged in professional development at the highest level. Please note that the tips in this section may also be quite helpful for individual use if you do not have a coach or mentor.

Development Activity	Suggested Resource(s) and Tips
Encourage someone you are mentoring to learn to enjoy traveling through international volunteer work. Connecting their passions to travel can increase their enjoyment of the experience.	• Global Volunteer Network can connect you with projects around the world (www.globalvolunteernetwork.org). • Go Volunteer lists volunteer programs around the world and shows reviews of the programs by active volunteers (www.go-volunteerabroad.com). • Inquire within organizations and activities you already participate in for global volunteer opportunities. • As a manager, arrange to do international corporate volunteer work with your team through an organization like World Action Teams (www.worldactionteams.org).
When coaching a direct report or mentee to enjoy traveling, ask open-ended questions to get them mentally ready.	• What are you excited about when you think about traveling to this other country? • What would make this travel experience extremely enjoyable for you? • What makes you nervous about traveling to this other country? What can you do to mitigate or eliminate these fears? • Think about your previous experiences with travel to new environments. What were your positive and negative experiences, and how did you respond to them? • What lessons can you take from past experiences to make your current experience very enjoyable? • Who can support you in preparing to travel to this new area? • Who can support you while you are traveling in the new area? • When you think ahead to the last day of your travels in this area, what are some things that you would like to be able to say about your experience there? How can you make sure that this vision becomes a reality?

Additional Reading

The readings listed here provide you with additional study of the Global Mindset capability in this section. You will find that many of these resources provide you with a specific and detailed look at using this capability in either a particular context or location.

Title: "Frequent Business Travelers across Europe: Career Aspirations and Implications"

Publication: *Thunderbird International Business Review*

Date: 2010

Authors: Barbara Demel and Wolfgang Mayrhofer

Executive Summary: This empirical article presents career aspirations of Austrian flexpatriates as well as perceived consequences of frequent flying on future careers, private life, and well-being. The results are compared with selected theoretical concepts from career and career-success literature.

Title: "The New Strategic Imperative: Understanding the Female Business Traveler"

Publication: *The International Business & Economics Research Journal*

Date: 2009

Author: Francine Newth

Executive Summary: This paper explores the characteristics, needs, and behaviors of women who travel on business and analyzes the data for potential segmentation. The study focuses exclusively on the female business traveler. The sample consists of 235 female business travelers from a variety of industries. The statistical methods include correlation analyses, factor analysis, and cluster analysis. The findings show that six factors explain 60.4 percent of the variance in characteristics, behaviors, and needs of female business travelers. Cluster analysis further identifies three clusters: the connective, the empowered, and the productive. The results show that there are three distinct types of women who travel on business. Strategies are suggested for organizations to use the findings to respond to female business travelers.

Title: "When Work Keeps Us Apart: A Thematic Analysis of the Experience of Business Travellers"

Publication: *Community, Work & Family*

Date: 2012

Authors: Helen Nicholas and Almuth McDowall

Executive Summary: While business travel is deemed important for organizational success and economic outcomes, little is known about the actual process of business traveling from the perspective of individuals who undertake such travel on a regular basis. Thus, the current qualitative study examined how business travelers (three women and eight men) attempt to find a balance between work and family by focusing on how time together and time apart are experienced.

Title: "Pulling the Plug on Culture Shock: A Seven-Step Plan for Managing Travel Anxiety"

Publication: *Journal of Global Business Issues*

Date: 2008

Author: Donald C. Smith

Executive Summary: Each year less than thirty million people in the United States travel overseas. Of those taking such a trip, approximately eight million are away on business. Given the pleasure and education that travel offers, it is interesting to explore why the number of travelers is so insignificant. In a country of 390 million people, only 10 percent of US citizens brave the new and exciting things world travel has to offer.

MONUMENT TO THE DISCOVERIES · LISBON, PORTUGAL

Vadim Petrakov / Shutterstock.com

5

Quest for Adventure

As shown in **Figure 5-1** on page 264, this chapter examines Quest for Adventure, which is a key dimension of Global Intellectual Capital. Quest for adventure is the essence of how willing you are to test yourself and to try new things. The popular American film character Indiana Jones is the perfect example of this. Indiana Jones is a professor of archaeology who travels to remote archaeological sites around the world to solve some of history's greatest mysteries, like the location of the biblical ark. He isn't on quests simply for the sake of adventure; he has deep personal and professional interests that compel him to immerse himself in new situations and places. It is a powerful combination of interest and willingness to explore the unknown that fuel his ability to do so.

Your line of work may not lead you in search of the lost ark, but there are still plenty of opportunities for real-life adventures that break you out of your routine. Are you willing to go beyond your comfort zone? Are you wiling to try new or different things? Your level of enthusiasm and willingness to do this characterize your own quest for adventure.

We are frequently asked why someone needs a quest for adventure to be a successful global leader. The answer to this question is embedded in the definition

GLOBAL MINDSET

Global INTELLECTUAL CAPITAL

Global Business Savvy

Knowledge of global industry

Knowledge of global competitive business and marketing strategies

Knowledge of how to transact business and assess risks of doing business internationally

Knowledge of supplier options in other parts of the world

Cosmopolitan Outlook

Knowledge of cultures in different parts of the world

Knowledge of geography, history, and important persons of several countries

Knowledge of economic & political issues, concerns, & hot topics of major regions of the world

Up-to-date knowledge of important world events

Cognitive Complexity

Ability to grasp complex topics quickly

Strong analytical and problem solving skills

Ability to understand abstract ideas

Ability to take complex issues and explain the main points simply and understandably

Global PSYCHOLOGICAL CAPITAL

Passion for Diversity

Enjoy exploring other parts of the world

Enjoy getting to know people from other parts of the world

Enjoy living in another country

Enjoy traveling

Quest for Adventure

Interest in dealing with challenging situations

Willingness to take risk

Willingness to test one's abilities

Enjoy dealing with unpredictable situations

Self-Assurance

Energetic

Self-confident

Comfortable in uncomfortable situations

Witty in tough situations

Global SOCIAL CAPITAL

Intercultural Empathy

Ability to work well with people from other parts of the world

Ability to understand nonverbal expressions of people from other cultures

Ability to emotionally connect to people from other cultures

Ability to engage people from other parts of the world to work together

Interpersonal Impact

Experience in negotiating contracts/agreements in other cultures

Strong networks with people from other cultures and with influential people

Reputation as a leader

Diplomacy

Ease of starting a conversation with a stranger

Ability to integrate diverse perspectives

Ability to listen to what others have to say

Willingness to collaborate

Figure 5-1

GLOBAL PSYCHOLOGICAL CAPITAL

of global leadership. A global leader is someone who must work effectively with people who come from different parts of the world. This means that the leader will interact with people who are very different than him or her. It doesn't matter where the leader is from, because the challenges of global leadership are the same. If you are German and you're dealing with a Chinese client or an American supplier, all of you come from different cultural and political backgrounds. These differences will require a willingness to deal with approaches that are different than yours and, in all likelihood, an interest in trying new approaches that make the partnerships work.

We have provided some useful tips in this chapter to help you push a little further beyond your current comfort zone. In this chapter, we will cover the following four components of quest for adventure:

- Interest in dealing with challenging situations

- Willingness to take risk

- Willingness to test one's abilities

- Enjoyment of dealing with unpredictable situations

The four capabilities that we are going to explore seem very similar at first glance, so let's begin with some points of distinction:

- Interest in dealing with challenging situations addresses a person's motivation to enter into complex situations.

- Willingness to take risk involves a person's motivation to enter into situations where he or she may have little knowledge or experience, which could lead to some degree of personal or professional failure.

- Willingness to test one's abilities refers to someone's motivation to develop his or her competence in a particular area (i.e., the difference between a person who is a novice, intermediate, or expert).

- Enjoyment of dealing with unpredictable situations involves both a person's tolerance for unpredictable situations, which on the high end would include enjoyment, and his or her ability to actually deal with it (e.g., solve it or manage it).

ROCK CLIMBER

Interest in Dealing with Challenging Situations

One of the authors saw different levels of interest in dealing with challenging situations in action with one of our client companies during a global strategy meeting. The problem was that the current markets that the client was in were not growing very fast. The client had reached the conclusion that in order to grow it needed to enter new markets (i.e., new countries). The trouble was that some of the executives felt uncomfortable with the idea of entering new markets, while others were quite excited about it. A few executives kept saying, "Do we really want to do this? It's too complicated, and there's too much risk. We don't know how these markets operate, and we probably will need to develop new products for these places." Executives in the other camp were saying, "Yes, it's complicated, and there is risk. But if we want to grow, we must go out there and learn. We have to push the envelope. We have to try new things." To the second group, the risks of sticking with their current markets outweighed the risks of exploring new markets.

Interest in dealing with challenging situations is built through experience over time, but it also has much to do with one's attitude. Think about a triathlete. A triathlon involves three sports: swimming, biking, and running. It is a complex event in that not only must the athlete be good at all three sports, she must know how to transition between all three. To get to that point, she had to master each of the three sports individually. She also had to have a positive attitude that her goals were achievable and worthwhile.

Reflect on your experiences with challenging situations in your profession. In all likelihood, you've had a combination of successes and challenges. Hopefully, you've been able to take what you've learned from difficult experiences and turn those learnings into success strategies for the future. This is critical for developing a positive interest in dealing with future challenges. If you have direct reports or people you mentor, this is an important point to remember. Once we've coached that person in remedying the situation, we should focus on what can be learned.

When similar new challenges arise, we should then coach that person to apply those new learnings. This is the only way forward. If we do not use failures as learning opportunities, it is quite likely that that person will have little interest in dealing with future challenges. Building this skill is an incremental process that requires personal reflection and supportive coaching. It's not just about teaching someone to fish, as the proverb would say, it is about developing the interest in fishing and the belief that that person can master fishing, especially when the fish are big and the waters are turbulent.

QUEST FOR ADVENTURE

SINGAPORE, SINGAPORE

Interest in Dealing with Challenging Situations in Action

As a non-Asian leader in a global Asian company headquartered in Singapore, I find that my biggest challenge is that there are low levels of innovation on my team.

KATHERINE JOHNSTON, MBA
Speaker, Author, and Consultant

"As a non-Asian leader in a global Asian company headquartered in Singapore, I find that my biggest challenge is that there are low levels of innovation on my team. I thought Eastern cultures were more reflective, but Singapore is different. There are big, open workspaces where desks are crowded closely together according to placement protocol. Everyone sits hunched over their desks, plugging away on PCs and phones. There is little time for reflection, which is critical for innovation. My team performs technical operations well, but I really struggle to have them identify creative ideas and innovation.

"The local and company culture do not foster innovative thinking. For instance, I have found that there are few, if any, meetings to discuss ideas. A leader in Singapore, at least in my company, assembles his employees around his desk, where they stand and each person gives a status update. There is no sharing of ideas or opportunities to ask questions, give input, or brainstorm. In my experience, the best ideas often emerge when people create together. That is why I have taken the initiative to change the culture of my team. While this is risky, in that it goes against both the local and company culture, I think it is necessary to create an environment for innovation. To that end, I have introduced a meeting structure with time built in to exchange ideas. At first, my team was reluctant to embrace this new approach, but now I am starting to see results."

This example was shared with Ms. Johnston by a coaching client.

DEVELOPMENT SUGGESTIONS
for Interest in Dealing with Challenging Situations

LEARN

Tips to learn about and begin developing the capability on your own. These tips involve self-directed learning, including reading, listening, watching, or observing, that you can do on your own at your own pace. They are most useful for novices in the capability, but are helpful for intermediate and advanced learners to keep knowledge current.

Development Activity	Suggested Resource(s) and Tips
Learn about positive psychology, a field that examines healthy mental states, to help shift your thinking about challenges to one of your opportunities.	Dr. Martin Seligman is one of the best-known authors and scientists in the area of learned optimism. He is a former president of the American Psychological Association: • You can use a number of free resources by Dr. Seligman and his team of researchers through the Positive Psychology Center (www.ppc.sas.upenn .edu). • Watch Dr. Seligman discuss positive psychology at a TED conference (www.ted.com/talks/martin_ seligman_on_the_state_of_psychology.html). • Read Dr. Seligman's book *Learned Optimism* (Seligman, 2006).
Learn about neurolinguistic programming (NLP) research on how to change your thought and behavior patterns. The methods do have some criticism in the scientific community for their real effectiveness, but they have a popular following among those who enjoy motivational techniques.	• The NLP and Coaching Institute's website offers workshops, publications, and free reports on NLP (www.nlpskills.com). • Richard Bandler's website offers workshops and publications on the subject of NLP (www.neurolinguisticprogramming.com). • Much of the work done by author Tony Robbins is influenced by neurolinguistic programming (www.tonyrobbins.com).
Build skills related to conflict management, as interpersonal conflict is a common, challenging situation.	• Take a class in conflict management through your local community college or university. • Read *Crucial Conversations* (Patterson, et al., 2011) to learn tools to resolve conflict when the stakes are high. • Read *Crucial Confrontations* (Patterson, et al., 2004) to learn about how to use six sources of influence with other people. • Both of the previous two books are offered in workshop format through VitalSmarts, which also hosts a newsletter, assessments, and other user tools (www.vitalsmarts.com). • You can browse academic resources on conflict management through the International Association for Conflict Management (www.iacm-conflict.org).

DEVELOPMENT SUGGESTIONS
for Interest in Dealing with Challenging Situations

CONNECT

Tips to learn about and continue developing the capability through others. These tips involve working with another person to learn from their experiences. They may involve asking questions, listening to and discussing experiences, forming a new relationship, deepening an existing relationship, or receiving feedback from someone who is acting as your mentor. These tips are useful for all levels of learners.

Development Activity	Suggested Resource(s) and Tips
Find support to keep you motivated and provide you with resources to deal with the challenging situation.	Ask yourself: • Can you realistically do this alone? Should you? • Who in your current network around the world can give you ideas, support, and resources for this situation? • Who do you know who has dealt with a situation like this in the past? Talk to these people to find out what they learned and how it benefitted them.
Create a team to help you deal with the challenging situation when you do not have one.	• Invite colleagues to join you in a focus group meeting to brainstorm ways to deal with the challenge. • Post an invitation to join a virtual focus group through LinkedIn and other social networks. • Call on consultants who have expertise in your area of interest.

DEVELOPMENT SUGGESTIONS
for Interest in Dealing with Challenging Situations

EXPERIENCE

Tips to learn about and develop skills in the capability through firsthand experience. These tips involve engaging in activities, such as exploring a new area, trying a new cultural activity, or participating in a specific business event. These tips are most useful for intermediate to advanced learners, and we suggest that novice learners prepare themselves for success by completing some of the tips in the Learn category first.

Development Activity	Suggested Resource(s) and Tips
Practice dealing with situations that may be challenging but not necessarily threatening to you, so you can develop more comfort with challenges.	• Do simulations or rehearsals of the challenging situation to build confidence and capability, so it's not overwhelming. • Volunteer for a challenging project or assignment. • Create challenges for yourself outside of your comfort zone in your daily life to build an aptitude for challenge (e.g., trying new foods, learning a new sport, interacting with new social groups, or learning new skills like dancing, singing, acting, or painting).

DEVELOPMENT SUGGESTIONS
for Interest in Dealing with Challenging Situations

EXPERIENCE

Tips to learn about and develop skills in the capability through firsthand experience. These tips involve engaging in activities, such as exploring a new area, trying a new cultural activity, or participating in a specific business event. These tips are most useful for intermediate to advanced learners, and we suggest that novice learners prepare themselves for success by completing some of the tips in the Learn category first.

Development Activity	Suggested Resource(s) and Tips
Once you have a challenging situation you are dealing with, use best practices to resolve it or manage it successfully.	• Draw a picture of success in your mind to determine what that would look like and what steps it will require. • Link a current passion you have with the challenging situation that gives you motivation to tackle it (e.g., helping others, learning something new, creating efficiencies, innovating). • Define the problem from multiple perspectives to see if it is truly a problem to be solved or if it is something to be better understood and managed. • Use mind mapping (e.g., breaking down all of the complexities of the issue into its smallest pieces) to fully understand the situation. • For each part of the issue, identify important versus urgent tasks to get a sense of the timeline for solving or managing the issue. • Set a timeframe for yourself or your team to resolve the situation or to create a management plan for it.
Debrief your experiences with a colleague or coach to maximize your learning and build your future confidence and competence.	Ask yourself: • What was your experience? What did you do? • How did you feel during the experience? What did you enjoy? What did you dislike? • What did you learn? How can you apply your learnings to similar situations in the future?

DEVELOPMENT SUGGESTIONS
for Interest in Dealing with Challenging Situations

COACH OR CONTRIBUTE

Tips to help others learn about and develop this capability. These tips involve coaching and mentoring others. They may include creating information or experiences for individuals, teams, or your organization. These tips are designed for those who are advanced in the capability and are useful development methods to keep advanced leaders in the capability engaged in professional development at the highest level. Please note that the tips in this section may also be quite helpful for individual use if you do not have a coach or mentor.

Development Activity	Suggested Resource(s) and Tips
When coaching direct reports or mentees, ask them open-ended questions to help them understand and increase their motivation to deal with the challenging situation.	• How would you describe your interest and motivation to deal with this challenge? • What is potentially exciting about this challenge for you? • What specifically makes you feel uncomfortable about the situation? What is the potential loss here? What's holding you back? • What are three metaphors that may be like this challenge? Pick the least fearful of the three for your mentee to focus on. • What could you potentially achieve in this situation that you would be proud of? What's in it for you? • What about this situation connects with your personal values and who you want to be as a leader? • If you couldn't fail, what would you do? • If a miracle happened overnight to resolve this situation, how would that look? • What are the potential risks if you don't engage in resolving the challenging situation?
When coaching, ask open-ended questions to help others determine how to approach the challenging situation successfully.	• Describe a similar difficulty you overcame. What steps did you take? How did you feel? • Describe a time you thought you would fail and didn't. What did you do? • How would a role model approach this? • How would your more successful twin do? • Start with a wildly successful end in mind, and back-cast. For example, "It's 2015 and I'm the VP of operations. In 2014, I accomplished x. In 2013, I completed y." • What skills do you currently possess that will support you in dealing with this challenging situation? • What do you not know about this situation that you need to learn to be able to address it well? • What environment do you need to create around you (and your team) to deal with this challenge? • How will you manage your stress while dealing with this situation? • Who will support you and motivate you during this situation (e.g., your supervisor, peers)? • What resources do you need to resolve the challenging situation? Where will you obtain them? • What type of training do you need to resolve the challenging situation or to be better prepared for a similar challenge in the future? • What goals and milestones will you set for success? How will you monitor and measure these?

Additional Reading

The readings listed here provide you with additional study of the Global Mindset capability in this section. You will find that many of these resources provide you with a specific and detailed look at using this capability in either a particular context or location.

Title: "Working in the Middle East: Western Female Expatriates' Experiences in the United Arab Emirates"

Publication: *International Journal of Human Resource Management*

Date: 2012

Authors: Edelweiss C. Harrison and Snejina Michailova

Executive Summary: This study is about the experiences of Western female expatriates working in the United Arab Emirates (UAE), a Muslim Arab country in the Middle East. We reveal these expatriates' own interpretations of their adjustment, cross-cultural training, and social ties and support experiences. On the basis of a survey of eighty-six female expatriates from Australia, New Zealand, the United Kingdom, and the United States and subsequent interviews with twenty-six of them, we find that Western women successfully adjust to life and work in the UAE despite significant cultural differences between their home countries and the UAE.

Title: "Improving the Probabilities of Success of Expatriate Managers in the Global Organisation of the 21st Century"

Publication: *International Journal of Human Resources Development and Management*

Date: 2011

Authors: Michael Harvey, Nancy Napier, and Miriam Moeller

Executive Summary: As globalization begins to accelerate, the need for personnel to staff organizations will reach a critical juncture. Two issues appear to be heading for conflict: (1) the need for adequate supply of global managers and (2) the need to change the staffing regimen of the past to meet the needs of the evolving global organizations. While there has been an ongoing debate in the academic literature about the effectiveness and the rate of success of expatriate managers, it is increasingly clear that selection, training/development, compensation, and performance appraisal of expatriate managers will have

GLOBAL PSYCHOLOGICAL CAPITAL

to change to reflect current environmental/political circumstances. We address the modifications that need to be made to the historic/traditional concept of expatriation to include creative solutions and means of implementing them as a way for expatriate managers to fit the staffing requirement of the twenty-first-century global organization. One might say that it could be a last-ditch effort to improve the probabilities of success of expatriate managers in global organizations.

Title: "Adjustment Elusiveness: An Empirical Investigation of the Effects of Cross-Cultural Adjustment on General Assignment Satisfaction and Withdrawal Intentions"

Publication: *International Journal of Intercultural Relations*

Date: 2012

Authors: Luísa Helena Pinto, Carlos Cabral-Cardoso, and William B. Werther, Jr.

Executive Summary: The research reported here explores the relationship between cross-cultural adjustment and general satisfaction with the assignment and withdrawal intentions. Responses from an international sample of 166 expatriates, currently assigned to thirty-nine countries, indicate that perceived cross-cultural adjustment does not predict expatriates' general assignment satisfaction, though satisfaction predicts withdrawal intentions.

Title: "Career Decision Making of Global Careerists"

Publication: *The International Journal of Human Resource Management*

Date: 2012

Authors: Vesa Suutari, Christelle Tornikoski, and Liisa Mäkelä

Executive Summary: The present study aims at increasing our understanding of (1) the elements that global careerists value most in their employment relationship, (2) the factors affecting their decisions to change employers or reject external job offers, and (3) the factors that are important to global careerists when considering their future career. By adopting a social exchange theoretical perspective, the results show that global careerists base their career-move decisions on two categories of returns: on motivational intangible and nonfinancial rewards and on financial rewards, which appear as secondary factors in their decision.

Title: "Personal Attributes of Expatriate Managers, Subordinate Ethnocentrism, and Expatriate Success: A Host-Country Perspective"

Publication: *The International Journal of Human Resource Management*

Date: 2010

Author: Klaus J. Templer

Executive Summary: This study had two objectives. First, to establish the relative importance of expatriate managers' job knowledge, relational leadership skills, and cultural openness and adaptability for expatriate success from the perspective of host-country national subordinates and to test whether these personal attributes are related to expatriate success criteria (expatriate work adjustment, subordinate commitment, subordinate job satisfaction, and unit performance). Second, to test whether host-country national subordinate ethnocentrism is related to expatriate work adjustment.

Willingness to Take Risk

One of our colleagues was scheduled to present a small workshop at a conference in Kuala Lumpur. When she arrived, however, she discovered that she was listed as a keynote speaker. She was surprised. There was nothing in the communication she had received that indicated this. While she had experience presenting keynote speeches at other conferences, she had prepared interactive material that was not suited for an audience of five hundred people. When she inquired to her hosts about the change, they said, "Our keynote speaker canceled, so we put you in his place. That is no problem, right?"

Someone without a willingness to take risk would have said, "No, that is a problem! I can't do this. I am not prepared." That person might even cast blame on the hosts for not communicating in advance. But our colleague was indeed willing to take a risk. Even though she was admittedly irritated at the change without notice and worried that she might not give a smooth presentation, she took the risk. She said the keynote speech went well, and the participants said they found it helpful.

What makes the difference between someone who avoids the risk and someone who is willing to take it? There is no simple answer, because what is considered risky is subjective. A risk is defined as an experience that exposes a person to danger, harm, or loss. For example, a novice traveler may find navigating an unfamiliar airport dangerous, fearing differences in safety standards and language differences that could lead to missed connections and abandonment in a foreign place. More experienced travelers, however, may feel quite comfortable even when the local language and airport procedures differ from what they are used to. They take the differences in stride and keep their eyes and ears open to navigate the foreign airport.

What our research has shown is that willingness to take risks requires a combination of experience and confidence that are built over time. Experience gives us the ability to quickly assess the level of risk involved and apply strategies we've

ZIPLINE THROUGH CLOUD FOREST · MONTEVERDE, COSTA RICA   Pattie Steib / Shutterstock.com

learned along the way to mitigate risks. Our experience also works to fortify our confidence. If we consistently avoid risks, we put ourselves in jeopardy of remaining nervous and potentially fearful of a situation in the future. It also stunts any possibility of learning and gaining confidence in that particular area. This is problematic for development, because we must continually learn in order to grow in our roles and in our careers.

For our colleague, she has found that a mantra (i.e., a phrase that helps someone transform their mood or motivation) helps her build the courage to take risks. She asks herself, "In light of eternity, what difference does it make?" This helps her put the risk into perspective and to remember to keep a sense of humor about her own discomfort. The tips in this chapter will provide you with a range of ideas to assess risk and build your comfort and confidence with taking risks, both small and large.

Visite el Rincón de las Locas →

TANGO • BUENOS AIRES, ARGENTINA

Willingness to Take Risk in Action

My experience coaching others has taught me that risk is self-defined, meaning that what is considered a risk differs for different people.

Susan Gebelein
CEO
Business and Leadership Consulting

My experience coaching others has taught me that risk is self-defined, meaning that what is considered a risk differs for different people. Some shy away from physical risks. Others may dread psychological risks, such as disagreements or difficult interpersonal situations, while others may be afraid to take business risks. Those who are more comfortable with risks often do not see their actions as risky. But those who have more trepidation, may have difficulty believing they can be successful or even survive the risk.

For example, I was working with a leader of a national American business who contemplated growing the business outside of his home country. During his investigation of this possibility, he encountered a number of potential risks. While he found that the cost of customizing the product design for each customer was less outside of his home country, this meant less control of the product. This frightened him. When he was approached by a representative from a Chinese company who was interested in producing the product, for example, he found himself nervous about the idea of doing business there. He had never done business in China before, and, frankly, he was nervous to even go there.

To be willing to take certain risks, it is helpful to do two things. First, you need to identify the risks you have taken in the past. This can get yourself out of the mindset that you are not a risk-taker. Second, you need to figure out the steps needed in your particular situation to make the risk more manageable. This may involve asking for help from an experienced colleague. It could also involve reading, building new skills, or doing anticipatory problem solving or crisis intervention. Some people find it helpful to look at what is the worst that can happen and then problem solve for that. Or, it may involve simply deciding that the risk is important enough to take even if you are very concerned about it. When all else fails, say to yourself, "Just because I am afraid, doesn't mean I'm not going to do it." Afterward, debrief the experience with a colleague or coach so that you can learn from the experience and increase your willingness to take risks in the future.

DEVELOPMENT SUGGESTIONS
for Willingness to Take Risk

LEARN

Tips to learn about and begin developing the capability on your own. These tips involve self-directed learning, including reading, listening, watching, or observing, that you can do on your own at your own pace. They are most useful for novices in the capability, but are helpful for intermediate and advanced learners to keep knowledge current.

Development Activity	Suggested Resource(s) and Tips
Learn about what risk means in business, how to assess the elements of a risk, and how to mitigate risk.	• Read a quick overview of risk management (www.whatisriskmanagement.net). • Read the International Organization of Standardization's (ISO) standards for risk management (ISO 31000) (www.iso.org/iso/home/standards/management-standards/iso31000.htm). • The Project Management Institute offers standards, training, and a certification for risk management (www.pmi.org). • The Risk Management Society has an informational website with links to its journal, workshops, and podcasts (www.rims.org).
Learn about positive psychology, a field that examines healthy mental states, to help shift your thinking about challenges to one of your opportunities.	Dr. Martin Seligman is one of the best-known authors and scientists in the area of learned optimism. He is a former president of the American Psychological Association: • You can use a number of free resources by Dr. Seligman and his team of researchers through the Positive Psychology Center (www.ppc.sas.upenn.edu). • Watch Dr. Seligman discuss positive psychology at a TED conference (www.ted.com/talks/martin_seligman_on_the_state_of_psychology.html). • Read Dr. Seligman's book *Learned Optimism* (Seligman, 2006).
Learn about general human motivation theories. There are many theories in this area, including those made famous by Abraham Maslow, B. F. Skinner, and Albert Bandura.	• For a very quick primer, read the "Theories of Motivation" blog post on About.com (http://psychology.about.com/od/psychologytopics/tp/theories-of-motivation.htm). • For a deeper look into nine theories, consider reading a book such as *Theories of Human Development* (Newman and Newman, 2007).
Learn about sports imagery to help motivate athletes to achieve higher performance and overcome injuries.	The Association for Applied Sport Psychology defines sports imagery and provides tips (www.appliedsportpsych.org/Resource-Center/Athletes/Articles/Sport-Imagery).

QUEST FOR ADVENTURE

DEVELOPMENT SUGGESTIONS
for Willingness to Take Risk

LEARN

Tips to learn about and begin developing the capability on your own. These tips involve self-directed learning, including reading, listening, watching, or observing, that you can do on your own at your own pace. They are most useful for novices in the capability, but are helpful for intermediate and advanced learners to keep knowledge current.

Development Activity	Suggested Resource(s) and Tips
Learn about personal visions, visioning practices, and vision boards in the personal development field.	There are many authors and life coaches in this field: • Martha Beck describes the benefits and steps to create a personal vision board (http://marthabeck.com/2008/07/the-subtle-tricks-to-building-an-effective-vision-board). • *Visioning: Ten Steps to Designing the Life of Your Dreams* (Capacchione, 2000) illustrates how to turn your goals into visual inspiration and uses reflection activities throughout. • *The Complete Idiot's Guide to Vision Boards* (Turner, 2009) includes instructions and photos on how to create your own vision board.
Learn about confidence boosters.	• Read *100 Ways to Boost Your Self-Confidence* (Goldsmith, 2010). • Read *Confidence Boosters!* (Cleghorn, 2011). • Learn about how to use visual imagery to boost self-confidence in *Visualize Confidence* (Rockefeller, 2007).
Read books about how to learn from failures.	• *Celebrate Your Mistakes* (Stammell and Field, 1996) includes seventy-seven risk-taking ideas from top companies. • *The Courage to Fail* (Mortell, 1992) discusses how to build resilience from failure. • *The Power of Failure* (Manz, 2002) discusses twenty-seven ways to turn setbacks into success. • *Learning from Life* (Center for Creative Leadership, 2007) is about turning life lessons into leadership experience.
Watch how role models and popular leaders take risks.	Watch films about famous leaders who took risks: • *Invictus* about South African leader Nelson Mandela (2009) • *The Iron Lady* about British leader Margaret Thatcher (2011) • *Ghandi* about Indian leader Mohandas Ghandi (1992) • *Schindler's List* about German leader Oskar Schindler (1993) • Watch *Forbes*'s slide show featuring thirty-four entrepreneurs, celebrities, politicians, and athletes discussing the greatest risks they have ever taken (www.forbes.com/2010/01/20/gucci-indy500-letterman-entreprenuer-management-risk-greatest_slide.html).

DEVELOPMENT SUGGESTIONS
for Willingness to Take Risk

CONNECT

Tips to learn about and continue developing the capability through others. These tips involve working with another person to learn from their experiences. They may involve asking questions, listening to and discussing experiences, forming a new relationship, deepening an existing relationship, or receiving feedback from someone who is acting as your mentor. These tips are useful for all levels of learners.

Development Activity	Suggested Resource(s) and Tips
Assemble a team to help you take a risk with more confidence and support.	Ask yourself: • Do you have the talent on your team to succeed? • Who do you need on your team to reduce the risks identified? What skills do they need? • Who do you already know who has the skills you need? • Who can you network with to identify the right people for the team?
Get coaching to support you before, during, and after the risky situation.	• Meet with your manager to prepare for the risk you are going to take by asking for ideas, resources, and support throughout the process. • Meet with colleagues who have faced similar risks to learn from their experiences. • Discuss your experiences after the fact with your manager, a colleague, or a personal coach to identify learnings you can use in the future.
Work with a consultant who has expertise in your field and with the cultures you are working with.	• Ask your manager and your human resources department for referrals to consultants with the expertise you are seeking. • Ask the consultant about real versus perceived risks in your situation. • Ask the consultant about cultural considerations in your situation.

DEVELOPMENT SUGGESTIONS
for Willingness to Take Risk

EXPERIENCE

Tips to learn about and develop skills in the capability through firsthand experience. These tips involve engaging in activities, such as exploring a new area, trying a new cultural activity, or participating in a specific business event. These tips are most useful for intermediate to advanced learners, and we suggest that novice learners prepare themselves for success by completing some of the tips in the Learn category first.

Development Activity	Suggested Resource(s) and Tips
Practice dealing with a risky situation to develop a level of comfort.	• Do simulations or rehearsals of the risky situation to build confidence and capability, so it's not overwhelming. • Volunteer for a risky project or assignment. • Create risk for yourself outside of your comfort zone in your daily life to build an aptitude for challenge (e.g., trying new foods, learning new skills, interacting with new social groups). • Develop the habit of dealing with progressively larger risks.
Once you have a risky situation you are dealing with, use best practices to resolve it or manage it successfully.	• If you are risk averse, break the perceived risk down into manageable portions. • Strategically approach the risky situation with a step-by-step plan. • Invite experts on the risky situation within and outside of your organization to help you quantify and analyze the risk involved. • Call on the risk management professionals in your organization to help you create a plan to reduce and manage risks.
Debrief your experiences with a colleague or coach to maximize your learning and build your future confidence and competence.	Ask yourself: • What was your experience? What did you do? • How did you feel during the experience? What did you enjoy? What did you dislike? • What did you learn? How can you apply your learnings to similar situations in the future?

DEVELOPMENT SUGGESTIONS
for Willingness to Take Risk

COACH OR CONTRIBUTE

Tips to help others learn about and develop this capability. These tips involve coaching and mentoring others. They may include creating information or experiences for individuals, teams, or your organization. These tips are designed for those who are advanced in the capability and are useful development methods to keep advanced leaders in the capability engaged in professional development at the highest level. Please note that the tips in this section may also be quite helpful for individual use if you do not have a coach or mentor.

Development Activity	Suggested Resource(s) and Tips
When coaching direct reports or mentees, ask them open-ended questions to help them understand and increase their motivation to take risks.	• What motivates you generally? • What is the risk involved in your mind? • What about this risk is attractive to you? What might you gain? • What is lost by taking this risk? What are you afraid of? • What is lost by not taking this risk? • Is the reward better than the risk? • What's the difference between a risk and a challenge for you? • What did you like doing as a child that was an adventure for you? What did you enjoy about these activities? • What do you need to learn about in this situation to quantify the risk and manage it? • What is getting in the way of taking this risk? • What have you learned from past risk taking that can help you here? • How do you think you can succeed and learn in this situation? • Who are some role models you have who are risk-takers? What characteristics do you like about them?
When coaching, ask open-ended questions to help others determine how to approach the risky situation successfully.	• What is the strategic direction you've been given or have defined to approach this risk? • Describe a similar situation you have taken successfully. What steps did you take? How did you feel? • Describe a time you thought you would fail and didn't. What did you do? • Thinking about past risk taking that didn't go well, what can you do differently this time? • What skills do you currently possess that will support you in dealing with this risky situation? • What environment do you need to create around you (and your team) to deal with this challenge? • What support system do you need to put in place? • Create a movie in your mind watching yourself be exceptionally effective in taking this risk. What do you see yourself doing?

Additional Reading

The readings listed here provide you with additional study of the Global Mindset capability in this section. You will find that many of these resources provide you with a specific and detailed look at using this capability in either a particular context or location.

....

Title: "Rewarding for Success in an International Assignment: The Case of Returning to an Uncertain Future"

Publication: *Journal of Business Studies Quarterly*

Date: 2010

Authors: Ileana Alvarado, Krystal A. Antoine, Gian-Carlo Cinquetti, Jorge Fernandez, Jabir Najair, Giuliana Scagliotti, and Bahaudin G. Mujtaba

Executive Summary: This case discusses how the decisions and communication from human resources (HR) management can be detrimental at times when placing expatriates. It also analyzes some of the problems that a firm can face along with recommended solutions that can prevent a reoccurrence. Recommendations, suggestions, and plans for practical alternatives are provided for HR professionals and expatriates. The case emphasizes the importance of clear communication between HR management and expatriates working abroad and starting repatriation. Multinational firms can use this case in order to improve their management and business structure.

....

Title: "Risk and Decision Making by Finance Executives: A Survey Study"

Publication: *International Journal of Managerial Finance*

Date: 2007

Author: Les Coleman

Executive Summary: When finance managers face decisions, they do not always make clinical evaluations using rational methodology, but systematically depart from utility maximization. This article addresses biases that are related to risk propensity and categorizes them under five headings: decision makers' characteristics and perception, reference levels, mental accounting and the assumption of mean reversion, the longshot bias or over-confidence, and the desire for immediate gratification. The research reported in the paper seeks to understand the mechanisms of these biases using a study of decision making by Australian finance executives in a setting that is representative of a typical business decision. This paper uses a case study that was designed to identify why decision makers facing choices will prefer a risky alternative. Data were collected using email contact and an electronic survey. Respondents (n=67) provided demographic data and answered questions that probed their attitudes and decision styles. Risk propensity was quantified by respondents' attitude toward a risky decision and was explained using independent variables related to decision maker traits. Just over half of the executives proved willing to take a risk, and almost half of the variance in their risk propensity was explained roughly equally by respondents: endowment, perception of risk's role in decisions, assessment of alternative choices, and expectation of the decision's outcome. Manipulation of the cases along four dimensions varied the decision's facts, but they proved only marginally significant to risk taking. The study provides a practical explanation of the risk-taking behavior of finance executives, confirms that context is more important to decisions than their content, and adds to the growing body of applied behavioral research in finance.

....

Title: "Negotiating the Risk or Risky Negotiations?"

Publication: *Financial Executive*

Date: 2009

Authors: Danny Ertel and Mark Gordon

Executive Summary: Economic downturns make the ordinary challenges of negotiating deals that actually deliver value much more difficult. Indeed, in today's environment, risk analysis is no longer just a question of challenging whether the integration team can deliver the savings, but whether a flawed deal can bring down the entire organization. For financial executives, the nightmares are not just about the big headline-grabbing M&A transactions. The simple fact is that most negotiators don't have the risk conversation with their counterparts often enough, and when they do, they don't do it well enough. Chief financial officers and controllers have a critical leadership role to play in ensuring that deal-makers and the business units they support think carefully about when and how to raise which risks during negotiation. In turbulent times, financial executives have an ever greater obligation to ensure that their teams negotiate in a way that will deliver deals where risks are well understood and well managed.

Title: "How to Increase a Company's Risk Taking"

Publication: *MIT Sloan Management Review*

Date: 2008

Author: Alden M. Hayashi

Executive Summary: What levers can an organization pull to become less risk averse? One solution has been to provide the CEO with stock options: the right to buy a company's stock at a prespecified price at a set date in the future. Do such incentives also lead to greater company risk taking? And what's the relationship between the two types of incentives—CEO and director stock options? Such questions were recently investigated by a team. In general, the CEOs in the study owned far more value in stock options than did the outside directors (an average of more than \$3.5 million versus about \$100,000). Not surprisingly, both types of incentives did indeed lead to greater company risk taking.

Title: "Are Female Executives More Risk-Averse than Male Executives?"

Publication: *Atlantic Economic Journal*

Date: 2006

Authors: Zahid Iqbal, O. Sewon, and H. Young Baek

Executive Summary: It is often argued that women are more risk averse than men. This paper provides additional evidence on this issue by examining the stock-selling behavior of male and female executives in response to stock option awards. When corporate executives sell shares of their firm upon new stock option awards, it is an indication that they are attempting to reduce risk through diversification of their personal portfolio. More rigorous stock sales by female executives would indicate that they are more risk averse than their male counterparts. However, this paper finds that male executives are more risk averse by engaging in higher diversification-related stock sales than the female executives. It is also found that the stock sales by male executives approximate the optimal hedge ratio.

Title: "Compensation Framing and the Risk-Taking Behavior of the CEO: Testing the Influence of Alternative Reference Points"

Publication: *Management Research*

Date: 2011

Authors: Martin Larraza-Kintana, Luis Gomez-Mejia, and Robert M. Wiseman

Executive Summary: This paper seeks to analyze how compensation framing influences the risk-taking behavior of the firm's CEO and the mediating role played by risk bearing. The study employs a sample of 108 US firms that issued an initial public offering in 1993, 1994, and 1995. A structural equation model is estimated, which explicitly considers the mediating effect of risk bearing on the compensation framing—risk taking relationship.

Title: "Gender and Risk: Women, Risk Taking and Risk Aversion"

Publication: *Gender in Management*

Date: 2010

Authors: Sylvia Maxfield, Mary Shapiro, Vipin Gupta, and Susan Hass

Executive Summary: Labeling women as risk averse limits the positive benefits both women and organizations can gain from their risk taking. The purpose of this paper is to explore women's risk taking and reasons for stereotype persistence in order to inform human resources practice and women's career development. The paper draws on literature about gender and organizations to identify reasons for the persisting stereotype of women's risk aversion. Using literature and concepts about risk appetite and decision making, the paper evaluates results of the Simmons Gender and Risk Survey database of 661 female managers. The paper finds evidence of gender neutrality in risk propensity and decision making in specific managerial contexts other than portfolio allocation. More in-depth research is needed to explore the gender-neutral motivators of risk decision making and to explore risk taking in a more diverse sample population. The paper explores why women's risk taking remains invisible even as they take risks and offers suggestions on how women and organizations may benefit from their risk-taking activities. The paper synthesizes evidence on risk taking and gender, and the evidence of female risk taking is an important antidote to persisting stereotypes. The paper outlines reasons for this stereotype persistence and implications for human resources development.

Title: "Leadership Attributes, Masculinity and Risk Taking as Predictors of Crisis Proneness"

Publication: *Gender in Management*

Date: 2011

Authors: Zachary Sheaffer, Ronit Bogler, and Samuel Sarfaty

Executive Summary: The purpose of this paper is to examine the extent to which leadership attributes, masculinity, risk taking, and decision making affect perceived crisis proneness. The paper draws mainly on the literature about gender, leadership, and organizational crises to explore whether masculinity predicts crisis proneness and the extent to which leadership attributes as well as risk-taking and decision-making styles are efficient predictors of perceived crisis preparedness (CP). Using pertinent literature and concepts, the paper evaluates a database of 231 female and male managers. As hypothesized, masculinity is positively associated, whereas transformational leadership is inversely associated with perceived CP. Both participative decision making and passive management predict a higher degree of perceived crisis proneness and so does risk taking. More in-depth research as well as a larger and more diverse sample are required to explore more definitively why and how masculinity is positively associated with crisis proneness. The paper provides preliminary evidence regarding the merits of feminine leadership traits as facilitators of CP. This finding does not, however, preclude the usefulness of masculine attributes in managing actual organizational crises. The findings appear particularly relevant given the current turbulent business environments and the increasing frequency and magnitude of corporate crises. The paper synthesizes evidence on CP proneness and gender, and the evidence of feminine attributes as an important antidote to perceived CP. The paper outlines reasons for this phenomenon and implications for placement of managers in current business arenas.

Title: "Risk Taking by Entrepreneur"

Publication: *The American Economic Review*

Date: 2009

Authors: Galina Vereshchagina and Hugo A. Hopenhayn

Executive Summary: Entrepreneurs bear substantial risk, but empirical evidence shows no sign of a positive premium. This paper develops a theory of endogenous entrepreneurial risk taking that explains why self-financed entrepreneurs may find it optimal to invest in risky projects offering no risk premium. Consistently with empirical evidence, the model predicts that poorer entrepreneurs are more likely to undertake risky projects. It also finds that incentives for risk taking are stronger when agents are impatient.

Willingness to Test One's Abilities

So far in our exploration of quest for adventure, we have looked at how to build an interest in dealing with challenging situations and the willingness to take risks. The first addressed a person's motivation to enter into complex situations. The second looked at how to build motivation to enter into situations where a person may have little knowledge or experience, which could lead to some degree of personal or professional failure. This brings us to willingness to test one's abilities. What we are referring to in this section is specifically someone's motivation to develop his or her competence.

Ability is defined as competence in an activity or occupation because of one's skill, training, or other qualification (www.dictionary.com). Ability is the difference between those who are novice, intermediate, or expert in a particular knowledge or skill. A novice, for example, may be quite interested in dealing with a challenging situation. He may also be willing to take risk. But his ultimate success will hinge on his ability to perform. Malcolm Gladwell's best-selling book *Outliers* (Gladwell, 2008) makes the point through multiple success stories that expert ability in any subject is the result of practice. While he acknowledges that some talented people have innate motivation and skill, they developed expert-level ability through ten-thousand hours of practice or more throughout their lives.

In business, we often focus on abilities in terms of technical skills. They are important. In global leadership, however, willingness to test one's abilities will likely have as much or more to do with a person's motivation to adapt their skills for different environments and to build strong cross-cultural relationships. This will determine who is willing to take on global responsibilities, a global role, or even a global assignment. This capability will also determine who will develop their career both up the proverbial career ladder as well as across geography and cultures.

EUROPEAN ATHLETIC CHAMPIONSHIPS 2010 · BARCELONA, SPAIN

Willingness to Test One's Abilities in Action

Sixteen years ago, when I first moved to the Washington, DC, area, I joined the DC Chamber of Commerce to promote my business in global leadership coaching.

BARRIE ZUCAL, MS
President and CEO
Global Coaches Network

Sixteen years ago, when I first moved to the Washington, DC, area, I joined the DC Chamber of Commerce to promote my business in global leadership coaching. A delegation from China came to visit, and I registered to attend a meeting with them that was to be followed by a lunch. Because I had lived in Taiwan and learned some Mandarin, I decided to test my abilities by speaking Mandarin when I introduced myself and my business to the Chinese. I thought it would be a nice way to bridge the culture gap.

I wrote my introduction in Mandarin, and I practiced it before the meeting. At the meeting, all of the delegates and Chamber members before me introduced themselves in English. When my turn came, I stood and started to introduce myself in Mandarin. While I was doing this, I could see the Chinese leaning forward, as if trying to understand what I was saying. I tried harder to speak, and still I could see that they didn't understand me. The Americans were looking at me with total fascination as I carried on.

I started laughing and said to the Chinese in English, "I am trying to speak Mandarin Chinese." It was quiet for a moment. Then they started laughing and congratulating me on my Mandarin. This broke the ice for the whole group.

WASHINGTON, D.C. • UNITED STATES OF AMERICA

Song Quan Deng / Shutterstock.com

DEVELOPMENT SUGGESTIONS
for Willingness to Test One's Abilities

LEARN

Tips to learn about and begin developing the capability on your own. These tips involve self-directed learning, including reading, listening, watching, or observing, that you can do on your own at your own pace. They are most useful for novices in the capability, but are helpful for intermediate and advanced learners to keep knowledge current.

Development Activity	Suggested Resource(s) and Tips
Learn about the differences between people who have higher versus lower needs for achievement.	• Dr. David McClelland developed the motivational needs theory that informs much of the work today on achievement. Dr. McClelland's 1961 seminal book, *The Achieving Society*, was reprinted in 2010 due to its current widespread use. • Dr. McClelland explores the relationship between motivation and emotions, values, and performance in *Human Motivation* (1987).
Learn about self-efficacy (i.e., how a person judges his or her own ability to achieve goals) and how to cultivate it.	• Dr. Albert Bandura developed the self-efficacy theory. • You can read a quick primer on self-efficacy theory at About .com (http://psychology.about.com/od/theoriesofpersonality/a/self_efficacy.htm). • For a more in-depth exploration, read *Self-Efficacy: The Exercise of Control* (Bandura, 1997).
Learn about how to build your self-confidence.	• *The Self-Esteem Workbook* has exercises and techniques to improve self-esteem (Schiraldi, 2001). • *The Self-Esteem Companion* (McKay, et al., 2005) has activities to realistically assess yourself and learn to focus on your strengths.

DEVELOPMENT SUGGESTIONS
for Willingness to Test One's Abilities

CONNECT

Tips to learn about and continue developing the capability through others. These tips involve working with another person to learn from their experiences. They may involve asking questions, listening to and discussing experiences, forming a new relationship, deepening an existing relationship, or receiving feedback from someone who is acting as your mentor. These tips are useful for all levels of learners.

Development Activity	Suggested Resource(s) and Tips
Find a mentor who believes in you and pushes you toward the goal.	• Ask your manager or a colleague to support you as you test your abilities. • Draw on your personal network (e.g., friends and family) to ask for active support while you work toward a goal. • Hire a personal coach to support you with your personal and professional growth.

DEVELOPMENT SUGGESTIONS
for Willingness to Test One's Abilities

CONNECT

Tips to learn about and continue developing the capability through others. These tips involve working with another person to learn from their experiences. They may involve asking questions, listening to and discussing experiences, forming a new relationship, deepening an existing relationship, or receiving feedback from someone who is acting as your mentor. These tips are useful for all levels of learners.

Development Activity	Suggested Resource(s) and Tips
Ask others who are successful at testing their own abilities about their personal success strategies.	• Identify who the stars are in your company, and ask to meet with one of them. • Ask your colleague about some of the crucibles he or she encountered to reach his or her current status and position. • Ask for advice on how to grow your abilities and/or career in the organization.

DEVELOPMENT SUGGESTIONS
for Willingness to Test One's Abilities

EXPERIENCE

Tips to learn about and develop skills in the capability through firsthand experience. These tips involve engaging in activities, such as exploring a new area, trying a new cultural activity, or participating in a specific business event. These tips are most useful for intermediate to advanced learners, and we suggest that novice learners prepare themselves for success by completing some of the tips in the Learn category first.

Development Activity	Suggested Resource(s) and Tips
Take on a challenge in something you already like to do.	• Identify a hobby or sport you already pursue that you would like to improve in to move from novice to intermediate or intermediate to expert. • Identify action steps to improve your abilities. • Set incremental timelines and goals. • Periodically reflect on your progress.
Identify a new activity or challenge that makes you nervous in the area in which you would like to test your abilities, and then give it a try.	Some ideas include the following: • traveling to a new part of the world where you do not speak the language or know anyone • joining a new organization or taking on a leadership role in an existing organization • trying a new sport or cultural activity (e.g., dance classes, new ethnic restaurants, language classes) • making new friends from another culture

DEVELOPMENT SUGGESTIONS
for Willingness to Test One's Abilities

EXPERIENCE

Tips to learn about and develop skills in the capability through firsthand experience. These tips involve engaging in activities, such as exploring a new area, trying a new cultural activity, or participating in a specific business event. These tips are most useful for intermediate to advanced learners, and we suggest that novice learners prepare themselves for success by completing some of the tips in the Learn category first.

Development Activity	Suggested Resource(s) and Tips
Determine the boundaries you need to maintain in a situation in order to safely test your abilities.	• Identify what makes you nervous about testing your abilities in the situation at hand. • Determine what you need to put in place or change in order to be willing to develop yourself in this area. • Make a plan for maintaining the boundaries you have identified.

DEVELOPMENT SUGGESTIONS
for Willingness to Test One's Abilities

COACH OR CONTRIBUTE

Tips to help others learn about and develop this capability. These tips involve coaching and mentoring others. They may include creating information or experiences for individuals, teams, or your organization. These tips are designed for those who are advanced in the capability and are useful development methods to keep advanced leaders in the capability engaged in professional development at the highest level. Please note that the tips in this section may also be quite helpful for individual use if you do not have a coach or mentor.

Development Activity	Suggested Resource(s) and Tips
When coaching direct reports or mentees, ask open-ended questions to help them identify their motivation to test their abilities and how they can increase it.	• Do you want to grow to the next level? Why or why not? • How would you describe your personal need for achievement? • What do you think it will take for you to grow to the next level? • What have been some prior successes you have had in growing your abilities? • What are your insecurities about testing your abilities? • What rewards exist for not taking risks or testing your abilities in your organization? • What's in it for you to test your abilities?
When coaching others, ask questions to help them identify ways to test their abilities.	• Make a list of ten tests of your ability that you want to pursue. • Start with a private personal goal to test your abilities rather than a public professional goal to make it safer to experience testing your abilities. • What boundaries do you need to maintain (e.g., work–life balance) while testing your abilities? How will you maintain these?

Additional Reading

The readings listed here provide you with additional study of the Global Mindset capability in this section. You will find that many of these resources provide you with a specific and detailed look at using this capability in either a particular context or location.

....

Title: "Capital Gains: Expatriate Adjustment and the Psychological Contract in International Careers"

Publication: *Human Resource Management*

Date: 2009

Authors: Arno Haslberger and Chris Brewster

Executive Summary: An expatriate assignment is an expatriate's opportunity to build career capital and a company's opportunity to generate social and Global Intellectual Capital.

....

Title: "Beyond Expats: Better Managers for Emerging Markets"

Publication: *McKinsey Quarterly*

Date: 2011

Author: Jeffrey A. Joerres

Executive Summary: The author proposes a new approach: pursuing a reverse expat strategy. Reverse expats spend a predetermined amount of time (often a month, though it could be more, depending on their experience level and the complexity of the business challenges involved) immersed in the company's established operations.

Title: "Recognising Diversity in Managing Work Life Issues of Flexpatriates"

Publication: *Equality, Diversity and Inclusion: An International Journal*

Date: 2011

Authors: Helene Mayerhofer, Angelika Schmidt, Linley Hartmann, and Regine Bendl

Executive Summary: The aim of this paper is to explore flexpatriates' perceptions of work–life balance (WLB) issues and identify possible adjustments of WLB programs to better meet the needs of flexpatriates. This paper investigates flexpatriates' challenges at the interface of personal and work lives and their perception of standard WLB programs and then proposes organizational adjustments to better meet the needs of flexpatriates.

Title: "'Adjustment' of the Independent Expatriate: A Case Study of Doug"

Publication: *Qualitative Research in Organizations and Management*

Date: 2010

Author: Steve McKenna

Executive Summary: The paper highlights ways in which qualitative research methods generally, and specifically when used in relation to expatriates, enable a fuller understanding of the processes of adjustment that expatriates experience and its relationship to their life as a work in progress. This type of research approach and analysis complements the more positivist study of expatriates. In some aspects, it supports research findings on adjustment, but it serves to humanize the independent expatriate and their experience.

Title: "Intercultural Knowledge Management: Exploring Models for Repatriation Competency Transfer in the Global Workplace"

Publication: *International Journal of Human Resources Development and Management*

Date: 2010

Author: Christine R. Velde

Executive Summary: Education is changing and becoming more global. Therefore, there is an increasing need for human resources managers to effectively manage the expatriation and repatriation processes of expatriates. The literature argues that the repatriation process from both the workplace and the employee's perspective remains problematic and has been neglected by both organizations and the research literature. Returning home and resettling into new roles is often traumatic for the expatriate. The literature reports that staff often leave their organizations following repatriation. This results in a loss of international knowledge and calls for a more strategic approach to repatriation. This exploratory paper, which draws on experience of expatriates and research literature in the field, argues for the development of new knowledge management frameworks and taxonomies, because globalization has forced expatriation and repatriation on to the strategic agenda.

. . . .

Title: "The Effects of Hardiness and Cultural Distance on Sociocultural Adaptation in an Expatriate Sales Manager Population"

Publication: *Journal of Personal Selling & Sales Management*

Date: 2011

Authors: Darin W. White, R. Keith Absher, and Kyle A. Huggins

Executive Summary: International corporations are increasingly concerned about expatriate executive attrition. There is an urgent need to develop methods for identifying the antecedents to successful expatriate performance. In choosing sales managers for international assignments, special attention should be paid to the candidate's psychological hardiness and cultural distance between the home and host countries.

Enjoyment of Dealing with Unpredictable Situations

One of us once worked with a person who had been in the same position for more than twenty years. She was good at her work and really enjoyed her colleagues. She especially liked the routine of knowing what to expect day in and day out. She had been offered higher-level jobs as well as jobs in other areas of the company, but she was happy where she was. In her personal life, she also enjoyed routine. Her family vacationed in the same camping spot each year, where they enjoyed the company of old friends who also made the annual pilgrimage there. Chances are you too have colleagues or friends who enjoy the routine of their work and lives.

Global leadership has little to offer in terms of routine. The work is complex, making unpredictable situations commonplace. And no matter how well a person has studied another culture, the experience of it is usually full of surprises. Global leadership work is not well-suited for everyone. This is why it is important to assess a potential global leader for his or her level of enjoyment in dealing with unpredictable situations, as well as their skill in forecasting potential situations.

Unpredictable is defined as something that is difficult or impossible to predict or foresee. Surprises happen: flights get canceled, employees go on strike, natural disasters occur, etc. However, many times there are warning signs to help us prepare: watching weather forecasts can help us predict canceled flights or natural disasters and keeping our ears open for news of employee discord can help us anticipate a strike, for example. So dealing with unpredictable situations involves being observant and informed to forecast when possible and taking unforeseen events in stride.

Enjoyment of unpredictable situations is a necessary quality for global leadership work, but enjoyment alone is not sufficient. Note that the capability says the situation must also be *dealt with*. Our research shows that successful leaders may view unpredictable situations as exhilarating problems to be solved, but they also work to understand the situations, resolve them, and, ultimately, transform them into more predictable situations in the future.

BULL RIDER • ONTARIO, CANADA

GLOBAL PSYCHOLOGICAL CAPITAL

J.T. Lewis / Shutterstock.com

Enjoyment of Dealing with Unpredictable Situations in Action

I was on my way to the Career Development Center to present my two-week evaluation of a training program in the U.A.E.

DOUG STUART, PH.D.
Development Coach and Intercultural Trainer

I was on my way to the Career Development Center to present my two-week evaluation of a training program in the U.A.E. A US-based technology transfer company had hired me to evaluate an English-language program they designed and implemented to train local hires for technical work in natural gas production. As a consultant, my job was to review the program and provide critical feedback.

It was late summer in the Gulf, and I was sweating in my sport coat, dress shirt, and tie, despite the ubiquitous air-conditioning. Arriving at the Center a little early, I learned that the local and expatriate heads of the institute were in a meeting with external visitors and that we would convene shortly. I was glad for a few minutes to go over my notes, because I had to report a difficult situation.

The goal of the course I reviewed was to produce employees who could study and conduct their work in English. Rapid progress in this eight-month English course was crucial to the students' subsequent success. About half of the teachers were expatriate native speakers, while the other half were native speakers of Arabic. All were competent, but the two groups had vastly different teaching styles. The Arabs were teaching in the text-based traditional style, with a heavy grammatical and written focus. In contrast, the expats were teaching with a lot of student interaction and speaking practice.

Because of the mixture of teaching styles, not all students were progressing as rapidly as desired. I had to recommend that some of the teachers be replaced by those who could teach in the more interactive style. There was pressure to hire local staff, and I knew it would be difficult to find Gulf Arabs comfortable with that style. The suggestion to replace local staff would be painful and embarrassing, both practically and politically. In the otherwise flamboyant world of Arab rhetoric, bad news is generally delivered privately and often indirectly.

As I waited in the anteroom, I overheard an alarming conversation. The center would hold a reception for the press and local dignitaries after our meeting to celebrate and publicize the great progress being made at the Center. They would announce that the program was a true opportunity for young local Arabs. I had not anticipated this. Because some of the press and local dignitaries had arrived early, they were invited to attend our meeting.

I recognized immediately that I could not deliver the report that I had prepared. Sweating a little more heavily, I pulled our expatriate department manager aside and told him I had to change our approach. For public consumption, I would now warmly report the excellent progress being made by the students due to the enthusiasm and talent for which they had been selected. I would also highlight the Center's excellent direction and the expertise and diligence of the English language staff. Furthermore, I would mention that through conversations with management and staff, we had discovered possibilities for further improving an already successful program. These "small changes," to be detailed in a later report, would be implemented over the coming months.

My evaluation report presentation was not as I had predicted or prepared for. But I knew that this desperate, tactical alteration was necessary to avoid a disaster at the public meeting. I was able to meet privately with the Center's director before my flight back to the United States to present the nature of these possibilities. And so, despite the bad news, face was saved.

Some of the recommended staffing changes did occur. The program was moderately successful by external standards, and the achievements of the Center were appreciated by the local community. A lucky bit of information at the last minute and some understanding of Arab culture had prevented a political disaster.

DEVELOPMENT SUGGESTIONS
for Enjoyment of Dealing with Unpredictable Situations

LEARN

Tips to learn about and begin developing the capability on your own. These tips involve self-directed learning, including reading, listening, watching, or observing, that you can do on your own at your own pace. They are most useful for novices in the capability, but are helpful for intermediate and advanced learners to keep knowledge current.

Development Activity	Suggested Resource(s) and Tips
Learn how to better predict unpredictable situations.	• *Predictable Surprises: The Disasters You Should Have Seen Coming and How to Prevent Them* (Bazerman and Watkins, 2008) offers insights on how to better forecast situations in your organization and minimize risks. • Read "Learning Cultures on the Fly" (in Advances in International Management, Javidan et al., 2007) by Richard M. Steers. • Learn about scenario planning in organizations by reading *Scenario Planning in Organizations: How to Create, Use, and Assess Scenarios* (Chermack, 2011) or *Scenario Planning: A Field Guide to the Future* (Wade, 2012).
Learn how others have successfully dealt with unpredictable situations.	*The Leadership Moment* (Useem, 1999) presents nine real-life stories of triumph and disaster during unpredicted situations.
Learn about positive psychology, a field that examines how to help shift your thinking about challenges to one of your opportunities.	• Dr. Martin Seligman is one of the best-known authors and scientists in the area of learned optimism. He is a former president of the American Psychological Association. • Use the free resources by Dr. Seligman and his team of researchers through the Positive Psychology Center (www.ppc.sas.upenn.edu). • Watch Dr. Seligman discuss positive psychology at a TED conference (www.ted.com/talks/martin_seligman_on_the_state_of_psychology.html). • Read Dr. Seligman's book *Learned Optimism* (Seligman, 2006).
Learn about neurolinguistic programming (NLP) research on how to change your thought and behavior patterns. The methods do have some criticism in the scientific community for their real effectiveness, but they have a popular following among those who enjoy motivational techniques.	• The NLP and Coaching Institute's website offers workshops, publications, and free reports (www.nlpskills.com). • Richard Bandler's website offers workshops and publications on the subject of NLP (www.neurolinguisticprogramming.com). • Much of the work done by author Tony Robbins is influenced by neurolinguistic programming (www.tonyrobbins.com).
Learn about how to become more adaptable.	• Read *AdaptAbility: How to Survive the Change You Didn't Ask For* (Ryan, 2009). • Read *Adaptability: The Art of Winning in an Age of Uncertainty* (McKeown, 2012). • Read *Adaptability: Responding Effectively to Change* (Center for Creative Leadership, 2007).

QUEST FOR ADVENTURE

DEVELOPMENT SUGGESTIONS
for Enjoyment of Dealing with Unpredictable Situations

CONNECT

Tips to learn about and continue developing the capability through others. These tips involve working with another person to learn from their experiences. They may involve asking questions, listening to and discussing experiences, forming a new relationship, deepening an existing relationship, or receiving feedback from someone who is acting as your mentor. These tips are useful for all levels of learners.

Development Activity	Suggested Resource(s) and Tips
Find a mentor who can support you while you solve or manage the situation that was not predicted.	• Ask your manager or a colleague to support you. • Draw on your personal network (e.g., friends and family) to ask for active support. • Ask an expert on the topic how he or she would deal with it. • Hire a personal coach to support you.
Determine what kind of support you need to work through the unpredicted situation, and connect with these sources of support.	Ask yourself: • Can you realistically do this alone? Should you? • Who in your current network around the world can give you ideas, support, and resources for this situation? • Who do you know who has dealt with a situation like this in the past? Talk to these people to find out what they learned and how it benefitted them.
Ask others who have successfully dealt with similar situations in your organization about their success strategies.	• Identify who in your company has successfully dealt with similar situations, and ask to meet with one of them. • Ask your colleague how he or she solved or managed the situation.
Create a team to help you deal with the unpredicted situation when you do not have one.	• Invite colleagues to join you in focus group meetings to brainstorm ways to deal with the situation. • Post an invitation to join a virtual focus group through LinkedIn and other social networks. • Call on consultants who have expertise in your area of interest.

DEVELOPMENT SUGGESTIONS
for Enjoyment of Dealing with Unpredictable Situations

EXPERIENCE

Tips to learn about and develop skills in the capability through firsthand experience. These tips involve engaging in activities, such as exploring a new area, trying a new cultural activity, or participating in a specific business event. These tips are most useful for intermediate to advanced learners, and we suggest that novice learners prepare themselves for success by completing some of the tips in the Learn category first.

Development Activity	Suggested Resource(s) and Tips
Become a better forecaster of situations in your organization.	• Think about your experiences in your organization in the long term, and identify trends you have noticed. • Keep current with industry journals and conferences. • Follow competitor news to identify situations they are facing that your organization may face. • Learn from past experience with unpredicted situations. Use what you learn to create contingency plans for the future when these situations resurface.
When you have an unpredicted situation you are dealing with, use best practices to resolve it or manage it successfully.	• Draw a picture of success in your mind to determine what that would look like and what steps it will require. • Link a current passion you have with the unpredicted situation that gives you motivation to tackle it (e.g., helping others, learning something new, creating efficiencies, innovating). • Define the problem from multiple perspectives to see if it is truly a problem to be solved or if it is something to be better understood and managed. • Use mind mapping (i.e., breaking down all of the complexities of the issue into its smallest pieces) to fully understand the situation. • For each part of the issue, identify important versus urgent tasks to get a sense of the timeline for solving or managing the issue. • Set a timeframe for yourself or your team to resolve the situation or to create a management plan for it.

QUEST FOR ADVENTURE

DEVELOPMENT SUGGESTIONS
for Enjoyment of Dealing with Unpredictable Situations

COACH OR CONTRIBUTE

Tips to help others learn about and develop this capability. These tips involve coaching and mentoring others. They may include creating information or experiences for individuals, teams, or your organization. These tips are designed for those who are advanced in the capability and are useful development methods to keep advanced leaders in the capability engaged in professional development at the highest level. Please note that the tips in this section may also be quite helpful for individual use if you do not have a coach or mentor.

Development Activity	Suggested Resource(s) and Tips
When coaching direct reports or mentees, ask open-ended questions to help them identify their motivation to deal with unpredictable situations.	• What have been your prior successes in dealing with unpredictable situations? • What is the reward versus the risk for dealing with the situation? • What are you afraid of? • How could you look at this situation as a game or a challenge rather than a risk? • When have you felt joy or exhilaration in an unpredicted situation? How can you recreate that for this situation?
When coaching others, ask questions to help them better deal with unpredicted situations.	• How are you currently feeling about this situation? • How do you plan to manage your stress or anxiety? • What support can you draw on to help you through this? • What one step can you take right now to solve or manage the situation?

Additional Reading

The readings listed here provide you with additional study of the Global Mindset capability in this section. You will find that many of these resources provide you with a specific and detailed look at using this capability in either a particular context or location.

....

Title: "Change Leaders: Creating Resilience in Uncertain Times"

Publication: *Leader to Leader*

Date: 2012

Author: Kathleen Allen

Executive Summary: The article discusses the effect of unpredictability of uncertainty on engineering and science-based companies. These companies are accustomed to calculating risk and acting on those calculations with a high degree of confidence, and hence, the effect is particularly troublesome for them. Business leaders must immediately take steps to make their organizations more flexible and resilient to the challenges of uncertainty. A resilient company will thrive in both good and bad times, and the key predictors of resilience are organizational structure and its associated policies.

....

Title: "Strategizing in an Unpredictable Climate: Exploring Corporate Strategies to Cope with Regulatory Uncertainty"

Publication: *Long Range Planning*

Date: 2011

Authors: Christian Engau and Volker H. Hoffmann

Executive Summary: Government regulation of business activities is increasing rapidly, exposing firms to considerable uncertainty and requiring managers to decide on appropriate strategic postures. To help managers make informed decisions, this study compiles a comprehensive overview of strategies to cope with regulatory uncertainty and illustrates their interdependencies and how they can be combined into overall coping postures, as well as offering management guidelines on deciding which to adopt. A literature review identifies a considerable variety of coping strategies, and we apply unique data from a worldwide cross-industry survey to categorize each into one of three types: offensive, defensive, or passive. We find that firms aiming to cope with the uncertainty associated with post-Kyoto regulation typically adopt one of four strategic postures, each characterized by a specific combination of these types: daredevils rely solely on offensive strategies, coordinators combine them with defensive ones, hedgers pursue strategies from all three categories, and gamblers choose not to specifically cope with uncertainty at all. We exemplify the strategies characteristic of each posture and illustrate their interdependencies by means of case studies in the European airline industry. We identify two main factors managers should consider particularly when deciding on their firm's strategic posture (the level of regulatory uncertainty they perceive and the firm's exposure to future regulations) and find that the higher the level of uncertainty, the broader the range of strategies applied, and the more future regulation seems likely to affect a firm, the more actively it seeks to cope with the associated uncertainty.

Title: "Decoding Resistance to Change"

Publication: *Harvard Business Review*

Date: 2009

Authors: Jeffrey D. Ford and Laurie W. Ford

Executive Summary: When a change initiative falters, the knee-jerk response can be to blame those who won't get on board. Jeffrey Ford, of Ohio State University, and Laurie Ford, of Critical Path Consultants, examine why that type of reaction is not only pointless but also potentially destructive. Drawing on their years of research and consulting work, the authors recommend seeing resistance for what it really is—feedback—and propose five ways for leaders to use that feedback to effect change more productively. In the early stages, if the only way to keep the conversation about change alive is to entertain highly charged discussions, so be it. A complete lack of feedback can sound the death knell for change. Employees need to know not only what will change but also why the new reality will be better. Don't be shy about offering explanations as directly as possible. People who resist change are often the ones most concerned about getting things right. Give them the chance to help you make a good change initiative better. Heed feedback even when it doesn't seem likely to yield objective improvements. The ownership people feel when you adopt their best ideas will pay off in ways you often cannot foresee. A legacy of bad change can inhibit your change effort, even if you had nothing to do with the unfortunate history. Acknowledging—and, if possible, correcting—past change failures is often essential to future success.

Title:　　　　"Designing Lobbying Capabilities: Managerial Choices in
　　　　　　　　　Unpredictable Environments"

Publication:　*European Business Review*

Date:　　　　2011

Authors:　　　Thomas Lawton and Tazeeb Rajwani

Executive Summary: The purpose of this paper is to explore how, in unpredictable policy environments, specific managerial choices play a vital role in designing lobbying capabilities through the choice of levels of investment in human capital, network relationships, and structural modification.

Title:　　　　"New Project? Don't Analyze—Act"

Publication:　*Harvard Business Review*

Date:　　　　2012

Authors:　　　Leonard A. Schlesinger, Charles F. Kiefer, and Paul B. Brown

Executive Summary: We all know how new projects happen in a predictable world: A team is assembled, a market analyzed, a forecast created, and a business plan written. Resources are then gathered, and the plan is set in motion. But how do you launch new projects in an unpredictable environment? What's the best way to do it in an age when the proliferation of data and opinion makes truly decisive analysis impossible; when faraway events have immediate, unexpected effects; and when economic malaise has made companies reluctant to take big bets on unproven ideas?

QUEST FOR ADVENTURE

PRESENTING TO A TEAM WITH CONFIDENCE

GLOBAL PSYCHOLOGICAL CAPITAL

Pressmaster / Shutterstock.cor

Self-Assurance

As shown in **Figure 6-1** on page 316, this chapter examines Self-Assurance, which is a key dimension of Global Intellectual Capital. Self-assurance refers to a leader's self-confidence and energy level. He needs to believe that he can successfully take on complex global work, and he needs to have the energy to juggle multiple roles, issues, and tasks at the same time. Consider the example of a leader put in a global role for the first time who does not have sufficient self-confidence. His company comes to him and says, "Starting tomorrow, you are now in a global role." Because he lacks confidence, he goes home and thinks, "I really don't know how to do this. I am not sure I'm going to succeed." He has insecurities and concerns about the probability of his success. These doubts in his mind will most likely not go away. They're going to affect every decision he makes. They're going to force him to be less decisive, to be constantly looking for affirmation or some kind of support. This will make it harder for him to work effectively with people from other parts of the world.

Some level of doubt is normal. It is, in fact, healthy to avoid becoming narcissistic (i.e., believing you are infallible). But a global leader must be reasonably confident to approach the work with composure, focus, grace, and success.

In this chapter, we will look at the four components of self-assurance:

- Energetic

- Self-confident

- Comfortable in uncomfortable situations

- Witty in tough situations

GLOBAL MINDSET

Global INTELLECTUAL CAPITAL

Global Business Savvy

Knowledge of global industry

Knowledge of global competitive business and marketing strategies

Knowledge of how to transact business and assess risks of doing business internationally

Knowledge of supplier options in other parts of the world

Cosmopolitan Outlook

Knowledge of cultures in different parts of the world

Knowledge of geography, history, and important persons of several countries

Knowledge of economic & political issues, concerns, & hot topics of major regions of the world

Up-to-date knowledge of important world events

Cognitive Complexity

Ability to grasp complex topics quickly

Strong analytical and problem solving skills

Ability to understand abstract ideas

Ability to take complex issues and explain the main points simply and understandably

Global PSYCHOLOGICAL CAPITAL

Passion for Diversity

Enjoy exploring other parts of the world

Enjoy getting to know people from other parts of the world

Enjoy living in another country

Enjoy traveling

Quest for Adventure

Interest in dealing with challenging situations

Willingness to take risk

Willingness to test one's abilities

Enjoy dealing with unpredictable situations

Self-Assurance

Energetic

Self-confident

Comfortable in uncomfortable situations

Witty in tough situations

Global SOCIAL CAPITAL

Intercultural Empathy

Ability to work well with people from other parts of the world

Ability to understand nonverbal expressions of people from other cultures

Ability to emotionally connect to people from other cultures

Ability to engage people from other parts of the world to work together

Interpersonal Impact

Experience in negotiating contracts/agreements in other cultures

Strong networks with people from other cultures and with influential people

Reputation as a leader

Diplomacy

Ease of starting a conversation with a stranger

Ability to integrate diverse perspectives

Ability to listen to what others have to say

Willingness to collaborate

Figure 6-1

Energetic

Energy level is an understudied aspect of leadership. We don't often talk about it, but you do need to be an energetic person to succeed in a global role. Why? Well, let's contrast two situations. In situation 1, you're dealing with people in your home country who are similar to you: same language, similar cultural background, and many shared values and assumptions in the workplace. In situation 2, you're dealing with people who are different from you in many ways and come from different parts of the world.

In situation 1, let's say you are a South African manager working with fellow South Africans. When you make a statement at work, it's very likely that your colleagues will understand you. They will understand the words you use, what you mean, and probably even the historical context behind why you are making that statement. Similarly, when your colleagues make a statement, it's very likely that you will understand them. This is because you are all working with similar understandings and experiences. Certainly, this is not always the case, but the more shared culture you have in a group the more fluid the communication tends to be.

Now in situation 2, let's say you are a South African manager working with Japanese colleagues. You may both be speaking the same language at work, but because his or her view of the world is different from yours, your brain is saying, "Now, wait a minute. I need to think about what was just said and figure out what this person means to communicate and why." Your brain has to work extra hard compared to situation 1. So simple communication takes more energy for you to understand and make sure that you are understood when you are working cross-culturally. And much deeper aspects of working relationships, like trust and rapport, take even more work.

If you have low energy, you can get exhausted very quickly in cross-cultural situations. Now, what happens when you're in a meeting and you're tired? You may become irritable and abrupt, or you may just stop participating. Either way, you may not make a good impression. The other people in the meeting, who happen

COMPETITIVE RUNNER

to be from other parts of the world, look at your behavior (e.g., body language, facial expressions) and may interpret it as lack of interest. They may not identify the fact that you are mentally worn out. They see you as a colleague who does not warrant their respect or attention.

This is a road block that will be hard to overcome. Your goal as a global leader is to get things done: to build relationships, to work with people from other parts of the world, to accomplish complex tasks. But if your colleagues see you as disinterested and insensitive, they will not be interested in working with you. So lack of energy can have huge implications in terms of your ability to work effectively with people from other parts of the world.

Learning to manage and sustain your energy level is critical. In this section, we provide you with tips to help you stay energetic on several levels: physical, mental, emotional, and behavioral. The tips you need to succeed will depend on your specific needs and may change over time. So we suggest you keep these lists handy to regularly try new methods to optimize your energy level.

SELF-ASSURANCE

INDEPENDENCE SQUARE ▪ ACCRA, GHANA   Felix Lipov / Shutterstock.cor

Energetic in Action

A senior finance executive, who several years earlier had led his team to a silver medal in the Olympics, took a newly developed role working in Ghana.

VALERIE WHITE, PH.D.
Principal
Change Perspectives

A senior finance executive, who several years earlier had led his team to a silver medal in the Olympics, took a newly developed role working in Ghana. His European-based company was looking to grow market share there. Taking this role meant leaving his wife and two children at home in the United Kingdom, where he would only be able to visit them sporadically. It also meant building a team of other new expats in the country, reporting to an unknown, South African–based manager who had a tough reputation. Furthermore, he would need to develop the local infrastructure to ensure the successful delivery of clean water supplies to remote areas of the country as part of the volunteer services project the company had committed to.

When this executive took the role, the economy was highly unstable. In the very likely scenario of the currency or economy failing, he would be unable to meet his plan. This would be reflected in his performance ratings, bonus, and perhaps reputation with the company. Yet none of these challenges kept him from taking the role. As his Olympic silver medal would show, he was an energetic person who was up to the challenge. He was determined to be successful in a bad economy and in personally and professionally risky circumstances. And so he was.

DEVELOPMENT SUGGESTIONS
for Energetic

LEARN

Tips to learn about and begin developing the capability on your own. These tips involve self-directed learning, including reading, listening, watching, or observing, that you can do on your own at your own pace. They are most useful for novices in the capability, but are helpful for intermediate and advanced learners to keep knowledge current.

Development Activity	Suggested Resource(s) and Tips
Learn how to use your mind to focus on the present and sustain your energy level.	• *The Power of Now* (Tolle, 2004) discusses how to stay in the present moment, which is what the author argues is all we really ever have control over. • *Relaxation Response* (Klipper and Benson, 2000) is a classic in the field about using your mind to affect how your body feels. • *The Seed: Finding Purpose and Happiness in Life* (Gordon, 2011) looks at the link between purpose and energy and how to strengthen it. • *Power of Full Engagement: Managing Energy Not Time Is the Key to High Performance and Personal Renewal* (Loehr and Schwartz, 2003) shares insights about how to manage energy rather than time to achieve high performance, health, happiness, and life balance. • *The Way We're Working Isn't Working: Four Forgotten Needs That Energize Great Performance* (Schwartz, 2010) discusses how to energize your performance. • Look at resources and publications by the Strozzi Institute, which specializes in the connections between mind, body, and impact (www.ranchostrozzi.com).
Take scientific self-assessments that help you determine where you draw energy from and provide you with tips on how to sustain it.	• Human Performance Institute's assessment (available in both a self-assessment and 360 version) provides an energy profile and recommendations on improving your energy (www.hpiinstitute.com). • The Myers-Briggs Type Indicator (MBTI) helps you determine whether your energy is usually drawn from internal feelings and ideas or from outside people and experiences (www.myersbriggs.org).
Learn about resilience (i.e., how to bounce back from difficult or demotivating experiences) to get your energy back after setbacks.	• *Psychology Today* provides a definition, articles, and tools to understand and build your resilience (www.psychologytoday.com/basics/resilience). • The American Psychological Association has a brochure on how to overcome difficult events called "The Road to Resilience" (www.apa.org/helpcenter/road-resilience.aspx). • *Resilience: Why Things Bounce Back* (Zolli and Healy, 2012) looks at resilience through the lens of scientific breakthroughs, ecological events, and leadership to discuss approaches for building a more resilient world. • *Developing Resilience: A Cognitive Behavioral Approach* (Neenan, 2009) provides guidance and tips for individuals to manage emotions and to move forward in difficult times. • *The Resilience Factor: 7 Keys to Finding Your Inner Strength and Overcoming Life's Hurdles* (Reivich and Shatte, 2003) includes a self-assessment and presents tips on how to overcome challenges in several areas of life.
Learn how to identify what is sapping your energy at work and how to sustain high performance.	Read *Sink, Float, or Swim* (Peltin and Rippel, 2009).

DEVELOPMENT SUGGESTIONS
for Energetic

CONNECT

Tips to learn about and continue developing the capability through others. These tips involve working with another person to learn from their experiences. They may involve asking questions, listening to and discussing experiences, forming a new relationship, deepening an existing relationship, or receiving feedback from someone who is acting as your mentor. These tips are useful for all levels of learners.

Development Activity	Suggested Resource(s) and Tips
Surround yourself with people who energize you.	• Personality assessments like Myers-Briggs Indicator (www.myersbriggs.org), DiSC (www.thediscpersonalitytest.com), and Insights (www.insights.com) will help you determine the personality types that energize you, but be cautious not to surround yourself with only people who are similar to you. Diversity of thought and behavior are important in global leadership and can be stimulating. • Regularly take breaks during your working day and week to call or meet with friends who energize you. • Take walks with colleagues instead of having sit-down meetings to add energy when it is needed. • Ask your high-energy colleagues how they sustain their own high energy.
Use active listening to stay engaged and energetic in conversations with colleagues.	• Read a quick overview of active listening with tips at MindTools (www.mindtools.com/CommSkll/ActiveListening.htm). • *The Wisdom of Listening* (Brady, 2003) discusses how to be fully present in conversations and relationships. • *Active Listening: Improve Your Ability to Listen and Lead* (Center for Creative Leadership, 2007) is a quick read on the basics of listening for managers. • *The Seven Powers of Questions: Secrets to Successful Communication in Life and at Work* (Leeds, 2000) discusses seven ways that questions can be used to open up conversations, better understand others, and achieve desired outcomes in a conversation.
Identify when you tend to be most energetic, during the day or night, and meet with people at those times when possible.	• Keep an energy log for one week, highlighting hours when you are more energetic and productive. • Ask friends, family, and colleagues what hours of the day they view you at your best.
Seek help from experts on how to identify what is sapping your energy and how to sustain high performance.	Tignum designs solutions for individuals and teams (www.tignum.com) through assessments, implementation of solutions, and measurement.

SELF-ASSURANCE

DEVELOPMENT SUGGESTIONS
for Energetic

EXPERIENCE

Tips to learn about and develop skills in the capability through firsthand experience. These tips involve engaging in activities, such as exploring a new area, trying a new cultural activity, or participating in a specific business event. These tips are most useful for intermediate to advanced learners, and we suggest that novice learners prepare themselves for success by completing some of the tips in the Learn category first.

Development Activity	Suggested Resource(s) and Tips
Take good physical care of yourself to maintain consistent and peak levels of energy.	Things to do at work: • Stretch after sitting every thirty minutes. • Stand up after every hour of sitting to move around. • When you begin to lose energy, physically change your position in a room. • Take a walk. • Exercise on a break at work, if possible, or before or after work daily. • Drink water throughout the day. • Eat healthy foods throughout the day. • Don't eat too much at lunch. • Take brief breaks with colleagues who are lively to talk and laugh. • Do brief energy-building activities during meetings (e.g., small group problem-solving, get-to-know-you activities, a mental challenge, a physical activity). • Look at additional tips by Healthy Companies International (www.healthycompanies.com). • Look at Dr. Jason Jones's resources, including a video series, on mental, physical, emotional, and spiritual energy (www.drjasonjones.com). Things to do at home to prepare for your workday: • Practice yoga, meditation, or other activities that relax you after work. • Take a break from any work responsibilities to focus on personal time and family time. • Get enough sleep. • Take regular vacations and personal time to recharge your batteries.

DEVELOPMENT SUGGESTIONS
for Energetic

EXPERIENCE

Tips to learn about and develop skills in the capability through firsthand experience. These tips involve engaging in activities, such as exploring a new area, trying a new cultural activity, or participating in a specific business event. These tips are most useful for intermediate to advanced learners, and we suggest that novice learners prepare themselves for success by completing some of the tips in the Learn category first.

Development Activity	Suggested Resource(s) and Tips
Actively manage your thoughts and emotions to sustain your passion and drive for your personal and professional goals.	• Set goals, especially during tough times, as working toward something that you feel passionate about will renew your energy. • Make progress on major projects by focusing on outcomes and benefits rather than the task, especially when you are not excited about the tasks you need to complete. • Make a list of things that are sapping your energy. Decide whether each is easy to change, important to change, not important to change, or not changeable. Start changing the easy things and those that are important to change. • Think of times in your life when you are filled with energy. What precipitates that energy? What thoughts and feelings do you have when in that state? What would you need to do or say or reframe to recapture those times of high energy?
Actively manage your behaviors to make them energetic. Energy often creates energy.	• Speak clearly in an upbeat manner. • Create an appearance of energy! • Use dynamic language to convey energy. • Visualize a person with high energy, and demonstrate the identified characteristics. • Have an alternative name for yourself that captures your spirit (e.g., Spark), and behave consistently like your alternative name. • Have someone else style coach you by taking a photo or video, watching it together, and talking about your energy level. • Identify when you tend to be most energetic, and leverage those times for interacting with others. • Do something in a compressed time frame to force energy.
Create an environment around you that is energetic.	• Surround yourself with people who energize you, and avoid those who drain you. • Use music to set the level of energy appropriate to the situation.

DEVELOPMENT SUGGESTIONS
for Energetic

COACH OR CONTRIBUTE

Tips to help others learn about and develop this capability. These tips involve coaching and mentoring others. They may include creating information or experiences for individuals, teams, or your organization. These tips are designed for those who are advanced in the capability and are useful development methods to keep advanced leaders in the capability engaged in professional development at the highest level. Please note that the tips in this section may also be quite helpful for individual use if you do not have a coach or mentor.

Development Activity	Suggested Resource(s) and Tips
When coaching direct reports or mentees, help them create a positive and energetic mental picture of their goals.	Ask your mentees to do the following, when appropriate: • Create a vision board (e.g., images that represent goals and success) using the electronic resource Pinterest (www.pinterest.com) or a simple paper version that can be posted in a visible spot. This can create a high mental energy for the goals. • Describe the end point of a project or task in positive terms, and identify something that you are passionate about achieving. • Visualize a high-energy person, describe that person's characteristics, and identify some characteristics you can adopt. • Follow the tips on managing physical, mental, and emotional energy throughout this chapter.

Additional Reading

The readings listed here provide you with additional study of the Global Mindset capability in this section. You will find that many of these resources provide you with a specific and detailed look at using this capability in either a particular context or location.

Title: "Being Global: How to Think, Act, and Lead in a Transformed World"

Publication: *Harvard Business Review Press*

Date: 2012

Authors: Angel Cabrera and Gregory Unruh

Executive Summary: In "Being Global," Cabrera and Unruh define a new context for global leadership, vividly illustrating both the challenges and the opportunities facing today's executives. How can you be effective? What new skills must you learn in order to be successful? What do international teams do to stay connected while still producing results on a regional scale? "Being Global" is written for leaders at all levels of their careers—whether in big business; small, private sector; or government—who aspire to think and act globally and who need some help getting there. Being a global citizen is just the starting point. Cabrera and Unruh provide the tools and guidance to help you develop even deeper leadership skills to benefit both you and your organization.

Title: "Developing Your Global Know-How"

Publication: *Harvard Business Review*

Date: 2012

Author: Keumyong Chung

Executive Summary: For up-and-coming executives, an overseas posting has long been a rite of passage, providing opportunities not available in their native country and experience that can be invaluable to their company both during the assignment and after their return home. How has the Great Recession affected this formula? *Harvard Business Review* spoke with the top human resources executives at four multinationals about how their companies are adapting global assignments to meet the demands of a changing world.

Title: "Expatriate Selection: Evaluating the Discriminant, Convergent, and Predictive Validity of Five Measures of Interpersonal and Intercultural Competence"

Publication: *Journal of Leadership & Organizational Studies*

Date: 2004

Authors: Andrea Graf and Lynn K. Harland

Executive Summary: Effective screening and selection of expatriates is a critical function in organizations, yet the use of paper-and-pencil instruments in expatriate selection is limited by the paucity of existing validity evidence. This study assessed the discriminant, convergent, and predictive validity of two Intercultural Competence measures (the Behavioral Assessment Scale for Intercultural Communication Effectiveness and the Intercultural Sensitivity Scale) and three Interpersonal Competence measures (the Interpersonal Competence Questionnaire, the Social Problem-Solving Inventory-Revised: Short Version, and the Self-Monitoring Scale).

Title: "In Search of Global Leaders"

Publication: *Harvard Business Review*

Date: 2003

Author: Daniel Meiland

Executive Summary: For all the talk about global organizations and executives, there's no definitive answer to the question of what we really mean by *global*. A presence in multiple countries? Cultural adaptability? A multilingual top team? We asked four CEOs and the head of an international recruiting agency—HSBC's Stephen Green, Schering-Plough's Fred Hassan, GE's Jeffrey Immelt, Flextronics's Michael Marks, and Egon Zehnder's Daniel Meiland—to tell us what they think. They share some common ground. They all agree, for example, that the shift from a local to a global marketplace is irreversible and gaining momentum. "We're losing sight of the reality of globalization. But we should pay attention, because national barriers are quickly coming down," Daniel Meiland says. "If you look ahead five or ten years, the people with the top jobs in large corporations . . . will be those who have lived in several cultures and who can converse in at least two languages."

Self-Confident

According to Merriam-Webster dictionary, *confidence* is the "faith or belief that one will act in a right, proper, or effective way." So self-confidence is having that faith and belief in yourself. These beliefs are determined by how a person thinks and feels at a very deep level. They develop over time, through experience, like many other aspects of Global Psychological Capital. But unlike other aspects of Global Psychological Capital, self-confidence is swayed heavily by how a person esteems his or her capabilities, not just by acquiring experience. This puts self-confidence in the realm of perception: "a physical sensation that is interpreted in light of experience" (www.merriam-webster.com).

The bad news here is that perception is reality. Leaders who believe that they will not succeed have usually charted the course for a difficult experience and a poor outcome. The good news is that perceptions are changeable. They are mental images that can be reframed, changed, and replaced with dedicated effort. Consider how these now-successful business people had to change their own perceptions of their experiences to get to the pinnacles of their success.

- Henry Ford, the inventor of the modern assembly line, went broke five times with failed businesses before founding Ford Motor Company.

- Soichiro Honda, founder of Honda, was turned down as an engineer for Toyota, and made scooters in his home until his neighbors encouraged him to start his own business.

- Akio Morita, founder of Sony, failed at selling his first product—a rice cooker that burned rice rather than cook it—before creating other products with his partners.

The following tips range from self-reflection to hands-on experience. This will allow you to start building your confidence privately, at first, and build to more public tests of yourself. This is a particularly important area to enlist the support

DRESSED FOR SUCCESS

of others as well. Draw on your support network. They will often be able to point out strengths that you are overlooking, as well as self-defeating behaviors that you would benefit by changing.

For those of you who have come to this chapter with an already solid sense of self-confidence, we invite you to particularly try out the Connect tips. Remember, confidence is largely about perception. Over-confidence can be a liability in global work, where others, especially those in more group-oriented cultures, perceive you as arrogant or even narcissistic. You may feel quite confident to enter into a project or relationship, while those around you withdraw due to your overbearing style. It is a useful reality check to be style coached (i.e., observed and critiqued by an objective colleague or coach). First impressions, after all, are hard to overcome.

SELF-ASSURANCE

ADDIS ABABA, ETHIOPIA

Self-Confident in Action

I came up through the ranks of the company very differently than my peers, and I could have never dreamed that I would become a marketing director leading the function in another continent.

VALERIE WHITE, PH.D.
Principal
Change Perspectives

"I came up through the ranks of the company very differently than my peers, and I could have never dreamed that I would become a marketing director leading the function in another continent. I was raised by my aunt, who told me that I had two choices after high school graduation: either complete trade school to become an electrician or get a job. I chose getting a job.

"I was hired for the third shift in the factory of a company that is now part of our larger organization. I absolutely loved the people and the work. I had a supervisor who recognized I had untapped talents, and he encouraged me to interview for a customer service job. I was in that role for three years and learned how much I loved working with people and customers. I started building real confidence and thinking that I might really be pretty good at this!

"I realized that I wanted to continue growing in the company and seek more challenging roles. But to do that, I had to build a solid foundation of knowledge in the field. That meant getting my college degree and a graduate degree, which I did in four years while working full-time. This would give me additional credibility and further build my self-confidence for higher-level roles.

"I also learned that perceptions really do matter! They are reality. I have a big mouth sometimes and will say things without thinking. I have found that because I do not feel intimidated by presenting to senior executives, I have to be particularly careful with what I say. Sometimes too much confidence makes me forget who I am speaking to. If I'm going to be perceived as a professional with executive presence, I need to think before I speak. This has taken some practice and coaching.

"As I have moved up through the organization to my current role as the head of marketing in Europe, I have continued to increase my level of confidence in handling whatever might come my way. I've done this by pursuing more challenges along the way. I plan to be in Europe for at least another two years, and then we'll see what happens. My family is behind me, and whatever is ahead I look forward to it!"

This example was shared with Dr. White by a coaching client.

DEVELOPMENT SUGGESTIONS
for Self-Confident

LEARN

Tips to learn about and begin developing the capability on your own. These tips involve self-directed learning, including reading, listening, watching, or observing, that you can do on your own at your own pace. They are most useful for novices in the capability, but are helpful for intermediate and advanced learners to keep knowledge current.

Development Activity	Suggested Resource(s) and Tips
Assess your level of self-confidence, which may include assessments on self-esteem or self-efficacy. Note that psychologists like Albert Bandura do distinguish between each of these, as the locus of control is different for each. However, issues with your self-confidence may be the result of low self-esteem or low self-efficacy, so taking various assessments in these areas will help you determine the cause(s) and work from there.	• Coach Sandy Goodwin offers a self-confidence assessment and coaching (www.innerconfidencecoach.com/Assessment-Test .pdf). • Human resources coach and author Joann Corley offers a comprehensive guide to emotional intelligence questions, including a section on self-confidence (www.joanncorley.com/ uploads/EQ-Interview._Assess.pdf). • Psychology Tools offers a self-esteem assessment and numerous resources (www.psychologytools.org/self-esteem .html). • Self-Esteem Daily offers an assessment, resources, and articles (http://eselfesteem.org).
Identify leaders you consider self-confident individuals, observe their behaviors, and take notes.	Ask yourself: • What does this person do in terms of behaviors and body language that shows self-confidence? • What does this person say that communicates self-confidence? • How does this person dress, groom, and carry himself that shows self-confidence? • How does this person interact with others that shows self-confidence?
Know your subject and the culture in which you are working by preparing mentally and through study.	• When you need to complete a task that is new to you or one where you do not feel confident, be sure to learn as much about the subject as possible and draw on your experienced colleagues to help you prepare to the best of your ability. • Learn the rules of behavior, including norms and taboos, for the culture you are working in. The book series *Kiss, Bow, or Shake Hands* (Morrison and Conaway, 2006) is available in editions for specific regions of the world and for certain business functions.

DEVELOPMENT SUGGESTIONS
for Self-Confident

LEARN

Tips to learn about and begin developing the capability on your own. These tips involve self-directed learning, including reading, listening, watching, or observing, that you can do on your own at your own pace. They are most useful for novices in the capability, but are helpful for intermediate and advanced learners to keep knowledge current.

Development Activity	Suggested Resource(s) and Tips
Learn about positive psychology, a field that examines healthy mental states, to help shift your thinking about challenges to one of your opportunities. Dr. Martin Seligman is one of the best-known authors and scientists in the area of learned optimism. He is a former president of the American Psychological Association.	• Review a number of the free resources by Dr. Seligman and his team of researchers through the Positive Psychology Center (www.ppc.sas.upenn.edu). • Watch Dr. Seligman discuss positive psychology at a TED conference (www.ted.com/talks/martin_seligman_on_the_state_of_psychology.html). • Read Dr. Seligman's book *Learned Optimism* (Seligman, 2006). • Read *Mindset: The New Psychology of Success* (Dweck, 2007).
Learn about building your self-confidence.	Read: • Pick the Brain's blog post "10 Ways to Instantly Build Self-Confidence" (www.pickthebrain.com/blog/10-ways-to-instantly-build-self-confidence) • Mind Tool's blog post and video "Building Self-Confidence" (www.mindtools.com/selfconf.html) • *Confidence: How Winning Streaks and Losing Streaks Begin and End* (Moss Kanter, 2006) • *10 Simple Solutions for Building Self-Esteem: How to End Self-Doubt, Gain Confidence, and Create a Positive Self Image* (Schiraldi, 2007) • *Unstoppable Confidence: How to Use the Power of NLP to Be More Dynamic and Successful* (Sayre, 2008)

DEVELOPMENT SUGGESTIONS
for Self-Confident

CONNECT

Tips to learn about and continue developing the capability through others. These tips involve working with another person to learn from their experiences. They may involve asking questions, listening to and discussing experiences, forming a new relationship, deepening an existing relationship, or receiving feedback from someone who is acting as your mentor. These tips are useful for all levels of learners.

Development Activity	Suggested Resource(s) and Tips
Ask someone in your organization to observe you and give you feedback on how you present yourself.	• Ask your manager or a colleague to give you feedback. • Have someone style coach you by taking a snap-shot or video, watching it together, and talking about it. • Contact your human resources representative for a referral to a coach who can help you build confidence.
Plan to have support in situations where you do not feel confident.	• Ask a supportive colleague to join you, when appropriate. • In cross-cultural situations, build relationships with colleagues before they are needed to build a support network. This can be done through frequent and pleasant social interactions in the workplace and by supporting others when they need it.

DEVELOPMENT SUGGESTIONS
for Self-Confident

EXPERIENCE

Tips to learn about and develop skills in the capability through firsthand experience. These tips involve engaging in activities, such as exploring a new area, trying a new cultural activity, or participating in a specific business event. These tips are most useful for intermediate to advanced learners, and we suggest that novice learners prepare themselves for success by completing some of the tips in the Learn category first.

Development Activity	Suggested Resource(s) and Tips
Manage your internal thoughts and emotions to feel self-confident.	• Tense and relax your muscles to reduce stress, or try deep breathing. • Think about a time when you were at your most confident meeting with people from another culture. What characteristics of the situation made you feel comfortable? What was your self-talk? What were your feelings? Try to capture those thoughts and feelings in situations where you feel less than confident. • Go into a quiet room. Close your eyes and visualize yourself conducting business with someone from another culture and acting completely self-confident. Repeat this exercise morning and evening for one week. • Ask yourself, if I were my more successful twin who always feels self-confident, what would I do? • Use a mantra that you say over and over to yourself, such as "I can do this." • Monitor your self-talk for negative messages. Replace them with a positive mantra. • Stay up-to-date with your own accomplishments and successes. Remind yourself of these regularly. • Visualize yourself as a confident person.
Manage your behavior to project self-confidence.	• Dress for success; your physical presence is tied to influence. Examine how your most successful colleagues dress and groom themselves in the culture where you are working. Then critically assess how you can improve. • Project self-confidence by standing up straight and generally using open, broad gestures.
Practice being self-confident through rehearsals and experience.	• Prepare yourself to be confident through rehearsals. Practice what you will say or do in the situation you have in mind. Role-play being a confident person. • Volunteer to speak at or host cross-cultural meetings at every opportunity. Eventually, interacting with people from other cultures will become second nature. • Take acting lessons through your local community college, theater, or university to learn how to project confidence through your voice and body language.

DEVELOPMENT SUGGESTIONS
for Self-Confident

COACH OR CONTRIBUTE

Tips to help others learn about and develop this capability. These tips involve coaching and mentoring others. They may include creating information or experiences for individuals, teams, or your organization. These tips are designed for those who are advanced in the capability and are useful development methods to keep advanced leaders in the capability engaged in professional development at the highest level. Please note that the tips in this section may also be quite helpful for individual use if you do not have a coach or mentor.

Development Activity	Suggested Resource(s) and Tips
When coaching direct reports or mentees to build their self-confidence, help them determine how they need to change or develop behaviors and thoughts to become more confident.	<ul><li>Use assessments, like those listed in the Learn sections of this chapter.</li><li>Ask them what it is they believe they need to do to become more confident.</li><li>Style coach them through observations and feedback, giving them your point of view on what they can do to better project self-confidence.</li></ul>
Help your direct reports or mentees recognize their own strengths that they can be proud of, and remind themselves of those strengths to boost their self-confidence.	<ul><li>Ask them to provide you with a résumé that you can use to identify their professional strengths and accomplishments.</li><li>Ask them to create a list of ten to fifteen personal or professional accomplishments they are proud of in the last five years.</li><li>Review the résumé and lists with them, and ask them what behaviors and thoughts they can use from their past successes to help them with their current challenges.</li></ul>
Help your direct reports or mentees change negative or self-defeating thoughts and behaviors by helping them reframe situations where they do not feel confident.	<ul><li>Ask them, what's the worst that can happen in this situation?</li><li>Suggest that they think of others in the room being as nervous as they are.</li><li>Coach them to believe in their ability to get promoted to the highest levels in the organization through positive self-talk.</li><li>Remind them that by pushing themselves to succeed in a few uncomfortable situations, they will quickly build confidence to tackle even greater challenges with ease.</li><li>Ask them to identify three things that they think about themselves that are negative and to reframe them as strengths.</li></ul>

SELF-ASSURANCE

Additional Reading

The readings listed here provide you with additional study of the Global Mindset capability in this section. You will find that many of these resources provide you with a specific and detailed look at using this capability in either a particular context or location.

....

Title: "Being Global: How to Think, Act, and Lead in a Transformed World"

Publication: *Harvard Business Review Press*

Date: 2012

Authors: Angel Cabrera and Gregory Unruh

Executive Summary: In "Being Global," Cabrera and Unruh define a new context for global leadership, vividly illustrating both the challenges and the opportunities facing today's executives. How can you be effective? What new skills must you learn in order to be successful? What do international teams do to stay connected while still producing results on a regional scale? "Being Global" is written for leaders at all levels of their careers—whether in big business; small, private sector; or government—who aspire to think and act globally and who need some help getting there. Being a global citizen is just the starting point. Cabrera and Unruh provide the tools and guidance to help you develop even deeper leadership skills, to benefit both you and your organization.

....

Title: "Developing Your Global Know-How"

Publication: *Harvard Business Review*

Date: 2012

Author: Keumyong Chung

Executive Summary: For up-and-coming executives, an overseas posting has long been a rite of passage, providing opportunities not available in their native countries and experience that can be invaluable to their companies both during the assignment and after their return home. How has the Great Recession affected this formula? *Harvard Business Review* spoke with the top human resources executives at four multinationals about how their companies are adapting global assignments to meet the demands of a changing world.

Title: "Expatriate Selection: Evaluating the Discriminant, Convergent, and Predictive Validity of Five Measures of Interpersonal and Intercultural Competence"

Publication: *Journal of Leadership & Organizational Studies*

Date: 2004

Authors: Andrea Graf and Lynn K. Harland

Executive Summary: Effective screening and selection of expatriates is a critical function in organizations, yet the use of paper-and-pencil instruments in expatriate selection is limited by the paucity of existing validity evidence. This study assessed the discriminant, convergent, and predictive validity of two Intercultural Competence measures (the Behavioral Assessment Scale for Intercultural Communication Effectiveness and the Intercultural Sensitivity Scale) and three Interpersonal Competence measures (the Interpersonal Competence Questionnaire, the Social Problem-Solving Inventory-Revised: Short Version, and the Self-Monitoring Scale).

Title: "In Search of Global Leaders"

Publication: *Harvard Business Review*

Date: 2003

Author: Daniel Meiland

Executive Summary: For all the talk about global organizations and executives, there's no definitive answer to the question of what we really mean by *global*. A presence in multiple countries? Cultural adaptability? A multilingual top team? We asked four CEOs and the head of an international recruiting agency—HSBC's Stephen Green, Schering-Plough's Fred Hassan, GE's Jeffrey Immelt, Flextronics's Michael Marks, and Egon Zehnder's Daniel Meiland—to tell us what they think. They share some common ground. They all agree, for example, that the shift from a local to a global marketplace is irreversible and gaining momentum. "We're losing sight of the reality of globalization. But we should pay attention, because national barriers are quickly coming down," Daniel Meiland says. "If you look ahead five or ten years, the people with the top jobs in large corporations . . . will be those who have lived in several cultures and who can converse in at least two languages."

SELF-ASSURANCE

Comfortable in Uncomfortable Situations

Think about your past global experience. What comes to mind when you read these words: awkward . . . unpleasant . . . unsettling . . . stressful . . . miserable . . . agonizing . . . intolerable . . . mortifying? Thinking once again about your global experience, what comes to mind when you read these words: assured . . . calm . . . collected . . . composed . . . confident . . . poised . . . serene . . . tranquil . . . suave?

Most likely, you can identify a situation for both word groups. This is because being comfortable in uncomfortable situations is highly subjective. We may define differently what it means to be comfortable and what constitutes an uncomfortable situation. And our definitions of these may change over time and with experience. Those of you who have interacted with children know that a small child may be very uncomfortable in the dark in his own room. There is a thriving business for nightlights as a result. As an adolescent, he may be exhilarated by the surprises to be discovered in dark places. We see similarly thriving businesses in haunted houses and suspense films. That said, we did say these feelings may change over time. They may not. There are adults who still don't want to enter a haunted house or see a suspense film. So while one may become more comfortable with some situations over time, there are also boundaries that need to be identified, recognized, and managed.

Boundaries are an important point of discussion, because your personal preferences will be challenged a lot in global situations. For example, if you do not drink alcohol—whether it be a preference or a strict moral code for you—this will be challenged in several cultures where drinking alcohol is a primary form of socializing during business. In this example, you may find yourself extremely uncomfortable and worried about offending your colleagues and business partners. Cross-cultural guides generally give the advice that it is important to partake in the local customs. So what do you do? This is an example of a boundary that you will maintain. It is not necessary to jeopardize your health or moral codes for the sake of cross-cultural bonding. But the situation must be dealt with with utmost respect. For example, having brushed up on local culture you could tell your host in advance of your visit that you understand that there may be alcohol at business dinners and that you are not able to partake. The advance notice will save your host embarrassment and help them prepare other colleagues to respect your needs.

The tips in this section are designed for you to grow your level of comfort where it is most needed. This may mean that you start with mildly uncomfortable situations and build to increasingly uncomfortable situations. For the more hearty, you may dive right into the tough situations. By stretching yourself continuously and exposing yourself to situations you may not know how to handle, you will discover hidden talents and expand your behavioral repertoire. You'll also gain a firm understanding of your personal limits and boundaries. We provide you with tips on managing those as well.

Comfortable in Uncomfortable Situations in Action

Pat, an English teacher, went to Japan as part of a sister-state teacher exchange program to teach English at a local government's international center.

ŞIRIN Z. KÖPRÜCÜ, MBA
International Business Consultant
StrategicStraits Inc.

Pat, an English teacher, went to Japan as part of a sister-state teacher exchange program to teach English at a local government's international center. She had been told that all workers in Japan have lockers in which they store coats and umbrellas and that these can often be found in a small room out of the way of the main open workspace. On her first day to the office, she was given the office tour, which included seeing the women's locker room. It was much like an American locker room but also had a relaxing area.

During the tour, Pat asked which locker would be hers. The women showing her around giggled and said someone would let her know. During the next few weeks, Pat inquired several times about her assigned locker. Cold weather was approaching, and she wanted to have a place to store her coat and boots. But she got the same answer each time: someone would let her know.

Over time Pat had become uncomfortable asking about her locker, but still wondered which one was hers. She wanted to follow the local protocol of putting her personal items in the right place. Finally, it dawned on her that the laughter could be a form of embarrassment, because there were no lockers available. Pat went into the locker room and surveyed the lockers. Sure enough, there were no available lockers.

Pat knew that continuing to ask would make her colleagues uncomfortable. So to ease her own discomfort with the situation, she decided to bring a tote bag to work each day to be able to tuck her coat and boots neatly under her desk. She and her colleagues never spoke about the lockers again. Everyone was now comfortable.

OSAKA, JAPAN

DEVELOPMENT SUGGESTIONS
for Comfortable in Uncomfortable Situations

LEARN

Tips to learn about and begin developing the capability on your own. These tips involve self-directed learning, including reading, listening, watching, or observing, that you can do on your own at your own pace. They are most useful for novices in the capability, but are helpful for intermediate and advanced learners to keep knowledge current.

Development Activity	Suggested Resource(s) and Tips
Familiarize yourself as much as possible with the environment where you will be presenting or working with others for the first time to create a sense of comfort.	• Do an informal visit of the site or a social visit with colleagues prior to important events or meetings. • Rehearse on-site when possible to gain familiarity.
Determine what it is about the situation that makes you uncomfortable, and prepare for that aspect.	• Think about the uncomfortable situation in-depth, and list all of the things that make you uncomfortable. • Identify resources and support to help you prepare yourself specifically in these areas.
Learn about how to build comfort in uncomfortable situations.	• Read *Think on Your Feet* (Woodall, 2009) to learn how to communicate well in stressful situations. • Read *Change Your Thinking, Change Your Life* (Tracy, 2003) on how to change your thinking to approach situations more confidently. • Read *The Talent Code* (Coyle, 2009) about how to maximize your potential in a variety of situations. • Read *Man's Search for Meaning* (Frankl, 2006), which is an exploration of how a deep sense of purpose can help us through the most difficult situations. In the case of the author, the difficult situations included experiences in Nazi concentration camps. This book has been rated among the most influential books for the last fifty years.
Learn techniques to manage stress and anxiety.	• Read HelpGuide's stress management blog "How to Reduce, Prevent, and Cope with Stress" (www.helpguide.org/mental/stress_management_relief_coping.htm). • Read Mayo Clinic's stress management blog "Stress Basics" (www.mayoclinic.com/health/stress-management/MY00435). • Read Mind Tool's stress management resource guide (www.mindtools.com/smpage.html). • Surf Jordan Friedman's stress reduction tips and videos (www.thestresscoach.com). • Read *Stress Relief Today: 297 Simple Techniques to Manage and Relieve Stress Today* (Jefferson, 2012). • Read *Stress Reduction for Busy People: Finding Peace in an Anxious World* (Groves, 2004).

SELF-ASSURANCE

DEVELOPMENT SUGGESTIONS
for Comfortable in Uncomfortable Situations

CONNECT

Tips to learn about and continue developing the capability through others. These tips involve working with another person to learn from their experiences. They may involve asking questions, listening to and discussing experiences, forming a new relationship, deepening an existing relationship, or receiving feedback from someone who is acting as your mentor. These tips are useful for all levels of learners.

Development Activity	Suggested Resource(s) and Tips
Learn about the people involved in an uncomfortable situation in advance when possible.	• Before important meetings or presentations, ask for the biographies of the people involved. • When you are leading a session, distribute biographies when possible. • When time allows, ask people to introduce themselves at the start of small-sized sessions.
Build relationships with colleagues prior to needing to work closely with them on a project to build comfort with them.	• Invite your colleagues to one-on-one lunch sessions or to go for a walk on a break to get to know one another. • Pay attention to connecting with your colleagues from other cultures, as those relationships can sometimes take longer to build. • Call your colleagues with expertise in areas you are working on to ask them for their insight and advice. Many people will take this as a compliment, and you will gain richer understanding of the issue.
Engage someone around you that you ordinarily pass by in conversation to build comfort speaking with new people.	• Talk to taxi drivers, maintenance personnel, janitors, administrative staff, and service professionals.

DEVELOPMENT SUGGESTIONS
for Comfortable in Uncomfortable Situations

EXPERIENCE

Tips to learn about and develop skills in the capability through firsthand experience. These tips involve engaging in activities, such as exploring a new area, trying a new cultural activity, or participating in a specific business event. These tips are most useful for intermediate to advanced learners, and we suggest that novice learners prepare themselves for success by completing some of the tips in the Learn category first.

Development Activity	Suggested Resource(s) and Tips
Manage your thoughts and emotions before and during an uncomfortable experience to reduce your anxiety and maintain your focus on a successful outcome.	• Before and during an uncomfortable global situation, use positive self-talk. Positive self-talk includes any statements that you use to coach yourself through an uncomfortable situation with more ease. For example, you may say, "This is an interesting experience for me. When I get through this, I'm going to share this as a funny story with my friends." • Think back to a time when you were in a similarly uncomfortable situation, and adopt strategies you used well then for your current situation. • Remind yourself why you are in the uncomfortable situation, and focus on your desired goal or outcome to stay motivated.
Prepare as thoroughly as possible before entering into the uncomfortable situation to manage your behavior while you are in it.	• Conduct a thorough risk assessment beforehand, identifying both realistic and unrealistic concerns. Then take the steps you can take to mitigate the risks. • Rehearse whatever you will be doing in an uncomfortable situation in a safe environment first. • Identify what success requires for you in your uncomfortable situation, and take steps to achieve it. • Do scenario planning (i.e., what will you say or do if certain events occur?).
Take steps to actively manage the uncomfortable situation while you are in it.	• When possible, break the uncomfortable situation into smaller, more manageable pieces by scheduling shorter but more frequent interactions. • Introduce yourself and others using credentials. Using credentials in first meetings can be helpful to establish credibility, especially in situations where you need to enlist the support or following of others. This also shows respect for those whom you are introducing. • In a group setting, speak early to reinforce your value and acceptance of ideas.

SELF-ASSURANCE

DEVELOPMENT SUGGESTIONS
for Comfortable in Uncomfortable Situations

EXPERIENCE

Tips to learn about and develop skills in the capability through firsthand experience. These tips involve engaging in activities, such as exploring a new area, trying a new cultural activity, or participating in a specific business event. These tips are most useful for intermediate to advanced learners, and we suggest that novice learners prepare themselves for success by completing some of the tips in the Learn category first.

Development Activity	Suggested Resource(s) and Tips
Practice engaging in uncomfortable situations for you to build your comfort and success strategies.	• Engage people who you would usually not have a conversation with (e.g., taxi driver, elevator operator, maintenance person, person sharing an elevator with you) to practice making conversation when it may feel awkward. • Try new activities and experiences that are out of your comfort zone (e.g., new sports, different foods, new film genres, friendships with different types of people, new cities). • Complete an international corporate volunteering experience to experience a new location or culture, such as those offered by World Action Teams (www.worldactionteams.com).
Complete a stress-reduction workshop to help you learn how to manage stress in uncomfortable situations.	• Jordan Friedman specializes in stress reduction workshops (www.thestresscoach.com). • Clarity Seminars offers stress, resiliency, and leadership training (www.clarityseminars.com).

DEVELOPMENT SUGGESTIONS
for Comfortable in Uncomfortable Situations

COACH OR CONTRIBUTE

Tips to help others learn about and develop this capability. These tips involve coaching and mentoring others. They may include creating information or experiences for individuals, teams, or your organization. These tips are designed for those who are advanced in the capability and are useful development methods to keep advanced leaders in the capability engaged in professional development at the highest level. Please note that the tips in this section may also be quite helpful for individual use if you do not have a coach or mentor.

Development Activity	Suggested Resource(s) and Tips
When coaching direct reports or mentees, help them mentally prepare for uncomfortable situations they will be facing.	Ask them to do the following: • Think about how they typically react to uncomfortable situations. What do they need to become comfortable? • Identify ways they best cope with stress and anxiety, and incorporate those techniques. • Think about an activity they are already enthusiastic about. What do they enjoy about that activity that they may be able to transfer to this new situation? • Describe what makes you uncomfortable about the situation. • Generate two to three strategies to minimize the discomfort.
When coaching direct reports or mentees, support them through uncomfortable situations.	Ask them to do the following: • Keep a journal of their experiences and feelings. • Remember why they are entering into this uncomfortable situation. Focus on the goal. • Identify their accomplishments and successes. Remind themselves of these and how they achieved them to maintain motivation. • Discuss their experiences and feelings after the uncomfortable situation to identify success strategies for the future.

SELF-ASSURANCE

Additional Reading

The readings listed here provide you with additional study of the Global Mindset capability in this section. You will find that many of these resources provide you with a specific and detailed look at using this capability in either a particular context or location.

....

Title: "Being Global: How to Think, Act, and Lead in a Transformed World"

Publication: *Harvard Business Review Press*

Date: 2012

Authors: Angel Cabrera and Gregory Unruh

Executive Summary: In "Being Global," Cabrera and Unruh define a new context for global leadership, vividly illustrating both the challenges and the opportunities facing today's executives. How can you be effective? What new skills must you learn in order to be successful? What do international teams do to stay connected while still producing results on a regional scale? "Being Global" is written for leaders at all levels of their careers—whether in big business; small, private sector; or government—who aspire to think and act globally and who need some help getting there. Being a global citizen is just the starting point. Cabrera and Unruh provide the tools and guidance to help you develop even deeper leadership skills to benefit both you and your organization.

....

Title: "Developing Your Global Know-How"

Publication: *Harvard Business Review*

Date: 2012

Author: Keumyong Chung

Executive Summary: For up-and-coming executives, an overseas posting has long been a rite of passage, providing opportunities not available in their native countries and experience that can be invaluable to their companies both during the assignment and after their return home. How has the Great Recession affected this formula? *Harvard Business Review* spoke with the top human resources executives at four multinationals about how their companies are adapting global assignments to meet the demands of a changing world.

GLOBAL PSYCHOLOGICAL CAPITAL

Title: "Expatriate Selection: Evaluating the Discriminant, Convergent, and Predictive Validity of Five Measures of Interpersonal and Intercultural Competence"

Publication: *Journal of Leadership & Organizational Studies*

Date: 2004

Authors: Andrea Graf and Lynn K. Harland

Executive Summary: Effective screening and selection of expatriates is a critical function in organizations, yet the use of paper-and-pencil instruments in expatriate selection is limited by the paucity of existing validity evidence. This study assessed the discriminant, convergent, and predictive validity of two Intercultural Competence measures (the Behavioral Assessment Scale for Intercultural Communication Effectiveness and the Intercultural Sensitivity Scale) and three Interpersonal Competence measures (the Interpersonal Competence Questionnaire, the Social Problem-Solving Inventory-Revised: Short Version, and the Self-Monitoring Scale).

Title: "In Search of Global Leaders"

Publication: *Harvard Business Review*

Date: 2003

Author: Daniel Meiland

Executive Summary: For all the talk about global organizations and executives, there's no definitive answer to the question of what we really mean by *global*. A presence in multiple countries? Cultural adaptability? A multilingual top team? We asked four CEOs and the head of an international recruiting agency—HSBC's Stephen Green, Schering-Plough's Fred Hassan, GE's Jeffrey Immelt, Flextronics's Michael Marks, and Egon Zehnder's Daniel Meiland—to tell us what they think. They share some common ground. They all agree, for example, that the shift from a local to a global marketplace is irreversible and gaining momentum. "We're losing sight of the reality of globalization. But we should pay attention, because national barriers are quickly coming down," Daniel Meiland says. "If you look ahead five or ten years, the people with the top jobs in large corporations . . . will be those who have lived in several cultures and who can converse in at least two languages."

COLLEAGUES SHARING A LAUGH

Witty in Tough Situations

We've all been in this situation: tension is building in a team meeting and at any moment tempers are likely to be lost. Suddenly, a team member makes a witty comment, everyone laughs, and the tension is broken. This happened recently with one of our colleagues during a trip to Peru. She had stepped out of a long meeting to grab a quick coffee. There were several restaurants nearby, so she thought she would only be gone for five minutes. But she didn't return for thirty minutes.

Her colleagues were worried and a bit perturbed that they had to wait on her for such a long time. When she returned with her coffee in hand, she was clearly frustrated and embarrassed to have been gone so long. She proceeded to explain that she found a restaurant that served coffee nearby, and she was thrilled to see that there were no customers waiting. She went to order her coffee at the counter, but was told she needed to go to the order window. She went to the next window and waited several minutes for someone to take her order. She was then given a ticket for another window where she was to pay. She proceeded to that window and waited several more minutes to pay for her drink. She was then directed to a third window to pick up her drink, where she again waited. Finally, when her long-awaited coffee was served, she asked for a lid and was directed to a fourth window where they served condiments and to-go containers.

While sharing her experience, she was clearly agitated and confused about the system. She told her Peruvian colleagues, "I do not understand why one must stand in four lines to get a simple cup of coffee in this country," to which a Peruvian colleague replied, "Well, our coffee is exceptionally good!" This had everyone laughing, and the tension was quickly dissipated. Her Peruvian colleague could have become offended by the insinuation that Peruvian service was poor and unnecessarily complicated. Instead, he made light of the situation in a way that both his Peruvian and foreign colleagues could appreciate.

What does it mean to be witty? According to Merriam-Webster dictionary, a witty person is "quick or ready to see or express illuminating or amusing relationships or insight." So while it does tend to have a lot to do with humor, it may also describe someone who points out interesting relationships between information. While being witty may involve humor or insight or both, it will always involve quick thinking combined with the ability to make connections between information and experiences.

This quality is particularly important in a global leader because cross-cultural interactions can sometimes be stressful, confusing, or frustrating. There is a caveat about being witty, however. One must understand the cultural dos and don'ts before trying to be witty in public. For instance, there are several enormously popular American comedians who use profanity, vulgarity, and political slander in their humor with great reception. These are inappropriate for the workplace generally, but also quite taboo in some other cultures. The risks are not just tied to reception; they may indeed cause legal or political problems. So be sure that you understand the culture well enough to know what is appropriate and what is inappropriate humor. You may want to test your witty comments on trusted local friends first. When in doubt, it's better to be quiet than to offend. For an entertaining look at a joke failing in a cross-cultural situation, watch this video of an Australian newscaster making a joke to the Dalai Lama during an interview (http://youtube/xlIrI80og8c).

Witty in Tough Situations in Action

A large American corporation was pursuing market opportunities in the Middle East. They had identified a Middle Eastern company as a potential customer.

MANSOUR JAVIDAN, PH.D.
Director of Najafi Global Mindset Institute
& Garvin Distinguished Professor

A large American corporation was pursuing market opportunities in the Middle East. They had identified a Middle Eastern company as a potential customer. The CEO set up an experienced team of executives to travel to the Middle Eastern country to start the process of negotiations with their counterparts. The team was headed by a senior American executive with years of experience in that region. We'll call him Joe. I was asked to join the negotiating team as an advisor.

Our first day of the visit went well, mostly socializing, exchanging gifts, and sharing basic factual information about the two companies and their broad strategies. The second day was the start of the more serious and detailed negotiations. Right after an early breakfast, we started the meeting with our counterpart team. After a smooth first hour, we realized the head of the counterpart team, Sam, was a very tough negotiator. His body language and his reaction to almost all of our ideas were negative and disinterested. By around 11 a.m., he seemed agitated and two of our team members were also visibly frustrated. The problem was not that they disagreed with our ideas. The problem was that they were not offering any alternatives or suggestions. They were just being obstinate. Tensions were high.

During the break, the head of our team and I had a brief chat. After the break, the head of our team, Joe, pleasantly made a suggestion. He said, "The last time I

OLD CAIRO, EGYPT

Victor V. Hoguns Zhugin / Shutterstock.com

was in this city, I had dinner at a very beautiful restaurant with magnificent views of the water. We started breakfast early today, and I am very hungry now. Our team would like to invite your team to lunch, and please invite any other colleagues you wish to join us."

The counterpart team was a bit surprised. They were not used to lunch at 11 a.m., and the cordial invitation was unexpected given the tension in the room. They were hesitating. Joe said, "I understand. We don't have to eat lunch immediately. We just love that part of the town, and we can go for a walk and visit the neighborhood as well." They made lunch reservations for 12 p.m. and began a leisurely stroll.

After we sat down, Joe started talking about his family and how he loves hunting and the outdoors. He started talking about his two sons studying at major universities in the United States. He was very cordial and shared several life experiences. The head of the counterpart team started warming up. He found a few common experiences and interests. He was also educated in the United States and shared a few things about his life as a student in the United States. Others started jumping in. We all started sharing and began to have a genuinely good time. We learned about each other's families and lives. By about 4 p.m., we had had a very pleasant lunch. Joe then invited us all to join him on a stroll through the neighborhood followed by some rest time before a 9 p.m. dinner. Because of the relationship building and wittiness that began emerging from the group, dinner that night was also lively. Tensions had dissipated.

At about 11 p.m., Joe, Sam, and I separated from the group for a cup of tea. Joe explained that our objectives were not solely business; we also needed to build long-term personal and business relationships. He asked Sam about his company's real interests and whether they also wanted to build this partnership. Sam replied, "Absolutely." Joe then said, "Okay, now that we have a common interest, how do you suggest we proceed?" Sam made a few suggestions about how to start the negotiations the next day, and we agreed. There was a big change of attitude and approach the next day. As an experienced global negotiator, Joe's ability to change course and move the process in a different direction were critical in saving the project.

DEVELOPMENT SUGGESTIONS
for Witty in Tough Situations

LEARN

Tips to learn about and begin developing the capability on your own. These tips involve self-directed learning, including reading, listening, watching, or observing, that you can do on your own at your own pace. They are most useful for novices in the capability, but are helpful for intermediate and advanced learners to keep knowledge current.

Development Activity	Suggested Resource(s) and Tips
Learn what humor means in your culture of interest. Note: Studies on cross-cultural humor consistently show that humor varies quite widely between cultures, so it is best to specifically examine it in the culture of interest rather than trying to find generalizations across cultures. However, you may find *Laughlab: The Scientific Quest for the World's Funniest Joke* (The British Association for the Advancement of Science, 2002) interesting. It discusses a scientific experiment to identify the funniest joke across cultures and the findings. It also has a website with the final report and the full list of jokes used in the study (www.laughlab.co.uk).	• Start by reflecting on what humor means and looks like in your own culture, so you can become aware of your current understanding of humor and how you use it. This understanding will help you determine how to modify your use of humor once you understand humor in the local culture. • Since humor is often tied to culture and history, make sure you develop a strong cosmopolitan outlook for the culture you are in by using the development tips in that chapter. This will help you understand what may or may not be funny in the local culture. • Watch local television programs, especially variety shows, to determine what is considered funny. • Ask local colleagues for recommendations on famous comedians in the culture. Watch their programs or performances to determine what are the characteristics of a funny person in this culture. • Observe local colleagues' interactions to see what they find humorous and how they react. For instance, some cultures frown on loud laughter in public. • Look for topics that are not taken lightly in the culture. It is usually wise to avoid humor about religion, race, politics, and sex or sexuality. Sarcasm is also problematic in many cultures. • Observe masters of ceremony at social events in the local culture to see how they use humor to liven up social events. • Read about the characteristics of humorous people in your culture of interest. • Instead of relying on your own translation of humor into the local culture, try to write down or memorize humorous comments or jokes you have heard go over well in that culture for your own future use.

DEVELOPMENT SUGGESTIONS
for Witty in Tough Situations

LEARN

Tips to learn about and begin developing the capability on your own. These tips involve self-directed learning, including reading, listening, watching, or observing, that you can do on your own at your own pace. They are most useful for novices in the capability, but are helpful for intermediate and advanced learners to keep knowledge current.

Development Activity	Suggested Resource(s) and Tips
Learn about the link between emotional intelligence and humor.	• Dr. Paul McGhee specializes in researching and writing about humor. You can read his article on the link between humor and emotional intelligence (www.laughterremedy.com/article_pdfs/Emotional%20Intelligence.pdf). • You can read more articles and research on humor by Dr. McGhee at the Laughter Remedy website (www.laughterremedy.com). There is a specific section on using humor in the workplace. • Read "Relating Sense of Humor to the Five Factor Theory Personality Domains and Facets" (Johnson and McCord, 2010) (http://paws.wcu.edu/mccord/pdf/Johnson-McCord-AJPR-2010.pdf).

DEVELOPMENT SUGGESTIONS
for Witty in Tough Situations

CONNECT

Tips to learn about and continue developing the capability through others. These tips involve working with another person to learn from their experiences. They may involve asking questions, listening to and discussing experiences, forming a new relationship, deepening an existing relationship, or receiving feedback from someone who is acting as your mentor. These tips are useful for all levels of learners.

Development Activity	Suggested Resource(s) and Tips
During tough situations, ask your local colleagues for their perspectives on the situation. This may result in one of them using wit to break the tension, which you can learn from. It will also help you understand the local point of view on the situation.	Ask your colleagues: • What is going on from your perspective? • If tension is identified, ask why there is tension. • How can this tension be resolved? • Is there anything interesting or funny in this situation from your perspective?

DEVELOPMENT SUGGESTIONS
for Witty in Tough Situations

CONNECT

Tips to learn about and continue developing the capability through others. These tips involve working with another person to learn from their experiences. They may involve asking questions, listening to and discussing experiences, forming a new relationship, deepening an existing relationship, or receiving feedback from someone who is acting as your mentor. These tips are useful for all levels of learners.

Development Activity	Suggested Resource(s) and Tips
Look for and build humor into your social network.	• Link up with funny colleagues on your various social networks. • Ask your current colleagues in that culture who the funniest or most popular people are that they know. Link up with those people. • Ask your colleagues from other parts of the world to explain what humor means to them and how it is used in their country. Also, ask what topics and behaviors to avoid when being humorous. • Subscribe to news feeds from local comedians. • Watch for humorous posts from your colleagues in other cultures to see what they find funny.

DEVELOPMENT SUGGESTIONS
for Witty in Tough Situations

EXPERIENCE

Tips to learn about and develop skills in the capability through firsthand experience. These tips involve engaging in activities, such as exploring a new area, trying a new cultural activity, or participating in a specific business event. These tips are most useful for intermediate to advanced learners, and we suggest that novice learners prepare themselves for success by completing some of the tips in the Learn category first.

Development Activity	Suggested Resource(s) and Tips
Prepare your thoughts and emotions before going into a tough situation to put it in perspective.	• Imagine you are in the tough situation already. Rather than dwelling on the negative aspects of the experience, think about what you can learn from it and how you can turn it into a funny story that you can subsequently relate to your friends. • Do or read something every day that makes you smile and lightens your mood, such as comics, cartoons, news parodies, or comedy videos on the Internet. Share it with others, as appropriate.

DEVELOPMENT SUGGESTIONS
for Witty in Tough Situations

EXPERIENCE

Tips to learn about and develop skills in the capability through firsthand experience. These tips involve engaging in activities, such as exploring a new area, trying a new cultural activity, or participating in a specific business event. These tips are most useful for intermediate to advanced learners, and we suggest that novice learners prepare themselves for success by completing some of the tips in the Learn category first.

Development Activity	Suggested Resource(s) and Tips
Manage your behavior while you are in a tough situation.	• Don't take yourself too seriously, and cultivate the ability to laugh at yourself. For example, if you are at a serious company meeting and you trip and fall, laugh at yourself. This will ease the tension, and others will laugh with you. • If culturally appropriate, smile to show warmth and friendliness to break tensions. • If you make a witty comment or tell a joke and it is not received well, quickly and sincerely apologize.
Take an improvisation or acting class to learn how to respond quickly and in witty ways to others' actions.	• Find an acting or improv class at your local university or community college. • Inquire about classes or workshops at your local community theater, comedy club, or improv theater.

DEVELOPMENT SUGGESTIONS
for Witty in Tough Situations

COACH OR CONTRIBUTE

Tips to help others learn about and develop this capability. These tips involve coaching and mentoring others. They may include creating information or experiences for individuals, teams, or your organization. These tips are designed for those who are advanced in the capability and are useful development methods to keep advanced leaders in the capability engaged in professional development at the highest level. Please note that the tips in this section may also be quite helpful for individual use if you do not have a coach or mentor.

Development Activity	Suggested Resource(s) and Tips
When hosting a team meeting or event where there are several cultures involved, incorporate humor from all cultures involved.	• Invite each person to submit one or more jokes that are funny in their culture that are also appropriate for the workplace. Share them throughout the event for entertainment purposes. This will help the team learn about what is humorous to their colleagues as well.

SELF-ASSURANCE

DEVELOPMENT SUGGESTIONS
for Witty in Tough Situations

COACH OR CONTRIBUTE

Tips to help others learn about and develop this capability. These tips involve coaching and mentoring others. They may include creating information or experiences for individuals, teams, or your organization. These tips are designed for those who are advanced in the capability and are useful development methods to keep advanced leaders in the capability engaged in professional development at the highest level. Please note that the tips in this section may also be quite helpful for individual use if you do not have a coach or mentor.

Development Activity	Suggested Resource(s) and Tips
When coaching direct reports or mentees on how to be witty in a tough situation, ask them open-ended coaching questions to get them to generate witty responses.	Ask them: • What is a metaphor you could compare this situation to? • What is something surprising or unexpected in this situation? • What would be a miracle that would transform this tough situation or resolve it? • What is it about this situation that your colleagues might find funny? • What are elements of this situation that your colleagues will not find funny and should be treated seriously? • What is the up side (i.e., something positive) about this situation? • How will this situation better prepare you and your colleagues? • What artifacts from the situation may be funny reminders of what has happened?

Additional Reading

The readings listed here provide you with additional study of the Global Mindset capability in this section. You will find that many of these resources provide you with a specific and detailed look at using this capability in either a particular context or location.

....

Title: "Being Global: How to Think, Act, and Lead in a Transformed World"

Publication: *Harvard Business Review Press*

Date: 2012

Authors: Angel Cabrera and Gregory Unruh

Executive Summary: In "Being Global," Cabrera and Unruh define a new context for global leadership, vividly illustrating both the challenges and the opportunities facing today's executives. How can you be effective? What new skills must you learn in order to be successful? What do international teams do to stay connected while still producing results on a regional scale? "Being Global" is written for leaders at all levels of their careers—whether in big business; small, private sector; or government—who aspire to think and act globally and who need some help getting there. Being a global citizen is just the starting point. Cabrera and Unruh provide the tools and guidance to help you develop even deeper leadership skills to benefit both you and your organization.

....

Title: "Developing Your Global Know-How"

Publication: *Harvard Business Review*

Date: 2012

Author: Keumyong Chung

Executive Summary: For up-and-coming executives, an overseas posting has long been a rite of passage, providing opportunities not available in their native countries and experience that can be invaluable to their companies both during the assignment and after their return home. How has the Great Recession affected this formula? *Harvard Business Review* spoke with the top human resources executives at four multinationals about how their companies are adapting global assignments to meet the demands of a changing world.

Title: "Expatriate Selection: Evaluating the Discriminant, Convergent, and Predictive Validity of Five Measures of Interpersonal and Intercultural Competence"

Publication: *Journal of Leadership & Organizational Studies*

Date: 2004

Authors: Andrea Graf and Lynn K. Harland

Executive Summary: Effective screening and selection of expatriates is a critical function in organizations, yet the use of paper-and-pencil instruments in expatriate selection is limited by the paucity of existing validity evidence. This study assessed the discriminant, convergent, and predictive validity of two Intercultural Competence measures (the Behavioral Assessment Scale for Intercultural Communication Effectiveness and the Intercultural Sensitivity Scale) and three Interpersonal Competence measures (the Interpersonal Competence Questionnaire, the Social Problem-Solving Inventory-Revised: Short Version, and the Self-Monitoring Scale).

Title: "In Search of Global Leaders"

Publication: *Harvard Business Review*

Date: 2003

Author: Daniel Meiland

Executive Summary: For all the talk about global organizations and executives, there's no definitive answer to the question of what we really mean by *global*. A presence in multiple countries? Cultural adaptability? A multilingual top team? We asked four CEOs and the head of an international recruiting agency—HSBC's Stephen Green, Schering-Plough's Fred Hassan, GE's Jeffrey Immelt, Flextronics's Michael Marks, and Egon Zehnder's Daniel Meiland—to tell us what they think. They share some common ground. They all agree, for example, that the shift from a local to a global marketplace is irreversible and gaining momentum. "We're losing sight of the reality of globalization. But we should pay attention, because national barriers are quickly coming down," Daniel Meiland says. "If you look ahead five or ten years, the people with the top jobs in large corporations . . . will be those who have lived in several cultures and who can converse in at least two languages."

COLLEAGUES SOCIALIZING

GLOBAL SOCIAL CAPITAL

7 Intercultural Empathy

8 Interpersonal Impact

9 Diplomacy

We have discussed Global Intellectual Capital and Global Psychological Capital. Global Intellectual Capital is what you know. Global Psychological Capital is your interest in engaging and leveraging what you know. So we've come to the final dimension of Global Mindset: Global Social Capital. It is about your behavioral propensities. These are your dispositions to interact with and build trust with people, especially those who are different from you.

Trust is critical to global work. If two people trust each other, they can work together. It really doesn't matter where they are from. If they trust each other, they interact more easily and get things done. Trust is essentially the lubrication of human relations. However, what trust means to a Chinese manager is not necessarily the same as what trust means to a Russian manager, or what trust means to an American manager. So how you end up trusting a Chinese manager is different from how you end up trusting an American manager. For example, in the Chinese culture, a big part of building trust is personal relationship: how much you socialize and how much you spend time together outside of work. In the US setting, trust is much more task-oriented: we have a task to do, so let's get together and get it done. People may or may not spend much time outside of work together at all. So the way that people in different parts of the world come to trust each other can differ greatly.

The drivers of trust are culture-specific, but the consequences are universal. For example, one of our authors was in a meeting with a group of Taiwanese, Korean, and American managers. The meeting was to discuss ways to improve teamwork within the group. A Taiwanese colleague said to her American colleague, "You know, when you all come to Taiwan to visit us, that is a very big deal to us. So two weeks prior to your arrival, we plan for your arrival. We make sure we are available every night to take you out, to make sure that you have a good time, because that is very important to us. Then you arrive in Taiwan, and you only go out with us for a day or two. After that you say, 'I'm tired. I want to go back to my room, check my emails, and do my work.' It's kind of disappointing." One of the American managers responded by saying, "Yes, you're right. But I'm not used to this. I don't go out with my colleagues every night. I can go out maybe two nights, but then I have other things that I need to do after work."

We see in the example that the whole notion of what it means to build a working relationship is different in the eyes of the Taiwanese colleague compared to the eyes of the American colleague. But they still have to work together. They still have to successfully manage that relationship. This is what Global Social Capital is all about.

As you can see in **Figure 1**, Global Social Capital consists of three main dimensions: intercultural empathy, interpersonal impact, and diplomacy. We'll provide you with a variety of useful tips to develop each.

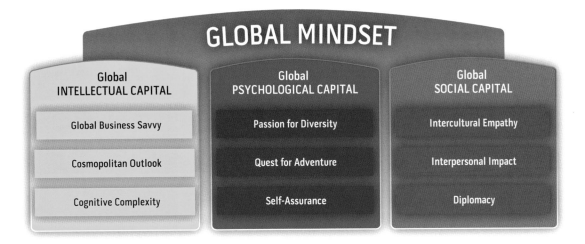

Figure 1

GLOBAL MINDSET

Global INTELLECTUAL CAPITAL

Global Business Savvy

Knowledge of global industry

Knowledge of global competitive business and marketing strategies

Knowledge of how to transact business and assess risks of doing business internationally

Knowledge of supplier options in other parts of the world

Cosmopolitan Outlook

Knowledge of cultures in different parts of the world

Knowledge of geography, history, and important persons of several countries

Knowledge of economic & political issues, concerns, & hot topics of major regions of the world

Up-to-date knowledge of important world events

Cognitive Complexity

Ability to grasp complex topics quickly

Strong analytical and problem solving skills

Ability to understand abstract ideas

Ability to take complex issues and explain the main points simply and understandably

Global PSYCHOLOGICAL CAPITAL

Passion for Diversity

Enjoy exploring other parts of the world

Enjoy getting to know people from other parts of the world

Enjoy living in another country

Enjoy traveling

Quest for Adventure

Interest in dealing with challenging situations

Willingness to take risk

Willingness to test one's abilities

Enjoy dealing with unpredictable situations

Self-Assurance

Energetic

Self-confident

Comfortable in uncomfortable situations

Witty in tough situations

Global SOCIAL CAPITAL

Intercultural Empathy

Ability to work well with people from other parts of the world

Ability to understand nonverbal expressions of people from other cultures

Ability to emotionally connect to people from other cultures

Ability to engage people from other parts of the world to work together

Interpersonal Impact

Experience in negotiating contracts/agreements in other cultures

Strong networks with people from other cultures and with influential people

Reputation as a leader

Diplomacy

Ease of starting a conversation with a stranger

Ability to integrate diverse perspectives

Ability to listen to what others have to say

Willingness to collaborate

Figure 7-1

DEVELOPING YOUR GLOBAL MINDSET

Intercultural Empathy

As shown in **Figure 7-1** on page 372, this chapter examines Intercultural Empathy, which is a key dimension of Global Social Capital. Intercultural empathy refers to how well you are able to emotionally connect with someone who comes from another part of the world. This takes the concept of a working relationship to a deeper level. We aren't just talking about transactional relationships where we do something for you and you do something for us in exchange. That may not require much personal connection at all, and as a result, when the tasks get really tough or inconvenient we may find that you are no longer willing to partner with us. You don't feel any compelling reason.

If we really want to have influence, where we can forge deep relationships that compel others to work with us on an ongoing basis, we have to focus on making real connections with others. This means we need to be good working partners ourselves. We have to have the ability to work well with others: to make contributions to the team, to show respect to each of our team members, and to follow through on our commitments. This sets a firm foundation for working relationships, but to reach the level of influence, we need to move beyond a focus on our personal working behaviors to a genuine interest in others. This means forming emotional connections with others (e.g., shared interests, common objectives), communicating effectively across cultures, and successfully engaging others to work together in the context of a team.

You may be very skilled at all of these behaviors in your own culture, but it can become a bit more tricky in cross-cultural situations. This is because these behaviors can look very different than what you are used to. For example, one of the authors was working with the management team of a Canadian company to discuss the Middle Eastern oil markets and Arab culture. They were thinking of investing in the oil industry in that part of the world and wanted to deepen their understanding of the culture. During the presentation, one of the Canadian managers raised a question about his confusion of nonverbal behavior that he had experienced in the region. He said, "When I'm in the Middle East meeting with some government officials or senior executives in Arab corporations, sometimes these individuals hold my hand. We walk and talk, but that person is holding my hand. I'm uncomfortable about that. Why do they hold my hand?"

In Canadian culture, it is not common for men to be seen holding hands unless they are a couple. In the Arab culture, a man holding another man's hand is common and is a sign of deep trust and friendship. This Canadian manager didn't understand that and was reluctant to ask his Arab colleagues about why they held hands. So he continued to feel uncomfortable during his visit to the region. Had he known that his colleague was holding his hand to show friendship and trust, he would have realized it was an important part of relationship building there. It is a way of emotionally connecting with another person. It may have still felt out of place for him from his own cultural reference, but he would have understood it.

In this chapter, we will provide you with tips to deepen your intercultural empathy in the following areas:

- ability to work well with people from other parts of the world

- ability to understand nonverbal expressions of people from other cultures

- ability to emotionally connect to people from other cultures

- ability to engage people from other parts of the world to work together

Ability to Work Well with People from Other Parts of the World

The ability to work well with people from other parts of the world is the foundation for intercultural empathy. It is essentially about personal leadership. Your colleagues need to see and believe that you are a team player. This means that you work well with others by showing them consistent respect and valuing what they bring to the team, both personally and professionally. It also means that you have integrity; you consistently follow through on your commitments and produce quality work. Respect and integrity will set a firm foundation for working relationships.

One of our colleagues once worked with a general manager for an international hotel chain who demonstrated exemplary intercultural empathy. The hotel staff was composed of Chinese, Russian, Mexican, Iranian, and American staff. This manager made a point to learn several phrases in each language to show respect and care for each of his employees. He spent the first hour or so of his day walking the hotel to personally greet each staff member. His greetings were not just in passing, he would actually stop in a room that was being cleaned and help make the bed or stop in the laundry room and fold towels alongside staff. His consistent daily interactions inspired the staff to interact with each other in the same way. While there were many cultural differences among staff members, especially language barriers, the sense of community that this manager built bridged cultures.

Intercultural empathy requires dedicated time and attention to working relationships. While it may seem challenging to take an extra hour during the day to spend time with employees like this manager, the investment of time and personal attention can be both personally and professionally rewarding for you and your entire team.

UNITED NATIONS ORCHESTRA • GENEVA, SWITZERLAND

Martin Good / Shutterstock.com

GLOBAL SOCIAL CAPITAL

Ability to Work Well with People from Other Parts of the World in Action

My global company needed to downsize substantially. Zixin, our Western-educated CEO, divided all employees worldwide into three groups: green, yellow, and red.

KATHERINE JOHNSTON, MBA
Speaker, Author, and Consultant

"My global company needed to downsize substantially. Zixin, our Western-educated CEO, divided all employees worldwide into three groups: green, yellow, and red. Green meant an employee definitely had a job, red definitely did not have a job, and yellow was uncertain. He then communicated the names in each grouping to all employees. Imagine the negative effect this had on all employees, not just the ones in the yellow and red groups. This required damage control.

"Zixin's intentions were good. For many years, many people acknowledged the need for downsizing, but no one, including the previous CEO, was willing to make the unpopular decision. Zixin expected a more positive reaction for finally taking action, especially from his senior management team, which included me. Unfortunately, Zixin's willingness to confront challenges and take risks was offset by an inability to work well with people from other cultures. He didn't really understand how his actions would be perceived in different cultural contexts. Working together, we were able to discuss how communication could be improved the next time such a situation arose, so that all parties felt respected."

* This example was shared with Ms. Johnston by a coaching client.

LONDON, ENGLAND

GLOBAL SOCIAL CAPITAL

QQ7 / Shutterstock.com

DEVELOPMENT SUGGESTIONS
for Ability to Work Well with People from Other Parts of the World

LEARN

Tips to learn about and begin developing the capability on your own. These tips involve self-directed learning, including reading, listening, watching, or observing, that you can do on your own at your own pace. They are most useful for novices in the capability, but are helpful for intermediate and advanced learners to keep knowledge current.

Development Activity	Suggested Resource(s) and Tips
Take assessments that measure your current cross-cultural competence and help you identify where to improve, so you may better work with diverse others.	• The Intercultural Development Inventory measures cross-cultural competence for individuals, groups, and organizations (www.idiinventory.com). • The Intercultural Communication and Collaboration Appraisal measures affective, cognitive, and behavioral aspects of cross-cultural competence (www.gpccolorado.com/intercultural-communication-and-collaboration-appraisal). • The Cultural Intelligence Center offers multiple assessments for cross-cultural competence in a variety of contexts (http://culturalQ.com). • The Cultural Orientations Indicator measures a person's work style preferences against ten dimensions of culture (www.tmcorp.com/Online-Learning/Assessments/Cultural-Orientations-Indicator-COI/56).
Take personality assessments that help you understand your own personal strengths and derailers in working with others.	• Hogan Assessments offers several leadership assessments that describe your behavioral tendencies and predict performance in the workplace (www.hoganassessments.com). • The Myers-Briggs Type Indicator identifies and describes your personality type, including how you interact with others (www.myersbriggs.org).
Read books on how to build cultural intelligence to work more effectively across cultures.	• *Leading with Cultural Intelligence: The New Secret to Success* (Livermore, 2009) includes practical tools, resources, and case studies. • *When Cultures Collide* (Lewis, 2005) examines global business in the context of sixty countries representing all major regions of the world. • *Cultural Intelligence: A Guide for Working with People from Other Cultures* (Peterson, 2004) includes case studies and illustrations to build cultural intelligence.

Watch cross-cultural training videos.	These companies offer previews and videos for purchase on multiple cross-cultural business topics:
	
	  • Aperian Global (e-learning modules) (www.aperianglobal.com)
	
	  • Atma Global (www.atmaglobal.com)
	
	  • Ideas and Training (www.ideasandtraining.com/Global-Business-Training.html)
	
	  • HumaNext (www.humanext.com/cross-cultural-training.html)

INTERCULTURAL EMPATHY

DEVELOPMENT SUGGESTIONS
for Ability to Work Well with People from Other Parts of the World

CONNECT

Tips to learn about and continue developing the capability through others. These tips involve working with another person to learn from their experiences. They may involve asking questions, listening to and discussing experiences, forming a new relationship, deepening an existing relationship, or receiving feedback from someone who is acting as your mentor. These tips are useful for all levels of learners.

Development Activity	Suggested Resource(s) and Tips
Determine what trust means in the culture of interest.	• Closely observe working relationships and team dynamics while you are in that culture. • Ask colleagues, both native locals and expatriates, to describe what it means to work well with people in this culture.
When working on multicultural teams, be inclusive and communicate openly.	• Make sure local employees from the culture are involved in your team and projects. • At the start of a project, openly discuss each person's expectations of how the team should work and communicate with one another. In some cultures, these meetings will best be done one-on-one and then presented by the manager. • During a project, check in periodically on how the team is working together. Find out what is going well and what needs to be improved. • After a project has ended, debrief the experience with the team or with each individual to learn how to make teamwork more productive and enjoyable in the future. • Find a trusted colleague or coach to debrief your experiences, so you can learn from your successes and challenges.

DEVELOPMENT SUGGESTIONS
for Ability to Work Well with People from Other Parts of the World

EXPERIENCE

Tips to learn about and develop skills in the capability through firsthand experience. These tips involve engaging in activities, such as exploring a new area, trying a new cultural activity, or participating in a specific business event. These tips are most useful for intermediate to advanced learners, and we suggest that novice learners prepare themselves for success by completing some of the tips in the Learn category first.

Development Activity	Suggested Resource(s) and Tips
Increase the frequency of your interactions with your colleagues around the world.	• Volunteer to lead global project teams or global meetings/calls. • Call your international colleagues periodically to personally connect with them about their roles and projects. • When working on a project, call your international colleagues to gain their unique perspectives and insights on your work.
Participate in an international volunteer project.	• Participate in a short-term international corporate immersion project led by organizations such as World Action Teams (www.worldactionteams.com). These programs allow you to work in corporate teams to understand regional and local issues firsthand on a team-based project. • Volunteer for a global nongovernmental organization or charity organization. You can find Global Journal's Top 100 Best NGO list (http://theglobaljournal.net/article/view/585). • The Development Studies program at University of Wisconsin-Madison lists major NGOs (http://devstudies.wisc.edu/resources_ngo.html).
Join social and networking groups aimed for globally working employees, and volunteer for a leadership role.	Some networking groups for globally working employees include the following: • InterNations (www.internations.org) • Transitions Abroad (www.transitionsabroad.com) • Escape Artist (www.escapeartist.com) • Expat Exchange (www.expatexchange.com)
Use Second Life to interact with people from other parts of the world.	Second Life (http://secondlife.com) is a website that hosts many live, virtual communities. While much of the website is geared toward social interests, there are virtual communities for businesses as well as international communities.

INTERCULTURAL EMPATHY

DEVELOPMENT SUGGESTIONS
for Ability to Work Well with People from Other Parts of the World

COACH OR CONTRIBUTE

Tips to help others learn about and develop this capability. These tips involve coaching and mentoring others. They may include creating information or experiences for individuals, teams, or your organization. These tips are designed for those who are advanced in the capability and are useful development methods to keep advanced leaders in the capability engaged in professional development at the highest level. Please note that the tips in this section may also be quite helpful for individual use if you do not have a coach or mentor.

Development Activity	Suggested Resource(s) and Tips
When coaching your direct reports or mentees on how to work well with people from other parts of the world, ask open-ended questions to help them identify how they can improve.	• In what ways is working well with your international colleagues critical to your success? How does it factor into your performance review and ultimate success with projects? • Reflecting on your experience working with your international colleagues, what is different about your interactions with them? What is similar? • Identify a time when you worked well with people from other parts of the world. Why and how did this happen? • Identify a time when you did not work well with people from other parts of the world. Why and how did this happen? • What concerns do you have about working with your international colleagues? • What do you enjoy about working with your international colleagues?
When you are coaching less senior or less experienced colleagues in your organization in how they can work well in a global culture, remind them of the behaviors that build and sustain trust.	According to our network of expert international executive coaches, these behaviors build and sustain trust cross-culturally: • Show respect to others as individuals and as representatives of another culture by learning about what respect looks like in their culture and acting appropriately. • Learn about the native cultures of your colleagues by showing interest and asking questions appropriately. • Remain open-minded about how different perspectives and cultural norms among your colleagues add value to the organization and interest to your working relationships. • Find commonalities between you and your colleagues that you can discuss and share. • Spend time with your colleagues to build interests and experiences together. • Ask for feedback about your working relationships with your colleagues. Invite their suggestions for improvement.

Additional Reading

The readings listed here provide you with additional study of the Global Mindset capability in this section. You will find that many of these resources provide you with a specific and detailed look at using this capability in a particular context or location.

....

Title: "Cultural Distance and Expatriate Job Satisfaction"

Publication: *International Journal of Intercultural Relations*

Date: 2011

Authors: Fabian Jintae Froese and Vesa Peltokorpi

Executive Summary: Despite its strong effect in domestic settings on job performance, organizational commitment, stress, and turnover intentions, job satisfaction has received little attention in the literature on expatriates. This paper analyzes the predictors of job satisfaction that may arise in an expatriate context.

....

Title: "Cross Culture Analysis: An Exploratory Analysis of Experiential Narratives and Implications for Management"

Publication: *Interdisciplinary Journal of Contemporary Research in Business*

Date: 2011

Authors: Shahzad Ghafoor, Fukaiha Kaka Khail, Uzair Farooq Khan, and Faiza Hassan

Executive Summary: Mergers, acquisitions, joint ventures, and numerous forms of partnerships have necessitated the intercourse between people of diverse cultural backgrounds in the same workplace. This has ultimately contributed to a considerable interest in the subject of cross-cultural learning. However, most studies in this area, though scanty, have addressed this subject from the organizational point of view. Thus, this study explores the area of cross-cultural learning from the perspective of the individual employee.

INTERCULTURAL EMPATHY

Title: "The Role of Communication Competencies in International Business Relationship Development"

Publication: *Journal of World Business*

Date: 2002

Author: David A. Griffith

Executive Summary: Effective communication between international business partners is critical for global success. Underlying national and organizational cultural differences in international business relationships creates hurdles to effective communication, hindering performance. To assist managers in understanding this issue, a model of communication effectiveness for international relationship development, derived from industry examples, theory, and a dataset consisting of 123 qualitative interviews conducted with American, Canadian, Chinese, and Japanese managers is presented. Further, in order to assist managers in the task of developing more effective communications, a six-step process aimed in directing managerial action is presented. By proactively managing its communications, a firm can develop stronger international business relationships facilitating the rapid response to market opportunities and challenges.

Title: "Making It Overseas"

Publication: *Harvard Business Review*

Date: 2010

Authors: Mansour Javidan, Mary Teagarden, and David Bowen

Executive Summary: The article presents two scenarios in which executives are employed overseas and focuses on the characteristics and skills needed to be an effective manager in a foreign country. The idea that successful leaders have a Global Mindset that is based on intellectual, psychological, and Global Social Capital is discussed. The article mentions how to take the Global Mindset Inventory and evaluate one's ability to be a business leader in a culturally different environment. A strategy is explained for creating a plan that will develop the three types of capital and nine attributes that define global leaders.

Title: "Developing International Executives: The Capacity-Building Approach"

Publication: *Development and Learning in Organizations*

Date: 2011

Authors: Anas Khan, Riad Khan, and Mohammad Habibur Rahman

Executive Summary: The purpose of this paper is to outline the development steps that should be undertaken by any executives who are to be sent on an expatriate assignment to take the lead in a foreign subsidiary location. It highlights the need to develop an understanding of the host country's business practices, cultural preferences, and operational methods.

Title: "Business Leaders as Citizens of the World: Advancing Humanism on a Global Scale"

Publication: *Journal of Business Ethics*

Date: 2009

Authors: Thomas Maak and Nicola Pless

Executive Summary: As the world is getting increasingly connected and interdependent, it becomes clear that the world's most pressing public problems such as poverty or global warming call for cross-sector solutions. The paper discusses the idea of business leaders acting as agents of world benefit, taking an active co-responsibility in generating solutions to problems. It argues that we need responsible global leaders who are aware of the pressing problems in the world, care for the needs of others, aspire to make this world a better place, and act in word and deed as global and responsible citizens.

Title: "Navigating Expatriate Leaders' Competencies"

Publication: *Leader to Leader*

Date: 2011

Author: Johnny D. Magwood

Executive Summary: The article focuses on the competencies of expatriate leaders, which are important in recognizing and appreciating the differences between home cultures and various host cultures within the reach of multinational companies (MNCs) through globalization. It states that MNC leaders commonly encounter challenges from stakeholders including suppliers, customers, and competitors, as well as balancing societal requirements and profits. It says that expatriate leaders are also confronted with differences in the workplace related to ethical standards. It discusses steps that should be taken by expatriate leaders in overcoming cultural differences relative to ethical and behavioral standards including establishing an inclusive work environment, understanding, and building ethics and values.

....

Title: "3 Skills Every 21st-Century Manager Needs"

Publication: *Harvard Business Review*

Date: 2012

Authors: Andrew L. Molinsky, Thomas H. Davenport, Bala Iyer, and Cathy Davidson

Executive Summary: Over the past decade, companies have become more global and employee groups more diverse than ever before. Organizations are less hierarchical and more collaborative. And today's offices are full of once unimaginable technological distractions. We asked experts in cross-cultural communication, information networks, and the science of attention what skills executives should cultivate to tackle these new challenges.

....

Title: "Developing Responsible Global Leaders through International Service-Learning Programs: The Ulysses Experience"

Publication: *Academy of Management Learning & Education*

Date: 2011

Authors: Nicola M. Pless, Thomas Maak, and Gunter K. Stahl

Executive Summary: A new challenge in executive education is to develop responsible global business leaders. We describe Project Ulysses, an integrated service-learning program that involves sending participants in teams to developing countries to work in cross-sector partnerships with nongovernmental organizations, social entrepreneurs, or international organizations. To understand how Ulysses participants learn from their experiences while abroad, we interviewed seventy participants and content-analyzed the learning narratives that they produced. We found evidence of learning in six areas: responsible mindset, ethical literacy, cultural intelligence, Global Mindset, self-development, and community building. We also identified a number of processes through which learning occurred at the cognitive, affective, and behavioral levels, including the process of resolving cultural and ethical paradoxes; constructing a new life-world, that is, developing a new perspective of self and the world; and making sense of the emotions experienced while on assignment. The results of a postprogram survey confirm the long-term effectiveness of Ulysses in developing and enhancing competencies that are critical for responsible global leadership.

....

Title:	"Global Leadership Teams: Diagnosing Three Essential Qualities"
Publication:	*Strategy & Leadership*
Date:	2012
Authors:	Robert J. Thomas, Joshua Bellin, Claudy Jules, and Nandani Lynton

Executive Summary: Companies that operate globally have to be adept at managing certain tensions: between global and local, between differentiated and integrated, and between many cultures and one organizational culture. So the authors aim to interview top managers to study how global leadership teams are coping with these challenges.

INTERCULTURAL EMPATHY

NONVERBAL CUES OF BOREDOM

Ability to Understand Nonverbal Expressions of People from Other Cultures

Nonverbal behaviors—body language, facial expressions, eye contact, silence—play a part in all human communication to varying degrees, but what those behaviors communicate across cultures can differ widely. Some cultures rely on body language more heavily than others to get their intended message across. For example, a German manager may be more likely to tell a direct report that she cannot attend a seminar she would like the company to pay for. He simply uses the words, "No, you cannot go." A Japanese manager may smile at the employee and say how nice that seminar sounds without committing to send her. The answer is no in both instances, but the communication of it is very different. In some cultures, what is not said is more important than what is said. The Japanese manager did not say yes, and that was the most important part of the message.

In cross-cultural work environments, the language of shared conversation may not be the native language of everyone involved. This means that nonnative speakers may supplement the language of conversation with nonverbal behavior: shaking or nodding the head, a broad gesture to describe a feeling, or pointing at objects to get the message across. Your ability to understand nonverbal expressions in the cultures in which you are working will help you more quickly understand communications correctly.

INTERCULTURAL EMPATHY

COLLEAGUES ENJOYING WORKING TOGETHER

GLOBAL SOCIAL CAPITAL

Ability to Understand Nonverbal Expressions of People from Other Cultures in Action

I was facilitating a teambuilding and strategic planning retreat for a federal government agency in Washington, DC. All of the participants were American, except for one Korean woman.

ŞIRIN Z. KÖPRÜCÜ, MBA
International Business Consultant
StrategicStraits Inc.

I was facilitating a teambuilding and strategic planning retreat for a federal government agency in Washington, DC. All of the participants were American, except for one Korean woman. As an icebreaker activity, I asked everyone to go around the room and share one thing about themselves that their colleagues didn't know. I had used this activity in past trainings to warm up groups and to emphasize that even when we think we know our coworkers, there is always something new to discover.

Each staff member offered some funny or interesting hobby or experience, until we reached the Korean participant. The Korean participant blushed, put her head down, and quietly said, "I don't have anything." I then (foolishly) replied, "Oh, come on. There has to be something you can share with us!" She kept her eyes on the floor and shook her head. She laughed nervously and said again, "I don't have anything." I kept trying to encourage her to participate. "No hobbies, special interests, surprising stories?" She shook her head, looking like she wanted the floor to swallow her up. So I said, "Okay, we'll come back to you later." And we moved on.

The Korean participant did not speak up in the large group at any time throughout the retreat, and I noticed that she rarely spoke in small group discussions either. Afterward, I wondered what had caused the participant to be so unwilling to participate in the icebreaker. Perhaps she was worried about her English skills or accent? Perhaps, valuing a more collectivist culture, she was not comfortable sharing anything about herself with the large group? Perhaps she was merely uncomfortable being forced to speak up in front of her manager and peers without preparation? Whatever the case, her nonverbal expressions were clearly telling me she was not comfortable participating. As a cross-cultural trainer, I scolded myself for having forced this woman into such an uncomfortable situation.

DEVELOPMENT SUGGESTIONS
for Ability to Understand Nonverbal Expressions of People from Other Cultures

LEARN

Tips to learn about and begin developing the capability on your own. These tips involve self-directed learning, including reading, listening, watching, or observing, that you can do on your own at your own pace. They are most useful for novices in the capability, but are helpful for intermediate and advanced learners to keep knowledge current.

Development Activity	Suggested Resource(s) and Tips
Learn about the general use of nonverbal behaviors in human communication.	Read the following books: • *The Definitive Book of Body Language* (Pease and Pease, 2006) • *What Every Body Is Saying: An Ex-FBI Agent's Guide to Speed-Reading People* (Navarro, 2008) • *The Silent Language of Leaders: How Body Language Can Help—or Hurt—How You Lead* (Goman, 2011)
Learn about cross-cultural communication, including the nonverbal expressions in different cultures.	• Read *Cross-Cultural Dialogues: 74 Brief Encounters with Cultural Difference* (Storti, 1994) to experience cultural differences through dialogues around the world. • Read *Guide to Cross-Cultural Communications* (Reynolds, et al., 2010), which focuses on business communications. • Read *Cross-Cultural Communication: Concepts, Cases, and Challenges* (Norales, 2006). • Use the app "Don't Get Me Wrong" by Judith Reker and Julia Grosse, which shows what different hand gestures mean around the globe.
Watch videos on nonverbal communication in different cultures. Some of these include firsthand descriptions and demonstrations by natives to a particular culture, while others include the experiences of foreigners in specific cultures.	• Watch a movie produced in the culture of interest. • Watch a documentary based in the culture of interest. • Watch native Thai and Filipino descriptions and demonstrations of nonverbal communications in their cultures (www.youtube.com/playlist?list=PL7C37EE2AB2B7A9CB). To find more like these in cultures of interest to you, search for "nonverbal communication" + your country or culture of interest. • The University of California, Berkeley, Media Center offers a series of videos for purchase on nonverbal communication, including several specific to differences across cultures (http://nonverbal.ucsc.edu/order.html).

DEVELOPMENT SUGGESTIONS
for Ability to Understand Nonverbal Expressions of People from Other Cultures

LEARN

Tips to learn about and begin developing the capability on your own. These tips involve self-directed learning, including reading, listening, watching, or observing, that you can do on your own at your own pace. They are most useful for novices in the capability, but are helpful for intermediate and advanced learners to keep knowledge current.

Development Activity	Suggested Resource(s) and Tips
Use a video without the sound to identify nonverbal expressions in a particular culture and discuss their meanings with others from the culture. This can be done with photos as well.	• Watch a movie produced in the culture of interest. • Watch a documentary based in the culture of interest. • Ask your local native colleagues to bring in pictures or video clips (or to demonstrate them personally) of common nonverbal expressions in the local culture.
Watch people who are known to be influential from a specific culture to see how they behave and what expressions they use.	Identify senior people in the organization, politicians, and other famous people from the culture of interest.
Learn about the varying importance and effect of nonverbal expressions by understanding the differences between high-context cultures and low-context cultures. Anthropologist Edward T. Hall originated the concept of high- and low-context cultures, wherein those in high-context cultures place great value on nonverbal expressions (e.g., body language, tone, silence, gestures) and those in low-context cultures more readily accept verbal and written communication at face value.	Read more about this concept and look at examples at ChangingMinds (http://changingminds.org/explanations/culture/hall_culture.htm).

DEVELOPMENT SUGGESTIONS
for Ability to Understand Nonverbal Expressions of People from Other Cultures

CONNECT

Tips to learn about and continue developing the capability through others. These tips involve working with another person to learn from their experiences. They may involve asking questions, listening to and discussing experiences, forming a new relationship, deepening an existing relationship, or receiving feedback from someone who is acting as your mentor. These tips are useful for all levels of learners.

Development Activity	Suggested Resource(s) and Tips
Make learning about nonverbal expressions a fun and interesting part of conversations with international colleagues.	When meeting with someone from another culture, ask them to describe or show you three nonverbal expressions from their culture. Share three of your own.

DEVELOPMENT SUGGESTIONS
for Ability to Understand Nonverbal Expressions of People from Other Cultures

CONNECT

Tips to learn about and continue developing the capability through others. These tips involve working with another person to learn from their experiences. They may involve asking questions, listening to and discussing experiences, forming a new relationship, deepening an existing relationship, or receiving feedback from someone who is acting as your mentor. These tips are useful for all levels of learners.

Development Activity	Suggested Resource(s) and Tips
Keep a cultural journal while you are in another culture to jot down observations and questions to explore further.	• When you observe an unknown nonverbal behavior, make a note to ask a native colleague about its meaning. • Periodically share your experiences and interpretations of those experiences with native colleagues to see if you are interpreting them correctly for the culture.
Seek feedback from a coach or colleague about the cross-cultural interpretations of your nonverbal behaviors.	• Ask a trusted coach or colleague to observe you for a few days and note nonverbal behaviors that may be problematic for the culture. • Have someone videotape you leading a meeting or presenting in another culture. Have your coach or colleague analyze your use of nonverbal behaviors.

DEVELOPMENT SUGGESTIONS
for Ability to Understand Nonverbal Expressions of People from Other Cultures

EXPERIENCE

Tips to learn about and develop skills in the capability through firsthand experience. These tips involve engaging in activities, such as exploring a new area, trying a new cultural activity, or participating in a specific business event. These tips are most useful for intermediate to advanced learners, and we suggest that novice learners prepare themselves for success by completing some of the tips in the Learn category first.

Development Activity	Suggested Resource(s) and Tips
Take advantage of every opportunity to interact face-to-face with your international colleagues, as nonverbal behaviors will add richness to the communication.	• Use Skype (www.skype.com) or other video conferencing software instead of telephone calls. • Plan and attend in-person meetings.
Prior to an international experience, participate in role-play exercises with a cross-cultural coach or a colleague who is native to the culture you'll be visiting to discuss varying meanings of nonverbal behaviors.	Incorporate photo, video, and magazine examples from the culture of interest to reference real-life nonverbal expressions you are likely to encounter.

INTERCULTURAL EMPATHY

DEVELOPMENT SUGGESTIONS
for Ability to Understand Nonverbal Expressions of People from Other Cultures

EXPERIENCE

Tips to learn about and develop skills in the capability through firsthand experience. These tips involve engaging in activities, such as exploring a new area, trying a new cultural activity, or participating in a specific business event. These tips are most useful for intermediate to advanced learners, and we suggest that novice learners prepare themselves for success by completing some of the tips in the Learn category first.

Development Activity	Suggested Resource(s) and Tips
Complete cross-cultural communication activities and role plays to improve your cross-cultural communication.	*52 Activities for Improving Cross-Cultural Communication* (Stringer and Cassiday, 2009) includes many types of activities for you to practice.

DEVELOPMENT SUGGESTIONS
for Ability to Understand Nonverbal Expressions of People from Other Cultures

COACH OR CONTRIBUTE

Tips to help others learn about and develop this capability. These tips involve coaching and mentoring others. They may include creating information or experiences for individuals, teams, or your organization. These tips are designed for those who are advanced in the capability and are useful development methods to keep advanced leaders in the capability engaged in professional development at the highest level. Please note that the tips in this section may also be quite helpful for individual use if you do not have a coach or mentor.

Development Activity	Suggested Resource(s) and Tips
When coaching your direct reports or mentees on how to understand nonverbal expressions of people from other cultures, ask open-ended questions to help them identify how they can improve.	• Considering your last experience in this culture, how much do you feel you understood of the nonverbal communication you received? Why did you feel this way? How can you improve your understanding? • Think of a situation where you successfully interpreted someone's nonverbal expression. What was it? How did you understand it? Then think of the reverse situation. Why didn't you understand it? • What do you do when you don't understand nonverbal behaviors? • What can you do to better understand nonverbal behaviors that you don't readily recognize without making judgments about them?

Additional Reading

The readings listed here provide you with additional study of the Global Mindset capability in this section. You will find that many of these resources provide you with a specific and detailed look at using this capability in a particular context or location.

....

Title: "The Nature of Language and Nonverbal Communication"

Publication: *Communicating Globally: Intercultural Communication and International Business*

Date: 2007

Authors: Roger N. Conaway, Wallace V. Schmidt, Susan S. Easton, and William J. Vardropein

Executive Summary: *Communicating Globally* integrates the theory and skills of intercultural communication with the practices of multinational organizations and international business. Chapter 5 specifically addresses the dimensions and intricacies of nonverbal communication from an intercultural perspective.

....

Title: "24 Business Communication Skills: Attitudes of Human Resource Managers versus Business Educators"

Publication: *American Communication Journal*

Date: 2011

Authors: David Conrad and Robert Newberry

Executive Summary: Several studies reveal that business needs communication skill competency and that business education must be sensitive to and understand the communication skill needs of business. Accordingly, ongoing research is needed to ascertain which specific communication skills business considers important and those college business educators consider important. Pressing beyond previous research, this study compares the communication skills business considered important and those business education considered important. The purpose is to determine if there is agreement or a gap between business and academic professionals regarding the relative importance of communication skills in business.

Title: "The Silent Language of Leaders: How Body Language Can Help—or Hurt—How You Lead"

Publication: *Jossey-Bass*

Date: 2011

Author: Carol Kinsey Goman

Executive Summary: Aspiring and seasoned leaders have been trained to manage their leadership communication in many important ways. And yet, all of their efforts to communicate effectively can be derailed by even the smallest nonverbal gestures such as the way they sit in a business meeting or stand at the lectern at a speaking engagement. In "The Silent Language of Leaders," Goman explains that personal space, physical gestures, posture, facial expressions, and eye contact communicate louder than words and, thus, can be used strategically to help leaders manage, motivate, and lead global teams and communicate clearly in the digital age.

Title: "'Who's There?': Differences in the Features of Telephone and Face-to-Face Conferences"

Publication: *Journal of Business Communication*

Date: 2012

Author: Dorothea Halbe

Executive Summary: A significant part of the work in business settings, especially in multinational projects, is done through talking over the phone in conference calls. The differences in the setting in comparison with face-to-face meetings create a new dynamic of talk and turn-taking because of the lack of body language.

Title:	"The Display of 'Dominant' Nonverbal Cues in Negotiation: The Role of Culture and Gender"
Publication:	*International Negotiation*
Date:	2011
Authors:	Zhaleh Semnani-Azad and Wendi L. Adair

Executive Summary: The current study extends prior negotiation research on culture and verbal behavior by investigating the display of nonverbal behaviors associated with dominance by male and female Canadian and Chinese negotiators. We draw from existing literature on culture, gender, communication, and display rules to predict both culture and gender variation in negotiators' display of three nonverbal behaviors typically associated with dominance: relaxed posture, use of space, and facial display of negative emotion.

COLLEAGUES SHARING A LAUGH

Ability to Emotionally Connect to People from Other Cultures

Emotional connection—these are two words we don't often discuss in the context of the workplace. It is unlikely your organization has a performance rating for how well you emotionally connect with others. However, it is a building block for a number of areas you probably are rated on: how well you work with your colleagues to accomplish tasks; your ability to influence customers, suppliers, and business partners; and a whole host of organizational values, dispositions, and attitudes. It is such an important building block for relationships that a whole field of study has arisen to better understand it. That field is called emotional intelligence and was popularized by Daniel Goleman. To really understand the concept, we have to closely examine what it means to make a connection and how emotions are involved.

A connection is a bond, a link, or a tie to another person. The bond could be over a shared experience where you built trust and have made memories together. The link could be a shared objective, like working on the same team or for the same organization. The tie could be a personal experience or hobby that you may not have shared at the same time but relate to (e.g., having lived in Dubai, a love of soccer). Connection, then, boils down to something you have in common.

Emotions are the glue that keeps two people connected. Surely you can think of an example of a colleague who has something in common with you, yet you don't feel a bond with this person. This is because of the subjective emotions we feel for the other person, despite our common experience. Raphael Cushnir, author of *The One Thing Holding You Back: The Power of Emotional Connection*, describes emotions as "messages from the brain that are delivered to the body." They are subjective feelings of like, dislike, joy, pain, etc.

In the workplace, it is especially important to manage these emotions in a professional way, because we must continue to see and work with colleagues even when we do not have an affinity for one another. If emotions are subjective, is there any hope for a positive emotional connection with that colleague you don't currently have a bond with? Yes, it is possible, but it takes concerted effort. There has to be a motivation to work on the relationship. A shared experience, link, or tie can be a good starting point to build from.

Emotional intelligence is critically important for developing several areas of Global Mindset, including passion for diversity (i.e., enjoy getting to know people from other parts of the world), intercultural empathy, intercultural impact, and diplomacy. This is because anyone who is working to develop his or her Global Mindset is most likely either preparing for or is currently in a role that requires building relationships with others from diverse cultures. Forging and building these relationships require the four types of abilities inherent to emotional intelligence: perceiving emotion, using emotions, understanding emotions, and managing emotions. These abilities allow a person to "monitor one's own and others' feelings and emotions, to discriminate among them and to use this information to guide one's thinking and actions" (Salovey and Mayer, 1990).

Let's consider the example of an American manager who is new to Thai culture and is meeting potential Thai business partners in their native country for the first time. The American manager extends his hand to shake his Thai colleague's hand. His Thai colleague appears surprised, pauses and looks at the manager's extended hand for a moment, and then puts his hands together near his forehead and bows. A person with well-developed emotional intelligence would quickly perceive the surprised facial expression, the pause, and the alternative greeting. This person would use his own emotions, perhaps embarrassment or surprise, to problem-solve the miscommunication while it was happening. This problem solving could be as simple as noting the appropriate greeting and demonstrating it in return. He would understand that the three nonverbal communications he received—a surprised facial expression, a pause, and an alternative greeting—reflected discomfort on the part of his Thai colleague and a desire to provide friendly guidance on the appropriate cultural greeting. The manager would then manage his emotions by remaining cordial and open to adapting to the local culture, rather than becoming frustrated or withdrawing from future interactions. Had the manager had low emotional intelligence, he might have missed or misread the nonverbal communication he received and continued trying to shake his Thai colleague's hand. This small cultural error could have had dire consequences for building business relationships in Thailand. This is because an extended hand in Thai culture means that someone is asking for money. This would certainly be considered very forward for a first introduction to potential business partners. Emotional intelligence allowed this manager to quickly recognize and adapt to the local cultural norms, which is especially important for developing the Global Mindset abilities captured in Global Social Capital.

We'll give you many tips in this chapter to help you build and strengthen emotional connections with diverse others. It is important to remember, though, that while cross-cultural studies have shown that many emotions are universal, their content and manner of expression vary considerably. So it is important not to make assumptions about how well you have bonded with someone from another culture until you have sufficient experience with that person. Relationships are always a work in progress.

INTERCULTURAL EMPATHY

TOKYO, JAPAN

Ability to Emotionally Connect to People from Other Cultures in Action

Emily was a very introverted senior manufacturing director who had difficulty trusting others' motives and often questioned how she would be perceived by senior management.

VALERIE WHITE, PH.D.
Principal
Change Perspectives

Emily was a very introverted senior manufacturing director who had difficulty trusting others' motives and often questioned how she would be perceived by senior management. When she was given the opportunity to co-lead a large facility in Japan, she and her family decided it would be beneficial for her career to have the overseas experience. The plant was struggling, and Emily had the knowledge to turn things around, if she could motivate the workers to make the changes.

Although Emily was well-versed in some of the cultural differences between American and Japanese workers, as her job frequently took her to Japan, she was not fully prepared for what she experienced. Through 360 feedback, Emily learned that the initial impressions she made on the people were not good. She was seen as cold, arrogant, and unapproachable. However, as people got to know her, their impressions of her shifted to that of someone who was open, had a quirky sense of humor, and was very knowledgeable about what needed to be changed. Emily realized that when she let her guard down, people in both the United States and Japan liked and respected her and were comfortable connecting with her as a person.

After several months in Japan, Emily was still puzzled by the fact that she could go out and spend a social evening with her direct reports, learn about their families and issues that night, and then have those topics be completely off-limits the next day at work. However, unlike in the past, she did not take this personally, but rather recognized under what circumstances people would open up to her as well as the appropriate ways that she could open up to them. As she continued to reach out, effectively use her wry humor, and make herself available to her people, her relationships with the workers in the Japanese plant improved. She found that their differences became interesting starting points to further build relationships.

DEVELOPMENT SUGGESTIONS
for Ability to Emotionally Connect to People from Other Cultures

LEARN

Tips to learn about and begin developing the capability on your own. These tips involve self-directed learning, including reading, listening, watching, or observing, that you can do on your own at your own pace. They are most useful for novices in the capability, but are helpful for intermediate and advanced learners to keep knowledge current.

Development Activity	Suggested Resource(s) and Tips
Learn about emotional intelligence (EQ).	• Review a brief overview, history, and list of assessments for EQ (http://psychology.about.com/od/personalitydevelopment/a/emotionalintell.htm). • Find articles and information about EQ tests and training (www.emotionalintelligence.net). This website is produced by the authors of *Emotional Intelligence 2.0* (Bradberry and Greaves, 2009). • Read *Emotional Intelligence: Why It Can Matter More Than IQ* (Goleman, 2005). • Read *Working with Emotional Intelligence* (Goleman, 2000).
Learn about the complexity of culture and how it manifests in behaviors, beliefs, and values using the iceberg model of culture, developed by anthropologist Edward T. Hall.	The iceberg model has been widely used and adapted since 1976: • You can read a summary of it at the Constant Foreigner (www.constantforeigner.com/iceberg-model.html). • You can read the original book that describes it: *Beyond Culture* (Hall, 1976).
Take assessments that measure your current cross-cultural competence and help you identify where to improve, so you may better work with diverse others.	• The Intercultural Development Inventory measures cross-cultural competence for individuals, groups, and organizations (www.idiinventory.com). • The Intercultural Communication and Collaboration Appraisal measures affective, cognitive, and behavioral aspects of cross-cultural competence (www.gpccolorado.com/intercultural-communication-and-collaboration-appraisal). • The Cultural Intelligence Center offers multiple assessments for cross-cultural competence in a variety of contexts (http://culturalQ.com). • The Cultural Orientations Indicator measures a person's work style preferences against ten dimensions of culture (www.tmcorp.com/Online-Learning/Assessments/Cultural-Orientations-Indicator-COI/56).
Assess your own biases toward and prejudices of others.	Project Implicit at Harvard hosts a series of online assessments to help identify biases and prejudices on a range of topics, including different races and personal characteristics (https://implicit.harvard.edu/implicit/demo).

DEVELOPMENT SUGGESTIONS
for Ability to Emotionally Connect to People from Other Cultures

LEARN

Tips to learn about and begin developing the capability on your own. These tips involve self-directed learning, including reading, listening, watching, or observing, that you can do on your own at your own pace. They are most useful for novices in the capability, but are helpful for intermediate and advanced learners to keep knowledge current.

Development Activity	Suggested Resource(s) and Tips
Read about the biological process of emotions and how they influence our behaviors toward others.	• Read *Crucial Conversations* (Patterson, et al., 2011), which discusses this process as well as how to manage it in high-stakes conversations. • Read about research findings on the link between mind and body through emotions: *Molecules of Emotions: The Science Behind Mind–Body Medicine* (Pert, 1999). • Read about the biology of emotions, and learn tips on how to master your emotions for positive results: *MindSight: The New Science of Personal Transformation* (Siegel, 2010).
Learn how emotional connections are formed, expressed, and sustained in the culture of interest.	• Learn about cultural norms through a local guidebook, CultureGram reports (www.culturegrams.com), or the GlobeSmart tool (www.aperianglobal.com). • Watch Aperian Global's (www.aperianglobal.com) series on interacting and doing business in different countries. • Watch a movie set in the culture of interest, and then discuss the emotional connections you saw with local natives or colleagues who have experience in this region. • Read fiction based in the culture of interest. You can browse travel fiction by region (http://librarybooklists.org/fiction/adult/travel.htm). • Observe how people in the culture interact with one another and show emotions in a work-related meeting. • Ask a local native colleague about his or her friends and family life to get a sense of what close relationships look like in the culture. Ask what it means to have a strong friendship in terms of the amount of time spent together, expectations, and sharing of feelings. • Ask colleagues or friends from the culture of interest how emotions are defined, manifested, and regarded in their culture.
Learn about sources of influence and how to leverage those for success in personal relationships.	• Take basic interpersonal skills training at your local community college or university. • Read *Influencer* (Patterson, et al., 2007), which discusses six sources of influence and illustrates their use through compelling case studies. • Read *Influence: Science and Practice* (Cialdini, 2008) to learn about sources of influence and how to inspire people to connect with you. • Read *Beyond Reason: Using Emotions as You Negotiate* (Fisher and Shapiro, 2006) to learn how to effectively connect with others over five key emotions.

DEVELOPMENT SUGGESTIONS
for Ability to Emotionally Connect to People from Other Cultures

CONNECT

Tips to learn about and continue developing the capability through others. These tips involve working with another person to learn from their experiences. They may involve asking questions, listening to and discussing experiences, forming a new relationship, deepening an existing relationship, or receiving feedback from someone who is acting as your mentor. These tips are useful for all levels of learners.

Development Activity	Suggested Resource(s) and Tips
Make a genuine connection with your colleagues from other cultures.	• Reach out regularly to colleagues in other cultures by phone, web, video conferencing, and in-person meetings when possible. • Ask about their families, hobbies, and profession. • Find common interests and experiences to discuss. • Ask them to describe a typical day in their life in their culture. • Ask them how relationships are built in their culture. • Ask them about local life (e.g., food, press, norms, roles, etc.) so you can make these connections in conversations with other local colleagues. • When you have observed reactions and emotions expressed by your colleagues from other cultures that you do not understand, ask your colleagues about those reactions and emotions at an appropriate time and in a nonjudgmental way to better understand them. • When there are differences of opinion, talk about them. Find out your colleague's point of view.
Find out how your behaviors are viewed in the culture so you can be aware and course-correct as needed.	• Ask a trusted colleague or coach from the culture of interest to help you identify behaviors you use well in this culture and those that you don't use well. • Ask for tips on how to improve your behaviors to better adapt to the culture. • Read *Culture from the Inside Out* (Cornes, 2004), and reflect on how your individual characteristics play a part in your view of the culture as well as how you are being viewed.
Attend meaningful local events with your local colleagues to share an important experience and to learn more through observation about how people in this culture emotionally connect.	• Attend a spiritual or religious ceremony or event. • Attend a sporting event. • Attend theater or another kind of performance art.

INTERCULTURAL EMPATHY

DEVELOPMENT SUGGESTIONS
for Ability to Emotionally Connect to People from Other Cultures

CONNECT

Tips to learn about and continue developing the capability through others. These tips involve working with another person to learn from their experiences. They may involve asking questions, listening to and discussing experiences, forming a new relationship, deepening an existing relationship, or receiving feedback from someone who is acting as your mentor. These tips are useful for all levels of learners.

Development Activity	Suggested Resource(s) and Tips
Ask colleagues or friends in the culture of interest about popular people in that culture, as these people may inspire emotions and connections.	Find out who are the top two or three popular: • sports stars • singers • actors • entertainers • heroes, both current and historical.

DEVELOPMENT SUGGESTIONS
for Ability to Emotionally Connect to People from Other Cultures

EXPERIENCE

Tips to learn about and develop skills in the capability through firsthand experience. These tips involve engaging in activities, such as exploring a new area, trying a new cultural activity, or participating in a specific business event. These tips are most useful for intermediate to advanced learners, and we suggest that novice learners prepare themselves for success by completing some of the tips in the Learn category first.

Development Activity	Suggested Resource(s) and Tips
Invite your colleagues from other cultures to participate with you in various activities and events to deepen your relationship.	You may consider inviting them to: • join you for meals both in restaurants and in your home • accompany you to a local cultural event, such as theater or an art show • participate in a social activity, such as a party or a sporting event • join you on an exploration of local sites • join you in a daily walk or other exercise.

DEVELOPMENT SUGGESTIONS
for Ability to Emotionally Connect to People from Other Cultures

EXPERIENCE

Tips to learn about and develop skills in the capability through firsthand experience. These tips involve engaging in activities, such as exploring a new area, trying a new cultural activity, or participating in a specific business event. These tips are most useful for intermediate to advanced learners, and we suggest that novice learners prepare themselves for success by completing some of the tips in the Learn category first.

Development Activity	Suggested Resource(s) and Tips
When interacting with colleagues from other cultures, remember to use behaviors that foster positive relationships with others.	Here are some behaviors that foster positive relationships with others: • In conversations, show genuine interest by seeking first to understand the other person before pushing to be understood. • Avoid making snap judgments. Keep an open mind as you work to understand the other person. • Pay attention to the emotions behind a conversation. What is not being said is often more powerful than what is being said. • Find common interest with others who are compatible with their cultural norms and socioeconomic status. • Avoid criticizing others. Find ways to compliment them on their strengths and contributions.
Use storytelling to open yourself up more to your colleagues through sharing of experiences and connect with them on a more personal level.	• Read *Tell to Win: Connect, Persuade, and Triumph with the Hidden Power of Story* (Guber, 2011) on how to use storytelling in business to influence and connect with others. • Read *The Leader's Guide to Storytelling: Mastering the Art and Discipline of Business Narrative* (Denning, 2011) about how to tell the right story at the right time. • Read *The Story Factor* (Simmons and Lipman, 2006) on the six types of stories you need to know and tell. • You can practice the art of storytelling by contributing a personal story to magazines like *The Sun* (www.thesunmagazine.org), *The New Yorker* (www.newyorker.com), or a magazine focused on social commentary in your region of the world.

DEVELOPMENT SUGGESTIONS
for Ability to Emotionally Connect to People from Other Cultures

COACH OR CONTRIBUTE

Tips to help others learn about and develop this capability. These tips involve coaching and mentoring others. They may include creating information or experiences for individuals, teams, or your organization. These tips are designed for those who are advanced in the capability and are useful development methods to keep advanced leaders in the capability engaged in professional development at the highest level. Please note that the tips in this section may also be quite helpful for individual use if you do not have a coach or mentor.

Development Activity	Suggested Resource(s) and Tips
When coaching your direct reports or mentees, ask open-ended questions to help them understand how they can better emotionally connect to people from other cultures.	Ask them: • What does emotional connection mean to you? What does it look like in terms of behaviors? • Think about people who you are close to. How did you become close? • Who is your best friend? Why? What does he or she do or not do that makes you so close? • What are three things you can do to better connect with your colleagues from other cultures? • What are three things that you do differently when you interact with people from another culture? Are these effective behaviors? • What do you believe your image is among your colleagues in other cultures? Do you agree or disagree? How can you make this image better reflect how you intend to be seen? • What stereotypes exist in your organization about colleagues from other cultures? What can you do to clear up these stereotypes among your colleagues? • Think about one person who lacks empathy. What are his or her attributes? • Think about one person who has high empathy. What are his or her attributes? How can you adopt these? • What are your top three emotional derailers in working relationships? What strategies can you take to minimize these? • Think about a person who is very good at emotionally connecting with others. What does he or she do to make these connections?

COACH OR CONTRIBUTE

Tips to help others learn about and develop this capability. These tips involve coaching and mentoring others. They may include creating information or experiences for individuals, teams, or your organization. These tips are designed for those who are advanced in the capability and are useful development methods to keep advanced leaders in the capability engaged in professional development at the highest level. Please note that the tips in this section may also be quite helpful for individual use if you do not have a coach or mentor.

Development Activity	Suggested Resource(s) and Tips
Help your direct reports or mentees better understand their own emotional connections with others through reading, assessments, and personal reflection.	<ul><li>Have them read *Crucial Conversations* (Patterson, et al., 2011) to understand their emotional reactions to others and how to manage those emotions and create productive dialogue.</li><li>Have them take assessments like the Myers-Briggs Type Indicator (MBTI) (www.myersbriggs.org), DiSC (www.thediscpersonalitytest.com), and Insights (www.insights.com) to understand their behavioral and emotional tendencies, and discuss the results with them.</li><li>When having difficulty connecting with people from other cultures, ask them to keep a journal noting what behaviors and reactions they are seeing in others and how they are interpreting them. Discuss their journal notes, and help clarify possible misinterpretations.</li></ul>
Provide your direct reports or mentees with helpful reminders about behaviors that foster positive relationships with others.	Here are some behaviors that foster positive relationships with others:<ul><li>In conversations, show genuine interest by seeking first to understand the other person before pushing to be understood.</li><li>Avoid making snap judgments. Keep an open mind as you work to understand the other person.</li><li>Pay attention to the emotions behind a conversation. What is not being said is often more powerful than what is being said.</li><li>Find common interest with others who are compatible with their cultural norms and socioeconomic status.</li><li>Avoid criticizing others. Find ways to compliment them on their strengths and contributions.</li></ul>

INTERCULTURAL EMPATHY

Additional Reading

The readings listed here provide you with additional study of the Global Mindset capability in this section. You will find that many of these resources provide you with a specific and detailed look at using this capability in a particular context or location.

....

Title: "The Effects of Cultural Intelligence on Expatriate Performance: The Moderating Effects of International Experience"

Publication: *International Journal of Human Resource Management*

Date: 2010

Authors: Lee Li-Yueh and Sukoco Badri Munir

Executive Summary: In recent years, cultural intelligence (CQ, or the ability that an expatriate has to adapt across cultures), cultural effectiveness (the ability to interact and communicate with host nationals), and cultural adjustment are regarded as three of the most important factors for expatriate performance. However, the interrelationships between these variables have largely been ignored. Moreover, the role of previous international experiences on the above interrelationships has also not been determined. This study focuses on how CQ and expatriates' experience affects cultural adjustment, cultural effectiveness, and expatriates' performance.

....

Title: "The Effects of Expatriate Demographic Characteristics on Adjustment: A Social Identity Approach"

Publication: *Human Resource Management*

Date: 2009

Authors: Jesse E. Olsen and Luis L. Martins

Executive Summary: As demand increases for expatriates to manage far-flung operations in a global economy, scholars and practitioners are focusing their attention on the factors that contribute to expatriate success. One such factor is the support that expatriates receive from host country nationals with whom they work.

GLOBAL SOCIAL CAPITAL

Title:	"Global Leaders' Virtues and Virtuous Performance"
Publication:	*Proceedings of the European Conference on Management, Leadership & Governance*
Date:	2010
Authors:	Arménio Rego and Miguel Pina Cunha

Executive Summary: In a globalized world, transnational companies are implicated in power relations with many other organizations, including states, responsible for millions of people's lives and livelihoods. Building positive organizational performance and contributing to the creation of a better planet requires having global leaders with positive qualities in senior positions in these organizations. In this paper, using Peterson and Seligman's (2004) framework, we explore how the character strengths and virtues of global leaders can make them more effective and better able to develop flourishing organizations and people within and around them in the contexts in which they operate. We start discussing the complex globalized context in which global leaders operate. Next, we explore the relevance of human strengths and virtues for global leaders' effectiveness and fostering of positive organizational performance. Finally, we integrate arguments and discuss how global leaders may combine different virtues for being effective and a source of positive organizational performance and social betterment.

GLOBAL SOCIAL CAPITAL

FACILITATING A TEAM DISCUSSION

Ability to Engage People from Other Parts of the World to Work Together

So far in intercultural empathy, we've spent our time looking at ourselves: our ability to work with other people around the world, our ability to understand nonverbal expressions of people from other cultures, and our ability to emotionally connect with people from other cultures. The last capability in intercultural empathy is focused on our ability to engage people from other parts of the world to work together. This shifts the focus away from how we manage our own behavior to how we influence the behavior of others. This is a much more sophisticated skill.

What does it mean to engage others to work together? To engage someone means "to induce to participate" (www.Merriam-Webster.com). It's about influence, and influence comes in many forms. For example, in the best-selling book *Influencer* (Patterson, et al., 2007), the authors list six sources of influence:

- Make the undesirable desirable.

- Surpass your limits.

- Harness peer pressure.

- Find strength in numbers.

- Design rewards and demand accountability.

- Change the environment.

Influence by definition means having the power or capacity to cause a direct or indirect effect on someone else (www.Merriam-Webster.com). There are six sources of influence because people are motivated by different things, especially across cultures, and because different situations require different approaches.

Influencer is a fascinating read because it illustrates through real-world cases how each of these sources of influence have been used successfully. For example, an international shipping company found that investing significant resources in training did little to resolve the costly problem of employees not filling shipping containers as full as possible. Training is a go-to solution for many companies. When in doubt, train, is the philosophy. But the company discovered that the sixth source of influence, change the environment, was key to resolving the issue. What did they do? They simply painted a "fill to here" line inside each shipping container. The problem was solved.

In contrast, another case in the book illustrates the importance of matching the influencing strategy to the motivations of the culture and the community. The World Health Organization (WHO) was working in Africa to try to eradicate Guinea Worm Disease—a terrible worm infestation in the human body that is transmitted through contaminated water. In this case, the strategy to change the environment did not work. Signs were posted in the village and near water sources to educate and warn villagers to use caution. Filtration devices were provided in homes as well. But the infestations were not improving. They found that infected persons were wading in water sources as they gathered water, thereby continuously recontaminating the water source. It was shameful to admit to having Guinea Worm Disease. Therefore, the source of influence the WHO put in place was to harness peer pressure. Villagers were asked to report infected people, so other villagers would know they should not enter the water source. This terrible disease has now been almost completely eradicated in many villages as a result.

So we see that cross-culturally we must know and use different influencing strategies to engage others. This is why the variety of tips in this chapter will be useful to you as you work to engage people from other parts of the world to work together more effectively.

Ability to Engage People from Other Parts of the World to Work Together in Action

We were anxious when it was announced that yet another American was appointed to lead our Nordic headquarters for a global American company.

KATHERINE JOHNSTON, MBA
Speaker, Author, and Consultant

We were anxious when it was announced that yet another American was appointed to lead our Nordic headquarters for a global American company. Bluntly put, his predecessor, Barb, had failed to integrate and engage employees during her two-year assignment. Her organization was highly stressed, but not particularly effective. Barb constantly made condescending remarks about Norwegians, confined her contact to the expat community, shunned language lessons, and tried to visit as many other European cities as possible during the weekends.

But the new appointee, Dave, surprised us all. We expected that he would come blazing in, announce his one-hundred-day plan, and immediately execute it in the supreme confidence that his ideas were best. Instead, he spent the first six weeks talking around. He hung out at the coffee bar and took long lunches with employees. He conducted many informal, one-on-one interviews about employees' experiences, ideas, and expectations. On the weekends, he and his family explored Norway, and he started weekly Norwegian lessons. "How hard can it be after Cyrillic?" he said, in his self-deprecating manner.

Dave built upon his previous and challenging experience of working in Russia to get a good start in Norway. After six weeks of talking around, he launched the first of several successful initiatives. His willingness to listen and incorporate others' ideas with his own quickly created a sense of collaboration. Everyone felt they had contributed. Dave was really adept at engaging people from other parts of the world to work together.

OSLO, NORWAY

Goran Bogicevic / Shutterstock.com

DEVELOPMENT SUGGESTIONS
for Ability to Engage People from Other Parts of the World to Work Together

LEARN

Tips to learn about and begin developing the capability on your own. These tips involve self-directed learning, including reading, listening, watching, or observing, that you can do on your own at your own pace. They are most useful for novices in the capability, but are helpful for intermediate and advanced learners to keep knowledge current.

Development Activity	Suggested Resource(s) and Tips
Watch or listen to world news from a variety of sources to have a current and broad understanding of cultures around the world.	• Read and watch world news in fifty languages at World News Network online (http://wn.com). • Read and watch BBC World News (www.bbc.co.uk/news/world). • Read and watch global news through GlobalPost online (www.globalpost.com). • Read and watch CNN International (http://edition.cnn.com). • Read and listen to NPR World News (www.npr.org/sections/world). • Read and watch region-specific news on Aljazeera (www.aljazeera.com). • Read the *Wall Street Journal* (available in editions for the United States, Asia, Europe, and the Americas) (http://online.wsj.com). • Read *The Economist* (www.economist.com). • Read the *Financial Times* (www.ft.com). • Read CNN Money (money.cnn.com/news/world). • Review Reuters (www.reuters.com). • Scan *Forbes* (www.forbes.com). • Read BBC (www.bbc.com). • Scan *Foreign Affairs* (www.foreignaffairs.com). • Read *BusinessWeek Asia* (www.businessweek.com/asia). • Review *China Business Review* (www.chinabusinessreview.com). • Read *BusinessWeek Europe* (www.businessweek.com/europe). • Scan Latin Finance (www.latinfinance.com). • Review Latin Focus (www.latin-focus.com). • Read *Latin Trade* (http://latintrade.com). • Review America Economia (www.americaeconomica.com).
Learn about cultural differences in work styles.	• Read the GLOBE studies: *Culture, Leadership, and Organizations: The GLOBE Studies of 62 Societies* (House, et al., 2004) and *Culture and Leadership across the World: The GLOBE Book of In-Depth Study of 25 Societies* (Chhokar, et al., 2007). • Look at side-by-side comparisons of cultures using Dr. Geert Hofstedes's dimensions (http://geert-hofstede.com). • Compare cultures by subscribing to the GlobeSmart tool through Aperian Global (www.aperianglobal.com). • Take a course through your local business school on doing business in a particular region of the world, such as "Regional Business Environment" courses at Thunderbird School of Global Business (www.thunderbird.edu).

DEVELOPMENT SUGGESTIONS
for Ability to Engage People from Other Parts of the World to Work Together

LEARN

Tips to learn about and begin developing the capability on your own. These tips involve self-directed learning, including reading, listening, watching, or observing, that you can do on your own at your own pace. They are most useful for novices in the capability, but are helpful for intermediate and advanced learners to keep knowledge current.

Development Activity	Suggested Resource(s) and Tips
Stay up-to-date on local interests and current events so you can talk about them and share them with others.	• You can find worldwide public holidays at Q++ Studio (www.qppstudio.net/publicholidays.htm). • You can search worldwide public holidays in several languages through Bank Holidays (www.bank-holidays.com). • Follow local news in your region for current events, like politics, sports, and entertainment. • Ask local colleagues about upcoming local events.
Learn popular proverbs in your culture of interest; they give a sense of the values and humor in that culture that you can connect with others over.	• Read local guidebooks such as Lonely Planet (www.lonelyplanet .com), Fodor's (www.fodors.com), Frommer's (www.frommers.com), and Rough Guides (www.roughguides.com), which often highlight some local proverbs or sayings. • Read books of idioms for the local culture. You can find them in local bookstores, or search for them online using the terms "idioms" or "slang" plus the language or country of interest.
Learn how to improve global collaboration.	Use the app "TMA World Mobile" by Roam Solutions, which provides you access to a library of skill videos, podcasts, tips, and resources to improve global collaboration and competitiveness.
Learn about sources of influence and how to leverage those for success when trying to engage people from other parts of the world to work together.	• Read *Influencer* (Patterson, et al., 2007), which discusses six sources of influence and illustrates their use through compelling case studies. • VitalSmarts offers training based on *Influencer* (www.vitalsmarts .com). • Read *Influence: Science and Practice* (Cialdini, 2008) to learn about sources of influence and how to inspire people to connect with you. • You will find articles and information about influence training at Dr. Cialdini's website (www.influenceatwork.com). • Read *Beyond Reason: Using Emotions as You Negotiate* (Fisher and Shapiro, 2006) to learn how to effectively connect with others over five key emotions.

GLOBAL SOCIAL CAPITAL

DEVELOPMENT SUGGESTIONS
for Ability to Engage People from Other Parts of the World to Work Together

CONNECT

Tips to learn about and continue developing the capability through others. These tips involve working with another person to learn from their experiences. They may involve asking questions, listening to and discussing experiences, forming a new relationship, deepening an existing relationship, or receiving feedback from someone who is acting as your mentor. These tips are useful for all levels of learners.

Development Activity	Suggested Resource(s) and Tips
Find out how people in the culture of interest engage with one another at work and how they view effective team and leader behaviors.	Ask local native employees: • What does a team look like and do in your culture? • What motivates workers in your culture? • What demotivates workers in your culture? • What does an effective leader do in your culture? • What does an effective leader not do in your culture? • What is your definition of a successful working relationship in your culture?
Involve local native employees as much as possible.	• Actively solicit the input of local native employees in projects, initiatives, decision making, policies, and programs. • Regularly discuss how the team is doing in working together and how they can work more effectively. • Use video or web conferencing to add a more personal connection in virtual team meetings.
Work closely with stakeholders in the culture of interest to understand their insights, needs, and concerns.	• Ask stakeholders for their insights on projects and initiatives. • Regularly touch base with them to discuss progress and their needs and concerns.
Make a point of meeting local customers, suppliers, and partners to form connections and to understand firsthand what their needs and concerns are.	Ask your local colleagues to arrange meetings with customers, suppliers, and partners prior to your arrival in the country to ensure you meet with them.
Talk to people in your organization who have experience working in the culture of interest.	Ask them to tell you about their successes and challenges.

INTERCULTURAL EMPATHY

DEVELOPMENT SUGGESTIONS
for Ability to Engage People from Other Parts of the World to Work Together

EXPERIENCE

Tips to learn about and develop skills in the capability through firsthand experience. These tips involve engaging in activities, such as exploring a new area, trying a new cultural activity, or participating in a specific business event. These tips are most useful for intermediate to advanced learners, and we suggest that novice learners prepare themselves for success by completing some of the tips in the Learn category first.

Development Activity	Suggested Resource(s) and Tips
Participate in an international corporate volunteering project to engage with people in another culture on a meaningful project.	These short-term projects led by organizations such as World Action Teams (www.worldactionteams .com) allow you to work in corporate teams to engage firsthand on a team-based project in a culture of interest.
Make sure to participate in social engagements in the local culture, as they are often important ways of forming positive and productive working relationships with others.	• Attend social engagements sponsored by the organization and by individuals within the organization. • Invite others to join you in social engagements. • Create opportunities to meet the families of your colleagues by inviting them to social events.
Practice good facilitation for the culture you are in by being sensitive to local culture when communicating and designing content for meetings and trainings.	• Observe meetings and trainings in the culture of interest, and note how facilitation differs from your current style. • Ask local colleagues to discuss facilitation best practices for the culture you are in. • After facilitating, ask for feedback from local colleagues about how you can improve.

DEVELOPMENT SUGGESTIONS
for Ability to Engage People from Other Parts of the World to Work Together

COACH OR CONTRIBUTE

Tips to help others learn about and develop this capability. These tips involve coaching and mentoring others. They may include creating information or experiences for individuals, teams, or your organization. These tips are designed for those who are advanced in the capability and are useful development methods to keep advanced leaders in the capability engaged in professional development at the highest level. Please note that the tips in this section may also be quite helpful for individual use if you do not have a coach or mentor.

Development Activity	Suggested Resource(s) and Tips
As a leader, create as many opportunities as possible for geographically dispersed teams to engage with one another.	<ul><li>Schedule meetings in different parts of the world where your team members are located.</li><li>Have meetings and conference calls chaired by people from different cultures.</li><li>Encourage your team members to contact others for input who are not co-located with them.</li><li>Regularly solicit input from all team members about how they can better engage with one another.</li></ul>
Consistently coach your direct reports and mentees to think globally and act locally.	<ul><li>Discuss the importance of having a high-level strategic view in the organization, while also understanding local needs and implementation requirements.</li><li>Provide examples to your team about how local implementation differs across cultures in your organization.</li><li>Invite colleagues who are from different countries to speak to your group about local needs and implementation for their countries.</li></ul>
Coach your direct reports and mentees on how to engage effectively in the cultures they are working in and across cultures within the team.	<ul><li>Share cultural differences that have surfaced in the past on the team and strategies to work with these differences.</li><li>Ask team members who are particularly effective at working in a particular culture of interest to share best practices.</li></ul>

Additional Reading

The readings listed here provide you with additional study of the Global Mindset capability in this section. You will find that many of these resources provide you with a specific and detailed look at using this capability in a particular context or location.

....

Title:　　　　　"Developing Global Leaders"

Publication:　*McKinsey Quarterly*

Date:　　　　　2012

Author:　　　　Pankaj Ghemawat

Executive Summary: The article focuses on methods global companies can use to attract talent and talks about five common myths concerning globalization. It states that a survey of senior executives found that 76 percent believed their organizations should develop global leadership capabilities, while around 30 percent of businesses in the United States failed to fully exploit international business opportunities due to the lack of internationally competent employees. It mentions that many companies are not fully globalized and talks about how experience alone is insufficient to develop an accurate Global Mindset. It comments on localization of subsidiary corporations and the need for a mixture of expatriate and local leadership. It talks about the difficulty in recruiting top talent due to competition from local companies.

....

Title:　　　　　"The New Global Manager: Learning Cultures on the Fly"

Publication:　*Organizational Dynamics*

Date:　　　　　2008

Authors:　　　Luciara Nardon and Richard M. Steers

Executive Summary: A major challenge facing managers today is how to deal with international partners and competitors that we simply don't understand. In many cases, the problem is not so much language differences as cultural differences. Two of the most commonly suggested strategies for succeeding include developing cultural fluency and developing a Global Mindset. While both of these strategies are useful, we suggest that the increasing intensity, time sensitivity, and diversity that characterizes today's global business environment may require a third approach.

We call it, simply, learning cultures on the fly. Drawing on intercultural interaction learning theory, we propose a new approach to succeeding abroad, through which personal learning in cross-cultural settings can be facilitated through social learning. In our view, an intercultural interaction is an opportunity for interdependent learning in which individuals both learn about each other's culture and negotiate effective ways of relating in relatively short order. To achieve this end, we suggest a four-pronged strategy for negotiating intercultural exchanges.

....

Title: "How to Cultivate Engaged Employees"

Publication: *Harvard Business Review*

Date: 2011

Author: Charalambos A. Vlachoutsicos

Executive Summary: Everybody knows that an empowered team enhances everyone's performance, including the manager's. Vlachoutsicos, of the Athens University of Economics and Business, argues that the vital, particular ingredient in buoying employees is fostering a sense of mutual dependence, or mutuality, every time you interact with subordinates.

LEADING A MEETING

GLOBAL SOCIAL CAPITAL

Andrey_Popov / Shutterstock.com

Interpersonal Impact

As shown in **Figure 8-1** on page 430, this chapter examines Interpersonal Impact, which is a key dimension of Global Social Capital. Interpersonal impact refers to a leader who has high interpersonal impact and exceptional influencing skills. Consider the example of former U.S. President Bill Clinton. Since his departure from office, he continues to be a major player in world affairs. This is because of his reputation as a leader and his tremendous network of personal and professional connections around the world. Many people are excited to work with him, and they enthusiastically recruit others to join them in projects such as the Clinton Global Initiative (CGI).

The work at CGI epitomizes President Clinton's skill in negotiating agreements and contracts in that its sole focus is to bring leaders together from around the globe to partner in solving some of the world's most difficult challenges. Leaders at CGI create agreements that they call commitments that outline how they will partner and how they plan to achieve their goals. Creating these commitments is an exercise in influence. So to participate in CGI, one must have three things: a positive reputation as a global leader, a strong network of contacts around the world, and high skill in negotiating agreements. These three things are the key components of our notion of Interpersonal Impact. Together, these qualities create trust and motivation from others to want to work with you.

In this chapter, we will cover each of the three components of interpersonal impact:

- Experience in negotiating contracts/agreements in other cultures

- Strong networks with people from other cultures and with influential people

- Reputation as a leader

GLOBAL MINDSET

Global INTELLECTUAL CAPITAL

Global Business Savvy

Knowledge of global industry

Knowledge of global competitive business and marketing strategies

Knowledge of how to transact business and assess risks of doing business internationally

Knowledge of supplier options in other parts of the world

Cosmopolitan Outlook

Knowledge of cultures in different parts of the world

Knowledge of geography, history, and important persons of several countries

Knowledge of economic & political issues, concerns, & hot topics of major regions of the world

Up-to-date knowledge of important world events

Cognitive Complexity

Ability to grasp complex topics quickly

Strong analytical and problem solving skills

Ability to understand abstract ideas

Ability to take complex issues and explain the main points simply and understandably

Global PSYCHOLOGICAL CAPITAL

Passion for Diversity

Enjoy exploring other parts of the world

Enjoy getting to know people from other parts of the world

Enjoy living in another country

Enjoy traveling

Quest for Adventure

Interest in dealing with challenging situations

Willingness to take risk

Willingness to test one's abilities

Enjoy dealing with unpredictable situations

Self-Assurance

Energetic

Self-confident

Comfortable in uncomfortable situations

Witty in tough situations

Global SOCIAL CAPITAL

Intercultural Empathy

Ability to work well with people from other parts of the world

Ability to understand nonverbal expressions of people from other cultures

Ability to emotionally connect to people from other cultures

Ability to engage people from other parts of the world to work together

Interpersonal Impact

Experience in negotiating contracts/agreements in other cultures

Strong networks with people from other cultures and with influential people

Reputation as a leader

Diplomacy

Ease of starting a conversation with a stranger

Ability to integrate diverse perspectives

Ability to listen to what others have to say

Willingness to collaborate

Figure 8-1

Experience in Negotiating Contracts/ Agreements in Other Cultures

Experience in negotiating contracts/agreements in other cultures refers to your skill (i.e., awareness, knowledge, and ability) in sharing resources, creating new ventures, or joint problem solving and how to specifically adapt your negotiations to the culture at hand. Dr. Karen S. Walch, a professor at Thunderbird School of Global Management, discovered through in-depth research in 2010 that the twenty-first-century focus on global interdependency and justice has created entirely new rules for negotiations today. She found that there are still some instances where the ruthless and selfish negotiation tactics of previous centuries may apply, namely where power is centralized and relationships may not matter. Generally, however, Dr. Walch found that the majority of negotiations today require understanding of the social context and collaboration with others in order to produce sustainable, prosperous, and satisfying agreements. This is because many of the current social, political, and economic problems in negotiations are the result of complex social connections, not simple win–lose power plays.

Even if you are an experienced and well-trained negotiator, it is important to reflect on how globalization and interdependency in the world of business today has created a very different environment for negotiations; a very uncertain and ambiguous environment requires different negotiation skills, which include not only intellectual and strategic analysis of what you want, but also the psychological curiosity and social diplomacy required for understanding the range of human and organizational needs in an interdependent world. The following tips are focused specifically on how to build your skills in cross-cultural negotiations for the twenty-first century.

INTERPERSONAL IMPACT

GLOBAL SOCIAL CAPITAL

NEGOTIATING A CONTRACT

Deklofenak / Shutterstock.com

Experience in Negotiating Contracts/Agreements in Other Cultures in Action

One of the first things that I observed when I became CEO of our company was that my American and European predecessors were not well received by some of our customers in Brazil and certain African countries.

VALERIE WHITE, PH.D.
Principal
Change Perspectives

"One of the first things that I observed when I became CEO of our company was that my American and European predecessors were not well received by some of our customers in Brazil and certain African countries. One of the effects this had was that the usually prolonged time it took to sign contracts became even longer. That is, if they were even able to successfully negotiate a deal. For each country and each customer, I know that there are unique differentiators, but certain approaches will always enhance success.

"My approach with every customer has been one of listening attentively and then being patient during negotiations. I come to the table with an open mind. I check my ego at the door and take ownership for making the relationship a success on both sides. That is what negotiation is all about in the service industry. Customers want to know that you understand their business. This means not only visiting job sites and engineering offices but also visiting contractors. I look to add value to our relationships by understanding how my customers approach the market and by helping them focus on the right thing to enhance their business.

"For example, is their primary drive increasing volume or just increasing revenues? You don't get to your bottom line without understanding what it will take to help the customer get to theirs. Listening, having patience, having market knowledge, and helping the customer to be properly focused have helped us decrease the time to deal finalization by 50 percent to 60 percent."

* This example was shared with Dr. White by a coaching client.

INTERPERSONAL IMPACT

GLOBAL SOCIAL CAPITAL

LEARN

Tips to learn about and begin developing the capability on your own. These tips involve self-directed learning, including reading, listening, watching, or observing, that you can do on your own at your own pace. They are most useful for novices in the capability, but are helpful for intermediate and advanced learners to keep knowledge current.

Development Activity	Suggested Resource(s) and Tips
Assess your own cultural and behavioral preferences using psychometric assessments, so you may be aware of them and manage them appropriately.	These tools measure cultural preferences: • The Intercultural Development Inventory measures cross-cultural competence for individuals, groups, and organizations (www.idiinventory.com). • The Cultural Orientations Indicator measures a person's work style preferences against ten dimensions of culture (www.tmcorp.com/Online-Learning/Assessments/Cultural-Orientations-Indicator-COI/56). These tools measure behavioral preferences: • The Myers-Briggs Type Indicator identifies and describes your personality type, including how you interact with others (www.myersbriggs.org). • Hogan Assessments offers several leadership assessments that describe your behavioral tendencies and predict performance in the workplace (www.hoganassessments.com). • DiSC (www.thediscpersonalitytest.com) and Insights (www.insights.com) offer assessments that describe your personality and behavioral preferences along four main types.
Specifically learn about the customs and norms in the culture of interest prior to a negotiation.	• Read books of cultural tips, such as the book series *Kiss, Bow, or Shake Hands* (Morrison and Conaway, 2006) before starting a negotiation. Editions are available for specific regions of the world and for certain business functions. • Learn about styles of communication to show respect (e.g., direct, indirect) and what is typical in the region you are in by using a tool such as GlobeSmart (www.aperianglobal.com). • Understand the values in that culture so you can leverage them in negotiation by taking the COI assessment (www.tmcorp.com/Online-Learning/Assessments/Cultural-Orientations-Indicator-COI/56) and by reading about culturally specific values in the GLOBE studies: *Culture, Leadership, and Organizations: The GLOBE Study of 62 Societies* (House, et al., 2004) and *Culture and Leadership across the World: The GLOBE Book of In-Depth Studies of 25 Societies* (Chhokar, et al., 2007).

INTERPERSONAL IMPACT

DEVELOPMENT SUGGESTIONS
for Experience in Negotiating Contracts/Agreements in Other Cultures

LEARN

Tips to learn about and begin developing the capability on your own. These tips involve self-directed learning, including reading, listening, watching, or observing, that you can do on your own at your own pace. They are most useful for novices in the capability, but are helpful for intermediate and advanced learners to keep knowledge current.

Development Activity	Suggested Resource(s) and Tips
Learn about the general use of nonverbal behaviors in human communication so you can be aware of their use and typical meanings.	Read the following books: • The *Definitive Book of Body Language* (Pease and Pease, 2006) • *What Every Body Is Saying: An Ex-FBI Agent's Guide to Speed-Reading People* (Navarro, 2008) • *The Silent Language of Leaders: How Body Language Can Help—or Hurt—How You Lead* (Goman, 2011)
Learn strategies for successful cross-cultural negotiations.	• Take Communicating and Negotiating with a Global Mindset at Thunderbird Executive Education (http://www.thunderbird.edu/executive_education/classroom_programs/communicating_negotiating.htm). • Attend courses on cross-cultural negotiations at your local colleges and universities. • Watch INSEAD professor Dr. Falcao's interview on how to avoid pitfalls in cross-cultural negotiations (http://youtube/-4GjCOipJIA). • Watch Negotiation Europe's video on cross-cultural negotiation tips (http://youtube/BII8PXGmSBk). • Find videos of interest on negotiation topics that are listed on the Harvard Program on Negotiations website (www.pon.harvard.edu/category/events/pon-film-series). • Read books on cross-cultural negotiation, such as *Negotiating Across Cultures: International Communication in an Interdependent World* (Cohen, 1997). You can also search for books specifically focused on negotiations in your culture of interest. • Read *Global Negotiation: The New Rules* (Graham and Requejo, 2008). • Read *Negotiating Globally: How to Negotiate Deals, Resolve Disputes, and Make Decisions Across Cultural Boundaries* (Brett, 2007). • Read *Culture and Conflict Resolution* (Avruch, 1998).

DEVELOPMENT SUGGESTIONS
for Experience in Negotiating Contracts/Agreements in Other Cultures

LEARN

Tips to learn about and begin developing the capability on your own. These tips involve self-directed learning, including reading, listening, watching, or observing, that you can do on your own at your own pace. They are most useful for novices in the capability, but are helpful for intermediate and advanced learners to keep knowledge current.

Development Activity	Suggested Resource(s) and Tips
Build your technical ability in negotiation and contract experience.	• Observe negotiations in your organization when possible, and ask to see how contracts are designed. • Learn how to produce a paper contract and seize opportunities to practice skills by working with your organization's legal counsel and negotiations experts.
Learn about ways to process information in your head so that you can fine-tune your cognitive abilities to stay sharp in negotiations.	Read Chapter 3 of this handbook on cognitive complexity where you will find many resources.

DEVELOPMENT SUGGESTIONS
for Experience in Negotiating Contracts/Agreements in Other Cultures

CONNECT

Tips to learn about and continue developing the capability through others. These tips involve working with another person to learn from their experiences. They may involve asking questions, listening to and discussing experiences, forming a new relationship, deepening an existing relationship, or receiving feedback from someone who is acting as your mentor. These tips are useful for all levels of learners.

Development Activity	Suggested Resource(s) and Tips
Build the relationship first before entering into negotiations.	Meet with your negotiation partners prior to formal meetings, if possible, to make introductions and begin to establish trust. This is particularly important in some cultures (e.g., Asian) where a large part of decision making happens prior to formal meetings.
Learn about prior negotiations in your organization to understand the history, available resources, and success strategies.	• Meet with colleagues who have signed contracts in the culture of interest to learn from their experiences and to understand what contracts/agreements already exist from your organization. • Ask people with experience in the country of interest to tell you about how relationships and trust are built in that country in the context of negotiations. • Talk to your legal department about their experience in the culture of interest.

DEVELOPMENT SUGGESTIONS
for Experience in Negotiating Contracts/Agreements in Other Cultures

CONNECT

Tips to learn about and continue developing the capability through others. These tips involve working with another person to learn from their experiences. They may involve asking questions, listening to and discussing experiences, forming a new relationship, deepening an existing relationship, or receiving feedback from someone who is acting as your mentor. These tips are useful for all levels of learners.

Development Activity	Suggested Resource(s) and Tips
Draw on cultural and language experts to ensure fluid communication and clear understandings.	• When entering a new country or region, revise standard contracts with experts to ask how issues would be handled in the specific region. • Establish relationships with the local embassy and other business groups who have expertise in the area. • When there is a difference in language, be sure to use an interpreter. This will help ensure understanding and can provide your team with guidance on the local cultural norms as well. • Ask others inside or outside your organization who have experience with contracts in this culture to mentor you. This may involve a local cultural and/or legal consultant who can provide you with insight in several key areas: local rules of engagement, ethical considerations pertinent to the negotiations, typical timelines and pace for negotiations, decision-making norms for the culture, and insights on who has real negotiation power and control among your negotiating partners.

DEVELOPMENT SUGGESTIONS
for Experience in Negotiating Contracts/Agreements in Other Cultures

EXPERIENCE

Tips to learn about and develop skills in the capability through firsthand experience. These tips involve engaging in activities, such as exploring a new area, trying a new cultural activity, or participating in a specific business event. These tips are most useful for intermediate to advanced learners, and we suggest that novice learners prepare themselves for success by completing some of the tips in the Learn category first.

Development Activity	Suggested Resource(s) and Tips
Role play a mock negotiation.	• Harvard's Program on Negotiation offers day- to week-long courses on negotiations that include mock negotiations (www.pon.harvard.edu). • If you are a college student, you can contact your local United Nations Association to locate your closest Model UN program where you can practice international negotiations in the context of the United Nations (www.wfuna.org). • Ask your colleagues who have negotiated in the culture of interest to practice a mock negotiation with you before you enter into a real one. • While role playing, have an experienced cultural advisor and negotiations expert observe you and provide feedback.

DEVELOPMENT SUGGESTIONS
for Experience in Negotiating Contracts/Agreements in Other Cultures

EXPERIENCE

Tips to learn about and develop skills in the capability through firsthand experience. These tips involve engaging in activities, such as exploring a new area, trying a new cultural activity, or participating in a specific business event. These tips are most useful for intermediate to advanced learners, and we suggest that novice learners prepare themselves for success by completing some of the tips in the Learn category first.

Development Activity	Suggested Resource(s) and Tips
Volunteer for a leadership role in your local community to practice group negotiations.	Some common community groups may include: • homeowner associations • parent/teacher/student groups • nonprofit groups • religious groups • sporting organizations.
Ask to join a negotiations team in your organization as an observer or as a participant.	• Ask your manager for recommendations on who to speak to about this. • Ask one of the experienced negotiations team members to debrief your experience with you.

DEVELOPMENT SUGGESTIONS
for Experience in Negotiating Contracts/Agreements in Other Cultures

COACH OR CONTRIBUTE

Tips to help others learn about and develop this capability. These tips involve coaching and mentoring others. They may include creating information or experiences for individuals, teams, or your organization. These tips are designed for those who are advanced in the capability and are useful development methods to keep advanced leaders in the capability engaged in professional development at the highest level. Please note that the tips in this section may also be quite helpful for individual use if you do not have a coach or mentor.

Development Activity	Suggested Resource(s) and Tips
When leading negotiations on a project in your organization, be sure to share your experience with others who will benefit from it.	• In a multinational company, share negotiation learnings in your region with those negotiating similar agreements and contracts in other regions. • Debrief with your colleagues after a successful or unsuccessful negotiation to discuss what went well and what went wrong. • Invite direct reports and mentees who need to build negotiation experience to shadow negotiations when appropriate or at least shadow pre- and post-negotiation meetings.
When coaching direct reports or mentees on how to successfully negotiate contracts or agreements in other cultures, provide guidance on best practices.	Create a brief job aid (e.g., handout, pamphlet, document) that highlights best practices for the organization, the industry, and the specific culture of interest.

INTERPERSONAL IMPACT

Additional Reading

The readings listed here provide you with additional study of the Global Mindset capability in this section. You will find that many of these resources provide you with a specific and detailed look at using this capability in a particular context or location.

....

Title: "Negotiations between Chinese and Americans: Examining the Cultural Context and Salient Factors"

Publication: *Journal of International Management*

Date: 2012

Authors: Asuman Akgunes and Robert Culpepper

Executive Summary: This paper examines differences in the cultural contexts of China and the United States as they relate to business negotiations and investigates differences in negotiating styles and practices. Recommendations for avoiding pitfalls and maximizing negotiating effectiveness are offered.

....

Title: "Descriptive Norms as Carriers of Culture in Negotiation"

Publication: *International Negotiation*

Date: 2011

Authors: Michele J. Gelfand, Janetta Lun, Sarah Lyons, and Garriy Shteynberg

Executive Summary: Research on culture and negotiation is critical for expanding theories of negotiation beyond Western cultures and for helping people to manage their interdependence in a world of increasing global threats and opportunities.

....

Title: "Cultural Differentiation of Negotiating Agents"

Publication: *Group Decision and Negotiation*

Date: 2012

Authors: Gert Jan Hofstede, Catholijn M. Jonker, and Tim Verwaart

Executive Summary: Negotiations proceed differently across cultures. For realistic modeling of agents in multicultural negotiations, the agents must display culturally differentiated behavior. This paper presents an agent-based simulation model that tackles these challenges, based on Hofstede's model of national cultures.

•••

Title: "Cross-Cultural Communication in Business Negotiations"

Publication: *International Journal of Economics and Finance*

Date: 2010

Author: Liangguang Huang

Executive Summary: All communication is cultural; it draws on ways we have learned to speak and give nonverbal messages. With the implementation of the Economic Reform and Opening policies, more and more Chinese companies do business with the foreigners. When negotiating with the delegates from different countries, cross-cultural communications play an important role. Culture differs from one another, which influences the style, the time, and the course of negotiations.

•••

Title: "The Influence of Culture in International Business Negotiations: A New Conceptual Framework and Managerial Implications"

Publication: *Journal of Transnational Management*

Date: 2010

Authors: Lalita Manrai and Ajay Manrai

Executive Summary: International business negotiations play a fundamental and critical role in just about every aspect of conducting business in today's global economy. The scope of international business negotiations spans goods and services; purchases of raw materials and supplies; distribution of products; advertising and market research activities; licensing and technology transfer agreements; setting up franchises and manufacturing operations; strategic alliances including joint ventures, mergers, and acquisitions; and much more.

INTERPERSONAL IMPACT

Title: "Negotiations, Chinese Style"

Publication: *The China Business Review*

Date: 2010

Author: Betsy Neidel

Executive Summary: To become or remain competitive in China, corporations may have to enter second- or third-tier cities, build relationships with regional and niche players, or cultivate deals in China's interior provinces. When working outside first-tier cities, where officials and local companies tend to be more attuned to Western deal-making styles, corporations can benefit from honing their Chinese-style negotiation skills, regardless of their level of experience in China. The objective of strategic preparation for negotiations is to gain insight into the negotiating partner's situation, intent, and capabilities and to identify areas of focus for discussions.

....

Title: "Cultural Impacts in International Negotiation"

Publication: *ADR Bulletin*

Date: 2010

Author: Simen Moen Nordbo

Executive Summary: The objective of this article is to examine the concept of culture, to review how Norwegian culture influences and determines negotiation processes and behaviors, and to give guidance on recommended approaches and behaviors in dealing with Norwegians.

....

Title: "Navigating the Rough Seas of Global Business Negotiation: Reflection on Cross-Cultural Issues and Some Corporate Experiences"

Publication: *International Journal of Business Insights & Transformation*

Date: 2010

Author: A. N. Sarkar

Executive Summary: The paper highlights some of the important aspects that need to be carefully considered for entering into successful international business negotiation through sound processes. In global negotiation, cross-cultural issues figure prominently and largely determine the success or failures of negotiations, especially for joint ventures.

....

Title: "A Traveler to Distant Places Should Make No Enemies: Toward Understanding Nigerian Negotiating Style"

Publication: *Journal of Applied Business and Economics*

Date: 2011

Authors: Samuel A. Spralls III, Patrick Okonkwo, and Obasi H. Akan

Executive Summary: The literature on international business negotiations, particularly that focusing on cultural negotiating styles, largely ignores Africa. In Africa, Nigeria is poised to escape poverty, achieve sustained growth, and make rapid gains in living standards. As worldwide economic interdependence continues to grow, collaborative agreements between companies in Nigeria and the United States will likely increase. A necessary precondition to the development of such agreements is the successful cross-cultural negotiation of the terms for their establishment.

....

Title: "An Analysis on Negotiation Styles by Religious Beliefs"

Publication: *International Business Research*

Date: 2011

Authors: Yu-te Tu and Heng-chi Chih

Executive Summary: This paper explores the effect of religious culture on negotiations. Specifically, we compare and contrast the effects of religious orientation on the negotiating styles of Greater China (Taiwan, Hong Kong, and China). The research aims to investigate the role of religious culture as a factor in shaping the negotiation styles of people with different religious beliefs.

INTERPERSONAL IMPACT

NETWORKING OVER THE PHONE

GLOBAL SOCIAL CAPITAL

Strong Networks with People from Other Cultures and with Influential People

Strong networks with people from other cultures and with influential people refer to your personal and professional network of colleagues across the world with whom you sustain a connection through periodic communication. Your ability to form and sustain these networks is determined by your general ability to network with others, your personal influence, and your proactive efforts to build your network cross-culturally.

Consider the example of Kiva Microfunds founders Jessica Jackley and Matt Flannery. Kiva is a nonprofit organization that allows people to lend money via the Internet to people in developing countries. What began as a test project to fund seven entrepreneurs in Africa in 2005 quickly turned into a successful and growing nonprofit. In 2005, Kiva funded $3,500 in loans; by 2006 it had reached $1 million in loan funding. Today, the loans are in the hundreds of millions.

How did two young, unknown entrepreneurs make this happen so quickly? It was because of the very strong networks they built across cultures and with influential people. They did this by facilitating real emotional connections between lenders and those in need. Their website (www.kiva.org) includes personal stories of each person who needs a loan, giving lenders the opportunity to personally connect with their entrepreneurs. They read about these people's life stories, their families, their business goals, and their dreams for better lives. This transformed the concept from one where people simply lend money to a personal mission to help another real person realize their dreams and create prosperity for their families. By doing this, Kiva has created a strong network with people from 220 countries.

INTERPERSONAL IMPACT

BEIJING, CHINA

Zhu Difeng / Shutterstock.com

Strong Networks with People from Other Cultures and with Influential People in Action

Years ago when I was working in China, my daughter came to visit and we went on a tour. While on the tour, we met a French family and an Indian family. The Frenchman and the Indian man were in China working for a company that had a partnership with a Chinese company.

BARRIE ZUCAL, MS
President and CEO
Global Coaches Network

Years ago when I was working in China, my daughter came to visit and we went on a tour. While on the tour, we met a French family and an Indian family. The Frenchman and the Indian man were in China working for a company that had a partnership with a Chinese company. They seemed like very nice people, and we had a lovely day with them.

The next day, I was in the hotel lobby and I heard the Frenchman and the Indian talking while they were waiting for their Chinese counterpart. Their whole conversation was about what was wrong with the way the Chinese worked and how the way that they worked was superior. They were bonding over their criticism of the Chinese while in China working in a partnership with the Chinese. This is not the way to build strong networks in other cultures.

Unfortunately, I have seen these situations occur all over the world with one person or one culture positioning themselves above another, with seemingly no concern for the effect of this on their ability to work well together. Strong networks have to start with a foundation of respect for each other and an appreciation of different working styles.

DEVELOPMENT SUGGESTIONS

for Strong Networks with People from Other Cultures and with Influential People

LEARN

Tips to learn about and begin developing the capability on your own. These tips involve self-directed learning, including reading, listening, watching, or observing, that you can do on your own at your own pace. They are most useful for novices in the capability, but are helpful for intermediate and advanced learners to keep knowledge current.

Development Activity	Suggested Resource(s) and Tips
Learn how to build trust in global business.	• Read *The Speed of Trust: The One Thing That Changes Everything* (Covey, 2006), which discusses how trust is the basis of the new global economy. • Read *Working GlobeSmart: 12 People Skills for Doing Business Across Borders* (Gundling, 2010), which highlights the importance of people skills in cross-cultural business environments. • Read *Trust Within Virtual Global Teams: Antecedents, Facilitators, and Sustainability Factors* (Chavaren, 2003), which discusses how to build trust across time, space, and cultures.
Learn how to build trust specifically in the culture of interest to you by looking at these themes: how hierarchy is viewed in the culture, what values are prevalent in the culture, and how people in the culture show respect to one another.	• Use the GlobeSmart tool (www.aperianglobal.com). • Obtain a Culture Gram report about the culture of interest (www.culturegrams.com). • Read about culturally specific values in the GLOBE studies: *Culture, Leadership, and Organizations: The GLOBE Study of 62 Societies* (House, et al., 2004) and *Culture and Leadership Across the World: The GLOBE Book of In-Depth Studies of 25 Societies* (Chhokar, et al., 2007).
Find out who the influential people are in the culture of interest to you.	• Read local society pages to become aware of who has influence. • Ask native local colleagues about influential people in the culture generally and specifically in your industry and organization.
Learn how to build strong networks.	• Surf *Entrepreneur*'s blog post "Five Rules for Building Strong Connections" (www.entrepreneur.com/article/220441), which includes video tutorials. • Read *The Connection Effect: Building Strong Personal, Professional, and Virtual Networks* (Dulworth, 2008). • Read *Networking for People Who Hate Networking: A Field Guide for Introverts, the Overwhelmed, and the Underconnected* (Zack, 2010).

DEVELOPMENT SUGGESTIONS
for Strong Networks with People from Other Cultures and with Influential People

CONNECT

Tips to learn about and continue developing the capability through others. These tips involve working with another person to learn from their experiences. They may involve asking questions, listening to and discussing experiences, forming a new relationship, deepening an existing relationship, or receiving feedback from someone who is acting as your mentor. These tips are useful for all levels of learners.

Development Activity	Suggested Resource(s) and Tips
Get to know your colleagues, business partners, suppliers, and customers.	• Build relationships before they are needed by periodically engaging people in your network in dialogue. • Build networking time into trips to headquarters and other locales. • Host people in your network after working hours. • Really get to know who the people in your network are by reading their biographies when available and asking them what they do outside of work. • Seek input from people in your network to enrich your work and to help you get to know them better. • Draw on shared passions by identifying shared interests and making the other person aware that you share that interest. • Host conversations through LinkedIn.
Be a valuable resource to people in your network to sustain and strengthen your relationship.	• When people in your network have a specific need, connect them to people who can help them. This can strengthen your relationship. • Behave in ways that make people in your network trust you by being visible and transparent, responding to their communications in a timely fashion, and doing what you say you will do.
Grow your network through connections you already have.	• Use your company directory to contact your colleagues in other countries. • Learn about your friends' friends (e.g., who they are, who they know), and ask to be connected to people of interest. • Be active on professional social networks like LinkedIn (www.linkedin.com). • Connect to your school's alumni network.
Create not just strong networks, but differentiated networks too.	• Involve yourself in both physical and virtual social networks. • Ask your colleagues who they think you should get to know in other countries where your organization operates. Ask your colleagues to introduce you to them. • Find a mentor in your industry or organization who can help you network with others. • Check your network against diversity criteria (e.g., age, culture, economic class) to make sure you have a diverse network. • Build a database of contacts so you can find people's contact details when needed. • Use the app "Society of International Business Leaders" by Phunware Inc., which shares common interest business expertise among global networks.

DEVELOPMENT SUGGESTIONS
for Strong Networks with People from Other Cultures and with Influential People

EXPERIENCE

Tips to learn about and develop skills in the capability through firsthand experience. These tips involve engaging in activities, such as exploring a new area, trying a new cultural activity, or participating in a specific business event. These tips are most useful for intermediate to advanced learners, and we suggest that novice learners prepare themselves for success by completing some of the tips in the Learn category first.

Development Activity	Suggested Resource(s) and Tips
Use common and effective door openers for networking.	• Discover the interests of other people in the country by asking local natives and reading guidebooks. Start conversations with others about these topics. • Be curious and open to learn about other cultures. Ask your colleagues about their specific interests and hobbies. • Identify a shared interest that you have with a colleague, and let them know that you have this in common. • Introduce colleagues to one another using thoughtful details about their positive characteristics and interests. This can expand your network.
Connect with local organizations in cultures of interest that will create an instant network for you to grow.	• Join chamber of commerce organizations in countries of interest. For example, AmChams is the name of US Chamber of Commerce organizations located in 102 countries across the world (www.uschamber.com/international/directory). • Contact people in your embassy and consulate in other countries. • Join Rotary International, which has chapters in many countries (www.rotaryinternational.org). • Find local and community groups on topics of interest to you through organizations like MeetUp (www.meetup.com). • Join Toastmasters International (www.toastmasters.org), where you can meet other professionals and build your speaking skills at the same time. • In your local town, identify government officials. Practice building relationships locally with them. • Participate in professional organizations for your industry and job function. • Join boards and foundations of groups that interest you, especially those in which you are an alumnus.

GLOBAL SOCIAL CAPITAL

EXPERIENCE

Tips to learn about and develop skills in the capability through firsthand experience. These tips involve engaging in activities, such as exploring a new area, trying a new cultural activity, or participating in a specific business event. These tips are most useful for intermediate to advanced learners, and we suggest that novice learners prepare themselves for success by completing some of the tips in the Learn category first.

Development Activity	Suggested Resource(s) and Tips
Actively network with stakeholders in your organization; they are influential people.	• Do a stakeholder assessment, identifying who the top ten stakeholders are for your work in your organization. Connect with them regularly. Ask one of them to be a professional mentor to you if appropriate and possible. • Ask your manager and your colleagues who they view as the most influential people in your organization, your industry, and the culture you are working in and why they are influential. Connect with them if possible. • Ask colleagues who are well-networked to introduce you to stakeholders and influential people when possible. Be sure to reciprocate.
Put yourself in a position to meet and interact with influential people in other cultures.	• Attend presentations where influential people are speaking, and meet them afterward. • Be active in leadership organizations. • Go to international conferences and actively work to develop networks there. • Attend local cultural events (e.g., music, food, film), and invite people in your network to join you. • Volunteer for a global cross-functional business team.
Build rapport by remembering people's names and at least one positive accomplishment or interest of that person.	• When you first meet someone, repeat his or her name back in response (e.g., "It's nice to meet you, Susan."). • Use the person's name in conversation, but don't overdo it. Once or twice is enough. • Find an opportunity to introduce the person you just met to another person, and use his or her name and a thoughtful detail about an accomplishment or interest. • Associate the person's name with something you can remember, such as another person with the same name or an image, song, or activity (e.g., George could inspire a picture of King George, a song by George Harrison, or a hike you once did in Georgia). • Mentally link an accomplishment or interest of the person to his or her name (e.g., Michael has a master's degree in economics; Barry loves boating).

INTERPERSONAL IMPACT

DEVELOPMENT SUGGESTIONS
for Strong Networks with People from Other Cultures and with Influential People

COACH OR CONTRIBUTE

Tips to help others learn about and develop this capability. These tips involve coaching and mentoring others. They may include creating information or experiences for individuals, teams, or your organization. These tips are designed for those who are advanced in the capability and are useful development methods to keep advanced leaders in the capability engaged in professional development at the highest level. Please note that the tips in this section may also be quite helpful for individual use if you do not have a coach or mentor.

Development Activity	Suggested Resource(s) and Tips
Network on behalf of other people.	• Introduce people you know to each other, and ask your acquaintances to do the same for you. • When people in your network have a specific need, connect them to people who can help them. This can strengthen your relationship.
Host networking events.	• Facilitate think tanks, where you invite several people in your network to join you in dialogue about a topic of importance to your function or industry. This can be done in person or virtually using conference calls or web or video meeting software. • Host a workshop for new and developing employees where more experienced colleagues share their wisdom and answer questions. • Take an active role in a professional organization where you help organize gatherings.
Help others achieve their goals.	• Host an exchange student. • Offer to be a mentor in your organization for new employees. • Offer to be a professional mentor through your local business school. • Spend quality time with your direct reports to mentor them.

COACH OR CONTRIBUTE

Tips to help others learn about and develop this capability. These tips involve coaching and mentoring others. They may include creating information or experiences for individuals, teams, or your organization. These tips are designed for those who are advanced in the capability and are useful development methods to keep advanced leaders in the capability engaged in professional development at the highest level. Please note that the tips in this section may also be quite helpful for individual use if you do not have a coach or mentor.

Development Activity	Suggested Resource(s) and Tips
When coaching your direct reports or mentees, ask open-ended questions to get them thinking about how they can better network.	Ask: • What currently impedes your networking efforts? • What worries do you have about networking? • How can you manage or resolve these worries? • Think about a time you have been successful forming business relationships with others. What did you do? How can you use that to build your network? • What organizations do you belong to that you can use to start building your network? • What organizations should you belong to to build your network in the direction you want to grow it? • Who do you know who can connect you with others you would like to meet? • How will networking help you be successful? • What are the consequences of not networking? • In two years, how would you like to see your professional network developed? What can you do now to make that happen? • Who do you know who is a successful networker who can mentor you on how to build your own network?

Additional Reading

The readings listed here provide you with additional study of the Global Mindset capability in this section. You will find that many of these resources provide you with a specific and detailed look at using this capability in a particular context or location.

Title: "Networking for Sales Success in Overseas Government Markets"

Publication: *Competitiveness Review*

Date: 2007

Authors: Felix Abeson and Michael A. Taku

Executive Summary: The purpose of this paper is to examine the relationship between sales networks and effectiveness in overseas government markets with a focus on overseas home-country officials and local key government officials. The practical implications of this study include the need for international sales managers to engage in networking involving their home-country official overseas as well as local government officials. Therefore, exporting advocacy is important. Also, the education and training of international sales people should emphasize the concept of sales network.

Title: "Influence of Culture on Relationship Development Processes in Overseas Chinese/Australian Networks"

Publication: *European Journal of Marketing*

Date: 2003

Authors: Gerry Batonda and Chad Perry

Executive Summary: This paper examines the effect of culture on inter-firm network development in international marketing. Differences and similarities between how overseas Chinese and Australian cultures affect network development and strategies for developing and maintaining quality and long-term relationship in cross-cultural networks were identified. Implications for practice emphasize the importance of cultural adaptation.

Title: "Mentoring across Global Boundaries: An Empirical Examination of Home- and Host-Country Mentors on Expatriate Career Outcomes"

Publication: *Journal of International Business Studies*

Date: 2008

Authors: Shawn M. Carraher, Sherry E. Sullivan, and Madeline M. Crocitto

Executive Summary: There has long been an interest in the effects of mentors on protégé career outcomes, especially with scholars now beginning to examine mentoring across national boundaries. Using survey information as well as company records for 299 expatriates (163 men, 136 women) in ten countries, we examined the effect of home- and host-country mentors upon expatriate effectiveness. We found that having a host-country mentor had a significant positive effect on the expatriate's organizational knowledge, organizational knowledge-sharing, job performance, promotability, and perceptions of teamwork.

Title: "Social Networks and Marketing Cooperation in Entrepreneurial Clusters: An International Comparative Study"

Publication: *Journal of International Entrepreneurship*

Date: 2009

Authors: Christian Felzensztein and Eli Gimmon

Executive Summary: The study focus is on the development of joint marketing activities between firms operating in a single industry sector, located in close proximity. The results suggest that social networking is important in facilitating inter-firm cooperation in marketing activities. The study also explores whether the levels of inter-firm cooperation differ between countries with distinctly different levels of social collectivism.

INTERPERSONAL IMPACT

Title: "Do Culture and Global Social Capital Impact the Networking Attributes of Indigenous Entrepreneurs?"

Publication: *Journal of Enterprising Communities*

Date: 2008

Author: Dennis Foley

Executive Summary: This paper provides a new perspective on the existence of Global Social Capital effects on networking for indigenous entrepreneurs.

Title: "Social Networks and Business Success: The Role of Subcultures in an African Context"

Publication: *The American Journal of Economics and Sociology*

Date: 2004

Author: Stein Kristiansen

Executive Summary: The main objective of this paper is to illuminate social and cultural preconditions for networking and success in business in an African context. By in-depth studies of small-scale entrepreneurs in the wood business in Tanzania, we find that people belonging to an Asian subculture probably have a better standing for entering and thriving in business, due to group cohesion, mobility, and level of education.

Title: "Western and Eastern Views on Social Networks"

Publication: *The Learning Organization*

Date: 2005

Author: Patricia Ordonez de Pablos

Executive Summary: The paper uses case study methodology to gather evidence of how world pioneering firms from Asia and Europe measure and report their social connections from a Western perspective. It examines the basic indicators firms use to measure these networks and the major issues managers should consider when measuring and reporting these knowledge-based resources.

Title: "Are Born Globals Really Born Globals? The Case of Academic Spin-Offs with Long Development Periods"

Publication: *Journal of International Entrepreneurship*

Date: 2012

Authors: Inger Pettersen and Anita Tobiassen

Executive Summary: In analysis, we identify networks that provide financial resources, knowledge, innovation and technology resources, marketing, and reputational resources. Networks acquired at different stages and network changes greatly affected growth and internationalization in the focal firms. We also find that networks and resources acquired in prefounding periods had great implications for growth and internationalization in the young firms.

Title: "Expatriates' Developmental Networks: Network Diversity, Base, and Support Functions"

Publication: *Career Development International*

Date: 2011

Authors: Yan Shen and Kathy E. Kram

Executive Summary: The purpose of this paper is to examine expatriates' developmental networks in terms of their structure and content. The study employed in-depth interviews with sixty-four expatriate professionals and managers in Singapore and China.

Title: "Influence of Social Networks on Internationalization of Russian SMEs"

Publication: *Proceedings of the World Conference of the International Council for Small Business*

Date: 2011

Author: Galina Shirokova

Executive Summary: In international entrepreneurship research, social networks are considered one of the most important factors in the process of internationalization. They help to make the decision to go abroad and facilitate the process of finding new international partners. Social networks provide necessary information and contacts. Entrepreneurial firms have to rely more on the social networks and personal contacts in the internationalization process comparatively with large companies as a result of their limited financial and human resources.

....

Title: "Networking: A Valuable Career Intervention for Women Expatriates?"

Publication: *Career Development International*

Date: 2011

Author: Susan Shortland

Executive Summary: The purpose of this paper is to report on female expatriates' views on the potential importance of a formalized women's network launched by management as a diversity intervention to aid women's career development in an oil, gas, and minerals extractive industries firm.

....

Title: "Culture, Cognition, and Collaborative Networks in Organizations"

Publication: *American Sociological Review*

Date: 2011

Author: Sameer B. Srivastava

Executive Summary: This article examines the interplay of culture, cognition, and social networks in organizations with norms that emphasize cross-boundary collaboration. In such settings, social desirability concerns can induce a disparity between how people view themselves in conscious (i.e., deliberative) versus less conscious (i.e., automatic) cognition. These differences have implications for the resulting pattern of intra-organizational collaborative ties.

Title: "International Entrepreneurial Capability: The Measurement and a Comparison Between Born Global Firms and Traditional Exporters in China"

Publication: *Journal of International Entrepreneurship*

Date: 2009

Authors: Man Zhang, Patriya Tansuhaj, and James McCullough

Executive Summary: This study presents the development and application of a new measure of international entrepreneurial capability. The data were collected from manufacturing firms in China, both traditional exporters and born global firms. Five key dimensions of international entrepreneurial capability were identified from the capability and entrepreneurship literature. After scale purification and validation, this new measure was used to examine the relationship between international entrepreneurial capability and global market performance. Born global firms are statistically different from traditional firms along three dimensions: international learning capability, international networking capability, and international experience.

INTERPERSONAL IMPACT

GLOBAL SOCIAL CAPITAL

STATUE OF GANDHI · SAN FRANCISCO, CALIFORNIA

Eric Broker Van Dyke / Shutterstock.com

Reputation as a Leader

Your reputation as a leader refers to how you consistently present yourself through your communication, presence, and behaviors to others. According to renowned industrial and organizational psychologist Dr. Robert Hogan, reputation is distinct from personal identity. Identity is how you view yourself on the inside. You may desire to be a collaborative leader, for instance. However, if you consistently micromanage your direct reports and devalue their ideas, then your reputation would actually demonstrate that you are an autocratic leader.

Reputation is how others view and experience you and is a much better predictor of performance than identity, according to Dr. Hogan. This is why it is critical when you are building your reputation as a leader to pay very close attention to your real-time communication, presence, and behaviors. They will paint a vibrant picture of who you really are as a leader and whether you are someone with whom people would be inclined to collaborate. Cross-cultural management research shows that there are some behaviors that work well across cultures to build one's management reputation: consistency, transparency, supportive behavior toward others, keeping promises, providing positive motivation, developing personal relationships, showing respect and care for others, and producing results.

While behaviors are key to this capability, we believe it is important for new and developing leaders to develop a personal vision prior to identifying appropriate behaviors. There are many tips in this section to help you craft a personal vision. This vision can be used as an important touchstone in your day-to-day life to remain focused on the behaviors that will help you build the reputation you desire.

INTERPERSONAL IMPACT

GUANAJUATO, MEXICO

Reputation as a Leader in Action

A nonprofit organization based outside the United States decided to buy a van through a grant offered by a US institution. But the van couldn't be delivered and placed in use before the termination of the grant period.

ŞIRIN Z. KÖPRÜCÜ, MBA
International Business Consultant
StrategicStraits Inc.

"A nonprofit organization based outside the United States decided to buy a van through a grant offered by a US institution. But the van couldn't be delivered and placed in use before the termination of the grant period. This was not allowable according to the grant terms.

"Leaders at the foreign nonprofit organization consulted with their US-based accounting firm. Their accountant was from the same country and was sympathetic to the situation. He suggested that the organization make up a receipt with a proper date on it that would show that the van had been delivered within the grant period. This was a solution the accountant and the foreign organization agreed upon together. However, after listening to both parties carefully and reflecting on this matter sympathetically, the accountant's supervisor had to reject the solution. He explained that this was against the law in the United States and that, as a result, the cost of the van could not be covered with the US grant funding. The accounting supervisor made a difficult decision that upheld the integrity of the firm and his reputation as a leader."

* This example was shared with Ms. Köprücü by a client.

DEVELOPMENT SUGGESTIONS
for Reputation as a Leader

LEARN

Tips to learn about and begin developing the capability on your own. These tips involve self-directed learning, including reading, listening, watching, or observing, that you can do on your own at your own pace. They are most useful for novices in the capability, but are helpful for intermediate and advanced learners to keep knowledge current.

Development Activity	Suggested Resource(s) and Tips
Evaluate your current reputation as a leader.	• Use a 360-assessment tool, such as the Global Mindset Inventory 360 version (www.globalmindset.com) to understand the views of your colleagues, manager, and others. • Listen to stories people are telling you about their experience of you, and evaluate how you can use this information to make positive changes. • Ask colleagues and supervisors who are important players in your function and industry to provide their opinion of your reputation and how you can strengthen it. • Look at your social media presence by reviewing the image your profiles convey and updating them accordingly. • Hire a publicist to evaluate your reputation and coach you on how to improve it.
Decide what reputation you aspire to.	• Read books that include strategies on how to build your reputation, such as *The Power of Reputation: Strengthen the Asset That Will Make or Break Your Career* (Komisarjevsky, 2012) and *Brand You Fifty: Fifty Ways to Transform Yourself from an Employee into a Brand That Shouts Distinction, Commitment, and Passion!* (Peters, 1999). • Think about which leaders resonate with you. Write down the main behaviors and qualities that you would like to adopt from them. • Reflect on the legacy you would like to create in the next five years, ten years, and at the end of your career. • Create an action plan describing how you will actively use the behaviors and reflect the qualities you aspire toward.

DEVELOPMENT SUGGESTIONS
for Reputation as a Leader

LEARN

Tips to learn about and begin developing the capability on your own. These tips involve self-directed learning, including reading, listening, watching, or observing, that you can do on your own at your own pace. They are most useful for novices in the capability, but are helpful for intermediate and advanced learners to keep knowledge current.

Development Activity	Suggested Resource(s) and Tips
Create a visual collage (i.e., a personal vision board) based upon your findings from reflecting on the reputation you aspire to that includes images and words that you can see daily. This will help keep you focused and motivated.	Here are some resources to help you create your personal vision board: • Martha Beck describes the benefits and steps to create a personal vision board (http://marthabeck.com/2008/07/the-subtle-tricks-to-building-an-effective-vision-board). • *Visioning: Ten Steps to Designing the Life of Your Dreams* (Capacchione, 2000) illustrates how to turn your goals into visual inspiration and uses reflection activities throughout. • *The Complete Idiot's Guide to Vision Boards* (Turner, 2009) includes instructions and photos on how to create your own vision board.
Study successful leaders in the culture of interest to see what is valued.	• Read stories of historical and current leaders in a culture who are considered admirable. This can be done using local guidebooks, such as Lonely Planet (www.lonelyplanet.com), Fodor's (www.fodors.com), Frommer's (www.frommers.com), and Rough Guides (www.roughguides.com). • Read *In the Eye of the Beholder: Cross-Cultural Lessons in Leadership from Project GLOBE* (Javidan, et al., 2006).

DEVELOPMENT SUGGESTIONS
for Reputation as a Leader

CONNECT

Tips to learn about and continue developing the capability through others. These tips involve working with another person to learn from their experiences. They may involve asking questions, listening to and discussing experiences, forming a new relationship, deepening an existing relationship, or receiving feedback from someone who is acting as your mentor. These tips are useful for all levels of learners.

Development Activity	Suggested Resource(s) and Tips
Build your reputation by proxy through relationships with others who are credible.	• Form a relationship with someone who already has a good reputation as a leader. • Ask colleagues and mentors with already strong leadership reputations to introduce you to others with whom you would like to connect. • Gain credibility with high-ranking people in your organization or industry by volunteering to work with them and proving your merit. • In other cultures, identify who the local connectors are (i.e., people who are trusted and respected) and work through them to meet business partners and suppliers. • Be a resource and connector for others to help build and expand your reputation as a leader.
Examine your current reputation in the culture of interest.	• Ask your local colleagues and business partners for their feedback on how your leadership style is viewed in the culture and how you can adapt it for success in that environment. • Be open to learning about the leadership cultures of your colleagues, business partners, suppliers, and customers.
Study successful leaders in the culture of interest to see what is valued.	Ask local colleagues who they value as leaders in the culture and why.

DEVELOPMENT SUGGESTIONS
for Reputation as a Leader

EXPERIENCE

Tips to learn about and develop skills in the capability through firsthand experience. These tips involve engaging in activities, such as exploring a new area, trying a new cultural activity, or participating in a specific business event. These tips are most useful for intermediate to advanced learners, and we suggest that novice learners prepare themselves for success by completing some of the tips in the Learn category first.

Development Activity	Suggested Resource(s) and Tips
Build your reputation as if it were your personal brand, and manage it actively.	The following tips were gathered from expert international executive coaches and are considered positive reflections of leadership across cultures: • Be visible among your staff and colleagues. • Treat even the most inexperienced employee with respect at all times. • Do what you say you will do. Commit to small steps if it makes it easier for you to ensure delivery. • Be a good communicator by being clear about your intentions and expectations. Use language that conveys action. • Make sure you understand others' comments and viewpoints. • Be adaptable and flexible to the local culture. • Do nice things for your employees and staff, such as recognizing them in a culturally appropriate way when they perform well. Be helpful to colleagues.
Practice your leadership by being active in social, professional, and philanthropic organizations.	• Find local and community groups on topics of interest to you through organizations like MeetUp (www.meetup.com). • Volunteer for leadership roles or create your own group to lead. • Participate in professional organizations for your industry and job function. Volunteer for leadership roles. • Join boards and foundations of groups that interest you, especially those in which you are an alumnus. • Volunteer for a leadership role in a community group, such as the following: homeowners association, parent/teacher/student groups, nonprofit groups, religious groups, or sporting organizations. • Debrief your experiences in these organizations with senior members, and ask them for feedback on how you are doing in your leadership role.

INTERPERSONAL IMPACT

DEVELOPMENT SUGGESTIONS
for Reputation as a Leader

COACH OR CONTRIBUTE

Tips to help others learn about and develop this capability. These tips involve coaching and mentoring others. They may include creating information or experiences for individuals, teams, or your organization. These tips are designed for those who are advanced in the capability and are useful development methods to keep advanced leaders in the capability engaged in professional development at the highest level. Please note that the tips in this section may also be quite helpful for individual use if you do not have a coach or mentor.

Development Activity	Suggested Resource(s) and Tips
As a manager of others, find out what your team needs to be successful and act on those things.	• Individually ask team members what they need to be successful in their roles and how you can support them. • Ask the team as a whole what they need from you as a leader to be successful. • Ensure that your team has the necessary resources to complete the job effectively. • Help your direct reports, mentees, and colleagues succeed by connecting them to people, resources, and information of interest to them. • Regularly reinforce goals, communicate project status, and praise good work in culturally appropriate ways. • Attend to social needs of the team, as culturally appropriate, by sponsoring team social events regularly. • Work to develop each individual on your team to meet the goals of his or her current position as well as his or her career goals.
When coaching your direct reports or mentees, ask open-ended questions to get them thinking about how they strengthen their reputation as a leader.	Ask: • What is your current reputation? How do you know? • Who should you talk to to get a candid idea of what your reputation currently is as a leader? • Who are two or three people you admire for their reputation as a leader? Why? • What qualities or behaviors would you like to adopt from leaders you admire? How will you make these a reality? • What learning, training, or behavior changes do you need to create the reputation you desire?

Additional Reading

The readings listed here provide you with additional study of the Global Mindset capability in this section. You will find that many of these resources provide you with a specific and detailed look at using this capability in a particular context or location.

....

Title: "The Leader's Role in Managing Reputation"

Publication: *Reputational Capital: Building and Maintaining Trust in the 21st Century*

Date: 2009

Authors: Gary Davies and Rosa Chun

Executive Summary: The leader of an organization has a central role in managing reputation. Leaders can personify their company to many stakeholders. Their personality will influence that of the organization they lead. In a crisis, internal and external stakeholders may insist that the leader accept a prominent role. Research indicates that while the reputation of the leader and organization are distinct from one another, they are strongly associated. Where the leader adopts the role of company spokesperson, nearly half of corporate reputation may emanate from his or her own image.

....

Title: "Don't Confuse Reputation with Brand"

Publication: *MIT Sloan Management Review*

Date: 2008

Authors: Richard Ettenson and Jonathan Knowles

Executive Summary: Many executives speak about corporate reputation and brand as if they are one and the same. They are not, and confusing the two can be costly—a lesson that companies like Nike and Walmart have learned the hard way. Focusing on reputation at the expense of brand can lead to product offerings that languish in the market. However, concentrating on brand and neglecting reputation can be equally dangerous, resulting in a lower stock price, difficulties in attracting top talent, and even product boycotts.

Title: "Satisfaction, Corporate Credibility, CEO Reputation and Leadership Effects on Public Relationships"

Publication: *Journal of Targeting, Measurement and Analysis for Marketing*

Date: 2011

Authors: Chang-hyun Jin and Hyun-chul Yeo

Executive Summary: The purpose of this study is to examine the effects that negative and positive news stories about corporate activities have on customer relationships with those companies. To test the proposed hypotheses, a two-by-two (positive versus negative news story; high versus low customer satisfaction) factorial design was implemented. The dependent variables are corporate credibility, CEO reputation for leadership, and customer perceptions of the quality of customer–company relationships.

Title: "Reputation Leadership"

Publication: *Leadership Excellence*

Date: 2010

Author: Nir Kossovsky

Executive Summary: Leaders know that reputation matters and that a good reputation brings countless benefits; and yet, most leaders don't appreciate fully the financial benefits of a good reputation or the costs of a damaged one.

Title: "Crisis Leadership: When Should the CEO Step Up?"

Publication: *Corporate Communications*

Date: 2009

Authors: Marela Lucero, Teng Kwang Alywin Tan, and Augustine Pang

Executive Summary: One explicit leadership role the CEO can play during crisis is to assume the role of being the organization's spokesperson. The CEO needs to step up to revise earlier statements or when the integrity of the organization is questioned. Additionally, the CEO should step up at the beginning of the crisis if the crisis pertains to organizational transgression or when the crisis becomes unbearable to organizational reputation.

Title: "Reputation, Trust and the Dynamics of Leadership in Communities of Practice"

Publication: *Journal of Management & Governance*

Date: 2006

Author: Paul Muller

Executive Summary: We argue that communities of practice adopt some specific patterns of internal organization where some of their members obtain a leadership status. Leaders contribute to cognitive advance of the community of practice by providing members with a consistent and coherent vision of its objectives.

Title: "The Importance of Reputation"

Publication: *Risk Management*

Date: 2008

Author: Ansi Vallens

Executive Summary: Reputation is a nebulous term. Reputation is how a company is perceived by its stakeholders, including customers, partners, employees, and regulators. According to a 2005 report by *The Economist* Intelligence Unit, reputation risk is the greatest risk facing global companies.

Title: "Managing Industry Reputation: The Dynamic Tension Between Collective and Competitive Reputation Management Strategies"

Publication: *Corporate Reputation Review*

Date: 2008

Authors: Monika I. Winn, Patricia Macdonald, and Charlene Zietsma

Executive Summary: To broaden understanding of the dynamics of collective reputation management, we conducted a longitudinal, qualitative study of two industries whose legitimacy was under sustained and intense attack by environmental stakeholders. Our study traces the emergence of, and dynamic tension between, collective and competitive reputation management and examines the motives for and effects of specific strategies used by the industry, individual firms, and groups of firms.

INTERPERSONAL IMPACT

FLAGS OF ALL NATIONS · UNITED NATIONS HEADQUARTERS · GENEVA, SWITZERLAND

GLOBAL SOCIAL CAPITAL

Diplomacy

As shown in **Figure 9-1** on page 474, this chapter examines Diplomacy, which is a key dimension of Global Social Capital. Diplomacy is a word that is usually associated with national governments. A diplomat is a person who represents his or her country abroad. Even though many global leaders work for private corporations, their work around the globe really begins as a representative for their country, their culture, and their organization. This is why diplomatic skills, like being a good conversation starter, being a good listener, integrating diverse perspectives, and being a good collaborator are equally important for government diplomats and global leaders alike. Global leaders need the support, collaboration, and cooperation of a variety of stakeholders from different parts of the world to achieve their objectives. This can only be achieved and sustained through diplomacy.

A global leader who has a high level of diplomacy is someone who starts from the premise that other people have very good ideas. They may be different from hers, but she is going to listen, explore those ideas, and figure out a way of building bridges between her way of doing things or seeing the world and their way. By showing the other people that she is willing to listen and that she respects their ideas, she in turn attracts their trust and respect. She makes everybody feel important, and this engages them to collaborate willingly toward mutual goals.

In this chapter, we will provide tips and resources for the four components of diplomacy:

- ease of starting a conversation with a stranger

- ability to integrate diverse perspectives

- ability to listen to what others have to say

- willingness to collaborate

DEVELOPING YOUR GLOBAL MINDSET

GLOBAL MINDSET

Global INTELLECTUAL CAPITAL

Global Business Savvy

Knowledge of global industry

Knowledge of global competitive business and marketing strategies

Knowledge of how to transact business and assess risks of doing business internationally

Knowledge of supplier options in other parts of the world

Cosmopolitan Outlook

Knowledge of cultures in different parts of the world

Knowledge of geography, history, and important persons of several countries

Knowledge of economic & political issues, concerns, & hot topics of major regions of the world

Up-to-date knowledge of important world events

Cognitive Complexity

Ability to grasp complex topics quickly

Strong analytical and problem solving skills

Ability to understand abstract ideas

Ability to take complex issues and explain the main points simply and understandably

Global PSYCHOLOGICAL CAPITAL

Passion for Diversity

Enjoy exploring other parts of the world

Enjoy getting to know people from other parts of the world

Enjoy living in another country

Enjoy traveling

Quest for Adventure

Interest in dealing with challenging situations

Willingness to take risk

Willingness to test one's abilities

Enjoy dealing with unpredictable situations

Self-Assurance

Energetic

Self-confident

Comfortable in uncomfortable situations

Witty in tough situations

Global SOCIAL CAPITAL

Intercultural Empathy

Ability to work well with people from other parts of the world

Ability to understand nonverbal expressions of people from other cultures

Ability to emotionally connect to people from other cultures

Ability to engage people from other parts of the world to work together

Interpersonal Impact

Experience in negotiating contracts/agreements in other cultures

Strong networks with people from other cultures and with influential people

Reputation as a leader

Diplomacy

Ease of starting a conversation with a stranger

Ability to integrate diverse perspectives

Ability to listen to what others have to say

Willingness to collaborate

Figure 9-1

Ease of Starting a Conversation with a Stranger

Consider a classic example of a person's ease in conversing with a stranger. You are waiting for an elevator. When it arrives, the doors open, and you see there is a passenger already on the elevator whom you don't know. Do you say hello? And if you do say hello, do you make any other conversation? Or do you find ways to keep yourself otherwise busy: checking your messages on your phone or watching the elevator light blink on each floor?

Certainly, there are times when we feel more sociable than others. But if you regularly find that you do not engage strangers in your daily life in conversation, such as taxi drivers, store clerks, and hotel personnel, it is important to consider why. Is it a question of discomfort or disinterest? Either way, this can be problematic in cross-cultural situations. Barring situations in which it may be unsafe to engage in conversations with a stranger (e.g., dark alleys at night, odd or threatening behavior), socializing in the context of daily activities is an important way to learn about culture and to build social networks. The following tips will provide you with some ideas on how you can gain more ease in conversing with strangers. So the next time that elevator door opens, feel good about striking up a conversation and maybe even meeting a new friend.

TALKING TO A TAXI CAB DRIVER

GLOBAL SOCIAL CAPITAL

Blend Images / Shutterstock.com

Ease of Starting a Conversation with a Stranger in Action

On a recent trip to Abu Dhabi, I was asked to lead and facilitate an executive global management seminar for a group of senior female executives, most of whom were Emirati.

CARI E. GUITTARD, MPA
Principal
Global Engagement Partners

On a recent trip to Abu Dhabi, I was asked to lead and facilitate an executive global management seminar for a group of senior female executives, most of whom were Emirati. The first morning, the tone in the room was notably formal and quiet. This was very different from similar seminars I had led in Dubai. Abu Dhabi, in general, is far more traditional and conservative in business settings.

I typically begin any meeting by building rapport. I do this by sharing some of my personal history and then engaging the group in rounds of opening questions to break the ice. With this group, however, I could sense they were not openly eager or ready to engage. They were silently and intently listening but reticent to participate. As the seminar is designed to be interactive, their silence proved challenging.

I decided to shift gears. I began asking them questions about their home and work lives generally. This shifted my role from that of facilitator and teacher to active listener. They were eager to share the pride they had in their families. This allowed for trust to build gradually, as each woman's story compelled another woman to share. From there, the conversation easily segued into the challenges they faced at work, which was the focus of our seminar. Once we reached a point of mutual trust, understanding, and intimacy, the remaining elements of the seminar flowed seamlessly. It took nearly a full half of the first day to establish this trust, but it clearly was critical to starting our conversation and deepening it throughout the workshop.

ABU DHABI CITY, UNITED ARAB EMIRATES

GLOBAL SOCIAL CAPITAL

ventdusud / Shutterstock.com

DEVELOPMENT SUGGESTIONS
for Ease of Starting a Conversation with a Stranger

LEARN

Tips to learn about and begin developing the capability on your own. These tips involve self-directed learning, including reading, listening, watching, or observing, that you can do on your own at your own pace. They are most useful for novices in the capability, but are helpful for intermediate and advanced learners to keep knowledge current.

Development Activity	Suggested Resource(s) and Tips
Learn how to sincerely greet someone in the culture of interest. This involves learning about the culture and learning some of the local language.	Resources to learn about the culture: • Subscribe to GlobeSmart to access country and cultural profiles (www.globesmart.com). • Visit Kwintessential country profiles (www.kwintessential.co.uk/resources/country-profiles.html). • Read *Kiss, Bow, or Shake Hands: The Bestselling Guide to Doing Business in More Than 60 Countries* (Morrison and Conaway, 2006). • Read guidebooks before traveling, such as Lonely Planet (www.lonelyplanet.com), Fodor's (www.fodors.com), Frommer's (www.frommers.com), and Rough Guides (www.roughguides.com). Resources to learn some of the local language: • Take a language course locally in the culture of interest through language institutes geared toward foreigners. • Take a language course at your local community college or university. • Learn a language online through Rosetta Stone (www.rosettastone.com). • Decide how you want to learn the language of interest through Berlitz (www.berlitz.com). Courses are offered in a variety of formats, including travel courses.
Learn icebreakers you can use to start conversations easily.	• Observe others at social gatherings to see what kinds of conversation starters they use with success, especially cross-culturally. Adapt those for your own use. Here are some conversation topics that will work well across most cultures: • Ask about local sporting events. • Discuss local dining and entertainment. • Ask questions about local cultural attractions. • Discuss important events, news, or history. • Ask about the weather. • For ideas on conversation starters, read *Over 600 Icebreakers and Games* (Carter, 2011) or *300+ Sizzling Icebreakers* (Puffett, 2010).

DEVELOPMENT SUGGESTIONS
for Ease of Starting a Conversation with a Stranger

LEARN

Tips to learn about and begin developing the capability on your own. These tips involve self-directed learning, including reading, listening, watching, or observing, that you can do on your own at your own pace. They are most useful for novices in the capability, but are helpful for intermediate and advanced learners to keep knowledge current.

Development Activity	Suggested Resource(s) and Tips
Learn the art of storytelling, as stories can engage others in dialogue with you.	Read a book on storytelling: • *The Leader's Guide to Storytelling: Mastering the Art and Discipline of Business Narrative* (Denning, 2011) • *Enchantment: The Art of Changing Hearts, Minds, and Actions* (Kawasaki, 2011) • *Tell to Win: Connect, Persuade, and Triumph with the Hidden Power of Story* (Guber, 2011) • *Fascinate: Your Seven Triggers to Persuade and Captivate* (Hogshead, 2010) • *Whoever Tells the Best Story Wins: How to Use Your Own Stories to Communicate with Power and Impact* (Simmons, 2007) Read about storytelling techniques and watch stories being told through storytelling organizations: • The International Storytelling Center: an international organization dedicated to inspiring and empowering people across the world to accomplish goals and make a difference by discovering, capturing, and sharing their stories (www.storytellingcenter.net) • Center for Digital Storytelling: an organization surfacing authentic voices from around the world through group process and participatory media creation (www.storycenter.org) • The National Storytelling Network: an American organization dedicated to advancing the art of storytelling in all avenues of life (www.storynet.org)

DEVELOPMENT SUGGESTIONS
for Ease of Starting a Conversation with a Stranger

LEARN

Tips to learn about and begin developing the capability on your own. These tips involve self-directed learning, including reading, listening, watching, or observing, that you can do on your own at your own pace. They are most useful for novices in the capability, but are helpful for intermediate and advanced learners to keep knowledge current.

Development Activity	Suggested Resource(s) and Tips
Learn how to give a good presentation or speech, as this can compel others to want to engage in conversation with you.	• Read *Boring to Bravo: Proven Presentation Techniques to Engage, Involve, and Inspire Your Audience to Action* (Arnold, 2010). • Read *Presentation Zen Design: Simple Design Principles and Techniques to Enhance Your Presentations* (Reynolds, 2011). • Read *Presentation Excellence: 25 Tricks, Tips, and Techniques for Professional Speakers and Trainers* (Casler and Weldon, 2010). • Watch videos of presentations from TED (Technology, Entertainment, Design) conferences (www.ted.com). The conferences are devoted to "ideas worth spreading" and the presentations are compelling. • Read Garr Reynold's Presentation Zen blog (including useful videos) (www.presentationzen.com).
Learn about how to actively listen to others, so you can remain in conversation with them once you get it started.	• Read a quick overview of active listening with tips at MindTools (www.mindtools.com/CommSkll/ActiveListening.htm). • *The Wisdom of Listening* (Brady, 2003) discusses how to be fully present in conversations and relationships. • *Active Listening: Improve Your Ability to Listen and Lead* (Center for Creative Leadership, 2007) is a quick read on the basics of listening for managers. • *The Seven Powers of Questions: Secrets to Successful Communication in Life and at Work* (Leeds, 2000) discusses seven ways that questions can be used to open up conversations, better understand others, and achieve desired outcomes in a conversation.

DIPLOMACY

DEVELOPMENT SUGGESTIONS
for Ease of Starting a Conversation with a Stranger

CONNECT

Tips to learn about and continue developing the capability through others. These tips involve working with another person to learn from their experiences. They may involve asking questions, listening to and discussing experiences, forming a new relationship, deepening an existing relationship, or receiving feedback from someone who is acting as your mentor. These tips are useful for all levels of learners.

Development Activity	Suggested Resource(s) and Tips
Gather tips on starting conversations from your colleagues who are very good at it.	• Notice who you would like to speak with because they interest you. • Ask to meet with the colleagues you have identified to discuss what they do to start up conversations.
Find out what the typical and appropriate conversation starters are in the culture of interest.	• Ask a local colleague what typical themes of conversation are in the culture and how to engage someone you don't know in a conversation. • If you don't have a colleague in the local culture, consult a cultural expert. Here are some conversation topics that will work well across most cultures: • local sporting events • local dining and entertainment • local cultural attractions. Ask trusted local experts for a list of conversation topics that are too sensitive to discuss. Here are some conversation topics that you will generally want to avoid discussing until a trusting relationship is established: • religion • politics • history • money/economics.

DEVELOPMENT SUGGESTIONS
for Ease of Starting a Conversation with a Stranger

EXPERIENCE

Tips to learn about and develop skills in the capability through firsthand experience. These tips involve engaging in activities, such as exploring a new area, trying a new cultural activity, or participating in a specific business event. These tips are most useful for intermediate to advanced learners, and we suggest that novice learners prepare themselves for success by completing some of the tips in the Learn category first.

Development Activity	Suggested Resource(s) and Tips
Develop your elevator speech (i.e., a thirty-second introduction about who you are and what you do), and practice it with a colleague. Introductions are an important part of first conversations.	• Ask a colleague to listen to your elevator speech and provide you with feedback on how you can improve it. • After practicing yours, invite your colleague to practice so you can learn from their elevator speech as well.
Practice starting conversations with people you do not know in your daily life (e.g., checker in food market, taxi driver).	• Set a goal to have at least one conversation a day with a stranger to practice this skill. • You can often start a conversation with a question or comment about the environment you are in or with a compliment on something you notice about the other person. • Have up-to-date knowledge of a variety of world events or local events that may come up in conversation. • Once you have the conversation started, you can deepen it with questions about the local town or cultural events. • Be sure to share something about yourself to contribute to the conversation, instead of making it an interrogation. • Do not complain, be negative, or use banalities, as they may turn off the conversation early. • Use the other person's name in conversation at least once or twice to personalize the conversation and to help you remember it. • If you are too nervous to start having conversations with strangers, role play having these conversations with a trusted colleague.

DEVELOPMENT SUGGESTIONS
for Ease of Starting a Conversation with a Stranger

COACH OR CONTRIBUTE

Tips to help others learn about and develop this capability. These tips involve coaching and mentoring others. They may include creating information or experiences for individuals, teams, or your organization. These tips are designed for those who are advanced in the capability and are useful development methods to keep advanced leaders in the capability engaged in professional development at the highest level. Please note that the tips in this section may also be quite helpful for individual use if you do not have a coach or mentor.

Development Activity	Suggested Resource(s) and Tips
When you are hosting a global team meeting or other cross-cultural event, incorporate social time and help facilitate conversations among the group to encourage others to practice starting conversations with others they may not know.	• Use nametags to make introductions easier. • Introduce others using thoughtful details about where they are from and what they do and highlighting some shared interest the two people may have. • Incorporate icebreaker activities, as appropriate, to facilitate conversations. For ideas on conversation starters, read *Over 600 Icebreakers and Games* (Carter, 2011) or *300+ Sizzling Icebreakers* (Puffett, 2010). • Incorporate some kind of local entertainment to provide a natural conversation piece for others.
When coaching direct reports or mentees on how to start a conversation with strangers, provide them with basic tips on how to start a conversation in the culture of interest, including cultural taboos to avoid.	Here are some conversation topics that will work well across most cultures: • local sporting events • local dining and entertainment • local cultural attractions. Ask trusted local experts for a list of conversation topics that are too sensitive to discuss. Here are some conversation topics that you will generally want to avoid discussing until a trusting relationship is established: • religion • politics • history • money/economics.

Additional Reading

The readings listed here provide you with additional study of the Global Mindset capability in this section. You will find that many of these resources provide you with a specific and detailed look at using this capability in a particular context or location.

....

Title: "A Conversation Analytic Approach to Business Information: The Case of Leadership"

Publication: *Journal of Business Communication*

Date: 2006

Author: Jonathan Clifton

Executive Summary: The way practitioners talk actively shapes an organization rather than just passively defining it. Thus, the long-held Aristotelian belief that language describes reality is being set aside for an approach whereby talk and organization are collapsed into one reflexive phenomenon. To put it simply, organizations are talk, and talk is organization.

....

Title: "Leadership Is a Conversation"

Publication: *Harvard Business Review*

Date: 2012

Authors: Boris Groysberg and Michael Slind

Executive Summary: Groysberg and Slind have identified four elements of organizational conversation that reflect the essential attributes of interpersonal conversation: intimacy, interactivity, inclusion, and intentionality. Intimacy shifts the focus from a top-down distribution of information to a bottom-up exchange of ideas.

DIPLOMACY

Title: "Idle Chatter"

Publication: *Entrepreneur*

Date: 2012

Author: Ross McCammon

Executive Summary: The article offers advice on how to speak to strangers and how to start conversations with others. Tips include listening to the other person, making eye contact, and speaking about the weather. Information is provided on the difference between small talk and schmoozing, as well as how to exit a conversation.

Title: "Using Storytelling, Conversation and Coaching to Engage"

Publication: *Strategic Communication Management*

Date: 2007

Author: Mike Pounsford

Executive Summary: In a media-rich world in which technology and social change is shifting control from the broadcaster to the audience, it is more and more difficult to cut through and reach increasingly demanding and cynical audiences. Therefore, despite the importance of blogs, user-controlled web space, discussion forums, and the like, the role of the visible leader and face-to-face conversation remains critical in order to create engaging places for people to work.

Ability to Integrate Diverse Perspectives

Integrating diverse perspectives is not synonymous with compromise. *Compromise* is defined as "an agreement or settlement of a dispute that is reached by each side making concessions" (Merriam-Webster). Essentially, each party has to give something up in a compromise. While compromise may be one way to integrate diverse perspectives where there are incongruent goals, many times in cross-cultural situations the goals are not necessarily incongruent. They are simply not understood or fully explored, leading people to assume compromise is the only way forward.

To illustrate this common problem, we sometimes incorporate cross-cultural negotiation simulations into our Global Mindset workshops. One such negotiation involves two international food manufacturers who are keen on acquiring a larger percentage of the local orange harvest from the supplier. Quantities are limited, and so the supplier may readily think that the decision is who to sell the oranges to. One manufacturer is a long-time trusted business partner, while the other is a potential new partner who is willing to pay top dollar. With only this information at hand, many of our novice participants go straight to deal making. However, our more experienced participants often have the savvy to ask questions about the objectives of those manufacturers. By exploring each of the perspectives fully, participants come to find that one distributor wants the fruit of the oranges for juice, while the other wants the rinds of the oranges for producing orange extract. With this knowledge, it is now possible to have a conversation about how to provide sufficient product to both manufacturers. Furthermore, participants discover that integrating diverse perspectives in this case ends up generating a much higher revenue for the supplier as well.

Integrating diverse perspectives requires respect for others' ideas and a generous amount of patience to be able to work toward understanding others' views. Until the other views are fully understood, you cannot reach consensus. Consensus

TEAM COLLABORATION

is critical to be able to move forward with decision making and action plans that are likely to be successful. Without consensus, the parties who do not agree or are not fully satisfied are unlikely to put their energy and resources into the final plans. It is common for our clients to share stories of how their cross-cultural business partners are not driven or seem apathetic. When we discuss the situations further, there is generally evidence that they were not fully on board at the time decisions were made for the particular projects in question. So, in actuality, the problem is not usually drive or apathy; it is lack of true consensus.

Clearly, negotiations and other high-stakes conversations do not always turn out to be a win-win for everyone. However, by learning how to fully explore and work toward integrating diverse perspectives, it opens the door to more possibilities than polarized discussions do and it makes reaching consensus on how to move forward possible. This section will provide you with tips and resources on how to create more of these possibilities in your global work.

ROME, ITALY

Ability to Integrate Diverse Perspectives in Action

A vice president of supply chain led a cost-reduction project with his team of supply chain leaders from India, China, the Americas, and the European Union.

SUSAN GEBELEIN
CEO
Business and Leadership, Consulting

A vice president of supply chain led a cost-reduction project with his team of supply chain leaders from India, China, the Americas, and the European Union. They needed to decide which suppliers to drop and which to add. In the first round of discussions, it was obvious that there was little agreement.

To integrate diverse perspectives, it is helpful to identify shared goals and then agree upon the criteria for decision making. In this situation, everyone agreed on the goal to reduce costs. But the points of disagreement were around the criteria for supplier inclusion or exclusion. There were differing values and cultural approaches at play on the team. Some wanted to stay with loyal suppliers who were reliable but who were also the most expensive. Others were concerned about canceling contracts with suppliers who were central employers in the community. Still others focused on cost savings with new suppliers. Another group argued that transportation costs and reliability among suppliers were key issues.

Once the team realized how many diverse perspectives were represented in the room, they were able to shift the conversation from one of competing values to one where they came together to decide on the criteria for inclusion. This required integrating all of these diverse perspectives. While the discussion of criteria was robust, they were able to reach agreements that satisfied the team as a whole.

DEVELOPMENT SUGGESTIONS
for Ability to Integrate Diverse Perspectives

LEARN

Tips to learn about and begin developing the capability on your own. These tips involve self-directed learning, including reading, listening, watching, or observing, that you can do on your own at your own pace. They are most useful for novices in the capability, but are helpful for intermediate and advanced learners to keep knowledge current.

Development Activity	Suggested Resource(s) and Tips
Learn about different cultural values and beliefs both generally and in the culture of interest, so you can identify these perspectives when they arise in conversations.	• Read the GLOBE studies: *Culture, Leadership, and Organizations: The GLOBE Study of 62 Societies* (House, et al., 2004) and *Culture and Leadership Across the World: The GLOBE Book of In-Depth Studies of 25 Societies* (Chhokar, et al., 2007). • Look at side-by-side comparisons of cultures using Dr. Geert Hofstedes's dimensions (http://geert-hofstede.com). • Compare cultures by subscribing to the GlobeSmart tool through Aperian Global (www.aperianglobal.com).
Understand your own perspectives and how they compare to other cultures, especially the culture of interest, by taking cross-cultural assessments.	• The Intercultural Development Inventory measures cross-cultural competence for individuals, groups, and organizations (www.idiinventory.com). • The Intercultural Communication and Collaboration Appraisal measures affective, cognitive, and behavioral aspects of cross-cultural competence (www.gpccolorado.com/intercultural-communication-and-collaboration-appraisal). • The Cultural Intelligence Center offers multiple assessments for cross-cultural competence in a variety of contexts (http://culturalQ.com). • The Cultural Orientations Indicator measures a person's work style preferences against ten dimensions of culture (www.tmcorp.com/Online-Learning/Assessments/Cultural-Orientations-Indicator-COI/56).

DEVELOPMENT SUGGESTIONS
for Ability to Integrate Diverse Perspectives

LEARN

Tips to learn about and begin developing the capability on your own. These tips involve self-directed learning, including reading, listening, watching, or observing, that you can do on your own at your own pace. They are most useful for novices in the capability, but are helpful for intermediate and advanced learners to keep knowledge current.

Development Activity	Suggested Resource(s) and Tips
Learn about cross-cultural negotiation techniques, which involve integrating diverse perspectives.	• Take Communicating and Negotiating with a Global Mindset at Thunderbird Executive Education (www.thunderbird.edu/executive_education/classroom_programs/communicating_negotiating.htm). • Attend courses on cross-cultural negotiations at your local colleges and universities. • Watch INSEAD professor Dr. Falcao's interview on how to avoid pitfalls in cross-cultural negotiations (http://youtube/-4GjCOipJIA). • Watch Negotiation Europe's video on cross-cultural negotiation tips (http://youtube/BII8PXGmSBk). • Find videos of interest on negotiation topics that are listed on the Harvard Program on Negotiations website (www.pon.harvard.edu/category/events/pon-film-series). • Read books on cross-cultural negotiation, such as *Negotiating Across Cultures: International Communication in an Interdependent World* (Cohen, 1997). You can also search for books specifically focused on negotiations in your culture of interest. • Read *Global Negotiation: The New Rules* (Graham and Requejo, 2008). • Read *Negotiating Globally: How to Negotiate Deals, Resolve Disputes, and Make Decisions Across Cultural Boundaries* (Brett, 2007). • Read *Culture and Conflict Resolution* (Avruch, 1998). • Read about finding third solutions (i.e., collaborative solutions) in *The Third Alternative* (Covey 2011).

DEVELOPMENT SUGGESTIONS
for Ability to Integrate Diverse Perspectives

LEARN

Tips to learn about and begin developing the capability on your own. These tips involve self-directed learning, including reading, listening, watching, or observing, that you can do on your own at your own pace. They are most useful for novices in the capability, but are helpful for intermediate and advanced learners to keep knowledge current.

Development Activity	Suggested Resource(s) and Tips
Read resources on storytelling, as they are useful in getting your own perspective across and can also be used to help integrate diverse perspectives when you are facilitating a group.	Read a book on storytelling: • *The Leader's Guide to Storytelling: Mastering the Art and Discipline of Business Narrative* (Denning, 2011) • *Enchantment: The Art of Changing Hearts, Minds, and Actions* (Kawasaki, 2011) • *Tell to Win: Connect, Persuade, and Triumph with the Hidden Power of Story* (Guber, 2011) • *Fascinate: Your Seven Triggers to Persuade and Captivate* (Hogshead, 2010) • *Whoever Tells the Best Story Wins: How to Use Your Own Stories to Communicate with Power and Impact* (Simmons, 2007) Read about storytelling techniques, and watch stories being told through storytelling organizations: • The International Storytelling Center: an international organization dedicated to inspiring and empowering people across the world to accomplish goals and make a difference by discovering, capturing, and sharing their stories (www.storytellingcenter.net) • Center for Digital Storytelling: an organization surfacing authentic voices from around the world through group process and participatory media creation (www.storycenter.org) • The National Storytelling Network: an American organization dedicated to advancing the art of storytelling in all avenues of life (www.storynet.org)
Learn how to build consensus.	• Read eHow's brief overview of how to build consensus in a team meeting (www.ehow.com/how_8014222_build-consensus-meetings.html). • Read *Consensus Through Conversation: How to Achieve High-Commitment Decisions* (Dressler, 2006). • Read *The Consensus-Building Handbook: A Comprehensive Guide to Reaching Agreement* (Susskind, et al., 1999). • Read *How to Make Collaboration Work: Powerful Ways to Build Consensus, Solve Problems, and Make Decisions* (Straus and Layton, 2002).

DEVELOPMENT SUGGESTIONS
for Ability to Integrate Diverse Perspectives

CONNECT

Tips to learn about and continue developing the capability through others. These tips involve working with another person to learn from their experiences. They may involve asking questions, listening to and discussing experiences, forming a new relationship, deepening an existing relationship, or receiving feedback from someone who is acting as your mentor. These tips are useful for all levels of learners.

Development Activity	Suggested Resource(s) and Tips
Learn about the unique array of perspectives in the culture of interest.	• Ask a local colleague to discuss the values and beliefs that are prevalent in the culture and how they arise in the context of business. • Ask a cultural expert to advise you on the values and beliefs in the culture of interest.
Go out of your way to learn about the perspectives of other people in depth.	When you hear a colleague present a diverse perspective, ask him or her more about it so you can understand it fully.
Meet privately with quieter people on your team to gather their perspectives.	When you identify people on your team who are not actively participating in team discussions, be sure to approach them privately to ask them for their perspectives so that everyone is heard.
Before going into a difficult or high-stakes conversation, role-play it with a colleague.	Brief your colleague on the perspectives that you anticipate encountering, so he or she can role-play realistic arguments.

DEVELOPMENT SUGGESTIONS
for Ability to Integrate Diverse Perspectives

EXPERIENCE

Tips to learn about and develop skills in the capability through firsthand experience. These tips involve engaging in activities, such as exploring a new area, trying a new cultural activity, or participating in a specific business event. These tips are most useful for intermediate to advanced learners, and we suggest that novice learners prepare themselves for success by completing some of the tips in the Learn category first.

Development Activity	Suggested Resource(s) and Tips
Prior to a meeting, prepare all participants with the information they need to participate fully and provide their unique perspectives.	• Circulate an agenda prior to the meeting. • Meet with quieter individuals prior to the meeting to discuss their ideas on how to make the meeting one where all ideas are heard. Incorporate those ideas into the meeting protocol.

DEVELOPMENT SUGGESTIONS
for Ability to Integrate Diverse Perspectives

EXPERIENCE

Tips to learn about and develop skills in the capability through firsthand experience. These tips involve engaging in activities, such as exploring a new area, trying a new cultural activity, or participating in a specific business event. These tips are most useful for intermediate to advanced learners, and we suggest that novice learners prepare themselves for success by completing some of the tips in the Learn category first.

Development Activity	Suggested Resource(s) and Tips
Establish guidelines for collaboration and decision making at the start of a meeting, so that all perspectives will be heard. If you are not the formal leader of the group, advocate that this be done.	• Start the meeting by gathering everyone's ideas and agreements on the guidelines that should be used for collaboration and decision making. • If there is a clear objective at the outset, keep it visible. • Establish a protocol that ensures that everyone has a turn to be heard. • When the conversation reaches a standstill due to competing perspectives, refer back to the shared objective and ask how the group can move toward the objective. • During the discussion, work to separate the problem from the solution when group members get stuck on a particular solution.
Listen to truly understand.	• Ask others for their perspectives. • Use active listening until the other person's viewpoint makes sense to you. This may include paraphrasing their ideas to see if you understood them correctly and asking clarifying questions. • Suspend judgment while listening. • Don't disagree with a perspective; repeat it to make sure you understood it correctly, and note it for consideration. • Use collaborative language, such as the word *and* instead of *but* when adding to an idea that you do not fully agree with. • Actively listen for common values and complimentary ideas, so you can find ways to link perspectives together later. • If you tend to over-participate in a meeting, volunteer to be the scribe or to take a pure facilitation role.

DEVELOPMENT SUGGESTIONS
for Ability to Integrate Diverse Perspectives

COACH OR CONTRIBUTE

Tips to help others learn about and develop this capability. These tips involve coaching and mentoring others. They may include creating information or experiences for individuals, teams, or your organization. These tips are designed for those who are advanced in the capability and are useful development methods to keep advanced leaders in the capability engaged in professional development at the highest level. Please note that the tips in this section may also be quite helpful for individual use if you do not have a coach or mentor.

Development Activity	Suggested Resource(s) and Tips
When coaching direct reports or mentees, ask open-ended questions to get them thinking about all of the perspectives on a specific issue.	• Imagine a 360-perspective on the issue. What are all of the perspectives you can think of? • What would be the benefit of integrating as many of these perspectives as possible? • When you think of all the diverse perspectives on the issue, how do you think you could stitch them together? • Thinking about all of these perspectives, what may be the common goal? • Thinking about each perspective individually, what resources are available to put that particular solution in place? What will be needed to implement each solution?

Additional Reading

The readings listed here provide you with additional study of the Global Mindset capability in this section. You will find that many of these resources provide you with a specific and detailed look at using this capability in a particular context or location.

....

Title: "Giving Voice to Diversity: An Interactive Approach to Conflict Management and Decision-Making in Culturally Diverse Work Environments"

Publication: *Journal of Business and Management*

Date: 2002

Authors: J. Broome Benjamin, Sara DeTurk, Erla S. Kristjansdottir, Tami Kanata, and Puvana Ganesan

Executive Summary: While there is much evidence to show that diversity of viewpoints and perspectives allows for more creative problem solving and decision making, there is also a great deal of research to indicate that cultural diversity presents one of the foremost challenges to organizations. This paper describes a process called Interactive Management (IM) and its application with employees of a large multinational technology company. IM was used in a set of workshops to help groups identify and structure barriers to effective communication in culturally diverse work environments.

....

Title: "Overcoming Barriers to Participation in Diverse Strategic Decision-Making Groups: A Leadership Perspective"

Publication: *International Journal of Business and Management*

Date: 2012

Authors: Robert L. Bjorklund and Svetlana S. Holt

Executive Summary: The authors acknowledge that diversity in institutions continues to be an urgent social, cultural, and national need, and that much is yet to be accomplished before that cause is satisfied. Where diversity has already happened in decision-making and problem-solving groups, there are consequences that require special handling. The paradoxical effect of bringing diversity to otherwise homogeneous groups is that differences, as important as they are, lead to communications difficulties that may actually reduce the likelihood of the advantage of the diverse membership.

....

Title: "When East and West Meet: An Essay on the Importance of Cultural Understanding in Global Business Practice and Education"

Publication: *Journal of International Business & Cultural Studies*

Date: 2009

Author: S. J. Chang

Executive Summary: As today's business decisions and choices are increasingly influenced by the diverse cultural backgrounds and perspectives of various corporate stakeholders, it is critical for business managers to have multicultural understanding. This motivates us to refine our business perspectives and approaches in the global arena as well as our educational philosophies on global business management.

....

Title: "Cross-Functional Team Decision-Making and Learning Outcomes: A Qualitative Illustration"

Publication: *Journal of Business and Management*

Date: 2002

Authors: Mark A. Clark, Susan D. Amundson, and Robert L. Cardy

Executive Summary: Members of cross-functional teams in a large, multi-site organization discuss their experience in completing various decision tasks, illustrating a confluence of research literature relating workgroup dynamics, information processing, and organizational learning.

Title: "Global Leaders Are Team Players: Developing Global Leaders Through Membership on Global Teams"

Publication: *Human Resource Management*

Date: 2000

Authors: Martha L. Maznevski and Joseph J. DiStefano

Executive Summary: Global teams today make an increasing number of decisions in multinational organizations, addressing challenges broad in scope and critical to performance. An additional role of global teams is discussed here, providing ideal training for future global leaders.

Title: "Diverse Perspectives: Minority Executives and Their Peers Tout the Benefits of Broader Representation in the C-Suite, Boardrooms"

Publication: *Modern Healthcare*

Date: 2012

Author: Ashok Selvam

Executive Summary: The article presents the perspectives of minority executives on the benefits of broader representation in the C-suite and boardrooms.

Ability to Listen to What Others Have to Say

One of our colleagues worked with a director in a multinational company who was, like many people at her level, very busy. She spent most of her days in meetings and carved little time out to interact with her staff. She was also a bureaucratic leader, with expectations that every project and task be reviewed by her personally. Given how busy she was, she was often quite delayed in her reviews. After patiently waiting for feedback and approval on documents that had been sent to the director a week earlier, our colleague tried several avenues to alert her that a major deadline was in jeopardy. Our colleague called her and left a message. Our colleague also sent her a few emails, but no response. The deadline passed. When the director returned to the office, she gave our colleague a stern warning about missing deadlines. When our colleague gently told the director that she had tried multiple times to get her attention about the pending deadline, the director said, "Well, you should have tried harder to get a hold of me."

Listening is something that we all begin learning as children. Those with the capacity to hear, however, sometimes take that for granted. Children who are hearing impaired perfectly illustrate what listening is really all about. For them, listening is done by observing and paying attention to their environment. It requires motivation to engage with others, to focus on them intently, and to figure out what it is they are communicating. Hearing-impaired people know all too well how valuable listening is to be able to interact with the world and form relationships.

In the business world, we spend a lot of time in communication training talking about active listening skills and behaviors. They are important and, as such, are included in the tips in this section as well. But the root of the problem in listening usually boils down to motivation. Do you want to hear what the other person has to say? Are you willing to take the time to listen? Are you willing to spend the energy needed to figure out not just what is being said, but what the other person

OPERA PERFORMANCE ▪ DNEPROPETROVSK, UKRAINE

Igor Bulgarin / Shutterstock.com

really is trying to communicate? Do you believe that listening is a form of showing respect to another person?

In the example with the director, she did not appear to be motivated to listen to the messages she was receiving. Instead of taking personal accountability for her failure to listen, she expected her employees to try harder to communicate with her. This is a fatal flaw in leadership, and one that is particularly perilous in global business where respect is paramount to relationship building. In cross-cultural interactions, listening is even more challenging given language differences, accents, differences in body language, and differences in what phrases and words actually mean in translation. This is why you must enter into cross-cultural interactions with a strong motivation to listen to what others have to say. This is the foundation for respectful and productive working relationships.

DIPLOMACY

YOKOHAMA, JAPAN

Ko Yo / Shutterstock.com

Ability to Listen to What Others Have to Say in Action

In a meeting that I facilitated, I observed a group of high-tech leaders from many regions of the world dismiss one of their Japanese colleague's comments without really listening to him.

SUSAN GEBELEIN
CEO
Business and Leadership, Consulting

In a meeting that I facilitated, I observed a group of high-tech leaders from many regions of the world dismiss one of their Japanese colleague's comments without really listening to him. While they initially appeared to be listening to his brief comments, they quickly moved on to their problem-solving discussion without giving his comments any real consideration. There were two contributing issues: the colleague's English was not strong, so it was difficult to understand his comments, and the group was not personally familiar with him. However, neither one of these issues was an acceptable reason to not listen to a colleague. Both are common in cross-cultural work.

A colleague of this Japanese man, who was also from Japan, watched this dismissive behavior happen three times. He then said to the group, "Perhaps you do not know my colleague well. He leads customer service for all of China, has about two hundred people reporting to him, and recently led a successful restructuring effort."

Immediately, the members of the group began to really listen and ask questions of the Japanese colleague each time he spoke. The problem they had come together to solve was how to restructure customer service operations. The resident expert on the issue in the room was the very person they were not listening to.

This is an important reminder that cross-cultural situations, especially where there are language differences, require patience and a commitment to really listen to and involve each person in the dialogue. Otherwise, we can miss out on golden opportunities to learn from one another.

DEVELOPMENT SUGGESTIONS
for Ability to Listen to What Others Have to Say

LEARN

Tips to learn about and begin developing the capability on your own. These tips involve self-directed learning, including reading, listening, watching, or observing, that you can do on your own at your own pace. They are most useful for novices in the capability, but are helpful for intermediate and advanced learners to keep knowledge current.

Development Activity	Suggested Resource(s) and Tips
Learn about the culture in which you will be communicating to identify things that interest you and motivate you to really get to know people in that culture.	• Read guidebooks before traveling, such as Lonely Planet (www.lonelyplanet.com), Fodor's (www.fodors.com), Frommer's (www.frommers.com), and Rough Guides (www.roughguides.com). • Do an Internet search for specifically how to transact business in your country of interest, including personnel practices, marketing, and distribution. • Subscribe to GlobeSmart (www.globesmart.com). • Visit Kwintessential country profiles (www.kwintessential .co.uk/resources/country-profiles.html). • Read *Kiss, Bow, or Shake Hands: The Bestselling Guide to Doing Business in More Than 60 Countries* (Morrison and Conaway, 2006).
Learn about your colleagues in the culture of interest to identify things about them that interest you in getting to know them personally.	Read professional biographies through your company directory and through LinkedIn profiles.
Learn about active listening techniques (e.g., using questions, nonverbal behavior, paraphrasing) to demonstrate that you are listening.	• Read a quick overview of active listening tips at MindTools (www.mindtools.com/CommSkll/ActiveListening.htm). • Take an interpersonal communications class at your local college or university. • *The Wisdom of Listening* (Brady, 2003) discusses how to be fully present in conversations and relationships. • *Active Listening: Improve Your Ability to Listen and Lead* (Center for Creative Leadership, 2007) is a quick read on the basics of listening for managers. • *The Seven Powers of Questions: Secrets to Successful Communication in Life and at Work* (Leeds, 2000) discusses seven ways that questions can be used to open up conversations, better understand others, and achieve desired outcomes in a conversation.

DEVELOPMENT SUGGESTIONS
for Ability to Listen to What Others Have to Say

CONNECT

Tips to learn about and continue developing the capability through others. These tips involve working with another person to learn from their experiences. They may involve asking questions, listening to and discussing experiences, forming a new relationship, deepening an existing relationship, or receiving feedback from someone who is acting as your mentor. These tips are useful for all levels of learners.

Development Activity	Suggested Resource(s) and Tips
Learn about your colleagues in the culture of interest to identify things about them that interest you in getting to know them personally.	• Arrange to spend social time with your colleagues. • Ask your colleagues questions about their professional role and about their personal interests, and listen intently to their responses. • Show interest by asking questions about what you are hearing and also by sharing some of your personal details that are of mutual interest. • Invite your colleagues who work in other cultures to speak to your team about their experiences.
Learn about listening techniques from your colleagues who are very good at it.	• Identify your colleagues who display superb listening skills. • Meet with them and ask them for their advice on how to be an exceptional listener. • Ask for feedback from them about ways that you could improve your own listening skills based on their observations.

DIPLOMACY

DEVELOPMENT SUGGESTIONS
for Ability to Listen to What Others Have to Say

EXPERIENCE

Tips to learn about and develop skills in the capability through firsthand experience. These tips involve engaging in activities, such as exploring a new area, trying a new cultural activity, or participating in a specific business event. These tips are most useful for intermediate to advanced learners, and we suggest that novice learners prepare themselves for success by completing some of the tips in the Learn category first.

Development Activity	Suggested Resource(s) and Tips
Create situations to listen to others.	Attend local business meetings or presentations in the local culture, and listen for the key points. Write down the key points as you understand them, and verify them with someone else who is there to see if you listened well.
While in interpersonal or group conversations, use active listening techniques to stay engaged with your colleagues and to work toward understanding them.	• Focus on listening. Do not type, check your phone, or engage in other behaviors that demonstrate that you are distracted. This is especially important when working to understand heavy accents. • Use eye contact, as appropriate for the culture. • Seek first to understand your colleague before adding your own personal opinion. • Check your understanding of what you have heard by paraphrasing it. • Reflect on any differences you observe between what is being said and what is actually meant. This may become clear through observing nonverbal behaviors. • Ask questions to find out more about statements that are made that you do not fully understand. • When appropriate, relate your own experience to show understanding and empathy. • When you have concerns or disagreements about what is being said, first listen for what is positive or a benefit of your colleague's ideas. Then share your concern.
Practice focused listening.	Attend an opera that is not in your native language. It will force you to focus on listening and deciphering communication.

COACH OR CONTRIBUTE

Tips to help others learn about and develop this capability. These tips involve coaching and mentoring others. They may include creating information or experiences for individuals, teams, or your organization. These tips are designed for those who are advanced in the capability and are useful development methods to keep advanced leaders in the capability engaged in professional development at the highest level. Please note that the tips in this section may also be quite helpful for individual use if you do not have a coach or mentor.

Development Activity	Suggested Resource(s) and Tips
Make effective listening a key capability and expectation on your own team.	• Discuss the importance of listening with each of your team members. Let them know it is an expectation. • As a team, discuss what it looks like to be an active listener in the context of the team's work. • Regularly provide your team with feedback on their listening skills and examples of what is working well and what can be improved. • Role model good listening. • In team meetings, be a good facilitator of dialogue for your team. When people are not being heard, invite them to share their thoughts. When people are over-participating and not listening to colleagues, actively invite others into the conversation to share their thoughts.
When leading virtual team meetings, demonstrate virtual active listening.	• Invite everyone on the line to individually share. If the meeting is large, use web-based meeting platforms to enable virtual chatting and other forms of active participation for the group. • Use people's names frequently to recognize that you have heard that person.

DIPLOMACY

Additional Reading

The readings listed here provide you with additional study of the Global Mindset capability in this section. You will find that many of these resources provide you with a specific and detailed look at using this capability in a particular context or location.

....

Title: "Listening and Leadership: An Investigative Study into the Listening Practices of United States Coast Guard Enlisted Officers in Charge"

Publication: *Regent University Website*

Date: 2004

Author: James K. Ellis

Executive Summary: The need for effective leadership is undisputed. What is unknown is the role of listening in leadership. Listening has been identified as the primary communication skill because it is the first communication skill acquired and, in comparison with speaking, reading, or writing, it is used more often the greater part of each day.

....

Title: "The Executive's Guide to Better Listening"

Publication: *McKinsey Quarterly*

Date: 2012

Author: Bernard T. Ferrari

Executive Summary: The article discusses the importance to executives of strong listening skills and describes three types of behavior that can help develop them. Respectful behavior toward others in a conversation including subordinates can encourage a free and open flow of information that can aid decision making.

Title: "Lending an Ear: Why Leaders Must Learn to Listen Actively"

Publication: *Leadership in Action*

Date: 2007

Author: Michael H. Hoppe

Executive Summary: The ability to listen effectively is an essential component of leadership. Most leaders know they need to be good listeners to be effective, but even though they may have the best intentions, they don't know specifically what to do (or not to do) to become better listeners. By learning the skills and behaviors of active listening, leaders can become more effective. Active listening involves six skills: 1. paying attention, 2. holding judgment, 3. reflecting, 4. clarifying, 5. summarizing, and 6. sharing. Each skill contributes to the active listening mindset, and each includes various techniques or behaviors.

Title: "Empathetic Listening as a Management Tool"

Publication: *Business Renaissance Quarterly*

Date: 2011

Authors: Joan Marques, Satinder Dhiman, and Richard King

Executive Summary: Empathetic listening, and enabling the other party to formulate his or her own answers through a gentle process of rephrasing and questioning, may very well become the key strategy for leaders who want to ensure a happier workforce and a more successful organization in the near future.

Title: "Good Listening Skills Make Efficient Business Sense"

Publication: *IUP Journal of Soft Skills*

Date: 2011

Author: D. B. Rane

Executive Summary: The ability to understand and give a response effectively to verbal communication is known as listening. The effectiveness in listening necessarily depends on the interrelationships between the sender and the receiver of the message, which is found to be a vital skill more particularly for the managers in business organizations while obtaining need-based information to perform their jobs successfully. The quality of relationships with others and job effectiveness

DIPLOMACY

largely depends on the listening ability of the individual concerned. Lack of listening ability at all the levels in the organizations leads to work-related problems. To become a good listener, one needs to practice and acquire special skills so that the vital information sent by the speaker is well received by the active listener. A lot of concentration and firm determination is required to become an active listener. Thus listening, among others, is one of the most essential skills one should have. Many people have bad listening habits and, hence, need to put a lot of effort to break these habits to become effective at work. This reveals that improvement in workplace productivity is possible by developing active listening and better communication at all the levels. This paper explains the process of listening, significance of active listening in business communication, concept of effective listening, and barriers to good listening and gives vital tips to become a good listener.

· ·

Title: "Developing Listening Skills"

Publication: *The American Salesman*

Date: 2010

Author: Michael E. Rega

Executive Summary: A wise man once explained, "People never learn anything with their mouths open. They can only learn by reading, by listening, by observing and by doing." If you are like most adults, you have not had training in listening since elementary school. Along the way, you may have picked up some bad habits. The first step is to review some common mistakes that prevent you from effectively using what you hear. Just as the prospect may have difficulty comprehending what you say, you also will need to concentrate on the skill of listening to achieve your objectives.

· ·

Title: "Learning to Listen: Guided Practice for Business Students"

Publication: *Allied Academies International Conference*

Date: 2011

Authors: Gary P. Schneider, Kathleen A. Simione, and Carol M. Bruton

Executive Summary: This case provides students with guided practice in listening as they learn skills and activities that can increase their level of active listening.

Title: "Reclaiming Rare Listening as a Means of Organizational Re-Enchantment"

Publication: *Journal of Organizational Change Management*

Date: 2011

Author: Jo A. Tyler

Executive Summary: The purpose of this paper is to contribute to a reclaiming of the potency of Rogerian listening in organizations. The paper views listening after Rogers, the father of active listening, as a process with potential to re-enchant organizations and the people who comprise them, in a move away from the popular view and professional training that fosters instrumentalized listening that deadens organizations and crushes the spirit of individuals.

FORMER U.S. PRESIDENT WILLIAM CLINTON RECEIVING HARRY S. TRUMAN AWARD FOR PUBLIC SERVICE 2009

GLOBAL SOCIAL CAPITAL

Willingness to Collaborate

What do Google, Apple, and Microsoft all have in common? Obviously, they are technology companies. What is not so obvious, though, is that they all were the result of collaborative partnerships. Chances are that you use at least one of their products daily in the course of business. They wouldn't exist without the willingness to collaborate among their respective founders. Collaboration has long been prized in business schools and corporations as a means of generating more and better ideas, for inspiring creativity, and for being a driver of innovation. But it is much more than that in today's business market. It is not just a tool; it has become a philosophy of doing business.

Business philosophy has largely been reset from one of rivalry to one of collaboration, even among the largest and most powerful companies in the world. Why? Because working together leads to greater success. This is particularly true in cross-cultural business where culturally specific business expertise is fundamental to success.

IBM and Cisco are two multinational giants that demonstrate how barriers are being broken down between CEOs, employees, customers, vendors, and even rivals. National boundaries are being bridged, corporate walls breached, and expertise shared. As economist Thomas Friedman has so simply put it, the world is flat. This means that willingness to collaborate is essential in the current global business environment. Collaboration itself will require that you actively share knowledge with others, are keen to learn from others, and are committed to working toward consensus.

MARRAKESH, MOROCCO

Willingness to Collaborate in Action

Several years ago, I had the opportunity to lead a high-profile Middle East CEO delegation to Washington, DC, for a series of collaborative meetings on Middle Eastern policies with senior appointees at the White House and State Department.

CARI E. GUITTARD, MPA
Principal
Global Engagement Partners

Several years ago, I had the opportunity to lead a high-profile Middle East CEO delegation to Washington, DC, for a series of collaborative meetings on Middle Eastern policies with senior appointees at the White House and State Department. The delegation was only due to be in town for a day and a half so we needed to maximize their time with each official.

The delegation was deeply prepared with notes, handouts to help guide the conversations, and briefing kits with the background on people they were due to meet as well as all of the policy positions of the administration. Each of the all-male delegation was impeccably dressed in the finest formal business attire—three-piece suit, silk tie, shined shoes, and fresh shave—all this despite the fact that they had just flown over seventeen hours and hadn't had a chance to catch even a glimpse of their respective hotel rooms. I have rarely seen a more focused, polished, prepared, or engaged group of CEOs.

We began with meetings at the Old Executive Office Building of the White House. Security, as expected, was extensive given that several members of the delegation were from countries that receive heightened security considerations. As we entered our meeting room, the administrative assistant placed us in a cozy living room space complete with mahogany table, high-backed leather chairs, and a large fireplace. The delegation was impressed, as this was a meeting place befitting their stature. Each took the liberty of straightening their ties, and then seated themselves around the large, formal table with their briefing notes.

Half an hour later, we were greeted hurriedly by a staffer. She gave no introduction, and simply informed us that our first point person was running late. There was no offer of a beverage or biscuit, despite the fact that it was early in the morning. Coffee, tea, or some caffeinated beverage was most certainly in order. So we sat in silence for another thirty minutes waiting.

To all of our dismay, the senior official we were supposed to meet with had been replaced at the last minute. His replacement was a very young, inexperienced new recruit who had no real experience in the Middle East. Not only was he not prepared, he was totally dispassionate about the group. Halfway through the delegation's briefing, he feigned an emergency and left the room, only to be replaced by another young staffer with even less interest in the topics at hand.

Needless to say, the collaborative meetings we had come for did not go well. There was no engagement or effort at real collaboration. We remained optimistic that the State Department would bring an entirely different, more organized, and engaging experience. So we headed over to Main State, where we had four back-to-back meetings scheduled.

Each meeting, in true American style, was scheduled for thirty minutes with five minutes in between for transit to a different meeting room. In our first meeting with one of the Under Secretaries, the delegation again methodically placed their materials in front of them, straightened their suits and ties, sat up straight, and waited. And waited. Fifteen minutes into our designated thirty-minute meeting slot, the official we were scheduled to meet with arrived apologizing and out of breath. She half-listened while our delegation gave her a full brief on their backgrounds and policy recommendations. Rather than asking questions, taking notes, or appearing remotely interested, she nodded, smiled, and then abruptly stood at the thirty-minute mark to say her good-byes.

It was a classic case of what I would call drive-by diplomacy, where the crises of the day took precedence over the delicate nature of seeding new collaborative relationships. The rest of our meetings at the State Department followed suit. We were exhausted from disappointment and low blood sugar. Not once had anyone in our meetings offered a refreshment.

I apologized on behalf of the entire government repeatedly and profusely throughout the day, even though I hadn't been employed there for years. I was so deeply embarrassed that this delegation was not treated with even the most basic forms of dignity and respect that any of us would show a stranger welcomed into our homes. In Middle Eastern culture, hospitality and warm welcomes are paramount for doing business in the region. And this experience left a sour taste in the delegates' mouths. As I was accompanying them back to the airport, one of the CEOs looked over at me and announced, "Aha! I now understand the secret to American diplomacy. You starve us; wait until we are completely exhausted, dehydrated, and dispirited; and THEN you have your way with us."

I am reminded of that delegation every time I hear a government official espouse the need for more public–private collaborative partners across the globe to help reinvigorate the global economy. I hope that one day the government will institute mandatory Global Mindset briefings for all of their employees and appointees in global roles—that and a beverage budget allocation. Diplomacy should never be conducted without proper refreshments.

DEVELOPMENT SUGGESTIONS
for Willingness to Collaborate

LEARN

Tips to learn about and begin developing the capability on your own. These tips involve self-directed learning, including reading, listening, watching, or observing, that you can do on your own at your own pace. They are most useful for novices in the capability, but are helpful for intermediate and advanced learners to keep knowledge current.

Development Activity	Suggested Resource(s) and Tips
Learn about how to collaborate in business contexts by reading books on the subject.	Read books such as: • *The Culture of Collaboration: Maximizing Time, Talent and Tools to Create Value in the Global Economy* (Rosen, 2009) • *Collaboration: How Leaders Avoid the Traps, Create Unity, and Reap Big Results* (Hansen, 2009) • *Harvard Business Review: Collaborating Effectively* (Harvard Business Press Books, 2011)
Learn collaboration strategies through workshops.	Take a workshop on collaboration such as: • The Culture of Collaboration Workshop (www.thecultureofcollaboration.com) • University of Wisconsin-Madison's experiential workshop, The Journey of Facilitation and Collaboration (www.journeyofcollaboration.com).
Learn about conflict management across cultures to help you understand and minimize obstacles to collaboration. Much of this literature is in the field of cross-cultural negotiations.	• Take the Intercultural Conflict Style Inventory (ICS) (www.icsinventory.com), which will help you understand your own approach to conflict and how it compares to other cultures. You can also take training through ICS to understand core conflict-resolution strategies across cultures. • Take Communicating and Negotiating with a Global Mindset at Thunderbird Executive Education (www.thunderbird.edu/executive_ education/classroom_programs/communicating_negotiating.htm). • Attend courses on cross-cultural negotiations at your local colleges and universities. • Watch INSEAD professor Dr. Falcao's interview on how to avoid pitfalls in cross-cultural negotiations (http://youtube/-4GjCOipJIA). • Watch Negotiation Europe's video on cross-cultural negotiation tips (http://youtube/BII8PXGmSBk). • Find videos of interest on negotiation topics that are listed on the Harvard Program on Negotiations website (www.pon.harvard.edu/ category/events/pon-film-series). • Read books on cross-cultural negotiation, such as *Negotiating Across Cultures: International Communication in an Interdependent World* (Cohen, 1997). You can also search for books specifically focused on negotiations in your culture of interest. • Read *Global Negotiation: The New Rules* (Graham and Requejo, 2008). • Read *Negotiating Globally: How to Negotiate Deals, Resolve Disputes, and Make Decisions across Cultural Boundaries* (Brett, 2007). • Read *Culture and Conflict Resolution* (Avruch, 1998).

DEVELOPMENT SUGGESTIONS
for Willingness to Collaborate

CONNECT

Tips to learn about and continue developing the capability through others. These tips involve working with another person to learn from their experiences. They may involve asking questions, listening to and discussing experiences, forming a new relationship, deepening an existing relationship, or receiving feedback from someone who is acting as your mentor. These tips are useful for all levels of learners.

Development Activity	Suggested Resource(s) and Tips
Learn about collaboration in the culture of interest.	• Ask your local colleagues to discuss what teamwork and collaboration look like in the culture of interest. • Work with a local cultural expert to discuss how collaboration works in the culture and strategies you can incorporate to be effective. • When entering into collaboration with diverse colleagues, openly discuss the ground rules and protocols for the collaboration.
Be open to learning from your colleagues.	• Ask for the opinions and suggestions of your colleagues regularly. • When you are faced with a new or particularly difficult business challenge, invite your colleagues to brainstorm solutions with you. • Prior to implementing a new product or service, consult with customers, suppliers, and business partners to incorporate their insights.

DEVELOPMENT SUGGESTIONS
for Willingness to Collaborate

EXPERIENCE

Tips to learn about and develop skills in the capability through firsthand experience. These tips involve engaging in activities, such as exploring a new area, trying a new cultural activity, or participating in a specific business event. These tips are most useful for intermediate to advanced learners, and we suggest that novice learners prepare themselves for success by completing some of the tips in the Learn category first.

Development Activity	Suggested Resource(s) and Tips
Spark and sustain your willingness to collaborate by identifying compelling reasons to engage in the work.	• Identify key objectives and outcomes that are meaningful for you. • Consider the benefits to you to enter into the collaboration. • Consider the positive results that may come out of the collaboration, even if you fear losing control or being vulnerable. • Consider what will be lost if you do not collaborate.

DIPLOMACY

DEVELOPMENT SUGGESTIONS
for Willingness to Collaborate

EXPERIENCE

Tips to learn about and develop skills in the capability through firsthand experience. These tips involve engaging in activities, such as exploring a new area, trying a new cultural activity, or participating in a specific business event. These tips are most useful for intermediate to advanced learners, and we suggest that novice learners prepare themselves for success by completing some of the tips in the Learn category first.

Development Activity	Suggested Resource(s) and Tips
Practice collaborating with others.	• Volunteer to serve in nonprofit organizations. • Volunteer for community service projects and events. • Volunteer for a leadership role in a professional, social, or community organization in which you belong. • Identify several issues/problems in your role that may benefit from a collaborative approach. Form a team to work on the issues together. • Identify your top three professional talents, and volunteer to be a resource to other groups in your organization who are working on those particular areas.
When entering into a collaboration, begin the partnership by discussing rules of engagement.	Start the meeting by gathering everyone's ideas and agreements on the guidelines that should be used for collaboration and decision making to make the process as smooth and as inclusive as possible. This may help you sustain your willingness to collaborate throughout the process.
Actively work on building consensus.	• Identify the positions on the issue held by each member of the group. • Weigh the pros/cons of each position, as well as the feasibility. • Do not make disagreements personal. • When there are disagreements, ask each group member what it would take to come to agreement. • If you anticipate high tension in the group, hire a dispute resolution expert who is familiar with the local culture to facilitate the meeting, such as a professional mediator or alternative dispute resolution (ADR) specialist. Your local university or community college communication departments may be able to make recommendations on facilitators. You can also do an Internet search of ADR specialists in your area. ICS Consulting (www.icsinventory.com) offers services to help managers resolve conflicts across cultures. • Keep in mind that conflict management, dispute resolution, and consensus building look different across cultures. Be sure to consult a local cultural expert and colleagues experienced in working with the local culture to ensure your success.

GLOBAL SOCIAL CAPITAL

DEVELOPMENT SUGGESTIONS
for Willingness to Collaborate

COACH OR CONTRIBUTE

Tips to help others learn about and develop this capability. These tips involve coaching and mentoring others. They may include creating information or experiences for individuals, teams, or your organization. These tips are designed for those who are advanced in the capability and are useful development methods to keep advanced leaders in the capability engaged in professional development at the highest level. Please note that the tips in this section may also be quite helpful for individual use if you do not have a coach or mentor.

Development Activity	Suggested Resource(s) and Tips
Help your direct report or mentee identify reasons to collaborate.	Ask them: • What are the key objectives and outcomes that are meaningful for you in this collaboration? • What benefits are there to you to enter into the collaboration? • What positive results may come out of the collaboration? • What will be lost if you do not collaborate? • What are the obstacles you see for collaboration? How can you plan for these and mitigate them?
When coaching direct reports and mentees on how to strengthen their collaboration skills, use the "yes, and" exercise.	Help your direct report or mentee change their language to be more collaborative. When they disagree with a statement, ask them to replace the use of the words *but* or *however* with *yes, and*. For example, if someone states they believe that changing vendors is the solution to a problem but your direct report disagrees, she may say, "Yes, changing vendors is one possible solution, and we should also consider how we can reduce costs with our current vendor." This inclusive language adds ideas toward solving the problem at hand without rejecting the ideas of others.
Help prepare your direct report or mentee for successful collaborations.	Ask them: • What does collaboration mean to you in the culture of interest? • If I were watching a movie of your collaborating, what would you be doing? • What do you intend to give to this collaborative effort?

Additional Reading

The readings listed here provide you with additional study of the Global Mindset capability in this section. You will find that many of these resources provide you with a specific and detailed look at using this capability in a particular context or location.

....

Title: "Improving Collaborative Learning and Global Project Management in Small and Medium Enterprises"

Publication: *International Journal of Advanced Corporate Learning*

Date: 2011

Authors: Marcus Birkenkrahe, Stefanie Quade, and Frank Habermann

Executive Summary: Globalization needs collaboration. In a multinational setting, traditional issues of collaboration are exacerbated because of language and culture. This problem is particularly felt by small- and medium-sized enterprises, which are traditionally not natural-born globals.

....

Title: "Rotating Leadership and Collaborative Innovation: Recombination Processes in Symbiotic Relationships"

Publication: *Administrative Science Quarterly*

Date: 2011

Authors: Jason P. Davis and Kathleen M. Eisenhardt

Executive Summary: Using a multiple-case, inductive study of eight technology collaborations between ten organizations in the global computing and communications industries between 2001 and 2006, this paper examines why some interorganizational relationships produce technological innovations while others do not. Comparisons of more and less innovative collaborations show that high-performing collaborative innovation involves more than possessing the appropriate structural antecedents (e.g., R&D capabilities, social embeddedness) suggested by prior alliance studies. Rather, it also involves dynamic organizational processes associated with collaboration partners' leadership roles that solve critical innovation problems related to recombination across boundaries.

Title: "New Business Models Through Collaborative Idea Generation"

Publication: *International Journal of Innovation Management*

Date: 2011

Authors: Martin J. Eppler, Friederike Hoffman, and Sabrina Bresciani

Executive Summary: Generating novel and sustainable business model ideas is a crucial yet challenging innovation task. A growing body of literature shows that artifacts, such as visual templates, objects, and sketches, can enhance team collaboration and creativity in innovation activities. Drawing on literature from diverse fields, we propose a model that aims to explain how artifacts can affect the team processes in developing new business model ideas, positing that they have an effect on creativity and collaboration. We report the results of an illustrative experimental study comparing the team processes of managers working on a business model innovation task. Teams were supported by different types of artifacts (a business model template; physical objects with sketching; or PowerPoint). The results indicate that using the template significantly increases perceived collaboration and decreases perceived creativity, hence showing that artifacts can have the power to shape teamwork for innovation tasks.

Title: "Collaboration: How Leaders Avoid the Traps, Create Unity, and Reap Big Results"

Publication: *Harvard Business Press*

Date: 2009

Author: Morten T. Hansen

Executive Summary: In "Collaboration," author Morten Hansen takes aim at what many leaders inherently know: in today's competitive environment, companywide collaboration is an imperative for successful strategy execution, yet the sought-after synergies are rarely, if ever, realized. In fact, most cross-unit collaborative efforts end up wasting time, money, and resources. How can managers avoid the costly traps of collaboration and, instead, start getting the results they need? In this book, Hansen shows managers how to get collaboration right through disciplined collaboration.

DIPLOMACY

Title: "Six Ingredients for Collaborative Partnerships"

Publication: *Leader to Leader*

Date: 2011

Author: Thomas Kayser

Executive Summary: New and experienced managers alike often lack the necessary mental maps and skills needed to be collaborative leaders capable of building effective partnerships within and across work teams. The author explains how three structural ingredients (shared goals, interdependence and complementary skills, and accountability) along with three behavioral characteristics (character, commitment, and authentic communication) can produce a multiplier effect that produces the synergy inherent in genuine collaborative partnerships.

Title: "Rewiring: Cross-Business-Unit Collaborations in Multibusiness Organizations"

Publication: *Academy of Management Journal*

Date: 2010

Authors: Jeffrey A. Martin and Kathleen M. Eisenhardt

Executive Summary: Cross-business-unit collaboration is central to large firms' value creation, yet empirical support for the prevailing view that a corporate process best fosters such collaboration has been unconvincing. This study of six firms asks how executives create collaborations that perform at high levels. Our emergent theory unexpectedly emphasizes that a BU-centric process led by multibusiness teams of general managers leads to better collaborations than a corporate-centric process.

Title: "Which Kind of Collaboration Is Right for You?"

Publication: *Harvard Business Review*

Date: 2008

Authors: Gary P. Pisano and Roberto Verganti

Executive Summary: Nowadays, virtually no company innovates alone. Firms team up with a variety of partners, in a wide number of ways, to create new technologies, products, and services. But what is the best way to leverage the power of outsiders? To help executives answer that question, Pisano, of Harvard Business School, and Verganti, of Politecnico di Milano, developed a simple framework focused on two questions: Given your strategy, how open or closed should your network of collaborators be? And who should decide which problems to tackle and which solutions to adopt? There are four basic modes of collaboration, say the authors.

....

Title: "An Approach to Assess Collaboration Readiness"

Publication: *International Journal of Production Research*

Date: 2009

Authors: Joao Rosas and Luis M. Camarinha-Matos

Executive Summary: The level of readiness of an organization to join a collaborative process depends on hard factors such as competency fitness or technological compatibility, but also on several other factors of a soft nature such as an organization's character, willingness to collaborate, or affectivity/empathy relationships.

....

Title: "Collaborative Strategic Planning: Three Observations"

Publication: *McKinsey Quarterly*

Date: 2012

Author: Olivier Sibony

Executive Summary: The article discusses drawbacks to social approaches to strategic planning. The author observes that while crowdsourcing can help generate new ideas and challenge existing plans, it's not likely to be an optimal way of identifying radical but necessary strategy shifts. He further notes that a free and open exchange of ideas requires courage on the part of participants to advance a proposal and risk seeing it attacked and refuted by others. In his view, crowd-based mechanisms are at risk of promoting conformity in thinking.

Title: "The Benefits of Collaboration between For-Profit Businesses and Nonprofit Arts- or Culture-Oriented Organizations"

Publication: *Advanced Management Journal*

Date: 2011

Authors: Larry Weinstein and John Cook

Executive Summary: The article discusses the benefits of for-profit businesses and nonprofit arts- or culture-oriented organizations partnerships. It explains the scope of the nonprofit arts- or culture-oriented organizations and their use as an effective vehicle by which business can demonstrate its commitments that meet with expectations. It cites several benefits that businesses can gain from an alliance with a nonprofit arts- or culture-oriented organizations partnership, including useful skills in meeting social responsibilities, creativity, and potential tax-deductibility of donations. It also mentions the financial support, managerial advice, and operational skills, as well as a source of volunteers in the partnership between organizations and businesses.

Najafi Global Mindset Institute Services

We are passionate about seeing our clients succeed. This is why we offer a number of development tools and services at Najafi Global Mindset Institute.

JENNIE L. WALKER, PH.D., PHR
Director of Global Learning & Market Development
Najafi Global Mindset Institute
Jennie.Walker@Thunderbird.edu

We trust that you have found the development suggestions, tips, and resources in this book to be valuable. We are passionate about seeing our clients succeed. This is why we offer a number of development tools and services at Najafi Global Mindset Institute. We have described them briefly here for your information, and we would love to continue to be a resource for you. Please contact us anytime with questions or join us for one of our workshops at www.globalmindset.com. We look forward to working with you!

Our products and services include the following:

- **GMI Self-Assessment Tool:** This psychometric instrument has been scientifically designed to produce results that are both valid and reliable. It is a self-assessment that measures an individual's readiness in all thirty-five capabilities of Global Mindset. You will receive a custom report that shows your individual scores and how they compare to a team score (if you take this assessment as part of a team) and our grand mean, which includes more than fifteen thousand global leaders from around the world. Your report also includes an individual development-planning section. This report can be debriefed individually or in teams during our custom Global Mindset Workshops.

- **GMI 360 Assessment Tool:** Like the GMI, this tool also has strong psychometric properties. It is designed to be used by an individual and his or her colleagues, supervisors, direct reports, business partners, clients, or customers. You and/or your coach will determine the group of people who will be assessing your Global Mindset. You also will complete a self-assessment. Your custom report will compare your self-assessment to the quantitative scores and qualitative feedback of your 360 raters. This is a terrific tool for in-depth leadership development. This tool also can be debriefed individually or as a team.

- **Global Mindset Workshops for Teams:** Our Global Mindset workshops are highly engaging, as we use a variety of activities and compelling information to make these development sessions come alive. We have a number of repeat clients as a result. Our most commonly requested session is four hours and includes an introduction to Global Mindset, activities, and a debrief session for individual and team GMI results. However, we often are asked to facilitate sessions ranging from five to eight hours, as well as multi-day workshops customized for the organization's development needs. We have facilitators located around the world.

- **Custom Individual and Team Coaching:** While our workshops are a great introduction to Global Mindset, we also work with our clients on an ongoing basis to provide additional Global Mindset coaching and development. Our custom Global Mindset coaching solutions, such as individual executive coaching, longer-term team coaching, and organizational development coaching, are valuable services for our clients who are working to make Global Mindset development a priority in their organizations at all levels. Please call us to discuss the specific needs of your organization.

- **GMI Certified Facilitator Certification:** Global Mindset development is a strong and growing need in many organizations. As such, some of these organizations have chosen to certify their own staff in-house to be able to debrief the GMI and facilitate Global Mindset workshops. Certification is also quite popular among executive coaches, global business consultants, and business school faculty and staff. We offer a robust two-day certification program for those who wish to become certified in the GMI. Those who wish to complete certification in the GMI 360 tool stay with us for an additional half-day beyond the GMI certification. Certification is valid for eighteen months.

- **Global Leader Assessment Center:** Our global leader assessment center, entitled *A Day in the Life of a Global Leader*, is a hands-on, experiential workshop designed to measure and develop leaders who are potential candidates for global assignments. Workshop participants simulate real-world business situations as if they were in a global leadership role. They are challenged over the course of 2.5 days to apply their Global Mindset knowledge, skills, and abilities throughout engaging, real-world scenarios. Participants receive comprehensive evaluation from multiple expert assessors, 360 feedback, and a tailored development plan that will help them take their leadership to the next level for success in a global role.

Acknowledgments

Thunderbird is a truly unique place. As the world's number-one ranked graduate school of international management, it is dedicated to helping individuals and corporations succeed in global environments. This mission inspired and guided our work, and we would first like to sincerely thank the Thunderbird community for its abundant support. Our interim president and CEO, Ambassador Barbara Barrett; our new president, Dr. Larry Penley; our chief operating officer, John Berndt; and our dean of faculty, Dr. Dale Davison, have been our constant supporters and advocates, as have been our Board of Trustees.

Our chairman of the Board of Trustees, Ann Iverson, calls our work "the soul of Thunderbird." The heart of our Institute, however, is Francis Najafi, a Thunderbird alum and trustee. He has funded our research and many activities over the past few years. He provided a generous financial gift that enabled us to renovate the Yount building on the Glendale campus of Thunderbird School of Global Management to be the home for Najafi Global Mindset Institute. He has been a valuable mentor, a strong supporter, and a very dear friend to us.

Our understanding of Global Mindset and how to develop it was shaped by many research partners, leadership development practitioners, and global managers and executives. Among our research partners, we would like to extend a warm thank you to Dr. Mary Teagarden, Dr. David Bowen, Dr. Femi Babarinde, Dr. Karen Walsh, Dr. Christine Pearson, and Dr. Amanda Bullough for their research insights. We are also grateful to Dr. Joy McGovern, the former head of client services at Najafi Global Mindset Institute. She helped us in our efforts to produce practical ideas and suggestions. We are also thankful to the executive coaches and academics who contributed to the extensive tips, resources, narratives, and case studies in the book. They are profiled in the About the Contributors section of the book, and we encourage you to get to know these fascinating individuals. They have synthesized decades of successful global work and research into golden nuggets that will benefit developing leaders for years to come. Among them, Sue Gebelein and Dr. Katherine Holt, were instrumental in helping us move this project toward publication with their generous publishing insights. Last, but certainly not least, we would like to acknowledge the hundreds of managers and executives in many corporations all over the world who had confidence in us and our work and participated in countless numbers of workshops and programs. Their ideas, self-reflections, and insights were immensely helpful to us, and this book is our gift back to them.

Personally, we are grateful to our spouses and families for energizing and motivating us throughout this journey. They have tolerated our travels and long days and nights and showed us support and love all the way. Without them, this book would not have been possible. You know who you are, and we love you.

Case Studies

The case studies in this section are designed to help both individuals and teams identify and analyze Global Mindset capabilities in global scenarios. They can be used for development of individuals, corporate teams, nongovernmental organization teams, or business students. Most of these cases are drawn from real-life scenarios where leaders were put in challenging cross-cultural situations. Each case is followed by several provocative discussion questions to help readers identify how Global Mindset capabilities were either used well or not. Teaching notes follow the discussion questions to help individuals or team facilitators debrief the questions.

Please note: These cases are copyrighted and may not be reproduced without permission. Individual personal use is permitted through the purchase of this book. Those who wish to obtain and distribute copies of these cases may contact Najafi Global Mindset Institute to purchase PDF copies: www.globalmindset.com.

Case Study Index and Synopses

....

Case Study 1: The Lived Experience of Developing a Global Mindset in South Africa
By Steven Segal, Ph.D.

This case discusses a native South African man's development of Global Mindset through his immersion into the city life of Johannesburg. The two worlds of this man are juxtaposed, revealing polar differences in life in his native Transkei compared to the bustle of Johannesburg. His challenges and, ultimately, successful adaptation to city life are described and discussed in terms of Global Mindset development.

Case Study 2: Preparing for a Crisis in Sudan
By Harison Yusoff, MS

A Malaysian human resources manager who is new to his role and new to operations in Khartoum, Sedan, is left in charge while his manager is away. During that time, an employee requires a minor medical procedure that turns tragic. The human resources manager is left to navigate a complex human disaster in a cross-cultural environment, both of which he is unprepared for.

Case Study 3: Caught in the Middle in Japan
By Lynda L. Moore, Ph.D.

Judy is a very internationally experienced middle manager in Japan who is reporting to a vice president with little Global Mindset. The case explores what makes Judy so effective, and her vice president, Jim, so ineffective. The case discusses strategies to build a Global Mindset at a senior level and how the organization can do a better job preparing executives for success in global roles.

Case Study 4: Risky Business in Iraq
By Zainubiah Abd Aziz

A high-risk trip to the 1997 Baghdad Oil and Gas Expo by exhibition employees from a Malaysian oil and gas company starts out as a lesson in cross-cultural differences. The employees discover just how different Iraqi culture is from their own Malaysian culture. An almost complete language barrier adds to the complications. But what starts out as a cross-cultural experience turns into a crisis for the Malaysian employees as the United States invades Iraq.

Case Study 5: A Global Acquisition Gone Sour in South Africa
By Harison Yusoff, MS

After acquiring a South African subsidiary, a corporate team from the Malaysian headquarters of an oil and gas company traveled to South Africa to meet with local management to work on aligning the subsidiary's business strategy with the parent company. The Malaysian team leader, an experienced expert in corporate strategy, told the team members prior to going that it would be a breeze. But things quickly went from bad to worse in South Africa.

Case Study 6: A US–Russian Academic Collaboration in Peril

By Yulia Tolstikov-Mast, Ph.D.

An international business professor from Russia decides to enlist the cooperation of a Russian colleague, located in Russia, to coordinate an American–Russian student project for a global management course. The semester-long project starts off well, but conflict ensues between the students within the first month. When the professor tries to enlist the support of her colleague to create a new course activity to get the students on the right track again, she encounters resistance. This case explores the complexities of working cross-culturally as well as misunderstandings that can happen within one's own culture.

Case Study 7: Leave No One Behind in Morocco

By Alfredo Behrens, Ph.D.

Western business people and their spouses attending a business gathering in Morocco took a day off for a bus tour. During the tour, one of the spouses suffered an accident, which required immediate first aid and transport to a medical facility. Under the advice of the English-speaking Moroccan tourist guide, the bus made a detour to his nearby village. While waiting for a helicopter evacuation of the injured woman, the bus left, leaving the businessman and his spouse behind with the tour guide. The case provides a forum to discuss culturally defined concepts like solidarity, loyalty, pragmatism, and cross-cultural relationships.

Case Study 1: The Lived Experience of Developing a Global Mindset in South Africa

STEVEN SEGAL, PH.D.
Senior Lecturer
Macquarie Graduate
School of Management

Abstract

This case discusses a native South African man's development of Global Mindset through his immersion into the city life of Johannesburg. The two worlds of this man are juxtaposed, revealing polar differences in life in his native Transkei compared to the bustle of Johannesburg. His challenges and, ultimately, successful adaptation to city life are described and discussed in terms of Global Mindset development.

The Case

The author of this case had a colleague who was a research academic at a university in Johannesburg, South Africa, who without even knowing it developed a Global Mindset. This person lived in two worlds: the rural world of his birthplace in Transkei (also in South Africa) and the urban area of Johannesburg.

Once a month, he flew from Johannesburg to Transkei to be with his extended family. Every time he made the flight, he underwent a metamorphosis. As he disembarked from the aircraft in Transkei, he would take off his workplace attire—his suit and tie—and replace them with his village clothing—a loin cloth. Once he had undergone this transformation, he would enter the village of his family. He would sit on the ground or squat comfortably amidst the elders of his tribe, knowing his place amidst them as part of a community. In the center of the gathering there was

TRANSKEI, SOUTH AFRICA

Luke Schmidt / Shutterstock.com

usually a wood fire, and the smoke would drift into his face in a way that did not disturb or distract him. Similarly, he would allow the flies to land on his face without having to flick them away or even notice them. He had an intrinsic respect for the order of authority in the tribe. He would talk only when it was his turn to speak and would respect the wisdom of the elders without even the hint of questioning them. Independence and even the idea of a self were just not part of the way of doing things.

On Sunday nights, he would hop on a flight to Johannesburg. By Monday morning, he would be dressed in a suit, ready for work in the so-called developed sector of the white economy. Here too he knew all the rules of the community, and he would enact them in his everyday dealing with people. He lived out the established patterns of authority. He knew how to argue his point at committee meetings and knew the importance of doing so as an individual in this kind of organizational setting to actualize his agenda. He knew the art of playing organizational politics, how to form networks, and how to communicate well in his role as a lecturer. He was also an extremely self-possessed and independent man.

It is tempting to say that the roles that he played came naturally and easily to him. But this would be incorrect. It was only after years of mastering the estrangement, pain, and bewilderment of grappling effectively with being a stranger in the world of the city that he began to master its ways. He moved as a young adult from the familiar and safe environment of Transkei to Johannesburg. During this transition, he was often alone and confused. All sorts of questions would pop up in his thoughts like, "Why are people in such a hurry in the city, and why are people so formal and unfriendly?" He even began to doubt himself and his ability to adapt to city life. He did not have a sense of belonging in the huge metropolis, and there was no embodied sense of the order to things that would give him a clear picture of what to do or how to be.

But he worked through the anxiety and uncertainty to slowly, but surely, adapt. He did this through a process of constant questioning that allowed him to become familiar with the ways of doing things in the city. This mastery should not be taken for granted. For every person new to Johannesburg who did master the city, there were hundreds who lost themselves to alcohol or other vices just to cope with the alienation of being a stranger in a new land. My colleague's understanding was hard-won. Because of his own struggles, he became an adept teacher helping others to learn to adapt to a new culture. He even did this for me and some of my peers.

On one occasion, we were doing research into tribal management practices, and he invited some of us to his tribal home in Transkei. He laughed in a very playful way at our bewilderment at not quite knowing how things got done and our awkwardness at what to do with ourselves in the new and unfamiliar culture. His laugh was not malicious. It was, in fact, playful and generous because, being highly attuned to our discomfort, he recognized our discomfort and helped us find our places in the community. Not only did he make us feel comfortable, he also created possibilities for us to understand. This helped us to reduce the sense of strangeness we felt in an unfamiliar setting. He was a very effective translator for the ways of the two worlds. This is a hard thing to do, but he was motivated to help us because he knew that we had the good will to want to listen beyond our boundaries. Both sides recognized the mutual generosity of spirit required for understanding an unfamiliar way of doing things. As a leader, our colleague helped us to find a sense of place and perspective amidst our confusion and sense of feeling out of place.

Discussion Questions

1. Describe the two worlds that the research academic from Transkei inhabited.

2. What made it possible for him to move between these worlds?

3. What are the Global Mindset attributes that you can see in this case? Use examples to back up your case.

4. Name and discuss some of the challenges involved in developing a Global Mindset.

5. Based on this case, how would you distinguish Global Mindset from cross-cultural education?

6. What thoughts about your own experience emerge from reading this case?

Teaching Notes

1.   Describe the two worlds that the research academic from Transkei inhabited.

The research academic was from a rural, native community where tradition was paramount. This included traditional dress, an established hierarchy with a deep respect for elders, and a prioritization of community over self.

His acculturation in Johannesburg allowed him to work equally well in that society where Western formal wear was the norm, society followed a different set of rules about order and hierarchy, and individual autonomy was prioritized over community. The pace of life between both was quite different, as was the degree of connection within the communities.

2.   *What made it possible for him to move between these worlds?*

We see a man who is comfortable moving between two cultures and two worlds. He was able to do this not through theoretical and abstract knowledge of the two cultures, but through an embodied knowledge of the two cultures. He knew his way around both without having to think about it, much like the art of riding a bicycle that becomes second nature over time. So too his understanding was based on a felt knowledge of the two cultures. He was quite at home in both of them. This was because of his well-developed Global Mindset.

3.   *What are the Global Mindset attributes that you can see in this case? Use examples to back up your case.*

This colleague mastered the art of being able to live in two worlds. This involved more than just the ability to translate from one world to another; it gave him a set of global competencies to use to navigate both worlds. The following list highlights the Global Mindset attributes possessed and displayed by the research academic from Transkei:

- In the face of uncertainty, he developed a quest for adventure, which is an ability to have faith taking a leap to immersing himself in others' ways of doing things.

- He developed the cosmopolitan outlook, which allowed him to not take his own worldview for granted when going into an unfamiliar situation.

- He developed an ability to adapt his own perspectives by listening to and exploring the views of others.

- He developed intercultural empathy to see other ways of doing things as legitimate and interesting alternatives, instead of reducing them to oddities.

- He developed an ability to appreciate and navigate uncertain situations.

- He learned to make decisions and take action in the face of the uncertainty or discomfort. He did not learn about the strange culture by thinking about it, but by immersing himself in it.

- He learned how to learn from mistakes that he made by modifying his actions and decisions appropriately.

- He developed a confidence in himself through his trial and error of navigating differences.

- He developed a sense of resilience to bounce back in the face of cultural missteps.

- He developed an ability to dialogue across cultures.

- He developed an ability to speak in the language of others and to listen to them using their cultural framework. As he would say, a person's world comes alive through the language they speak. To see a person's worldview and thus work effectively with them is to be able to see things through their language.

- He learned how to enable other people to learn about cultures by guiding them in immersion experiences. This included a profound ability to listen and pick up on nonverbal cues. He was able to turn their anxiety into learning opportunities.

- He developed a sense of psychological flexibility. This was not only a tolerance, but also an actual enjoyment of the uncertainty and ambiguity in cross-cultural interactions.

4. *Name and discuss some of the challenges involved in developing a Global Mindset.*

In this case, the research academic from Transkei faced extreme loneliness and isolation while learning to navigate a new culture. Many others have not fared as well and have turned to vices to cope with these challenges. His adaptation required patience, persistence, keen observation, open-mindedness, and flexibility.

5. *Based on this case, how would you distinguish Global Mindset from cross-cultural education?*

A big difference between cross-cultural interactions and having a Global Mindset is that cross-cultural interactions often do not involve reciprocal understanding. In our research excursion to Transkei, we were having a cross-cultural experience because we did not understand his culture the way he understood ours. We saw his culture through the lens of our own. He had a Global Mindset that allowed him to fully understand and navigate both worlds. He was a leader who was able to translate and interpret between cultures. He helped us understand ethnic black culture, the way of being in this culture, and the expectations and assumptions within the society.

This is a challenge for many people from Western cultures who tend to take their cultural knowledge as the standard by which Asian and African cultures want to be educated, without a complementary understanding of the Asian or African culture. In contrast, Asian and African people tend to have an appreciation of both their own way of doing things and Western ways of being, because they are generally exposed to both and have to learn both ways of being.

The colleague of the author was not only very helpful but also very adamant that we develop a reciprocal understanding of African tribal culture in its own terms. He cautioned us not to reduce it or redefine it in Western standards, as had been the custom of centuries of colonialism. This was not just about African pride; it was pragmatic. If we wanted to know our way about African culture, we needed to understand its ways of doing things. So, too, if we want to understand Asian cultures and their effect on organizations and management, we need a more reciprocal understanding. This understanding allows us to know our way about and see into the culture in a way that we could not otherwise do through our own cultural lens. The challenge to develop a more symmetrical understanding is especially important in view of the rise of China and the Asian century, where expecting the other to understand management practices in Western terms is not going to be good enough in the future.

6. *What thoughts about your own experience emerge from reading this case?*

Although it would be incorrect, a little knowledge about the autobiography of Nelson Mandela suggests that we are writing about Nelson Mandela here. In his journey into developing a Global Mindset, he too went through the alienation of living in between the familiarity of his homeland and the strangeness of urban life. In the face of extreme adversity, he was able to dwell in the anxiety and uncertainty of the unknown long enough to develop a mastery of the two worlds. This enabled him to dialogue between the two, being mindful of the vulnerabilities, values, and aspirations of the people of both worlds. This helped him architect the rainbow nation of South Africa. Furthermore, he was quite open to being transformed by the new way of life in the city, while preserving the identity of his heritage. And more than this, he was able to rise above personal threats to his identity to be able to listen to his enemy. While the path that we are talking about here is the one that was traversed by Mandela, the person in this case is an ordinary leader. He may not stand out on any world stage, but he demonstrates that developing a Global Mindset is possible and creates extraordinary opportunities to expand our own lives and those of others.

Case Study 2: Preparing for a Crisis in Sudan

HARISON YUSOFF, MS
Learning Manager
PETRONAS Leadership
Centre

Abstract

A Malaysian human resources manager who is new to his role and new to operations in Khartoum, Sedan, is left in charge while his manager is away. During that time, an employee requires a minor medical procedure that turns tragic. The human resources manager is left to navigate a complex human disaster in a cross-cultural environment, both of which he is unprepared for.

The Case

Ravi, one of our native Malaysian staff members with a technical background, was posted to Sudan in 1999 for three years. Ravi's tenure there began as a training supervisor with the Greater Nile Petroleum Operating Company. This is a joint venture between four companies—China's CNPC (40 percent), Malaysia's PETRONAS (30 percent), Canada's Talisman (25 percent), and the National Oil Company of Sudan Sudapet (5 percent). The venture later emerged to be a major contributor to PETRONAS's overseas production and revenue.

Ravi was sent to Sudan to help set up the joint venture for the human resources department. He was promoted to deputy human resource manager in October 1999 where his role primarily involved assisting the human resources manager to plan and implement company policies and processes to drive performance and

KHARTOUM, SUDAN

Imagine Images, Alastair Pidgen / Shutterstock.com

productivity. He also oversaw the well-being of staff and their administrative needs during the setup of the joint venture.

On a Tuesday afternoon in December 1999, Ravi was informed that a Malaysian staff member had been admitted to the local hospital in Khartoum. The human resources manager, Jamila, was away for the week, leaving Ravi in charge. He rushed to the hospital to visit the young engineer, Ahmad. He found him quite cheerful despite his complaint of a nagging pain in the lower abdomen.

"The doctor said it is appendicitis and will involve only a minor operation," Ahmad told Ravi.

"I would strongly advise that we get the opinion of our panel doctor in Dubai," Ravi responded. "If you could just give me a few hours to make the arrangements, I can get you on a flight to Dubai by tonight and you can have the operation as soon as we can arrange for it."

Ravi's effort to persuade Ahmad to attend to his medical needs in Dubai were unsuccessful.

"It's okay," said Ahmad. "I heard the doctors here are just as reputable, and I want to get it done with. I have so much work to finish that I cannot afford any more time away. There have been too many delays on this project."

Looking at Ravi's worried frown, Ahmad continued with a smile. "Anyway, I am planning to go back for a long leave to Kuala Lumpur right after we complete the first phase of this project. I will have plenty of time to rest and recuperate then," Ahmad said.

Even though Ravi tried to convince Ahmad to delay the surgery, it was to no avail. Ahmad went through with the procedure at the hospital in Khartoum the following day.

That Wednesday, Ravi received a call from the hospital in Khartoum informing him that Ahmad had died due to excessive bleeding after the surgery. Ravi was shocked. For a few hours after that, he could hardly remember what he had done. He was in a mad scramble to prepare the report for his superiors and to make the necessary arrangements.

Ravi was completely unprepared for the emotional and administrative nightmare that ensued. According to Ravi, the hospital administrators seemed very uncooperative and did not see the urgency of the situation. To get the body released and flown back to Kuala Lumpur involved intricate communication and negotiation techniques that Ravi had not been prepared to perform.

When Ravi's boss, Jamila, returned from her trip, she realized how traumatic the situation must have been for Ravi. He was new in the position and there was no policy or procedure in place to guide him. His offshore experience called for him to be prepared for technical crises, but this kind of situation was totally new for him. It was a disaster of the human kind. It was through sheer providence that Ravi managed to coordinate the administrative matters and overcome the multitude of challenges, which among the most critical was making arrangements for deporting the body from Sudan to Malaysia.

The human resources manager reported that the incident was a crucial learning experience for the organization. According to Jamila, "Not only did we lack the standard processes, what was particularly glaring at that time was that there was nothing in place to help someone of Ravi's level cope with the consequences of the distressful situation and get him back on track. Not only did he feel inadequate for not being able to persuade Ahmad to seek medical care in Dubai in the first place, but the maddening runaround and massive paperwork in Khartoum took a toll on his well-being as well. Due to the stress he suffered, Ravi became more taciturn and was overly particular with processes and procedures in regard to health and medical matters."

Ravi admitted that he became quite paranoid, wondering if there could be another crisis just around the corner. It was energy-sapping for him. Jamila observed that Ravi took some time to revert to his normal self. When he finally appeared more stable, Jamila heaved a sigh of relief. She said, "Ravi is a very valuable team member. The organization is fortunate to have him back in shape." But the entire situation begs the question: are other organizations prepared to address these kinds of complex human disasters in cross-cultural environments?

Discussion Questions

1. How could someone in Ravi's position be more equipped to manage his responsibilities in a new environment and a new culture during both normal circumstances and emergencies?

2. What training would have been useful to help the overseas staff prepare for crisis situations and perform well during traumatic experiences?

3. Do you believe there is a difference in intensity or stress in an international working environment compared to a local environment? How can the overseas staff cope with stress?

Teaching Notes

1. *How could someone in Ravi's position be more equipped to manage his responsibilities in a new environment and a new culture during both normal circumstances and emergencies?*

Research at Najafi Global Mindset Institute at Thunderbird School of Global Management shows that developing the competencies of a Global Mindset equip staff for success in new environments and in new cultures. The three main components of Global Mindset—Global Intellectual Capital, Global Psychological Capital, and Global Social Capital—provide a useful framework for development to navigate the complexities of global work. In this case, Jamila was right to say that a standard operating procedure would have provided a framework, but realistically it alone would not help staff navigate the complex cultural issues at play.

Ravi needed both an operations framework and the framework of a Global Mindset for success in his position. Here are some competencies in Global Mindset that would have been helpful for him:

*   He would have benefitted from development in global business savvy and cosmopolitan outlook to understand how to do business in the local culture in the context of the cultural norms.

*   Training in intercultural empathy would have provided useful techniques on how to communicate more effectively with local Sudanese people. Establishing credibility and trust go a long way in getting cooperation from others. Ravi would have benefited from learning the art and science of persuading people from different cultures and backgrounds. Learning how to influence

may have helped Ravi get his message across more strongly to Ahmad as well.

- Helping a global staff build interpersonal impact for daily work as well as crisis situations would pay huge dividends for the organization, such as building strong networks with people from other cultures and with influential people to be able to count on them for assistance and to mitigate obstacles especially in emergencies. They would also gain ideas and skills for negotiating agreements in the local culture. Without these skills, staff in global roles will find it a constant challenge to establish their reputation as someone to be respected.

2. *What training would have been useful to help the overseas staff prepare for crisis situations and perform well during traumatic experiences?*

Jamila had reiterated the importance of having standard operating procedures to handle challenging situations. But more importantly, preparation for global roles involves selecting people with the right psychological makeup who are motivated to learn about and overcome challenges. Once that is in place, the right development programs can help strengthen the skills to deal with crises. No matter how strong and motivated the person is, there should be a program in place to help stabilize the person after a harrowing incident. Failure to provide this will be detrimental for any organization that aspires for success at the global level.

Staff who will be posted in global positions should be thoroughly trained to handle stress and to be provided with a list of resources they can call on to get help when needed. Global staff should be reminded that when they really need help, they should just reach out to their bosses, friends, colleagues, and social networks—someone is bound to be able to help. Remember: you are not alone!

3. *Do you believe there is a difference in intensity or stress in an international working environment compared to a local environment? How can the overseas staff cope with stress?*

In a foreign environment, normal ways of doing things may be vastly different from what we are used to at home, creating discomfort and potentially more stress than in our home environments. This stress can be magnified if overseas staff are not thoroughly prepared to manage new and unpredictable situations. The rule of thumb is: "Prepare for the unexpected." They should be conditioned to be psychologically resilient, enabling them to cope in difficult situations. This can be done through experiential training activities, such as job shadowing.

Stress-reduction techniques are also important. Taking frequent effective exercise may help, combined with sufficient relaxation. Overseas staff must also be encouraged to build strong social networks abroad so they have the friends and support to not only cope with but also enjoy their environment.

Case Study 3: Caught in the Middle in Japan

LYNDA L. MOORE, PH.D.
Professor, Simmons
School of Management

Abstract

Judy is a very internationally experienced middle manager in Japan who is reporting to a vice president with little Global Mindset. The case explores what makes Judy so effective and her vice president, Jim, so ineffective. The case discusses strategies to build a Global Mindset at a senior level and how the organization can do a better job preparing executives for success in global roles.

The Case

Judy sighed as she looked at her cup of tea. "I really don't know what to do. I feel as though I can't win in this case and am tired of being put in the middle." She had invited her colleague Susan, another American, to meet her for tea to discuss her concerns about her present position. Susan looked her in the eyes. "You really can't worry about this. They can't expect you to play all of these roles simultaneously. Can't you just talk to your manager?"

Judy didn't know what to think. She had been in her current role as an information technology (IT) account manager for Jim Acker, vice president of Japan development, in a large multinational pharmaceutical firm for one year. Her role was to partner with him to provide the technology for a team of seven hundred predominately male Japanese employees. She managed the staff in Japan and

TOKYO, JAPAN

Singapore and collaborated with colleagues to meet the needs of all clients in the Asia–Pacific region.

Jim Acker was known as a manager who demanded results. He was a no-nonsense kind of guy: straight to the point and arrogant. Recently she had suggested to him that he try to communicate with the team in a less direct, confrontational manner. His response was that he was the manager in charge and that they should adapt to him.

Judy thought about how his leadership and management style was typical of the other Americans who were sent to the region over the past two to three years. Their US headquarters sent its US-based executives to gain experience in other markets to develop their global leadership skills. Each executive was provided with a one-hundred-page cross-cultural guide on how to succeed in Japan. But the advice on adapting to local culture obviously went unheeded. Jim was no different. He never socialized with the team, and he preferred to go out only with other American executives whenever possible. He focused only on the work, and when he asked team members if they had questions he accepted their silence as understanding and agreement.

Meanwhile, projects were not meeting deadlines and everyone was concerned. Several of the team members approached Judy. They were able to confide in Judy, because she had earned their trust over the last few months. She did this by respecting their need for slow change and group consensus that was common in the culture. They felt Jim was ineffectual and believed they had no reason to trust him. While the team expressed their frustrations to Judy, Jim also expressed his frustration about the team performance to her. She was in the middle.

Judy was no stranger to working across cultures. She had worked the last ten years outside of the United States, specifically working in Brussels, China, and Japan. Her first ten years at the company were spent in the United States. She was chosen for her current assignment as part of a new leadership development program to increase the pipeline of executives with knowledge and experience in global markets. She was one of four women outside of the United States who was nominated for this program. Her sponsor was the vice president of the division, whom Jim Acker reported to. The vice president acknowledged Judy's successful track record working outside the United States.

In her support role, Judy felt she was walking a fine line. She initially played it quiet with her team in meetings with Jim. She knew he wanted to be seen as the voice of authority. The Japanese team had given her feedback that she needed to speak up more on their behalf, yet she knew that previous bosses also had been unwilling to receive feedback about the need to adjust their leadership to local cultural norms. She knew that Jim thought he could bully his way through.

How could she play an effective role in bridging the gap between the team and her boss? She was worried about being seen as aligning too much with one or the other, in which case she would lose the trust of the other and become ineffective in her role. Furthermore, as a woman leader she was concerned about being seen as too aggressive by the Japanese or too soft by her American boss. Her success in this role was an important part of her plan to advance in the company.

Discussion Questions

1. What Global Mindset attributes have helped Judy to reach this position? What does Judy need to be successful in this role?

2. What might Jim do in this case to allow his team to save face and maintain his authority? What Global Mindset attributes would be helpful?

3. What might the company do to increase the effectiveness of American executives in international assignments? How might they specifically enhance the usefulness of the executive guides on how to succeed in another culture?

Teaching Notes

1. *What Global Mindset attributes have helped Judy to reach this position? What does Judy need to be successful in this role?*

   Judy has obviously gained many Global Mindset attributes that have allowed her to be successful in prior positions outside the United States. Her global business savvy was developed through work experience in several countries, including Japan. Her Global Psychological Capital appears to be high, because she has sought out assignments in different parts of the world and obviously enjoys learning about new cultures. Judy must have Global Social Capital as well, as she has developed the trust of her Japanese team and demonstrated the intercultural empathy necessary to do so. She is clearly willing to collaborate and work with different perspectives. Judy needs to be reminded that these attributes and skills have gotten her to this point in her career and that she can draw upon them in this situation to effectively communicate with both her boss and the IT team.

2. *What might Jim do in this case to allow his team to save face and maintain his authority? What Global Mindset attributes would be helpful?*

   Jim appears to lack many of the skills necessary to be effective as a leader working with a culturally diverse team in another region of the world. He has fallen into the classic cross-cultural management and communication trap of expecting everyone to adapt to his style of working and communicating. Had he spoken to others, including Judy, to sincerely learn more about the culture, he would have learned that he must gain the trust of his team in order to work effectively. Therefore, socializing was critical to his ability to get the job done. It is not clear if Jim has the Global Psychological Capital to be effective in this role, particularly the enjoyment of getting to know people in other parts of the world. But, most importantly, Jim's intercultural empathy, interpersonal impact, and diplomacy appear to be underdeveloped, which is what is crucial at this stage to gain trust from his team and meet his objectives. He seems to lack these critical Global Social Capital dimensions: the ability to work well with people from other parts of the world, to emotionally connect with his team, and to see why he may be contributing to the miscommunication and lack of trust between him and his team.

Being ostracized is one of the worst things that can happen to a Japanese person, who are raised to be part of a group and depend on others. Therefore, when making requests it often takes more time, because the person asked usually consults others in the group to reach a consensus. Because avoiding conflict and trouble is extremely important in Japan, diplomatic language is often used rather than the direct approach. Jim needs to adjust his style to these considerations and adapt to the local norm of saving face in order to win the team's respect and effectively meet his business goals. This could be a valuable leadership development lesson for Jim if he is open to listening to both his team and Judy. Judy could be a very important ally in his ability to work effectively with his team and complete his international assignment successfully.

3. *What might the company do to increase the effectiveness of American executives in international assignments? How might they specifically enhance the usefulness of the executive guides on how to succeed in another culture?*

It appears that the company has not assessed the skills necessary for someone like Jim to succeed in an overseas assignment, such as by taking the Global Mindset Inventory (GMI). Learning to interpret behavior from outside one's cultural perspective is crucial to success. Jim needs to understand that a lack of active participation in team meetings in Japan does not imply team dysfunction but rather a different cultural explanation for good team membership.

Merely assigning a country survival guide will not be enough to help executives adapt their behavior. A local mentor with knowledge of the country could help guide Jim, and expat groups might help Jim to see his own cultural bias provided that he is not socializing with them for the sake of escaping the local culture. Global Mindset attributes could be screened through the use of instruments such as the GMI and peer and supervisor performance ratings. This would help the company with more effective and successful employee deployment, development, and global talent management.

Case Study 4: Risky Business in Iraq

Abstract

Zainubiah Abd Aziz
Learning Specialist
PETRONAS Leadership
Center

A high-risk trip to the 1997 Baghdad Oil and Gas Expo by exhibition employees from a Malaysian oil and gas company starts out as a lesson in cross-cultural differences. The employees discover just how different Iraqi culture is from their own Malaysian culture. An almost complete language barrier adds to the complications. But what starts out as a cross-cultural experience turns into a crisis for the Malaysian employees when the United States invades Iraq.

The Case

PETRONAS, a Malaysian oil and gas company, embarked on a globalization strategy in 1985. As a result, many new joint ventures and working partnerships were initiated. The policy has benefited the organization substantially over time. The initial incremental revenue has grown sizeable over the years. Globalization has made an incredibly positive effect on the organization.

In 1997, PETRONAS management started eyeing the Middle East market, particularly Iraq. As the competition there is high with a level playing field, PETRONAS saw an opportunity there. To begin knocking at the door of a country, it is necessary to showcase the organization. Coincidently, PETRONAS received an invitation to participate in the Baghdad Oil and Gas Expo.

BAGHDAD, IRAQ

"It's all set. We are participating in the Iraq Expo," said Hisham, manager of the international corporate exhibition group in PETRONAS. He was speaking to his team of executives, graphic and exhibit designers, and technical assistants, among whom included an employee named Jaafar. "And management has decided to send you, Jaafar, to head the exhibition team." Hisham continued on a high note, "Expectations are high, Jaafar. Let's ensure everything goes smoothly, okay?"

The team was also informed by their colleagues in the exploration division that the exhibition could be very challenging. Iraq was going through sanctions under the regime of the late Saddam Hussein. There was concern that since Iraq had been invaded by the United States previously, it may happen again in the near future. Political tensions were high between the two countries.

Jaafar had completed international assignments in a few other countries in Asia and Europe. His role in the department involved managing exhibitions, coordinating sponsorship of corporate social responsibility programs, and formulating stakeholder management programs. He was excited about the opportunity to explore Iraq, to get to know the people, and, most importantly, to test his own ability. To him, if he could survive this trip to Iraq, he would be able to survive anywhere. "Can you tell me more about this operation, so that I can make the necessary preparations?" Jaafar asked.

Hisham was happy with Jaafar's immediate acceptance and willingness to take up the challenge. As planned, the preparations for the journey to Iraq started. Jaafar and another two colleagues entered Iraq by land through Jordan, because flights to the country were not permitted. Administrative and logistical coordination was arranged earlier with the help of the Malaysian Embassy. However, the travel arrangements were only made for the segments of the trip through Jordan.

Once Jaafar and his colleagues arrived in Iraq, they were on their own. They traveled in three SUVs from Aman, Jordan, to Baghdad. The journey took them through 1,200 kilometers of desert country with only sporadic villages and shanty towns. They had to pass through twenty fully armed army check-points along the way. As Jaafar had been advised, he brought with him cartons of cigarettes and Coca-Cola to give to the guards at the check-points. Jaafar and his team breathed a sigh of relief that these tokens seemed to do the job, despite the communication barriers.

Along the journey, Jaafar discovered that not a single Iraqi army personnel could speak English. Because Jaafar and his team could not speak Arabic, they had to use the Jordanian driver as their translator. Jaafar could not have imagined how they would have survived without him. Once they arrived in Baghdad, the driver returned to Aman, and Jaafar and his team checked in to the Al-Hamra Hotel. But due to the great rapport Jaafar built with the Jordanian driver, the driver had recommended an Iraqi colleague who spoke English to drive Jaafar and his team while they were in Baghdad.

The Iraqi driver's name was Imaddin, and he became more than just a driver for Jaafar. This was because Imaddin appreciated the respectful treatment and friendship he received from Jaafar. For example, during meal times, Imaddin brought Jaafar to restaurants. As was customary, Imaddin would wait outside. But Jaafar insisted that Imaddin eat with him and his team. This small gesture created a bond between them. And this bond saved Jaafar from injury on another occasion when Imaddin prevented a physical fight with a local authority who demanded money from Jaafar in exchange for his services. Imaddin's support made Jaafar's initial entre in Iraq easier, but there were many more challenges to come.

Jaafar found working with Iraqis to be quite challenging. It was beyond anything he had faced before, but it was also stimulating. It was the nonverbal communication that made him realize how different Malaysians and Iraqis communicated. Iraqi voices were often very loud and the people expressed themselves with attention-grabbing hand gestures and body movements. Jaafar was very interested to learn about these differences. He hoped his observations would help him interpret the nonverbal communication better, so he could interact more effectively with the Iraqis.

Jaafar realized how crucial it was to connect with the people they encountered so they could smoothly manage their hotel stay, exhibition setup, and the related logistics and management of facilities and materials in connection to the exhibition. At times, Jaafar was reminded of a Malaysian proverb: chickens and ducks are not able to communicate with each other. Because he only had body language and hand gestures to fall back on, he began to master the game of charades.

At the early stage of exhibition preparation, prior to leaving Malaysia, there were many forms that the office had to fill out to comply with the conditions provided by the organizer. Among the forms included the exhibitor's requirement for the booth setting. Jaafar had already stipulated the necessity for a few basic facilities and requirements, like electrical appliances and the assignment of a carpenter to set up the booth. Yet the day before the expo when he arrived at the hall, Jaafar discovered that nothing had been prepared for them by the organizer. After investigating, which was not an easy task considering the language barrier, the organizers confirmed they had received the request form but did not seem concerned about providing the requested resources. Jaafar was stunned for a moment and racked his brain to think of his next course of action.

Immediately, Jaafar knew that he needed to go shopping for electrical appliances, carpets, and stationeries. His driver Imaddin was a good source to determine where to obtain these items. As supplies were limited in Iraq, Imaddin was extraordinarily helpful. While setting up the booth, there were other exhibitors who were also setting up their booths with the help of local carpenters and electricians. As Jaafar had substantial experience as an exhibitor, most of the appliances he used were portable. Suddenly, the sound of the noisy carpenters at work became silent, because all of them stopped working to witness the new gadgets that Jaafar and his team were using that they had never seen before. At first, this attention made them feel a bit uncomfortable, but they marched on with their task. Upon completion, their exhibitor colleagues were so amazed with the result that they gave Jaafar and his team a round of applause. Jaafar rose to the occasion and took a bow gracefully.

Jaafar was aware there was risk in going to Iraq, but he hadn't realized the magnitude of it. Although he had gathered as much information as possible, the situation was even more unpredictable than imagined and far from being comfortable. During Jaafar's short stint in Iraq, he got his first insight of what it is like to be in a war zone. Every night after the sirens were generated, the city of Baghdad was blanketed by complete darkness within seconds. This was followed by unidentifiable flying objects that he was told were Army surveillance devices. It gave Jaafar and his team the shock of a lifetime in the beginning, and later they began worrying about not being able to leave. Getting stuck in the middle of the Iraq war was not an attractive option.

The fear grew greater after the fourth day of the exhibition. That day, Jaafar, his team, and some Malaysian students who were in Iraq were called in by the Malaysian Embassy in Iraq for a critical briefing. They received information that there was a possibility that the United States was going to attack Iraq soon. The Malaysians were advised to be cautious and to bring their passports everywhere they went. In the event of an emergency, all Malaysians had to report to the Embassy, whereby an escape route would be activated.

The following evening, Jaafar observed a rally by Iraqi men in the street who were shouting and protesting. They were all armed, shooting in the air and looking furious. It was later shared that there had been an announcement by Iraqi officials that the United States was about to attack. In Jaafar's experience, this only happened in movies. All he could think about was his family and how much he wanted to go home to them.

Discussion Questions

1. How was Jaafar able to form good relationships with his drivers in such a short period of time? What aspects of Global Mindset did he draw on to make this possible?

2. What did Jaafar do to try to understand and communicate with the Iraqis in light of the language barrier? What aspects of Global Mindset did he draw on?

3. How did Jaafar and his team overcome the setback of their booth not being ready? What aspects of Global Mindset did Jaafar use to get his booth successfully set up?

4. The case ends with Iraq going to war while Jaafar and his team are still there. This is a particularly large crisis compared to what most internationally working employees will face, but how can an organization ensure that its employees are well prepared for any kind of crisis while abroad?

Teaching Notes

1. *How was Jaafar able to form good relationships with his drivers in such a short period of time? What aspects of Global Mindset did he draw on to make this possible?*

    Jaafar's passion for diversity and intercultural empathy helped him form these cross-cultural relationships. He enjoyed getting to know people from Iraq and exploring a new place, even though the conditions were not what he was used to. He was quick to form emotional connections with the drivers by showing a genuine interest in them and treating them as more than equals; he treated them as friends.

2. *What did Jaafar do to try to understand and communicate with the Iraqis in light of the language barrier? What aspects of Global Mindset did he draw on?*

Jaafar was a keen observer of nonverbal communication. He quickly picked up on tones of voice, gestures, and other body language to interpret what was being said to him. In exchange, he also used nonverbal communication to try to get his message across. Once again, he drew on his skills in intercultural empathy to communicate cross-culturally. Jaafar could have better prepared for the trip by making arrangements prior to traveling to have a dedicated translator. This would have helped him overcome the language barrier.

3. *How did Jaafar and his team overcome the setback of their booth not being ready? What aspects of Global Mindset did Jaafar use to get his booth successfully set up?*

Jaafar's ability to think on his feet was tested when the exhibition booth was not set up as requested. His previous experience certainly helped give him the needed spontaneity to get the booth up and running. But it was his combination of intercultural empathy and quest for adventure that helped him to achieve results in a short time in an environment with limited resources. His intercultural empathy was instrumental in gaining the friendship of Imaddin, who was able to help him quickly secure needed resources. Hamadi's quest for adventure motivated him to embrace the challenges before him and achieve results. He also showed wittiness while handling the stress of the situation when he took a bow.

4. *The case ends with Iraq going to war while Jaafar and his team are still there. This is a particularly large crisis compared to what most internationally working employees will face, but how can an organization ensure that its employees are well prepared for any kind of crisis while abroad?*

While no degree of preparedness can ensure that internationally working employees do not end up in crisis situations, there are some things that can be done to prepare them. From an organizational perspective, employees can be equipped with risk-management plans. In Jaafar's case, this was registration through the Malaysian Embassy and briefings on the potential security concerns in the area prior to going.

From a selection and training perspective, Jaafar showed the importance of selecting employees for high-risk assignments who have a strong Global Mindset overall and a particularly deep degree of development in Global Psychological Capital. He had the motivation and resilience needed to navigate a complex and stressful situation, due to his Global Psychological Capital. He also showed the importance of having a deep cosmopolitan knowledge. He was up-to-date with important world events as well as knowledge on geography, history, economic, and political issues. This helped him to understand the new cultural environment and adapt to it the best he could. Again, he would have been better prepared with a local guide and translator, but Jaafar did a pretty good job without having these resources. Finally, Jaafar's high degree of intercultural empathy and diplomacy allowed him to quickly form connections with locals that both helped him complete his tasks and sustained him emotionally during his stay in Iraq. So it is clear that all three areas of Global Mindset are important to develop in employees prior to sending them on high-risk international assignments.

Case Study 5: A Global Acquisition Gone Sour in South Africa

HARISON YUSOFF, MS
Learning Manager
PETRONAS Leadership
Centre

Abstract

After acquiring a South African subsidiary, a corporate team from the Malaysian headquarters of an oil and gas company traveled to South Africa to meet with local management to work on aligning the subsidiary's business strategy with the parent company. The Malaysian team leader, an experienced expert in corporate strategy, told the team members prior to going that it would be a breeze. But things quickly went from bad to worse in South Africa.

The Case

As a brand and communication specialist with PETRONAS, a multinational Malaysian Oil & Gas company, Fatimah had traveled to over forty countries worldwide in her role to advocate and institutionalize the PETRONAS global brand. Her key missions in PETRONAS's overseas offices included:

- helping to design and institute the brand through each specific country office

- guiding in the design and development of PETRONAS communication materials and collaterals, which included supervision of local information gathering and video and photo shoots

- disseminating and communicating the PETRONAS brand to overseas staff.

CAPE TOWN, SOUTH AFRICA

Richard Cavalleri / Shutterstock.com

In the late 1990s, among the newest PETRONAS acquisition was Engen Limited in South Africa. This subsidiary was involved in refining crude oil and marketing refined petroleum products. Soon after acquiring Engen Limited, PETRONAS management emphasized the need to align its business strategy with that of PETRONAS's overall scope and direction. A team was formed for this particular task, including Fatimah.

Fatimah felt extremely excited to be a part of the team. She had never been to South Africa and was very keen to learn more about the place her hero Nelson Mandela hailed from. She was also excited to work with one of PETRONAS's experts on corporate strategies, Ali. During the first team meeting, he said the best approach would be to formulate the corporate strategy together with the South Africans. And so they all planned their travel to South Africa.

Prior to leaving for Cape Town, the group met to discuss the agenda and expectations for the meeting.

"An acquisition such as this provides a great opportunity for us to create a compelling new brand aligned to the mother brand," Ali said.

"But can we achieve that in three days?" Fatimah worried aloud. She remarked that it would be difficult to get anything concrete if things were done in a rush. "Perhaps this could be positioned as the first get-together, marking an initial cohesive meeting of minds, and then we can have follow-up meetings in the near future," Fatimah suggested.

But Ali interjected as the team leader. "We cannot afford to spend too much time dawdling. Speed is of the essence." Observing Fatimah's doubts, Ali assured her, "Don't worry, we have done this in the past with other subsidiaries. It's going to be a breeze!"

The meeting itinerary was drawn out precisely prior to leaving. It was designed to ensure that every minute in Cape Town would be well spent.

The team arrived in Cape Town on Wednesday evening after an eight-hour flight. They were met by an administrative officer who bade them a warm welcome and escorted them to the Victoria & Alfred Hotel Waterfront. This was an elegant venue that offered a spectacular view of the harbor and Table Mountain.

The following day, Fatimah and her team arrived for the meeting at the Engen office. Apart from Fatimah and Ali, the other members of the Malaysian entourage included two other managers. Their South African counterparts comprised a team leader, three other managers, and two young officers. Both teams introduced themselves briefly, and the discussion commenced almost immediately. It was all very professional and business-like. The meeting wrapped up at 8 p.m. that day, and Ali reminded everyone to be punctual the next day, as they had a lot more to cover and decide on.

The following day, Ali continued the agenda in the same place they left off. As the day went on, Fatimah could feel that their South African counterparts were not happy with the way the meeting was being conducted. Their body language demonstrated their displeasure and obvious disapproval. Fatimah tried to subtly interrupt Ali's momentum with signals and hints, but he did not seem to get the drift.

As Ali went on and on with the meeting, the Malaysian team realized that they were not getting the support from the local staff as they had hoped. Disagreements ensued. One after the other, recommendations were rejected outright. Things quickly went from bad to worse. When the meeting ended, everyone was tired and frustrated.

On the way back to the hotel, the Malaysian team discussed how the day went. The team members encouraged Ali to slow the pace a bit, so they could work toward winning the trust and agreement of the South Africans.

The next day was a Saturday. Because it was a weekend, only two of the South African members attended the meeting. The rest did not even inform the Malaysian team that they would not be coming. Even though Ali really made efforts to salvage the situation, the two South Africans were very explicit that they were not happy with the Malaysian's insistence to have the meeting on a weekend. Things were going nowhere, and decisions could not be made without the rest of the South African team present. The meeting had to be adjourned.

Both parties were upset and viewed each other unfavorably. The Malaysian team leader felt that the South Africans lacked commitment and drive and were unsupportive simply for the sake of being critical. The South Africans thought the Malaysians were not sensitive to their culture and viewed them with suspicion and mistrust. Fatimah had the sad affirmation that her initial worry had been justified.

Being a people person, Fatimah suggested that the Malaysian team focus more on relationship building. The team leader and the entourage agreed to extend their stay to resolve the situation.

For the remainder of the weekend in Cape Town, Fatimah visited the famous marketplace and shopping areas with her South African colleagues and bought souvenirs and knick-knacks they recommended. The South Africans were delighted with their guest's attitude. Because she had made an effort earlier to read the book on Nelson Mandela and his life and time in prison, Fatimah was able to conduct intellectual conversations related to the topic that her South African colleagues held dear to their hearts. She and the team also visited the prison where Mandela was jailed, which was an extraordinary historical landmark and showcase.

Fatimah was particularly good at forming relationships with her South African colleagues, because she had a well-developed quest for adventure and passion for diversity. She loved exploring new places and meeting new people.

On the final day, Fatimah conducted a session on brand communication in which she was able to communicate the PETRONAS brand messages to all the local staff, from the janitor to the head of operations. The key people stayed after the session for a comprehensive meeting to discuss what they would need to do as a follow-up for the strategy.

The Malaysian team learned a valuable lesson. If only they had been equipped with essential Global Mindset knowledge and skills, they could have avoided the quandary they got themselves into.

Discussion Questions

1. What did the Malaysian team overlook when planning for the meeting in South Africa?

2. What would have been a more effective approach to communicate with and show respect to the South African team members?

Teaching Notes

1. *What did the Malaysian team overlook when planning for the meeting in South Africa?*

    In South Africa, the Malaysian team was not prepared with the understanding of the culture and working norms of the South African staff. This is a classic case of not having a well-developed cosmopolitan outlook or intercultural empathy. Without this understanding, the Malaysian team viewed the South Africans as lacking commitment, when really commitment for the South Africans just looked different than the way the Malaysian team demonstrated it.

    According to the GLOBE research analysis of management and leadership behaviors for South Africa, individualism ranks very high (among the white population sample) in this culture. A high individualism ranking indicates that individuality and individual rights are paramount within the society. Work–life balance is critical for South Africans. After work and during weekends, South Africans plan for recreation and individual or family activities, which they are reluctant to forego unless there is a major crisis. Their preference for individualism led them to resent the way the Malaysian entourage assumed that they should comply with the way things had been planned from Kuala Lumpur. Because the Malaysians continued to push through their agenda with no regard for the South Africans' reluctance, they were perceived to be arrogant and condescending. The South Africans became unwilling to cooperate with them.

2. *What would have been a more effective approach to communicate with and show respect to the South African team members?*

    The Malaysian team would have been more effective had they begun communication with the South African team prior to leaving for South Africa. This would have allowed the two teams to start building trust through collaborative design of the team meeting. If the Malaysian team leader had been able to establish a favorable image both before arriving in South Africa and during his first impression, he could have been successful in better influencing the South Africans. They might even have accepted the pace due to the time constraints.

The Malaysian team leader should have started local interactions with social time for the two teams to get to know one another and break the ice. He could have initiated a teambuilding exercise. Both of these efforts would have been helpful to build intercultural empathy and interpersonal impact among the teams. Also, if opportunities were provided for the South Africans to give comments and feedback from the beginning, and if the Malaysians had listened to their views and accommodated their needs and preferences, things could have proceeded in a more amicable manner.

Case Study 6: A US–Russian Academic Collaboration in Peril

YULIA TOLSTIKOV-MAST, PH.D.
Assistant Professor Global
Leadership, IndianaTech

Abstract

An international business professor from Russia decides to enlist the cooperation of a Russian colleague, located in Russia, to coordinate an American–Russian student project for a global management course. The semester-long project starts off well, but conflict ensues between the students within the first month. When the professor tries to enlist the support of her colleague to create a new course activity to get the students on the right track again, she encounters resistance. This case explores the complexities of working cross-culturally as well as misunderstandings that can happen within one's own culture.

The Case

It is exciting and challenging to teach international courses. In addition to the traditional tasks of formulating course objectives and selecting appropriate books and delivery methods, there is another very critical task: designing effective assignments. Those assignments should help increase students' intercultural awareness, understanding, and skills. Although there are numerous methods that prove their effectiveness in accomplishing these education goals, it is still not a very easy task to move students from awareness to adopted behavior in a

MOSCOW, RUSSIA

Andrey Bayda / Shutterstock.com

semester-long course. The most effective methods involve cultural immersion, but that is not always possible in classes that do not include the time or resources for travel abroad.

Dr. Reznik was ready to face these challenges, as she was preparing to teach a global management course. Dr. Reznik was originally from Russia and had moved to the United States fifteen years prior. To stay connected with her homeland, she visited Russia every three years. She also remained close to her college friends who became professors in Russia. So she thought while designing her syllabus, "Russian–American collaboration can be the culminating assignment in my class! It could be a semester-long project where students can practice applying acquired knowledge to enhance a wide range of important skills." Dr. Reznik was certain that she had a strong knowledge of Russian culture and that it would be easy to coordinate this project with one of her professor friends in Russia.

The next morning, Dr. Reznik called one of her friends in Russia. She was excited to walk away from the call with the feeling that they had had a great conversation and that the Russian professor was completely on board with the project. A Russian university also fully committed to providing any necessary logistical support (e.g., conference rooms, large screens for Skype discussions) and assigned the best students majoring in international business to represent the university by participating in the project.

A day before the start of the semester, Dr. Reznik was feeling very proud of the upcoming project. She was excited for the learning opportunity that it would create for both American and Russian students. All of the main challenges were reconciled, including a starting day of the project (Russian university has a different length of a semester), project deadlines, Skype sessions (considering time difference between countries), and cultural differences that could potentially influence the project. In addition, Dr. Reznik designed preproject activities to ensure that both groups of students had similar global business knowledge: knowledge of a global industry selected for the project, understanding of global marketing strategies, and knowledge of business transactions and risk factors involved in a Russian–American business collaboration. Finally, both sides planned to discuss each other's cultures, including the historical perspective on Russian–American relations, important current events, knowledge of each other's economic and political issues, as well as cultural values and beliefs. Dr. Reznik agreed to be the primary professor leading the project.

The first several weeks of the semester were exuberating! American students were very excited to engage in a live project, and Russian students were honored to be part of the semester-long international activity. Both Russian and American groups demonstrated creativity as they came up with introductory videos that they posted on YouTube. Both groups also engaged in preproject activities learning about each other's cultures and mastering global business knowledge.

Trouble started during week four. American students found that the project presented complexity that went beyond cultural differences. One of these complexities included that neither the American nor the Russian students were certain how to approach uncomfortable situations. For example, when there were disagreements among the students on both sides, they were not sure how to do it and still maintain good relationships. Also, Russian students demonstrated lack of confidence when it came to initiating tasks. They completely relied on the American students to direct the project. American students, in their turn, were confused. They had perceived the Russian students to be motivated, creative, and proactive, as this is what they learned about Russian students from their introductory videos, but this was not what they were experiencing as the project went forward. The students were dealing with the kind of complexity faced by typical global operations on a daily basis.

Dr. Reznik saw her students getting more confused and frustrated. She did anticipate some of the challenges, but was surprised to see them losing confidence and motivation that early in the project. After careful consideration, she decided to introduce a new activity that could potentially help both the American and the Russian students accomplish their joint work. Dr. Reznik crafted an email to her Russian colleague where she explained why a new short activity should be introduced and how this activity, combined with additional class discussions, could assist the Russian and American students.

The next morning, when she opened her email, she found the following email from the Russian professor: "I CANNOT BELIEVE THAT YOU ARE CHANGING THE COURSE OF THE PROJECT!!!!!!!!! I TRUSTED YOUR EXPERTISE IN DESIGNING AND LEADING A STRONG COLLABORATIVE PROJECT. BUT IT SEEMS THAT IT HAS NOT BEEN WORKING RIGHT FOR US. MY STUDENTS WILL CONTINUE WITHOUT ANY NEW ACTIVITIES, ADDITIONAL DISCUSSIONS, OR READINGS!!!! SEMESTER STILL IS NOT OVER AND I WILL TRY TO MAKE IT WORK ON MY OWN!!!"

Puzzled, Dr. Reznik replied to the email. Her tone was reserved but direct as she asked for clarifications. She was offended and thought this would be the last time she would engage in further collaborative projects with her Russian friend. The reply from the Russian professor came the same day. The tone was apologetic, and it seemed that the Russian professor was puzzled herself, thinking that the tone of her initial email was appropriate and not aggressive.

Sitting in her office drinking tea, Dr. Reznik reflected on the situation. What did she overlook in her planning? What went wrong? How could she move forward with the project? And what should she say to her Russian friend?

Discussion Questions

1. What Global Mindset attributes did Dr. Reznik exhibit? Explain using examples from the case.

2. Being from Russia herself, why did Dr. Reznik get frustrated while working with her Russian friend?

3. What other preproject activities could have been helpful for both the American and Russian students? Explain how these activities could have differed from the activities introduced to the students.

4. As a student or professional, have you been involved in similar situations? How were the challenges approached or resolved? Which Global Mindset elements were used in the situation? What could you have done differently using Global Mindset dimensions?

Teaching Notes

1. *What Global Mindset attributes did Dr. Reznik exhibit? Explain using examples from the case.*

   Dr. Reznik invested a good amount of time in setting up the project activities and discussing them with the Russian university. It was a proactive step to align learning objectives and to make sure that the university (and not only a professor) supported the initiative (and would provide needed assistance). These types of collaborative projects are new to Russia, and considering the culture's strong power distance orientation, it is necessary to engage the university administration in all decisions. Dr. Reznik showed a high level of cosmopolitan outlook and diplomacy in doing this.

2. *Being from Russia herself, why did Dr. Reznik get frustrated while working with her Russian friend?*

   Although Dr. Reznik is originally from Russia, she adopted western project management skills (e.g., assertiveness, individual leadership). As a result, she took initiative in the project design and coordination and did not include the Russian professor in decision making. Because of that, Dr. Reznik overlooked challenges that the Russian professor faced, including her weak ability to conduct debriefings (because in Russia most classes are conducted as lectures), lack of international experience, pressure from the university administration to have an exemplary international project, and hesitance to ask questions or provide suggestions to her American colleague.

   Dr. Reznik's reaction to the email from the Russian professor was a result of miscommunication by both sender and receiver. What the Russian professor meant to communicate was:

   > "It's already midnight, but I need to respond to Dr. Reznik's email so that she can receive it before she leaves work today. I'm trying to be responsive. I will also type in uppercase, so that she understands how important this project is for us. I am surprised that she wants to introduce changes to the project, but I trust her professional judgment in designing the project and do sense that both American and Russian students experience difficulties. At the same time, I am very concerned with my administration's reaction toward the proposed project changes.

They need to approve changes, and I am not sure if they are open to it at this stage of the project. I think it's better if I continue without changes. I understand the overall goals and can lead my students independently."

Dr. Reznik, however, interpreted this email as a screaming disagreement with her suggestions and a disrespectful comment that the Russian professor wanted to proceed on her own. This was a premature conclusion driven by emotions that she should have explored more fully through dialogue.

3. *What other preproject activities could have been helpful for both American and Russian students? Explain how these activities could have differed from the activities introduced to the students.*

Dr. Reznik designed a detailed preproject training that should have oriented students in cultural differences and helped to build global business knowledge. This was designed to build the students' global business savvy and cosmopolitan outlook. However, at the same time, Dr. Reznik did not put training or resources in place to help students develop the necessary cognitive complexity they needed to work through challenging issues. As a result, students were unable to grasp complex issues, respond to abstract ideas, or translate complex situations into simple action steps.

More specifically, it seemed that American students treated the relationships with their colleagues as transactional (e.g., exchange of emails). When they did not receive replies, they assumed it was due to a lack of reply by their colleagues rather than understanding the multitude of challenges faced by their Russian colleagues in communicating. The Russian students often had unreliable Internet connections, they had limited teamwork experience, and they were accustomed to lecture rather than discussions in courses. This, combined with the Russian students' perception that the Americans should be the ones guiding the project, led to the disconnects between the two teams of students. The American students, in particular, needed to be developed in intercultural empathy, to be able to understand the challenges of their international counterparts and develop skills in emotionally connecting with them. Because all of these factors are real-world issues faced in global corporations as well, these are the kinds of realities Dr. Reznik should have prepared the students for.

Finally, to minimize or even prevent challenges, Dr. Reznik could have administered the Global Mindset Inventory to both Russian and American students to help them understand their own Global Mindsets, especially in the area of Global Psychological Capital. For example, how open-minded are the students to working with diverse others? Are they ready to take risks? Students could have also discussed their own cultural values and how their cultures are seen through the lenses of others. Activities that encourage reflection and self-analysis could have helped increase students' self-awareness and understanding of their decisions. In addition, Dr. Reznik could have incorporated role-playing sessions to practice diplomacy, negotiation, and the ability to engage people from other parts of the word to work together. This role playing could have exposed students to the importance of Global Social Capital and provided opportunities to practice critical Global Mindset skills.

4. *As a student or professional, have you been involved in similar situations? How were the challenges approached or resolved? Which Global Mindset elements were used in the situation? What could you have done differently using Global Mindset dimensions?*

The responses to this question will be drawn out in a discussion of the personal/professional experiences of the participants.

How the American–Russian University Collaboration Ended

In her email to her Russian colleague, Dr. Reznik suggested having a reflection session. During this session (which could have been done separately by both cultural groups), students would have an opportunity to openly discuss challenges and acknowledge their own mistakes. In addition, Dr. Reznik offered to facilitate a Global Mindset discussion for both Russian and American students. This discussion could have provided thinking points for students (e.g., How important are self-assurance and passion for diversity in international collaborations? Why should I have intercultural empathy or diplomacy?). Finally, Dr. Reznik hoped to engage the groups of Russian and American students in designing joint strategies (and negotiating common meanings of activities) that would help them overcome future challenges and assure successful work on their projects.

The Russian professor was apprehensive to introducing any changes to the project agenda. In her follow-up email to Dr. Reznik, she shared that she was very concerned about the proposed changes, because she would have to explain them to her department chair, who was inflexible when it came to making changes in the middle of the semester. He was also the designated project coordinator on the Russian side. Given the concerns, the reflection sessions would not be possible for the Russian students.

Dr. Reznik proceeded with the reflection session for her American students. She spent several weeks helping her students reflect, learn, and adjust. In fact, a reflection activity became a mandatory part of each class meeting. During that reflective time, Dr. Reznik concentrated on increasing students' Global Mindsets. This also allowed Dr. Reznik herself to reflect on her own Global Mindset and to initiate specific steps to integrate some of the dimensions into her behavior.

Case Study 7: Leave No One Behind in Morocco

ALFREDO BEHRENS, PH.D
Professor of Leadership
and Cross Cultural
Management, FIA
Business School, Brazil

Abstract

Western business people and their spouses attending a business gathering in Morocco took a day off for a bus tour. During the tour, one of the spouses suffered an accident, which required immediate first aid and transport to a medical facility. Under the advice of the English-speaking Moroccan tourist guide, the bus made a detour to his nearby village, where the injured woman received rustic first aid. The remaining busload of businesspeople waited anxiously around the bus, wanting to leave. While waiting for helicopter evacuation of the injured woman, the bus left, leaving the businessman and his spouse behind with the tour guide. The case provides a forum to discuss culturally defined concepts like solidarity, loyalty, pragmatism, and cross-cultural relationships.

This case was inspired by a scene in the film Babel *(2006). Although several details from the film have been changed to craft this for both practitioners and students of international business, the use of the film clip, with permission of the copyright owners, may add visual interest to the discussion of this case.*

The Case

A business gathering in Morocco offered its participants a one-day bus tour of the country. About forty Western businesspeople and their spouses signed up

OLD MEDINA, MOROCCO

and took off. Life was comfortable enough inside the tall, air-conditioned bus, but the scenery was barren. It was all sand and rocks—no life to be seen. The road was paved, but looked like at any moment it could disappear under a sandstorm, leaving the passengers disoriented in a foreign land.

Far from their five-star hotel, one of the spouses, Susan, suffered what appeared to be a broken ankle while touring a local historical site. Susan stepped back off a path to take a photo and lost her footing in a hole in the ground. Not only did her ankle appear broken, she was bleeding quite strongly from where a bone fragment had come through her skin.

Susan's husband, Richard, was panicked to have his spouse badly injured in the middle of nowhere. Anwar, the English-speaking tour guide, suggested that the bus make a detour to his nearby village for immediate care. The other business people suggested they drive on to the larger city, but Richard agreed they should stop somewhere close for first aid.

As the bus drove into the village, the passengers became nervous. They had been told not to go too far away from tourist centers due to safety concerns. The village was very foreign to them, and they talked nervously about whether they should actually stop. Their trust in Anwar and concern for Susan made them cooperative with the stop. Anwar told them they could call for emergency care from the village.

Susan received rustic first aid in the tour guide's household. This did seem to help stabilize her bleeding. Everyone was relieved that a helicopter ambulance was also successfully called from the only village telephone. But after a long wait, they were becoming anxious to leave. The bus could not be left idling with the air-conditioner on, because the driver needed to conserve the fuel to return to town. It became well over 100 degrees on the bus, and everyone was uncomfortable. They could not stay on the bus any longer, as it was hotter on the bus than outside.

The group was growing increasingly impatient with the seemingly endless wait. Anwar's family served them all hot tea as a gesture of hospitality and to calm their visible anxiety, but no one would accept the tea. They were afraid to drink it.

One of Richard's colleagues, Oliver, a stout Englishman, decided to convince Richard that he should stay with his spouse in the village, while the bus took everyone else back to the familiar hotel in the city. Richard was not keen on staying alone with his injured wife in the village and refused. He was also fearful that if the helicopter ambulance did not arrive, they would have no way back to the city for the night. Oliver and Richard began to argue heatedly. Richard even threatened Oliver that if he left them behind he should fear for his own safety. Anwar intervened, saying that the helicopter ambulance should arrive shortly and that there was no need for violence. He suggested that everyone else step outside and let Richard try to call the helicopter ambulance once more.

Everyone returned to the bus, and Richard made the call. But while Richard was calling, the group convinced the bus driver to leave. They quickly departed before Richard or Anwar could stop them. Richard, Susan, and Anwar were all left behind in the village, with no security that the helicopter ambulance was on its way.

Discussion Questions

1. How would you describe the Global Mindset of the group?

2. How would you describe the Global Mindset of Richard?

3. How would you describe the Global Mindset of Anwar?

4. What would you have done in this situation if you were part of the larger group? If you were Richard? If you were Anwar?

Teaching Notes

1. How would you describe the Global Mindset of the group?

The group failed to display cosmopolitan outlook in understanding the local culture; instead they feared it. It was likely their limited Global Psychological Capital that created the many fears they had. The tourists initially showed interest in diversity by signing up to a bus tour of the surroundings. However, it is one thing to see the unfamiliar world through the windows of an air-conditioned bus and quite another to be exposed to the unfamiliar people, with their goats, smells, and sounds. This dose of reality made them anxious to leave.

In terms of Global Social Capital, the group showed little self-assurance. They mostly seemed apathetic rather than energetic or self-confident.

Intercultural empathy was mostly lacking among the group, who would not socialize with the locals, nor partake in their food or drink, much less allow themselves to enter into their homes to see how they lived. They did not show basic understanding that the tea, having been boiled, was safe to drink. The group was overwhelmed by the differences and was not able to decipher the villagers' nonverbal expressions, which were showing them solidarity through kind gestures to make them feel comfortable. The group also failed in terms of diplomacy by rejecting all that was offered as a gift. Incapable of connecting, the group could only think of fleeing. The need to flee overcame any possibility of exploring life in the village or of getting to know the people.

The case of this business tourist group illustrates how important developing Global Mindset is prior to having a cultural immersion. Had the group had a better understanding of local life and how to interact well with diverse others, they may not have chosen to panic. Instead, they may have used the stopover as an unexpected opportunity to learn more about the local culture.

2. *How would you describe the Global Mindset of Richard?*

Richard had challenge thrust upon him, which he could not refuse to face. He needed to help his wife. Richard's Global Psychological Capital proved strong. He showed an interest in going to the local village and working with the locals to obtain medical care for his wife. He showed passion for diversity and quest for adventure through these actions.

From a Global Social Capital perspective, Richard was self-assured. He was able to deal effectively with people whose language he could not understand, and he was able to connect with them to get their assistance and support. However, he did not show much diplomacy in dealing with Oliver or the rest of the group when he was confronted with their desire to leave. In this sense, he failed to integrate diverse points of view. In acting this way, Richard failed to persuade the crowd, who decided it was better to sneak away than face Richard a second time.

The personal nature of the crisis for Richard likely clouded his judgment and ability to integrate diverse perspectives. This is where it could have been helpful for other members of the group to have developed Global Mindsets to assist Richard with the crisis and help manage the needs of the group.

3. *How would you describe the Global Mindset of Anwar?*

Anwar showed strong Global Psychological Capital in being a leader of foreign tour groups and in learning to speak English. His passion for diversity and quest for adventure led him to a position with a travel agency. However, his Global Social Capital appeared somewhat low, in that he was quick to help two of the group members, but essentially ignored the needs of the rest.

This is likely because Anwar had no fear of the village. He viewed his people as hospitable and warm. He lacked the ability to read the tourists' nonverbal expressions of anxiety, nor could he assuage their worries when they voiced them. Anwar, as the leader of the group, should have found a way to integrate the perspectives and needs of everyone.

4. *What would you have done in this situation if you were part of the larger group? If you were Richard? If you were Anwar?*

Those brought up in America, Canada, Northern Europe, or some of their former colonies may tend to take a pragmatic stance favoring the rule of universal laws such as majority rule. Those brought up in more collectivist environments are likely to take a stance supporting those who most need help, rather than the majority. Pragmatists are likely to argue that it would be fair to fire Anwar, who sided with Richard and Susan, rather than taking the majority to a safer place. Those brought up in Latin American or Mediterranean countries, less bound to pragmatist considerations, will likely give greater weight to those in need as more deserving of help than the healthy ones.

References

Abeson, Felix, and Michael A. Taku. "Networking for Sales Success in Overseas Government Markets." *Competitiveness Review* 17, no. 3 (2007): 162–69.

Akgunes, Asuman, and Robert Culpepper. "Negotiations between Chinese and Americans: Examining the Cultural Context and Salient Factors." *Journal of International Management* 7, no. 1 (2012): 191–200.

Albescu, Felicia, Irina Pugna, and Dorel Paraschiv. "Cross-Cultural Knowledge Management." *Informatica Economica* 13, no. 4 (2009): 39–50.

Allen, Kathleen. "Change Leaders: Creating Resilience in Uncertain Times." *Leader to Leader* no. 63 (2012): 13–18.

Alvarado, Ileana, Krystal A. Antoine, Gian-Carlo Cinquetti, Jorge Fernandez, Jabir Najair, Giuliana Scagliotti, and Bahaudin G. Mujtaba. "Rewarding for Success in an International Assignment: The Case of Returning to an Uncertain Future." *Journal of Business Studies Quarterly* 1, no. 4 (2010): 110–18.

Armstrong, Steven J., and Andrew Hird. "Cognitive Style and Entrepreneurial Drive of New and Mature Business Owner-Managers." *Journal of Business and Psychology* 24, no. 4 (2009): 419–30.

Arnold, Kristin. *Boring to Bravo: Proven Presentation Techniques to Engage, Involve, and Inspire Your Audience to Action*. Austin: Greenleaf Book Group Press, 2010.

Avruch, Kevin. *Culture and Conflict Resolution*. Washington, DC: US Institute of Peace, 1998.

Baghai, Mehrdad, Steve Coley, David White, and Stephen Coley. *The Alchemy of Growth*. New York: Basic Books, 2000.

Bandura, Albert. *Self-Efficacy: The Exercise of Control*. New York: Worth Publishers, 1997.

Barbarinde, Olufemi. Personal Interview, 2012.

Bateman, Thomas S. "Leading with Competence: Problem-Solving by Leaders and Followers." *Leader to Leader* no. 57 (2010): 38–44.

Batonda, Gerry, and Chad Perry. "Influence of Culture on Relationship Development Processes in Overseas Chinese/Australian Networks." *European Journal of Marketing* 37, no. 11 (2003): 1548–74.

Bazerman, Max H., and Michael D. Watkins. *Predictable Surprises: The Disasters You Should Have Seen Coming and How to Prevent Them*. Boston: Harvard Business School Press, 2008.

Bender, Silke, and Alan Fish. "The Transfer of Knowledge and the Retention of Expertise: The Continuing Need for Global Assignments." *Journal of Knowledge Management* 4, no. 2 (2000): 125–37.

Benjamin, J. Broome, Sara DeTurk, Erla S. Kristjansdottir, Tami Kanata, and Puvana Ganesan. "Giving Voice to Diversity: An Interactive Approach to Conflict Management and Decision-Making in Culturally Diverse Work Environments." *Journal of Business and Management* 8, no. 3 (2002): 1–26.

Billing, Tejinder K., Debmalya Mukherjee, Ben L. Kedia, and Somnath Lahiri. "Top Executives' International Expertise Commitment: Exploring Potential Antecedents." *Leadership & Organization Development Journal* 31, no. 8 (2010): 687–704.

Birdinshaw, Julian, Cyril Bouquet, and Tina C. Ambos. "Managing Executive Attention in the Global Company." *MIT Sloan Management Review* 48, no. 4 (2007): 39–45.

Birkenkrahe, Marcus, Stefanie Quade, and Frank Habermann. "Improving Collaborative Learning and Global Project Management in Small and Medium Enterprises." *International Journal of Advanced Corporate Learning* 4, no. 4 (2011): 32–38.

Bjorklund, Robert L., and Svetlana S. Holt. "Overcoming Barriers to Participation in Diverse Strategic Decision-Making Groups: A Leadership Perspective." *International Journal of Business and Management* 7, no. 6 (2012): 49–57.

Bradberry, Travis, and Jean Greaves. *Emotional Intelligence 2.0*. San Diego: TalentSmart, 2009.

Brady, Mark. *The Wisdom of Listening*. Somerville, MA: Wisdom Publications, 2003.

Brasfield, David W., James P. McCoy, and Mary Tripp Reed. "Effect of Global Business Curriculum on Student Attitudes." *Business Education Innovation Journal* 3, no. 2 (2011): 73–81.

Brett, Jeanne M. *Negotiating Globally: How to Negotiate Deals, Resolve Disputes, and Make Decisions across Cultural Boundaries*. San Francisco: Jossey-Bass, 2007.

British Association for the Advancement of Science, The. *Laughlab: The Scientific Quest for the World's Funniest Joke*. London: Arrow Books, 2002.

Bryon, Mike. *How to Pass Diagramatic Reasoning Tests*. London: Kogan Page, 2008.

Bussing-Burks, Marie. *Starbucks*. Westport, CT: Greenwood, 2009.

Cabrera, Angel, and Gregory Unruh. *Being Global: How to Think, Act, and Lead in a Transformed World*. Boston: Harvard Business Review Press, 2012.

Cameron, Gordon. *Trizics*. North Charleston, SC: Createspace, 2010.

Capacchione, Lucia. *Visioning: Ten Steps to Designing the Life of Your Dreams*. New York: Putnam, 2000.

Cappelli, Peter, Harbir Singh, Jitendra Singh, and Michael Useem. *The India Way*. Boston: Harvard Business Press, 2010.

Carbasho, Tracy. *Nike*. Westport, CT: Greenwood, 2010.

Carraher, Shawn M., Sherry E. Sullivan, and Madeline M. Crocitto. "Mentoring across Global Boundaries: An Empirical Examination of Home- and Host-Country Mentors on Expatriate Career Outcomes." *Journal of International Business Studies* no. 39 (2008): 1310–26.

Carter, Jennifer. *Over 600 Icebreakers and Games*. Wiltshire, England: Hope Books, 2011.

Carter, Philip. *The Complete Book of Intelligence Tests*. West Sussex, England: John Wiley & Sons, 2005.

Casler, Carlton, and Joel Weldon. *Presentation Excellence: 25 Tricks, Tips, and Techniques for Professional Speakers and Trainers*. Phoenix: CLB Publishing House, 2010.

Center for Creative Leadership. *Learning from Life*. Greensboro, NC: Center for Creative Leadership, 2007.

—— *Active Listening: Improve Your Ability to Listen and Lead*. Greensboro, NC: Center for Creative Leadership, 2007.

—— *Adaptability: Responding Effectively to Change*. Greensboro: Center for Creative Leadership, 2007.

Chang, S. J. "When East and West Meet: An Essay on the Importance of Cultural Understanding in Global Business Practice and Education." *Journal of International Business & Cultural Studies* 2 (2009): 1–13.

Chavaren, Oliver. *Trust within Virtual Global Teams: Antecedents, Facilitators, and Sustainability Factors*. Lincoln, NE: iUniverse, 2003.

Cheng, Shu-Ling, and Hae-Ching Chang. "Cognitive Complexity Implications for Research on Sustainable Competitive Advantage." *Journal of Business Research* 63, no. 1 (2010): 67–70.

Chermack, Thomas J. *Scenario Planning in Organizations: How to Create, Use, and Assess Scenarios*. San Francisco: BK Business, 2011.

Chhokar, Jagdeep S., Felix C. Brodbeck, and Robert J. House. *Culture and Leadership across the World: The GLOBE Book of In-Depth Studies of 25 Societies*. New York: Psychology Press, 2008.

Cholle, Francis. *The Intuitive Compass*. San Francisco: Jossey-Bass, 2011.

Chung, Keumyong. "Developing Your Global Know-How." *Harvard Business Review* (March 1, 2011): 1–7.

Cialdini, Robert B. *Influence: Science and Practice*. Boston: Pearson Education, 2008.

Clark, Mark A., Susan D. Amundson, and Robert L. Cardy. "Cross-Functional Team Decision-Making and Learning Outcomes: A Qualitative Illustration." *Journal of Business and Management* 8, no. 3 (2002): 217–38.

Cleghorn, Patricia. *Confidence Boosters!* London: Orchid Publications, 2011.

Clerkin, Thomas A. "Assessment Issues in Estimating Managerial Potential in a Global Context." *International Management Review* 7, no. 1 (2011): 5–9.

Clifton, Jonathan. "A Conversation Analytic Approach to Business Information: The Case of Leadership." *Journal of Business Communication* 43 (July 2006): 201–19.

Clouse, Mark Alan, and Michael D. Watkins. "Three Keys to Getting an Overseas Assignment Right." *Harvard Business Review* (October 1, 2009): 1–8.

Cohen, Raymond. *Negotiating across Cultures: International Communication in an Interdependent World.* Washington, DC: US Institute of Peace, 1997.

Coleman, Les. "Risk and Decision Making by Finance Executives: A Survey Study." *International Journal of Managerial Finance* 3, no. 1 (2007): 108–24.

Coleman, William, and Alina Sajed. *Fifty Key Thinkers on Globalization.* London: Routledge, 2013.

Conaway, Roger N., Wallace V. Schmidt, Susan S. Easton, and William J. Vardropein. "The Nature of Language and Nonverbal Communication." In Communicating Globally: Intercultural Communication and International Business. Thousand Oaks, CA: Sage Publications, 2007.

Conrad, David, and Robert Newberry. "24 Business Communication Skills: Attitudes of Human Resource Managers versus Business Educators." *American Communication Journal* 13, no. 1 (2011): 4–22.

Cornes, Alan. *Culture from the Inside Out.* Boston: Nicholas Brealey Publishing, 2004.

Covey, Stephen R. *The Third Alternative.* New York: Free Press, 2011.

Covey, Stephen M. R. *The Speed of Trust: The One Thing that Changes Everything.* New York: Free Press, 2006.

Coyle, Daniel. *The Talent Code.* New York: Bantam, 2009.

Cushnir, Raphael. *The One Thing Holding You Back: The Power of Emotional Connection.* New York: HarperOne, 2008.

D'Arcy, Jan. *Technically Speaking.* Columbus, OH: Battelle Press, 1998.

Davidson, Daniel. *101 Money Saving Travel Tips.* Little Man Productions, 2012. http://www.amazon.com/Money-Saving-Travel-eGuidebooks-ebook/dp/B007RTTZ7G.

Davies, Gary, and Rosa Chun. "The Leader's Role in Managing Reputation." In *Reputational Capital: Building and Maintaining Trust in the 21st Century*, edited by Joachim Klewes and Robert Wreschniok, 311–23. Manchester, England: Springer, 2009.

Davis, Jason P., and Kathleen M. Eisenhardt. "Rotating Leadership and Collaborative Innovation: Recombination Processes in Symbiotic Relationships." *Administrative Science Quarterly* 56, no. 2 (2011): 159–201.

de Bono, Edward. *Six Thinking Hats.* Boston: Little, Brown, and Company, 1999.

Del Missier, Fabio, Timo Mäntylä, and Wändi Bruine Bruin. "Decision-Making Competence, Executive Functioning, and General Cognitive Abilities." *Journal of Behavioral Decision Making* 25, no. 4 (2012): 331–51.

Deloitte. "The Challenge of Complexity in Global Manufacturing: Trends in Supply Chain Management." Last modified March 2, 2010. http://www.deloitte.com/view/en_GX/global/insights/deloitte-research/2d61c5275d0fb110VgnVCM100000ba42f00aRCRD.htm.

Demel, Barbara, and Wolfgang Mayrhofer. "Frequent Business Travelers across Europe: Career Aspirations and Implications." *Thunderbird International Business Review* 52, no. 4 (2010): 301–11.

Denning, Stephen. *The Leader's Guide to Storytelling: Mastering the Art and Discipline of Business Narrative.* San Francisco: John Wiley & Sons, 2011.

Diugwu, Ikechukwu. "Knowledge Acquisition and Sharing: A Sustainable Source of Competitive Advantage in Supply Chains." Proceedings of the International Conference on Global Intellectual Capital, Knowledge Management & Organizational Learning, Bangkok, Thailand, October 2011.

Doherty, Noeleen, Michael Dickmann, and Timothy Mills. "Exploring the Motives of Company-Backed and Self-Initiated Expatriates." *Human Resource Management* 22, no. 3 (2011): 595–611.

Dragoni, Lisa, In-Sue Oh, Paul Vankatwyk, and Paul E. Tesluk. "Developing Executive Leaders: The Relative Contribution of Cognitive Ability, Personality, and the Accumulation of Work Experience in Predicting Strategic Thinking Competency." *Personnel Psychology* 64, no. 4 (2011): 829–64.

Dressler, Larry. *Consensus through Conversation: How to Achieve High-Commitment Decisions.* San Francisco: Berrett-Koehler Publishers, 2006.

Dulworth, Michael. *The Connect Effect: Building Strong Personal, Professional, and Virtual Networks.* San Francisco: Berrett-Koehler Publishers, 2008.

Dweck, Carol. *Mindset: The New Psychology of Success.* New York: Ballantine Books, 2007.

Earley, P. Christopher, and Elaine Mosakowski. "Cultural Intelligence." *Harvard Business Review* (October 2004): 139–46.

Elliott, Bob, and Kevin Carroll. *Make Your Point*. New York: Second Avenue Press, 2005.

Ellis, James K. "Listening and Leadership: An Investigative Study into the Listening Practices of United States Coast Guard Enlisted Officers in Charge." Regent University. 2004. http://www.regent.edu/acad/global/publications/dissertations.cfm.

Engau, Christian, and Volker H. Hoffmann. "Strategizing in an Unpredictable Climate: Exploring Corporate Strategies to Cope with Regulatory Uncertainty." *Long Range Planning* 44, no. 1 (2011): 42–63.

Eppler, Martin J., Friederike Hoffman, and Sabrina Bresciani. "New Business Models through Collaborative Idea Generation." *International Journal of Innovation Management* 15, no. 6 (2011): 1323–52.

Ernst & Young. "Global Mobility Risk Advisory: Taking Hold of Global Mobility Cost." Last modified 2010. http://www.ey.com/Publication/vwLUAssets/2011_HC_Global_Mobility_Risk_Advisory/$FILE/EY_HC_GM_Risk_Advisory_engl.pdf.

Ertel, Danny, and Mark Gordon. "Negotiating the Risk or Risky Negotiations?" *Financial Executive* (May 7, 2009). http://www.amazon.com/Negotiating-risky-negotiations-DEALS-DEALMAKERS/dp/B00292MUVY.

Ettenson, Richard, and Jonathan Knowles. "Don't Confuse Reputation with Brand." *MIT Sloan Management Review* 49, no. 2 (2008): 19–21.

Felzensztein, Christian, and Eli Gimmon. "Social Networks and Marketing Cooperation in Entrepreneurial Clusters: An International Comparative Study." *Journal of International Entrepreneurship* 7, no. 4 (2009): 281–91.

Ferrari, Bernard T. "The Executive's Guide to Better Listening." *McKinsey Quarterly* (February 2012). http://unm2020.unm.edu/knowledgebase/university-leadership-and-governance/2-better-listening-skills-mckinsey-1202.pdf.

Fisher, Roger, and Daniel Shapiro. *Beyond Reason: Using Emotions as You Negotiate*. New York: Viking, 2006.

Foley, Dennis. "Does Culture and Global Social Capital Impact on the Networking Attributes of Indigenous Entrepreneurs?" *Journal of Enterprising Communities* 2, no. 3 (2009): 204–24.

Ford, Jeffrey D., and Laurie W. Ford. "Decoding Resistance to Change." *Harvard Business Review* 87, no. 4 (2009): 99–103.

Frankl, Viktor. *Man's Search for Meaning.* Boston: Beacon Press, 2006.

Freeman, Susan, Kate Hutchings, and Sylvie Chetty. "Born-Globals and Culturally Proximate Markets." *Management International Review* 52, no. 3 (2012).

Froese, Fabian Jintae, and Vesa Peltokorpi. "Cultural Distance and Expatriate Job Satisfaction." *International Journal of Intercultural Relations* 35, no. 1 (2011): 49–60.

Gannon, Martin J. *Paradoxes of Culture and Globalization.* Thousand Oaks, CA: Sage Publications, 2007.

Gebelein, Susan, Kristie J. Nelson-Neuhaus, Carol J. Skube, David G. Lee, Lisa A. Stevens, Lowell W. Hellervik, Brian L. Davis, and Lynn Marasco. *Successful Manager's Handbook.* Minneapolis: PreVisor, 2010.

Gelfand, Michele J., Janetta Lun, Sarah Lyons, and Garriy Shteynberg. "Descriptive Norms as Carriers of Culture in Negotiation." *International Negotiation* 16, no. 3 (2011): 361–81.

Ghafoor, Shahzad, Fukaiha Kaka Khail, Uzair Farooq Khan, and Faiza Hassan. "Cross Culture Analysis: An Exploratory Analysis of Experiential Narratives and Implications for Management." *Interdisciplinary Journal of Contemporary Research in Business* 3, no. 5 (2011): 335–51.

Ghemawat, Pankaj. "Developing Global Leaders." *McKinsey Quarterly* (June 2012). https://www.mckinseyquarterly.com/Developing_global_leaders_2985.

—— *World 3.0.* Boston: Harvard Business Review Press, 2011.

—— "Remapping Your Strategic Mind-Set." *McKinsey Quarterly* (August 2011). http://www.mckinseyquarterly.com/Remapping_your_strategic_mind-set_2837.

—— "The Cosmopolitan Corporation." *Harvard Business Review* 89, no. 5 (May 2011): 92–99.

—— *Redefining Global Strategy.* Boston: Harvard Business Review Press, 2007.

Gilkey, Roderick, and Clint Kilts. "Cognitive Fitness." *Harvard Business Review* (November 1, 2007). http://hbr.org/product/cognitive-fitness/an/R0711B-PDF-ENG.

Gillis, John, Jr. "Building a Global Leadership Pipeline." *Chief Learning Officer* (January 2012): 26–29.

Giroux, Isabelle. "Problem Solving in Small Firms: An Interpretive Study." *Journal of Small Business and Enterprise Development* 16, no. 1 (2009): 167–84.

Gladwell, Malcolm. *Outliers.* New York: Little, Brown, and Company, 2008.

Global Intelligence Alliance. "Global Market Intelligence Survey 2009." April 2009. http://www.globalintelligencecc.com/cc/index. php?option=com_virtuemart&page=shop.registration&Itemid=28&link=glo bal-market-intelligence-survey-2009/GIA_WhitePaper_2009_04_Global_MI_ Survey.pdf.

Goldsmith, Barton. *100 Ways to Boost Your Self-Confidence.* Franklin Lakes, NJ: The Career Press, 2010.

Goleman, Daniel. *Working with Emotional Intelligence.* New York: Bantam, 2000.

Goman, Carol Kinsey. *The Silent Language of Leaders: How Body Language Can Help—or Hurt—How You Lead.* San Francisco: Jossey-Bass, 2011.

Gordon, Jon. *The Seed: Finding Purpose and Happiness in Life.* Hoboken, NJ: John Wiley & Sons, 2011.

Graf, Andrea, and Lynn K. Harland. "Expatriate Selection: Evaluating the Discriminant, Convergent, and Predictive Validity of Five Measures of Interpersonal and Intercultural Competence." *Journal of Leadership & Organizational Studies* 11, no. 2 (2004): 46–62.

Graham, John L., and William Hernandez Requejo. *Global Negotiation: The New Rules.* New York: Palgrave MacMillan, 2008.

Green, Stephen, Fred Hassan, Jeffrey Immelt, Michael Marks, and Daniel Meiland. "In Search of Global Leaders." *Harvard Business Review* (August 1, 2003). http://hbr.org/product/in-search-of-global-leaders/an/R0308B-PDF-ENG.

Griffith, David A. "The Role of Communication Competencies in International Business Relationship Development." *Journal of World Business* 37, no. 4 (2002): 256–65.

Griffiths, Chris. "Solving Problems." *Leadership Excellence* 29, no. 4 (2012): 5–10.

Groves, Dawn. *Stress Reduction for Busy People: Finding Peace in an Anxious World.* Novato, CA: New World Library, 2004.

Groysberg, Boris, and Michael Slind. "Leadership Is a Conversation." *Harvard Business Review* (June 1, 2012). http://hbr.org/product/leadership-is-a-conversation/an/R1206D-PDF-ENG.

Guber, Peter. *Tell to Win: Connect, Persuade, and Triumph with the Hidden Power of Story*. New York: Crown Business, 2011.

Guillén, Mauro F., and Esteban García-Canal. "How to Conquer New Markets with Old Skills." *Harvard Business Review* 88, no. 11 (2010): 118–22.

Gundling, Ernest. *Working GlobeSmart: 12 People Skills for Doing Business across Borders*. Mountain View, CA: Davies-Black Publishing, 2010.

Gupta, Anil K., Vijay Govindarajan, and Haiyan Wang. *The Quest for Global Dominance*. San Francisco: Jossey-Bass, 2008.

Halbe, Dorothea. "'Who's There?': Differences in the Features of Telephone and Face-to-Face Conferences." *Journal of Business Communication* 49, no. 1 (2012): 48–73.

Hall, Edward T. *Beyond Culture*. New York: Anchor Books, 1976.

Hansen, Morten T. *Collaboration: How Leaders Avoid the Traps, Create Unity, and Reap Big Results*. Boston: Harvard Business School Publishing, 2009.

Harrison, Edelweiss C., and Snejina Michailova. "Working in the Middle East: Western Female Expatriates' Experiences in the United Arab Emirates." *International Journal of Human Resource Management* 23, no. 3 (2012): 625–44.

Harvard Business Press Books. *Harvard Business Review: Collaborating Effectively*. Boston: Harvard Business Press Books, 2011.

Harvey, Michael, Nancy Napier, and Miriam Moeller. "Improving the Probabilities of Success of Expatriate Managers in the Global Organisation of the 21st Century." *International Journal of Human Resources Development and Management* 11, no. 2/3/4 (2011): 141–66.

Haslberger, Arno, and Chris Brewster. "Capital Gains: Expatriate Adjustment and the Psychological Contract in International Careers." *Human Resource Management* 48, no. 3 (2009): 379–97.

Hayashi, Alden M. "How to Increase a Company's Risk Taking." *MIT Sloan Management Review* 49, no. 2 (2008): 6–7.

Heijes, Coen. "The Broad Dimensions of Doing Business Abroad." *The Business Review* 8, no. 1 (2007): 93–99.

Hessenbruch, Arne. "Demystifying Electricity Pricing." Global Business Hub. November 15, 2012. http://www.boston.com/business/blogs/global-business-hub/2012/11/demystifying_el.html.

Hofstede, Gert Jan, Catholijn M. Jonker, and Tim Verwaart. "Cultural Differentiation of Negotiating Agents." *Group Decision and Negotiation* 21, no. 1 (2012): 79–98.

Hogshead, Sally. *Fascinate: Your Seven Triggers to Persuade and Captivate.* New York: HarperCollins Publishers, 2010.

Holt, John W., Jr., Jon Stamell, and Melissa Field. *Celebrate Your Mistakes.* Scarborough, NY: Irwin Professional Pub, 1996.

Hoppe, Michael H. "Lending an Ear: Why Leaders Must Learn to Listen Actively." *Leadership in Action* 27, no. 4 (2007): 11–14.

House, Robert J., Paul John Hanges, Mansour Javidan, Peter W. Dorfman, and Vipin Gupta. *Culture, Leadership, and Organizations: The GLOBE Studies of 62 Societies.* Thousand Oaks, CA: Sage Publications, 2004.

Huang, Liangguang. "Cross-Cultural Communication in Business Negotiations." *International Journal of Economics and Finance* 2, no. 2 (2010): 196–99.

Iqbal, Zahid, O. Sewon, and H. Young Baek. "Are Female Executives More Risk-Averse than Male Executives?" *Atlantic Economic Journal* 34, no. 1 (2006): 63–74.

Javidan, Mansour, Mary Teagarden, and David Bowen. "Making It Overseas." *Harvard Business Review* (April 1, 2010). http://hbr.org/product/making-it-overseas/an/R1004L-PDF-ENG.

Javidan, Mansour, Peter W. Dorfman, Mary Sully de Luque, and Robert J. House. "In the Eye of the Beholder: Cross-Cultural Lessons in Leadership from Project GLOBE." Academy of Management *Perspectives* 20, no. 1 (2006): 67–90.

Jefferson, D. K. *Stress Relief Today: 297 Simple Techniques to Manage and Relieve Stress Today.* CreateSpace Independent Publishing Platform, 2012. http://www.amazon.com/Stress-Relief-Today-Techniques-ebook/dp/B0079JHOF4.

Jin, Chang-hyun, and Hyun-chul Yeo. "Satisfaction, Corporate Credibility, CEO Reputation and Leadership Effects on Public Relationships." *Journal of Targeting, Measurement and Analysis for Marketing* 19 (June 13, 2011): 127–40.

Joerres, Jeffrey A. "Beyond Expats: Better Managers for Emerging Markets." *McKinsey Quarterly* (May 2011). http://www.mckinseyquarterly.com/Beyond_expats_Better_managers_for_emerging_markets_2802.

Johnson, Andrew, and David M. McCord. "Relating Sense of Humor to the Five Factor Theory Personality Domains and Facets." *American Journal of Psychological Research* 6, no. 1 (January 20, 2010). http://paws.wcu.edu/mccord/pdf/Johnson-McCord-AJPR-2010.pdf.

Johnson, P. Fraser, Robert D. Klassen, Michiel R. Leenders, and Amrou Awaysheh. "Selection of Planned Supply Initiatives: The Role of Senior Management Expertise." *International Journal of Operations & Production Management* 27, no. 12 (2007): 1280–302.

Karr, Susan Schott. "Critical Thinking: A Critical Strategy for Financial Executives." *Financial Executive* 25, no. 10 (2009): 58–61.

Kawasaki, Guy. *Enchantment: The Art of Changing Hearts, Minds, and Actions.* New York: Portfolio Trade, 2011.

Kayser, Thomas. "Six Ingredients for Collaborative Partnerships." *Leader to Leader* no. 61 (2011): 48–65.

Khan, Anas, Riad Khan, and Mohammad Habibur Rahman. "Developing International Executives: The Capacity-Building Approach." *Development and Learning in Organizations* 25, no. 2 (2011): 10–14.

Klipper, Miriam Z., and Herbert Benson. *Relaxation Response.* New York: HarperTorch, 2000.

Komisarjevsky, Chris. *The Power of Reputation: Strengthen the Asset That Will Make or Break Your Career.* New York: American Management Association, 2012.

Kossovsky, Nir. "Reputation Leadership." *Leadership Excellence* 27, no. 5 (2010): 7–8.

Kosta, Joy. "Opening Our Mind to Paradoxical Thinking." Human Capital Institute. March 8, 2012. http://www.hci.org/lib/opening-our-mind-paradoxical-thinking.

Kristiansen, Stein. "Social Networks and Business Success: The Role of Subcultures in an African Context." *The American Journal of Economics and Sociology* 63, no. 5 (2004): 1149–71.

Larraza-Kintana, Martin, Luis Gomez-Mejia, and Robert M. Wiseman. "Compensation Framing and the Risk-Taking Behavior of the CEO: Testing the Influence of Alternative Reference Points." *Management Research* 9, no. 1 (2011): 32–55.

Lawton, Thomas, and Tazeeb Rajwani. "Designing Lobbying Capabilities: Managerial Choices in Unpredictable Environments." *European Business Review* 23, no. 2 (2011): 167–89.

Leeds, Dorothy. *The Seven Powers of Questions: Secrets to Successful Communication in Life and at Work*. New York: The Berkley Publishing Group, 2000.

Lewis, Richard D. *When Cultures Collide*. Boston: Nicholas Brealey Publishing, 2005.

Livermore, David. *Leading with Cultural Intelligence: The New Secret to Success*. New York: American Management Association, 2009.

Li-Yueh, Lee, and Sukoco Badri Munir. "The Effects of Cultural Intelligence on Expatriate Performance: The Moderating Effects of International Experience." *International Journal of Human Resource Management* 21, no. 7 (2010): 963–81.

Loehr, Jim, and Tony Schwartz. *The Power of Full Engagement: Managing Energy Not Time Is the Key to High Performance and Personal Renewal*. New York: The Free Press, 2003.

Lohman, Margaret C. "Cultivating Problem-Solving Skills through Problems-Based Approaches to Professional Development." *Human Resources Development Quarterly* 13, no. 3 (2002): 243–61.

Lovvorn, Al S., and Chen Jiun-Shiu. "Developing a Global Mindset: The Relationship between an International Assignment and Cultural Intelligence." *International Journal of Business & Social Science* 2, no. 9 (2011): 275–83.

Lucero, Marela, Teng Kwang Alywin Tan, and Augustine Pang. "Crisis Leadership: When Should the CEO Step Up?" *Corporate Communications* 14, no. 3 (2009): 234–48.

Maak, Thomas, and Nicola Pless. "Business Leaders as Citizens of the World: Advancing Humanism on a Global Scale." *Journal of Business Ethics* 88, no. 3 (2009): 537–50.

Manrai, Lalita, and Ajay Manrai. "The Influence of Culture in International Business Negotiations: A New Conceptual Framework and Managerial Implications." *Journal of Transnational Management* 15, no. 1 (2010): 69–100.

Manz, Charles C. *The Power of Failure*. San Francisco: Berrett-Koehler Publishers, 2002.

Magwood, Johnny D. "Navigating Expatriate Leaders' Competencies." *Leader to Leader* no. 62 (2011): 7–10.

Marketing Week. "Global Marketing: Overcoming a Little Local Difficulty." (October 2008): 28–29.

Marques, Joan, Satinder Dhiman, and Richard King. "Empathetic Listening as a Management Tool." *Business Renaissance Quarterly* (April 1, 2011). http://www.highbeam.com/doc/1P3-2374269391.html.

Martin, Jeffrey A., and Kathleen M. Eisenhardt. "Rewiring: Cross-Business-Unit Collaborations in Multibusiness Organizations." *Academy of Management Journal* 53, no. 2 (2010): 265–81.

Maxfield, Sylvia, Mary Shapiro, Vipin Gupta, and Susan Hass. "Gender and Risk: Women, Risk Taking and Risk Aversion." Gender in Management 25, no. 7 (2010): 586–604.

Mayerhofer, Helene, Angelika Schmidt, Linley Hartmann, and Regine Bendl. "Recognising Diversity in Managing Work Life Issues of Flexpatriates." *Equality, Diversity and Inclusion: An International Journal* 30, no. 7 (2011): 589–609.

Maznevski, Martha L., and Joseph J. DiStefano. "Global Leaders Are Team Players: Developing Global Leaders through Membership on Global Teams." *Human Resource Management* 39, no. 2–3 (2000): 195–208.

McCammon, Ross. "A Small Talk Survival Guide for the Achmooze-Averse." *Entrepreneur* (June 19, 2012). http://www.entrepreneur.com/article/223775#.

McClelland, David C. *The Achieving Society*. Eastford, CT: Martino Fine Books, 2010.

—— *Human Motivation*. New York: Cambridge University Press, 1987.

McIntyre, Nancy H., Michael Harvey, and Miriam Moeller. "The Role of Managerial Curiosity in Organizational Learning: A Theoretical Inquiry." *International Journal of Management* 29, no. 2 (2012): 659–76.

McKay, Matthew, Patrick Fanning, Catharine Sutker, and Carole Honeychurch. *The Self-Esteem Companion*. Oakland, CA: New Harbinger Publications, 2005.

McKenna, Steve. "'Adjustment' of the Independent Expatriate: A Case Study of Doug." *Qualitative Research in Organizations and Management* 5, no. 3 (2010): 280–98.

McKeown, Max. *Adaptability: The Art of Winning in an Age of Uncertainty*. London: Kogan Page, 2012.

Molinsky, Andrew L., Thomas H. Davenport, Bala Iyer, and Cathy Davidson. "3 Skills Every 21st-Century Manager Needs." *Harvard Business Review* (January 2012): 1–6.

Morieux, Yves. "Smart Rules: Six Ways to Get People to Solve Problems Without You." *Harvard Business Review* (September 1, 2011). http://hbr.org/product/smart-rules-six-ways-to-get-people-to-solve-proble/an/R1109D-HCB-ENG.

Morrison, Terri, and Wayne A. Conaway. *Kiss, Bow, or Shake Hands: The Bestselling Guide to Doing Business in More than 60 Countries*. Avon, MA: Adams Media, 2006.

Mortell, Art. *The Courage to Fail*. New York: McGraw-Hill, 1992.

Mortenson, Mark, and Michael O'Leary. "Managing a Virtual Team." *Harvard Business Review* (April 16, 2012). http://blogs.hbr.org/cs/2012/04/how_to_manage_a_virtual_team.html.

Moss Kanter, Rosabeth. *Confidence: How Winning Streaks and Losing Streaks Begin and End*. New York: Crown Publishing Group, 2006.

Muller, Paul. "Reputation, Trust and the Dynamics of Leadership in Communities of Practice." *Journal of Management & Governance* 10, no. 4 (2006): 381–400.

Nardon, Luciara, and Richard M. Steers. "The New Global Manager: Learning Cultures on the Fly." *Organizational Dynamics* 37, no. 1 (2008): 47–63.

Navarro, Joe, and Marvin Karlins. *What Every Body Is Saying: An Ex-FBI Agent's Guide to Speed-Reading People*. New York: HarperCollins Publishers, 2008.

Neenan, Michael. *Developing Resilience: A Cognitive Behavioral Approach*. New York: Routledge, 2009.

Neidel, Betsy. "Negotiations, Chinese Style." *The China Business Review* 37, no. 6 (2010): 32–41.

Newman, Barbara M., and Phillip R. Newman. *Theories of Human Development*. Mahwah, NJ: Lawrence Erlbaum Associates, 2007.

Newth, Francine. "The New Strategic Imperative: Understanding the Female Business Traveler." *The International Business & Economics Research Journal* 8, no. 11 (2009): 51–64.

Nicholas, Helen, and Almuth McDowall. "When Work Keeps Us Apart: A Thematic Analysis of the Experience of Business Travellers." *Community, Work & Family* 15, no. 3 (2012): 335–55.

Nisbett, Richard. *The Geography of Thought*. New York: The Free Press, 2004.

Norales, Francisca O. *Cross-Cultural Communication: Concepts, Cases, and Challenges*. New York: Cabria Press, 2006.

Nordbo, Simen Moen. "Cultural Impacts in International Negotiation." *ADR Bulletin* 12, no. 2 (2010): 1–8.

O'Brien, Emma, and Phillipa Robertson. "Future Leadership Competencies: From Foresight to Current Practice." *Journal of European Industrial Training* 33, no. 4 (2009): 371–80.

O'Grady, Jason D. *Apple Inc*. Westport, CT: Greenwood, 2008.

Olsen, Jesse, E., and Luis L. Martins. "The Effects of Expatriate Demographic Characteristics on Adjustment: A Social Identity Approach." *Human Resource Management* 48, no. 2 (2009): 311–28.

Pablos, Patricia Ordonez de. "Western and Eastern Views on Social Networks." *The Learning Organization* 12, no. 5 (2005): 436–56.

Parmigiani, Anne, and Will Mitchell. "The Hollow Corporation Revisited: Can Governance Mechanisms Substitute for Technical Expertise in Managing Buyer–Supplier Relationships?" *European Management Review* 7, no. 1 (2010): 46–70.

Patterson, Kerry, Joseph Grenny, Ron McMillan, and Al Switzler. *Crucial Conversations*. New York: McGraw-Hill, 2011.

—— *Crucial Confrontations*. New York: McGraw-Hill, 2004.

Patterson, Kerry, Joseph Grenny, David Maxfield, and Ron McMillan. *Influencer*. New York: McGraw-Hill, 2007.

Pease, Barbara, and Allan Pease. *The Definitive Book of Body Language*. New York: Bantam Dell, 2006.

Pecotich, Anthony, and Steven Ward. "Global Branding, Country of Origin and Expertise." *International Marketing Review* 24, no. 3 (2007): 271–96.

Peltin, Scott, and Jogi Rippel. *Sink, Float, or Swim*. Munich, Germany: Redline-Verlag, 2009.

Pert, Candace B. *Molecules of Emotions: The Science Behind Mind–Body Medicine*. New York: Touchstone, 1999.

Peters, Tom. *Brand You Fifty: Fifty Ways to Transform Yourself from an Employee into a Brand that Shouts Distinction, Commitment, and Passion!* New York: Alfred A. Knopf Inc., 1999.

Peterson, Brooks. *Cultural Intelligence: A Guide for Working with People from Other Cultures*. Yarmouth, ME: Intercultural Press, 2004.

Pettersen, Inger, and Anita Tobiassen. "Are Born Globals Really Born Globals? The Case of Academic Spin-Offs with Long Development Periods." *Journal of International Entrepreneurship* 10, no. 2 (2012): 117–41.

Pinto, Luísa H., Carlos Cabral-Cardoso, and William B. Werther, Jr. "Compelled to Go Abroad? Motives and Outcomes of International Assignments." *The International Journal of Human Resource Management* 23, no. 11 (2012): 2295–314.

—— "Adjustment Elusiveness: An Empirical Investigation of the Effects of Cross-Cultural Adjustment on General Assignment Satisfaction and Withdrawal Intentions." *International Journal of Intercultural Relations* 36, no. 2 (2012): 188–99.

Pisano, Gary P., and Roberto Verganti. "Which Kind of Collaboration Is Right for You?" *Harvard Business Review* 86, no. 12 (2008): 78–86.

Pless, Nicola M., Thomas Maak, and Gunter K. Stahl. "Developing Responsible Global Leaders through International Service-Learning Programs: The Ulysses Experience." *Academy of Management Learning & Education* 10, no. 2 (2011): 237–60.

Pounsford, Mike. "Using Storytelling, Conversation and Coaching to Engage." *Strategic Communication Management* 11, no. 3 (2007): 1363–87.

Puffett, Michael. *300+ Sizzling Icebreakers*. London: Monarch, 2010.

Rahimi, Gholamreza, Alireza Razmi, and Qader Vazifeh Damirch. "The Role of Cultural Intelligence in Achievement of Iran's Small and Medium Enterprise Managers." *Interdisciplinary Journal of Contemporary Research in Business* 3, no. 5 (2011): 720–27.

Ramalu, Subramaniam A/L Sri, Wei Chuah Chin, and Raduan Che Rose. "The Effects of Cultural Intelligence on Cross-Cultural Adjustment and Job Performance amongst Expatriates in Malaysia." *International Journal of Business & Social Science* 2, no. 9 (2011): 59–71.

Rane, D. B. "Good Listening Skills Make Efficient Business Sense." *IUP Journal of Soft Skills* 5, no. 4 (2011): 43–51.

Ranieri, Kathryn L. "Toward Group Problem Solving Guidelines for 21st Century Teams." *Performance Improvement Quarterly* 17, no. 3 (2004): 86–105.

Rega, Michael E. "Developing Listening Skills." *The American Salesman* 45, no. 5 (2010): 3–7.

Rego, Arménio, and Miguel Pina Cunha. "Global Leaders' Virtues and Virtuous Performance." Proceedings of the European Conference on Management, Leadership & Governance, Wroclaw, Poland, October 2010.

Reivich, Karen, and Andrew Shatte. *The Resilience Factor: 7 Keys to Finding Your Inner Strength and Overcoming Life's Hurdles.* New York: Broadway Books, 2003.

Reynolds, Garr. *Presentation Zen Design: Simple Design Principles and Techniques to Enhance Your Presentations.* Berkeley: New Riders, 2011.

Reynolds, Sana, Deborah Valentine, and Mary Munter. *Guide to Cross-Cultural Communications.* Upper Saddle River, NJ: Prentice Hall, 2010.

Rockefeller, Kirwan. *Visualize Confidence.* Novato, CA: New World Library, 2007.

Rodrik, Dani. *The Globalization Paradox.* New York: W. W. Norton & Company, 2011.

Rosas, Joao, and Luis M. Camarinha-Matos. "An Approach to Assess Collaboration Readiness." *International Journal of Production Research* 47, no. 17 (2009): 4711–35.

Rose, Raduan Che, Subramaniam Sri Ramalu, Jegak Uli, and Naresh Kumar Samy. "Expatriate Performance in International Assignments: The Role of Cultural Intelligence as Dynamic Intercultural Competency." *International Journal of Business & Management* 5, no. 8 (2010): 76–85.

—— "Expatriate Performance in Overseas Assignments: The Role of Big Five Personality." *Asian Social Science* 6, no. 9 (2010): 104–13.

Rosen, Evan. *The Culture of Collaboration: Maximizing Time, Talent and Tools to Create Value in the Global Economy.* San Francisco: Red Ape Publishing, 2009.

Ryan, M. J. *AdaptAbility: How to Survive the Change You Didn't Ask For.* New York: Crown Archetype, 2009.

Saksena, Sonny. "Managing Complexity: How to Capture Latent Value from Products, Customers, and Operations." *Business Performance Management Magazine* (August 1, 2007). http://bpmmag.net/mag/managing_complexity_products_customers_0807.

Salovey, Peter, and John D. Mayer. "Emotional Intelligence." *Imagination, Cognition, and Personality* 9, no. 3 (1990): 185–211.

Sarkar, A. N. "Navigating the Rough Seas of Global Business Negotiation: Reflection on Cross-Cultural Issues and Some Corporate Experiences." *International Journal of Business Insights & Transformation* 3, no. 2 (2010): 48–63.

Sayre, Kent. *Unstoppable Confidence: How to Use the Power of NLP to Be More Dynamic and Successful.* New York: McGraw-Hill, 2008.

Schiraldi, Glenn R. *10 Simple Solutions for Building Self-Esteem: How to End Self-Doubt, Gain Confidence, and Create a Positive Self Image.* Oakland, CA: New Harbinger Publications, 2007.

___ *The Self-Esteem Workbook.* Oakland, CA: New Harbinger Publications, 2001.

Schlesinger, Leonard A., Charles F. Kiefer, and Paul B. Brown. "New Project? Don't Analyze—Act." *Harvard Business Review* 90, no. 3 (2012): 154–58.

Schneider, Gary P., Kathleen A. Simione, and Carol M. Bruton. "Learning to Listen: Guided Practice for Business Students." Allied Academies International Conference, Las Vegas, October 2011. http://www.alliedacademies.org/public/proceedings/Proceedings29/IACS%20Proceedings%20Fall%202011.pdf.

Schwartz, Tony, Jean Gomes, and Catherine McCarthy. *The Way We're Working Isn't Working: Four Forgotten Needs that Energize Great Performance.* New York: Free Press, 2010.

Scott, Missy. *Harley-Davidson.* Westport, CT: Greenwood, 2008.

Scott, Virginia. *Google.* Westport, CT: Greenwood, 2008.

Seligman, Martin E. P. *Learned Optimism.* New York: Pocket Books, 2006.

Selvam, Ashok. "Diverse Perspectives: Minority Executives and Their Peers Tout the Benefits of Broader Representation in the C-Suite, Boardrooms." *Modern Healthcare* (2012). http://www.modernhealthcare.com/article/20120407/MAGAZINE/304079968.

Semnani-Azad, Zhaleh, and Wendi L. Adair. "The Display of 'Dominant' Nonverbal Cues in Negotiation: The Role of Culture and Gender." *International Negotiation* 16, no. 3 (2011): 451–79.

Senge, Peter M. *The Fifth Discipline.* New York: Doubleday, 2006.

Sheaffer, Zachary, Ronit Bogler, and Samuel Sarfaty. "Leadership Attributes, Masculinity and Risk Taking as Predictors of Crisis Proneness." *Gender in Management* 26, no. 2 (2011): 163–87.

Shen, Yan, and Kathy E. Kram. "Expatriates' Developmental Networks: Network Diversity, Base, and Support Functions." *Career Development International* 16, no. 6 (2011): 528–52.

Shirokova, Galina. "Influence of Social Networks on Internationalization of Russian SMEs." Proceedings of the World Conference of the International Council for Small Business, Split, Croatia, July 2011.

Shortland, Susan. "Networking: A Valuable Career Intervention for Women Expatriates?" *Career Development International* 16, no. 3 (2011): 271–92.

Sibony, Olivier. "Collaborative Strategic Planning: Three Observations." *McKinsey Quarterly* (May 2012): 94–97.

Siebdrat, Frank, Martin Hoegl, and Holger Ernst. "How to Manage Virtual Teams." *MIT Sloan Management Review* (2009). http://sloanreview.mit.edu/the-magazine/2009-summer/50412/how-to-manage-virtual-teams.

Siegel, Daniel J. *MindSight: The New Science of Personal Transformation.* New York: Bantam Books, 2010.

Simmons, Annette. *Whoever Tells the Best Story Wins: How to Use Your Own Stories to Communicate with Power and Impact.* New York: American Management Association, 2007.

Simmons, Annette, and Doug Lipman. *The Story Factor.* Cambridge, MA: Basic Books, 2006.

Sirkin, Hal, Jim Hemerling, and Arindam Bhattacharya. *Globality.* New York: Business Plus, 2008.

Smith, Donald C. "Pulling the Plug on Culture Shock: A Seven Step Plan for Managing Travel Anxiety." *Journal of Global Business Issues* 2, no. 1 (2008): 41–48.

Spralls, Samuel A., III, Patrick Okonkwo, and Obasi H. Akan. "A Traveler to Distant Places Should Make No Enemies: Toward Understanding Nigerian Negotiating Style." *Journal of Applied Business and Economics* 12, no. 3 (2011): 11–25.

Srivastava, Sameer B. "Culture, Cognition, and Collaborative Networks in Organizations." *American Sociological Review* 76, no. 2 (2011): 207–33.

Steers, Richard M. "Learning Cultures on the Fly." In *Advances in International Management*, edited by Timothy Devinney, Torben Pedersen, and Laszlo Tihanyi, 171–90. Bingley, England: Emerald Group Publishing, 2007.

Steger, Manfred B. *Globalization: A Very Short Introduction*. Oxford: Oxford University Press, 2009.

Steinwascher, William Henry, and Rajagopal. "Analytical Perspectives on the Integration and Diffusion of Knowledge in Multicultural Business Schools to Build Global Image." *ICFAI Journal Of Knowledge Management* 7, no. 3–4 (2009): 64–79.

Storti, Craig. *Cross-Cultural Dialogues: 74 Brief Encounters with Cultural Difference*. Boston: Intercultural Press, 1994.

Straus, David, and Thomas C. Layton. *How to Make Collaboration Work: Powerful Ways to Build Consensus, Solve Problems, and Make Decisions*. San Francisco: Berrett-Koehler Publishers, 2002.

Stringer, Donna M., and Patricia A. Cassiday. *52 Activities for Improving Cross-Cultural Communication*. Boston: Nicholas Brealey Publishing, 2009.

Stroppa, Christina, and Erika Spiess. "Expatriates Social Networks: The Role of Company Size." *The International Journal of Human Resource Management* 21, no. 13 (2010): 2306–22.

Susskind, Lawrence, Sarah McKearnan, and Jennifer Thomas-Larmer. *The Consensus Building Handbook: A Comprehensive Guide to Reaching Agreement*. Thousand Oaks, CA: Sage Publications, 1999.

Suutari, Vesa, Christelle Tornikoski, and Liisa Mäkelä. "Career Decision Making of Global Careerists." *The International Journal of Human Resource Management* 23, no. 16 (2012): 3455–78.

Sviokla, John. "Getting Buy-In for Abstract Ideas." *Harvard Business Review* (November 13, 2009). http://blogs.hbr.org/sviokla/2009/11/getting_buyin_for_abstract_ide.html.

Templer, Klaus J. "Personal Attributes of Expatriate Managers, Subordinate Ethnocentrism, and Expatriate Success: A Host-Country Perspective." *The International Journal of Human Resource Management* 21, no. 10 (2010): 1754–68.

Thomas, Robert J., Joshua Bellin, Claudy Jules, and Nandani Lynton. "Global Leadership Teams: Diagnosing Three Essential Qualities." *Strategy & Leadership* 40, no. 3 (2012): 25–29.

Thornton, Paul B. "Why Some Leaders Succeed and Others Fail." *Leader to Leader* no. 60 (2011): 17–21.

Tolle, Eckhart. *The Power of Now*. Novato, CA: New World Library, 2004.

Tracy, Brian. *Change Your Thinking, Change Your Life*. Hoboken, NJ: John Wiley & Sons, 2003.

Triandis, Harry C. "Cultural Intelligence in Organizations." *Group & Organization Management* 31, no. 1 (2006): 20–26.

Tu, Yu-te, and Heng-chi Chih. "An Analysis on Negotiation Styles by Religious Beliefs." *International Business Research* 4, no. 3 (2011): 243–53.

Turner, Marcia Layton. *The Complete Idiot's Guide to Vision Boards*. New York: Penguin Group, 2009.

Tyler, Jo A. "Reclaiming Rare Listening as a Means of Organizational Re-Enchantment." *Journal of Organizational Change Management* 24, no. 1 (2011): 143–57.

Useem, Michael. *The Leadership Moment*. New York: Three Rivers Press, 1999.

Vallens, Ansi. "The Importance of Reputation." *Risk Management* 55, no. 4 (2008): 36–42.

Velde, Christine R. "Intercultural Knowledge Management: Exploring Models for Repatriation Competency Transfer in the Global Workplace." *International Journal of Human Resources Development and Management* 10, no. 4 (2010): 297–309.

Vereshchagina, Galina, and Hugo A. Hopenhayn. "Risk Taking by Entrepreneurs." *The American Economic Review* 99, no. 5 (2009): 1808–30.

Vesterby, Vincent. "Measuring Complexity: Things that Go Wrong and How to Get It Right." *Emergence: Complexity and Organization* 10, no. 2 (2008): 90–101.

Vlachoutsicos, Charalambos A. "How to Cultivate Engaged Employees." *Harvard Business Review* 89, no. 9 (2011): 123–26.

Wade, Woody. *Scenario Planning: A Field Guide to the Future*. Hoboken, NJ: John Wiley & Sons, 2012.

Wang, Barbara Xiaouyu, and Harold Chee. *Chinese Leadership*. New York: Palgrave Macmillan, 2011.

Wang, Yu-Lin, and Emma Tran. "Effects of Cross-Cultural and Language Training on Expatriates' Adjustment and Job Performance in Vietnam." *Asia Pacific Journal of Human Resources* 50, no. 3 (2012): 327–50.

Weinstein, Larry, and John Cook. "The Benefits of Collaboration between For-Profit Businesses and Nonprofit Arts- or Culture-Oriented Organizations." *Advanced Management Journal* 76, no. 3 (2011): 4–9.

White, Darin W., R. Keith Absher, and Kyle A. Huggins. "The Effects of Hardiness and Cultural Distance on Sociocultural Adaptation in an Expatriate Sales Manager Population." *Journal of Personal Selling & Sales Management* 31, no. 3 (2011): 325–37.

Winn, Monika I., Patricia Macdonald, and Charlene Zietsma. "Managing Industry Reputation: The Dynamic Tension between Collective and Competitive Reputation Management Strategies." *Corporate Reputation Review* 11, no. 1 (2008): 35–55.

Woodall, Marian K. *Think on Your Feet*. Bend, OR: Professional Business Communications, 2009.

Zack, Devora. *Networking for People Who Hate Networking: A Field Guide for Introverts, the Overwhelmed, and the Underconnected*. San Francisco: Berrett-Koehler Publishers, 2010.

Zaraysky, Susanna. *Travel Happy, Budget Low*. Cupertino, CA: Kaleidomundi, 2009.

Zhang, Man, Patriya Tansuhaj, and James McCullough. "International Entrepreneurial Capability: The Measurement and a Comparison between Born Global Firms and Traditional Exporters in China." *Journal of International Entrepreneurship* 7, no. 4 (2009): 292–322.

Zolli, Andrew, and Anne Marie Healy. *Resilience: Why Things Bounce Back*. New York: Free Press, 2012.

About the Authors

MANSOUR JAVIDAN, PH.D.
Director of Najafi Global Mindset Institute
and Garvin Distinguished Professor

Multiple award-winning executive educator and author whose teaching and research interests span the globe, Dr. Javidan is the former dean of research, Garvin Distinguished Professor and founding director of Najafi Global Mindset Institute at Thunderbird School of Global Management, the world's number-one ranked business school in international business. His current research is focused on scientifically identifying and defining the essential attributes of global leadership, resulting in the Global Mindset Inventory, an assessment tool that measures an individual's potential to work effectively with others who come from different parts of the world. He is also past president and chairman of the Board of Directors for the world-renowned research project on executive performance and leadership, titled GLOBE (Global Leadership and Organizational Behavior Effectiveness). Dr. Javidan has been designated an Expert Advisor (Global Leadership) by the World Bank and a Senior Research Fellow by the US Army and is widely published in journals such as *Harvard Business Review, Journal of International Business Studies*, and *Academy of Management Perspectives*.

JENNIE L. WALKER, PH.D., PHR
Director of Global Learning & Market Development
Najafi Global Mindset Institute

Dr. Walker's research and work focus on the most effective methods to develop individuals and teams for success in complex, diverse, and increasingly global environments. She has worked in adult learning and performance since 1995 and has specialized in corporate leadership development since 2002, designing and delivering leadership programs for several *Fortune* 500 companies in multiple industries. Her specialized area of expertise is on the degree to which different development methods quantitatively and qualitatively affect global leadership development. She is a frequent presenter at professional conferences, including the Society for Human Resources Management (SHRM), Academy of International Business (AIM), American Society for Training and Development (ASTD), and the American Educational Research Association. Dr. Walker writes a monthly blog on global leadership topics for SHRM entitled We Know Next, and has been published in *AIB Insights, The MBA Women's Guide to Success,* and *Human Resources People and Strategy Journal.* Her work has included regional, national, and global audiences.

About the Contributors

Many of the development suggestions, resources, and examples in this book were the result of expert advice from our contributors. This esteemed group includes expert international executive coaches, senior human resources development professionals, highly regarded business consultants, and prestigious academics. While some of our contributors are specifically named in the examples that they have provided throughout the book, most are only listed in this section. We would like to sincerely thank all of our contributors for the wisdom they have imparted. Please take a moment to get to know them. They are a fascinating group of people.

ZAINUBIAH ABD AZIZ
Learning Specialist, PETRONAS Leadership Centre

Ms. Aziz has more than fifteen years of experience in human resources. She has served as both a generalist and a consultant, providing human resources solutions to multiple organizations. She currently focuses on leadership development in PETRONAS Leadership Centre. Ms. Aziz has a degree in economics and a diploma in human resources management and is pursuing a master of science in human resources development.

OLUFEMI BABARINDE, PH.D.
Associate Professor, Global Studies
Thunderbird School of Global Management

Dr. Babarinde's areas of expertise include doing business in Sub-Saharan Africa, business issues in South Africa, doing business in Europe, international development, and regional integration agreements. Included in his highly regarded research are the integration process of the European Union, African regionalism, and the European Union's external relations, particularly with less-developed countries, Sub-Saharan Africa, and the United States. He has authored/coauthored several articles, and some of his most recent publications include "Africa Is Open for Business: A Continent on the Move" (2009) and "Bridging the Economic Divide in the Republic of South Africa: A Corporate Social Responsibility Perspective" (2009).

ALFREDO BEHRENS, PH.D.
Professor of Leadership and Cross-Cultural Management at FIA Business School, Brazil

Dr. Behrens holds a Ph.D. from the University of Cambridge and lectures at FIA Business School on leadership and cross-cultural management issues. His latest book is on organizational leadership in Latin America: *Shooting Heroes to Reward Cowards, a Sure Path to Organizational Disaster*, available in English on Kindle and published in Portuguese by Beï, 2011. He also wrote *Culture and Management in the Americas*, published by Stanford University Press in 2009, on Kindle, in print, and available in an earlier Portuguese edition by Editora Saraiva: *Cultura e Administração nas Américas*. He also has written numerous academic articles, is a member of the Editorial Board of Thunderbird International Business Review, and is the recipient of many international awards.

MARGARET BUTTERISS, M.SC.
Principal, M A Butteriss & Associates

Ms. Butteriss is a senior-level global executive coach and leadership development and organization effectiveness consultant. An expert in the field since 1978, she has worked with leading multinational companies in the United States, Canada, and Europe as a senior management team member and consultant. Her thirty-plus years of hands-on global business experience and knowledge, combined with her executive coaching experiences, enable her to offer her clients insights into leading and managing global and domestic organizations and meeting the challenges faced during business and personal transitions. Ms. Butteriss's last book was *Coaching the Corporate MVP: Challenging and Developing High Potential Employees* (Jossey Bass).

Dale G. Caldwell, MBA
CEO, Strategic Influence, LLC

Mr. Caldwell has over fifteen years of experience as a coach, organizational consultant, trainer, and facilitator. In addition, he spent over ten years as either a corporate CEO or director of human resources. His experience dealing with the pressures that executives face in a dynamic business environment has provided him with unique coaching insights into ways to effectively deal with these challenges. He developed and trademarked an innovative approach to leadership called Intelligent Influence that he uses to maximize the influence of clients in his executive coaching practice.

Arvind Deshmukh, MBA
Manager of Operations, Najafi Global Mindset Institute

Mr. Deshmukh is an experienced professional in business development, account management, marketing strategy, and customer relationship management. He currently manages operations at Najafi Global Mindset Institute including psychometric instrument administration and reporting, information technology management, and customer service.

Sue Gebelein
CEO, Business and Leadership Consulting

Ms. Gebelein is an entrepreneurial business leader, C-level coach, and business advisor to leaders in companies in the United States, Europe, and Asia-Pacific. She specializes in growth strategies for leaders and companies, advising companies and coaching leaders in vision, strategy execution, and team alignment. She designs and facilitates leadership capability building programs and processes, including developing global leadership mindset. She was an executive with Personnel Decisions International (PDI) for twenty-five years, responsible for PDI's leadership-development services and products and a member of the executive team that grew the company to a thirty-office, full-service global consulting firm. She was the primary author and editor of both *The Successful Manager's Handbook* and *The Successful Executive's Handbook*. Ms. Gebelein is on the Executive Committee for Human Resources People and Strategy.

CARI GUITTARD, MPA
Principal, Global Engagement Partners

Ms. Guittard leads a global affairs portfolio for Global Engagement Partners, focusing on public and corporate diplomacy efforts as well as support and advisory work in a variety of strategic communications, public–private partnerships, and tri-sector engagement efforts. She is a former cybersecurity specialist for the US Department of State, with particular expertise in the Middle East, Southeast Asia, Latin America, and Asia. She also served for eight years as the founding executive director of Business for Diplomatic Action, the only private-sector nonprofit organization whose mission was to enlist the US business community in public diplomacy and global engagement efforts. Ms. Guittard serves as adjunct faculty for the University of Southern California Annenberg School's Masters of Public Diplomacy Program as well as HULT International Business School's Dubai campus, teaching courses in corporate diplomacy and geopolitical risk, international negotiations, and women's leadership.

HÉCTOR GUTIÉRREZ, MBA
President and Founding Partner, The GTZ Group

Mr. GuTiérreZ is a sought-after management strategy, business operations, M&A and structures consultant, as well as entrepreneur. He has helped multinational and Latin American clients build strategic management direction and establish information platforms across their businesses. Mr. GuTiérreZ has been the owner or partner in seven companies in three countries through the GTZ Group.

KATHERINE HOLT, PH.D.
Founding Member, Peakinsight Global Networks

Dr. Holt has coached executives throughout Asia-Pacific for the past twenty years. Her forte is team coaching, working with multiple levels of leaders simultaneously to accelerate their individual and collective performance. Her firm provides global talent management and leadership development consulting in forty countries. She has published articles about global leadership and served as ghost editor for *Awaken, Align, Accelerate* by MDA Consulting. After receiving ASTD's Gordon Bliss award for lifetime professional service, Dr. Holt became a CPLP Fellow in 2012.

WILLIAM C. HORST, PH.D.
President and Founder, Horst Consulting Partners, LLC

Dr. Horst is an executive coach and psychologist who partners with executives and organizations on leadership development. His executive coaching includes extensive work with individual executives as well as coaching executive teams both live and virtually. Dr. Horst brings over twenty-five years of experience in global organizations and with global executives to his consulting and coaching practice. He works with a wide range of companies including mining, financial services, utilities, technology, and family businesses. He uses the Global Mindset Inventory (GMI) in teaching global leadership and developing global leaders through coaching. He also uses the GMI as part of his assessment practice for developing leadership continuity in organizations.

KARINE JAFFREDO BALTZLEY
Founder, Differences Matter, Inc.

Ms. Jaffredo Baltzley provides global learning expertise, ranging from consulting to coaching, to designing and delivering leadership and global diversity programs throughout the world. She has more than a decade of experience helping clients navigate particularly challenging cross-cultural situations. Her extensive global experience includes interventions in the United States, Europe, the Middle East, Africa, and Asia, which have been delivered in English, French, and Spanish to all levels of leadership. She is certified in a number of tools, such as the Intercultural Development Inventory and the Global Mindset Inventory, and is certified to deliver the GenderSpeak Workshops.

KATHERINE JOHNSTON, MBA
Speaker, Author, and Consultant

Ms. Johnston provides leadership development programs, seminars, and keynote speeches for Norwegian and international companies. Ms. Johnston is coauthor of *Boss or Buddy: Balancing Act for Today's Leaders* (in Norwegian, 2009) and delivers Boss&Buddy leadership programs. Currently, she is writing a book about Scandinavian leadership style, as well as building a practice around creating Global Mindset and developing global leaders. Ms. Johnston has twenty-five years of experience working in the Americas, Europe, Russia, and Asia. She looks forward to conducting several annual intercultural communication seminars for young professionals in Africa over the next four years.

ŞIRIN Z. KÖPRÜCÜ, MBA
International Business Consultant, StrategicStraits, Inc.

Ms. Köprücü has fifteen years of international business experience as a marketer and trainer in the pharmaceutical, health communications, association, and training industries. She is the founder of StrategicStraits, Inc., an organization where she partners with other specialist trainers and consultants to help internationally working clients achieve economic sustainability through Global Mindset development. She designs customized programs to develop specific Global Mindset skills, serves as a volunteer leader in the International Section Council of the American Society of Association Executives (ASAE), and is a faculty member with ASAE University. Ms. Köprücü has lived and worked in the United States, Turkey, the United Kingdom, Switzerland, and Germany.

CHARISSE KOSOVA, MA
Manager of Global Learning & Development, IOR Global Services

Ms. Kosova is engaged in promoting learning and development initiatives. She designs curricula for and supports IOR's international network of trainers to ensure that they offer IOR's expatriate assignees the tools to develop as intercultural professionals. She also works directly with multinational corporate clients whose employees at all levels are striving to develop skills to work and communicate more effectively across cultures, both face-to-face and virtually. She is certified in several cultural assessment tools, as well as in e-learning instructional design, and workplace learning and performance coaching. A native of Chicago, Ms. Kosova has lived and worked in Morocco, Japan, and the United Kingdom, in both corporate and non-profit positions.

DAVID MAHER
Executive Director, World Action Teams

Mr. Maher is the executive director of World Action Teams, whose mission is to develop leaders who create value for business and society. World Action Teams does this by partnering with corporations to design and deliver discovery experiences for leaders in rapidly growing global markets. As a leadership and executive development consultant, Mr. Maher's particular expertise is in the facilitation of a more developed self and global awareness through assessments, executive coaching at both the formal and informal level, and facilitation of truly experiential education in the international arena. Mr. Maher is certified to debrief the Global Mindset Inventory, is a certified Wilderness First Responder, is a certified grant writer, and has received a CLP Leadership Certification.

PAUL MAYER
Head of Human Resources, Americas
ALTANA AG

With over thirty years of experience in all aspects of human resources, Mr. Mayer has worked in a variety of business settings that include ultraprecise manufacturing, utilities, consumer products, research, medical devices, aerospace, and chemical manufacturing. Some of the areas for which he has had responsibility are compensation and benefits, staffing, safety, training and development, acquisition evaluation, employee communications, employee evaluations, organizational development, employee relations, and labor relations.

LYNDA L. MOORE, PH.D.
Professor, Simmons School of Management

Professor Moore has taught for over thirty years at the Simmons School of Management. Professor Moore teaches MBA and executive courses in gender, diversity and leadership, Global Mindset, culturally intelligent leadership, and cross-cultural comparative analysis of women leaders. She is chair of the Organizational Behavior and Management Department and faculty affiliate of the Center for Gender and Organizations. Dr. Moore's research and numerous publications focus on women in global leadership, gender, diversity, and leadership across cultures and the development of culturally sensitive leadership models. Professor Moore is a fellow of the Leadership Trust Foundation, teaches at the Indian School of Business, and was the recipient of a Fulbright fellowship to the United Arab Emirates.

STACEY MURPHY, MBA
Executive Coach and Management Consultant,
Beacon Consulting

Ms. Murphy is a business coach and consultant who has helped leaders and organizations communicate with clarity and focus for more than twenty years. She has a distinctive blend of functional and business expertise, spanning strategic planning, finance, investor relations, merger and transition management, and leadership development, giving her a broad, big picture perspective. She specializes in executive assessment and development, delivering assessment-center services to global clients. As a coach, she is sought out to work with global and emerging leaders, helping them to become more compelling influencers, stronger relationship managers, and more strategic leaders. She is also adjunct faculty in the Department of Business at Caldwell College, where she teaches creativity, innovation, and competitive advantage, along with other business courses.

JOY MCGOVERN, PH.D.
Principal, The McGovern Group

Dr. McGovern is an industrial/organizational psychologist who has spent the last twenty years as a leadership consultant and business developer to *Fortune* 50 corporations, nonprofits, and universities across a wide range of industries and services. Prior to that, she spent ten years working inside organizations in leadership development positions. She is a sought-after and frequent presenter on her work for organizations such as the American Psychological Association and the Society of Industrial/Organizational Psychologists. She is also the author of *The Return on Investment Study of Executive Coaching*. Dr. McGovern has been quoted extensively in a wide variety of media outlets, including the *Wall Street Journal*, *Fortune*, and the *New York Times*, and she has been interviewed on CNN, CNBC, and Reuters World News.

SIDNEY A. NACHMAN, PH.D.
Principal, Sound Insight Consulting

Dr. Nachman has extensive experience as a coach, organizational consultant, trainer, and facilitator. He has coached hundreds of leaders and executive teams in the United States, Canada, Asia Pacific, India, and the Middle East. In his work, he applies insights from the behavioral sciences, action learning, and psychological and 360 assessments to help leaders expand their individual and organizational capabilities and performance. He was a founding member and codesigner of the New York University (NYU) Management Simulations Project Group and has provided professional development for MBA and undergraduate business students at NYU, Dartmouth, and the University of Michigan.

SATISH PRADHAN, MA
Chief, Group HR, Tata Sons Limited

Mr. Pradhan heads the Tata Group human resources function. Prior to joining the group in April 2001, he was with ICI, Plc., in London at the head office as organization design & development manager (Group HR). During the last thirty years, he has worked with Steel Authority of India, CMC, ICI India, Brooke Bond Lipton India, Ltd. (now Unilever India), and ICI, Plc., in various capacities in the human resources area. He is on the boards of various Tata group companies, professional bodies, and nongovernmental organizations, and is a Chartered Fellow of the Chartered Institute of Personnel and Development.

Maria Seddio, MA
Founder and CEO of CorpTalk, LLC

Ms. Seddio is founder and CEO of CorpTalk, an executive coaching and organizational development firm specializing in transformational leadership and organizational readiness. She works closely with C-level executives and global organizational leaders to integrate systems thinking, community building–based designs, and the power of conversation into more interconnected, innovative, agile business models. Known for her thought leadership on future workplace topics and the changing role of leaders, Ms. Seddio is a frequent conference presenter, discussion host, and participant in executive learning forums.

Steven Segal, Ph.D.
Senior Lecturer, Macquarie Graduate School of Management

Dr. Segal lectures and conducts research in a range of areas, including leading with a Global Mindset, philosophy of management, and executive coaching. He is a registered psychologist and practicing executive coach. He has published numerous articles as well as a book called *Business Feel*, which has been translated into Mandarin.

Alan L. Siegel, Ph.D.
Principal, Siegel Organizational Consulting

Dr. Siegel is an organizational psychologist and global executive coach working with senior leaders in Europe, Asia, Latin America, and North America for over twenty-five years. His passion is helping companies ensure continuity of global leadership talent through high energy, business-focused assessment and development programs. His transformational coaching work focuses on accelerating transition and effect in new leadership roles for global leaders and high potentials. Dr. Siegel's extensive experience as an organizational consultant and executive coach has enabled him to partner with senior leaders to shape their careers and the future of their businesses. He continues to explore his interest and understanding of what makes global leaders successful.

Doug Stuart, Ph.D.
Development Coach and Intercultural Trainer

Dr. Stuart's interest and expertise is the field of intercultural assessment. He is licensed to interpret numerous intercultural instruments, and he consults with clients on their choice of selection and development instruments for their global workforce. His overview of tools was published in the SAGE publication, *Contemporary Leadership and Intercultural Competence*. His most recent article, "Taking Stage Development Theory Seriously: Implications for Study Abroad," was published in Stylus's *Student Learning Abroad* 2012.

Molly Takeda, Ph.D.
Professor, Consultant, and Blogger

Dr. Takeda has over twenty-five years of experience consulting, training, researching, teaching, and serving the international business and leadership community. As a business professor, she has designed international business curricula, taught in MBA and EMBA programs in Asia, Australia, and the United States, and published over twenty articles in academic journals. She has consulted with firms that are globalizing, designed and conducted training programs, and coached global executives relying on her expertise in global strategy, management, and leadership development systems. Dr. Takeda has lived and worked in the United States, South America, Europe, and Asia.

Yulia Tolstikov-Mast, Ph.D.
Assistant Professor Global Leadership, IndianaTech

Dr. Tolstikov-Mast is an assistant professor at the Ph.D. program in global leadership at the Indiana Institute of Technology. In addition to teaching research and leadership courses, she assists in the program development and serves as a liaison to the International

Center of Indiana. Dr. Tolstikov-Mast holds a bachelor of arts degree in linguistics from Rostov State Pedagogical University, Russia; a master's degree in professional communication from Purdue University; and a Ph.D. in communication from the University of Memphis. Her current research interests include organizational culture and change in transnational organizations, Russian followership, and development of Russian the business class.

KAREN S. WALCH, PH.D.
Associate Professor, Thunderbird School of Global Management

Dr. Walch has an academic background in international negotiation, cultural competencies, and political economy. She has several decades of experience in various business and academic contexts, including insurance, law, tourism, aquaculture, security studies, and MBA graduate education. Dr. Walch's interests are in the area of political and social-psychological factors in communication and negotiation. She has authored many articles and books, including her most recent book, *Seize the Sky: 9 Secrets of Negotiation Power.*

VALERIE WHITE, PH.D.
Principal, Change Perspectives

Dr. White has been an executive coach in *Fortune* 500 companies throughout the United States, Europe, and Asia for nearly twenty years. She has done extensive leadership assessment and feedback and has written and contributed to several senior-level global assessment centers. She offers clients new and highly effective ways to more rapidly and happily set and reach goals, and she is routinely asked for additional coaching and insights. Valerie is coauthor of *First Impressions: What You Don't Know About How Others See You* (Bantam Books, 2004). The book is being published in seventeen languages and was nominated for a Books for a Better Life Award.

HARISON YUSOFF, MS
Learning Manager, PETRONAS Leadership Centre

Ms. Yusoff has more than ten years of experience as a manager and leader in public relations, including corporate communications, community relations, and corporate social investment programs. During that time, she managed several high-level public relations and media campaigns. She also has extensive experience in teaching and academia and has authored/coauthored a number of articles for local and international publications. Her master's degree is in managerial psychology.

BARRIE ZUCAL, MS
President and CEO, Global Coaches Network

Ms. Zucal has twenty-five years' experience working with global leaders in the United States, the Middle East, and Asia as a therapist to them and their families and as their global leadership coach. Based on this experience, she now designs and delivers cutting-edge global leadership development programs that provide truly global coaches for global leaders. She also coaches global leaders and trains and certifies experienced executive coaches to become global leadership coaches. Her clients are leaders in global business, government, and EMBA programs. Currently, she is preparing women for senior-level global roles, because she believes that the world needs them now.

Index

Note: *f* represents a figure